EDITED BY
KOON TECK KOH,
TARKINGTON J NEWMAN AND
MUHAMMAD SHUFI BIN SALLEH

Coaching Values and Life Skills through Physical Education and Sports
A Practical Toolkit

Designed cover image: Coach talking to soccer players; Getty Image

First published 2025
by Routledge
4 Park Square, Milton Park, Abingdon, Oxon OX14 4RN

and by Routledge
605 Third Avenue, New York, NY 10158

Routledge is an imprint of the Taylor & Francis Group, an informa business

© 2025 selection and editorial matter, Koon Teck Koh, Tarkington J Newman and Muhammad Shufi Bin Salleh; individual chapters, the contributors

The right of Koon Teck Koh, Tarkington J Newman and Muhammad Shufi Bin Salleh to be identified as the authors of the editorial material, and of the authors for their individual chapters, has been asserted in accordance with sections 77 and 78 of the Copyright, Designs and Patents Act 1988.

All rights reserved. No part of this book may be reprinted or reproduced or utilised in any form or by any electronic, mechanical, or other means, now known or hereafter invented, including photocopying and recording, or in any information storage or retrieval system, without permission in writing from the publishers.

Trademark notice: Product or corporate names may be trademarks or registered trademarks, and are used only for identification and explanation without intent to infringe.

British Library Cataloguing-in-Publication Data
A catalogue record for this book is available from the British Library

ISBN: 978-1-032-68864-0 (hbk)
ISBN: 978-1-032-71678-7 (pbk)
ISBN: 978-1-032-68865-7 (ebk)

DOI: 10.4324/9781032688657

Typeset in Galliard
by SPi Technologies India Pvt Ltd (Straive)

"The authors' work refers to the educational value of physical education and sports (PES) and researches and analyzes in depth the values and skills that are developed through experiential sports and social activities which determine behaviours and life attitudes. Olympic Games and Olympic Education highlight the cultural and educational value of PES. This comprehensive book is an excellent tool for practitioners to understand the goals, methods, means and theories of PES. It also highlights the ways we can move from theory to practice and evaluate the relevant values-oriented educational programmes."

— **Ng Ser Maing**, *Vice President, International Olympic Committee*

"A/P Koh Koon Teck's book is a compelling read for coaches, physical education teachers, and any organization leader with sports programmes for youth. It is exceptional in that it gives practical handles for how values and life skills can be effectively taught to youth. It is not just lip service, but the authors show how it can be seamlessly integrated into coaching as an approach. Better yet, it is transferable to other arenas of life. With this, our youth will be more ready for the future."

— **Liew Wei Li**, *Director-General of Education, Singapore*

"Character and Citizenship Education is at the heart of the education system in Singapore. It is a key pillar in our approach to the holistic development of Singaporean students' values, character, social-emotional well-being, and citizenship dispositions. This book provides much-needed evidence-based research and strategies to meet the changing education landscape. I am impressed by the pedagogy of intentionality—integrating content knowledge with values and life skills through context-specific activities and guiding learners to reflect on their experiences and transform them into new knowledge. I highly recommend this book to educators and practitioners!"

— **Professor Liu Woon Chia**, *Director, National Institute of Education, Nanyang Technological University, Singapore*

"Sport Singapore strongly believes that sport is an excellent platform to shape our youths into capable, resilient and adaptable adults who contribute to our society in various roles. Singapore's President Tharman Shanmugaratnam famously said that "sport made me", and indeed sport can play a big part in helping individuals to acquire the skills needed to thrive well into the future. This is reflected in our Vision 2030 aspiration of enabling Singaporeans to *Live Better Through Sport*. This book provides compelling evidence-based practical ideas to develop and integrate values-driven practices. A must read, especially for all our teachers and coaches."

— **Alan Goh**, Chief Executive Officer, Sport Singapore

"I am delighted to endorse the textbook, "Coaching Values and Life Skills through Physical Education and Sports: A Practical Toolkit", which brings together researchers from around the globe to facilitate a comprehensive understanding of the necessary knowledge and tools to effectively teach values and life skills through physical education and sports. The chapters in this book are broken down into six parts, and they include a broad range of relevant theories, historical and current empirical research, that both researchers and practitioners should find useful in their daily practices."

— **Professor Gordon Bloom**, Chair, Department of Kinesiology & Physical Education, McGill University, Canada

"Central to the development of young people learning to adapt to a dynamic society is the ability to shape why they do what they do within a values-based framework. Practitioners need guidance in shaping the moral values and good character of young people in and through physical education and sport (PES). This book provides evidence-based practical ideas to apply in these unique settings. Koon Teck brings together prominent international scholars and practitioners to create a must-have resource to effectively teach values and life skills."

— **Professor Cliff Mallett OAM**, School of Human Movement and Nutrition Sciences, University of Queensland, Australia

Coaching Values and Life Skills through Physical Education and Sports

This impactful resource guide is for international educators and practitioners involved in physical education and sports (PES) who want to learn evidence-based approaches to the teaching of values and character education.

Through a systematic approach to teaching and evaluating values and character education, this book bridges the gap between theory and practice. It offers empirical evidence and strategies to show how values and character can be internalised through carefully designed experiences, active participation, and regular reinforcement, without compromising the time needed to learn sports skills – a common concern raised by PE teachers and sports coaches. Results from case studies have also revealed that values can be transferred beyond the context of physical education lessons and sports through a collaborative approach and effective communication between teachers, coaches, and parents. Key strategies based on empirical evidence are highlighted in this book. It also highlights an Asian perspective on values and life skills training through physical education and provides readers with step-by-step implementation guidelines to simplify some complex strategies in developing values and life skills through PES seamlessly.

The book provides useful information to anyone engaged in developing young people in, and through, sports. In particular, it will be of great value to pre-service and in-service teachers and coaches for implementing effective strategies to balance teaching sports skills, values, and life skills effectively in PES.

Koon Teck Koh is an Associate Professor at the Physical Education and Sports Science (PESS) Academic Group, National Institute of Education (NIE), Nanyang Technological University (NTU), Singapore. His research areas are in sports coaching and pedagogy. He has published more than 100 publications, including peer-reviewed journal articles, books, book chapters, and professional articles. He is also a registered FIBA coach and coach developer recognised by FIBA and Sports Singapore. Dr. Koh held numerous prominent appointments at the international and local levels. These include President of the ASEAN Council of Physical Education and Sports, Executive Board member of the World Association for Basketball Coaches, FIBA Technical Commission, Chairman of the FIBA Asia Coaches Committee, Head, PESS/NIE/NTU, President of the Basketball Association of Singapore, President of the Singapore Physical Education Association, and Executive Council member of the Singapore National Olympics Council (SNOC).

Tarkington J Newman is an Associate Professor at the University of Kentucky College of Social Work and the Director of the Sports Social Work (SSW) Research Lab. Additionally, they serve as the Research Committee Chair for the Alliance of Social Workers in Sports (aswis.org). Through the SSW Research Lab, Dr. Newman is committed to serving youth populations (ages 10–24) who are socially vulnerable and/or at risk for behavioural and mental health problems. Dr. Newman's research focuses on promoting critical positive youth development (CPYD) through sports and other forms of physical activity, specifically related to the development and transfer of normative life skills (e.g., emotional regulation, communication, teamwork, leadership) and social justice life skills (e.g., antiracism, LGBTQ+ allyship, healthy masculinity, mental health literacy).

Muhammad Shufi Bin Salleh is a Teaching Fellow in the Physical Education and Sports Science Department at the NIE, NTU, Singapore.

Contents

List of Contributors   x
Preface   xiii
Acknowledgements   xvii

PART 1
WHAT ARE VALUES AND LIFE SKILLS?   1

Values and Life Skills: Definition and Importance in Physical Education and Sports   **One**   3
Koon Teck Koh

Schools: An Ideal Platform to Teach Values and Life Skills   **Two**   16
Fernando Santos and Marta Ferreira

Physical Education and School Sports, the Natural Setting for Values and Life Skills   **Three**   29
Scott Pierce, Emily Jones and Andrew Eberline

PART 2
SCIENCE OF LEARNING   43

Understanding Youth Sports through Experiential Learning   **Four**   45
Levone Lee, Anne Stauffer, Sandy Nino, Ellison Blumenthal and Tarkington J Newman

The Development of Life Skills through Sports from the Bioecological Theory Lens   **Five**   58
Vitor Ciampolini, Juarez Vieira do Nascimento and Michel Milistetd

Six Practical Approaches to Teaching Values and Life Skills — 74
Samantha Bates, Dawn Anderson-Butcher and Kylee Ault-Baker

PART 3
MYTH OF CHARACTER EDUCATION — 89

Seven Values and Life Skills Are Learnt When Participating in PES (Physical Education and Sports) Context — 91
Zhihua Yin and Yue Xu

Eight Values and Life Skills Are Learnt When Participating in Activities — 106
Zarizi Ab Rahman

Nine Diverse Values and Life Skills Learnt from Sports Context — 118
Eiichiro Fukami

Ten Caught or Taught? Situating Approaches for Coaching Life Skills through Sports — 128
Martin Camiré

PART 4
THE ART OF TEACHING VALUES AND LIFE SKILLS — 141

Eleven The Intentional Approach to Teaching Values and Life Skills — 143
Yvonne Seng

Twelve Preparing Coaches to Teach Life Skills: The Need for a Behaviour Change Perspective in Coach Education Programmes — 165
Carlos Ewerton Palheta and Michel Milistetd

Thirteen Integration — 179
Swee Meng Wong, Alice Koh and Thomas Yong

Fourteen Practical Strategies for Using a Trauma-Informed Approach to Support Life Skills Transferability through Physical Education and Sports 198
Kalyn McDonough and Jenn M Jacobs

PART 5
THEORY TO PRACTICE 213

Fifteen Whole-School Approach 215
Ferdinand Xie Fai Mar and Koon Teck Koh

Sixteen Teaching Values and Life Skills to Different Age Groups 228
Koon Teck Koh and Muhammad Shufi Bin Salleh

PART 6
HOW WE KNOW IT HAS WORKED 243

Seventeen Strategies to Evaluate the Intentional Teaching of Values and Life Skills in Sports 245
Koon Teck Koh and Shun Xin Koong

Eighteen Strategies to Evaluate the Intentional Teaching of Values and Life Skills in Sports: Sports Singapore's Perspective 258
Eliza Tan, David Chin, Noor Hisham, Caleb Khoo and Federico Carreres

Nineteen Sports-Based Life Skills Interventions: Psychological Needs and Psychological Well-Being 289
Ken Hodge

Index 303

Contributors

Zarizi Ab Rahman, Faculty of Education, Universiti Teknologi MARA, Puncak Alam Campus, Selangor, Malaysia

Dawn Anderson-Butcher, Ph.D., LISW-S, CMPC, The Ohio State University, College of Social Work, USA

Kylee Ault-Baker, Ph.D., CMPC, The Ohio State University, College of Social Work, USA

Samantha Bates, Ph.D., LISW-S, The Ohio State University, College of Social Work, USA

Ellison Blumenthal, MSW, MS, University of New Hampshire, Department of Social Work, USA

Martin Camiré, School of Human Kinetics, University of Ottawa, Canada

Federico Carreres, University of Alicante, Spain

David Chin, Republic Polytechnic, Singapore

Vitor Ciampolini, Federal University of Santa Catarina, Departamento de Educação Física, Brazil

Andrew Eberline, Ph.D., School of Kinesiology and Recreation, Illinois State University, Normal, Illinois, USA

Marta Ferreira, Escola Superior de Educação, Politécnico do Porto, Porto, Portugal

Eiichiro Fukami, School of Sports Sciences, Waseda University, Japan

Noor Hisham, Punggol Secondary, Singapore

Ken Hodge, University of Otago, New Zealand

Jenn M Jacobs, Department of Kinesiology and Physical Education, Northern Illinois University, USA

Emily Jones Ph.D., School of Kinesiology and Recreation, Illinois State University, Normal, Illinois, USA

Alice Koh, Student Development Curriculum Division, Ministry of Education Singapore, Singapore

Caleb Khoo, St. Hilda's Secondary, Singapore

Koon Teck Koh, Physical Education and Sports Science, National Institute of Education, Singapore

Shun Xin Koong, Physical Education and Sports Science, NIE, Singapore

Levone Lee, MSW, University of Kentucky, College of Social Work, USA

Ferdinand Xie Fai Mar, Physical Education and Sports Science, NIE, Singapore

Kalyn McDonough, UNESCO Core International Faculty, University of Melbourne, Australia

Michel Milistetd, Federal University of Santa Catarina, Departamento de Educação Física, Brazil

Juarez Vieira do Nascimento, Federal University of Santa Catarina, Departamento de Educação Física, Brazil

Tarkington J Newman, Ph.D., MSW, MS, University of Kentucky, College of Social Work, USA

Sandy Nino, University of Kentucky, College of Social Work, USA

Carlos Ewerton Palheta, Sports Pedagogy Research Center (NuPPE), Federal University of Santa Catarina, Florianópolis, Brazil

Scott Pierce, Ph.D., School of Kinesiology and Recreation, Illinois State University, Normal, Illinois, USA

Muhammad Shufi Bin Salleh, Physical Education and Sports Science, NIE Singapore

Fernando Santos, Escola Superior de Educação, Politécnico do Porto, inED, Centro de Investigação e Inovação em Educação, Porto, Portugal

Yvonne Seng, Psychology and Child and Human Development, NIE, Singapore

Anne Stauffer, MSW, University of Kentucky, College of Social Work, USA

Eliza Tan, Sports Singapore, Singapore

Swee Meng Wong, Physical, Sports and Outdoor Education Branch (Sports Education), Student Development Curriculum Division, Ministry of Education Singapore, Singapore

Yue Xu, Department of Physical Education and Sports Sciences, University of Limerick

Zhihua Yin, College of Physical Education and Health, East China Normal University, China

Thomas Yong, Student Development Curriculum Division, Ministry of Education Singapore, Singapore

Preface

Childhood and adolescence are critical developmental periods featuring rapid physical, psychological, and social growth that influence trajectories of long-term health and well-being. Youth developmental scholarship has long recognised the critical importance of learning transferable values and life skills (Danish et al., 1993; Gould & Carson, 2008; Fraser-Thomas et al., 2005; Hodge et al., 2013; Hellison, 2003). Whereas *values* are conceptualised as principles and beliefs that guide behaviour and the standard by which actions are judged to be good or desirable, *life skills* are recognised as intrapersonal and interpersonal skills (i.e., actionable behaviours) that enable individuals to manage the demands, challenges, and stressors of everyday life (Koh et al., 2014). In other words, while values provide guidelines for behaviour (e.g., work ethic), life skills are the resultant behaviours (e.g., discipline). Values and life skills are important mechanisms that not only help promote positive long-term development but also help to prevent the onset and/or adherence to behavioural health problems, such as aggressive and violent behaviours (Newman et al., 2023). Throughout the last several decades and around the world, physical education and sports (PES) settings have been recognised as being uniquely effective learning environments for the development and transfer of life skills and values (Bruner et al., 2023; Qi et al., 2020; Vella et al., 2016).

Given the importance of teaching values and life skills in PES settings, this book is intended to be a resource for PES scholars, practitioners, and students alike. The book represents a culmination of international, interdisciplinary, and interprofessional expertise and is organised into six sections. In Part 1 (WHAT ARE VALUES AND LIFE SKILLS?), **Koh** (Chapter 1) provides a contemporary perspective on values and life skills and their relevance to PES educators. Additionally, **Santos and Ferreira** (Chapter 2) discuss the role of schools in developing critical thinking and reflexive skills that may enable youth to challenge the status quo in pursuit of a justice society. Finally, **Pierce, Jones, and Eberline** (Chapter 3) examine the inherent structure and demands of PES, and discuss the role of the PES educator within a systems-based approach.

Part 2 (Science of Learning) begins with **Lee, Stauffer, Nino, Blumenthal, and Newman** (Chapter 4) and builds upon the Coaching on the Wave Model to discuss the utility of experiential learning theory when teaching life skills and values in PES. Also, through a theoretical lens, **Ciampolini, Nascimento, and Milistetd** (Chapter 5) propose a model to frame the development of life skills and values through the four dimensions of bioecological theory. This section ends with practical approaches to teaching values and life skills by **Bates, Anderson-Butcher, and Ault-Baker** (Chapter 6), in which they reflect upon existing frameworks.

In Part 3 (Myth of Character Education), **Yin and Xu** (Chapter 7) provide a unique cultural perspective of why, what, and how PES educators teach values and life skills when using physical activities in China, whereas **Rahman** (Chapter 8) provides insight into a Malaysian PES context and a PES curriculum for promoting the development of motor skills, values, and life skills. Additionally, **Fukami** (Chapter 9) discusses the potential of using a member-centred team management approach to teach values and life skills within Japanese school athletic clubs. **Camiré** (Chapter 10) ends this section by situating the most prevalent approaches known to facilitate the development of values and life skills, as well as offering concrete, practical strategies for PES educators.

Part 4 (The Art of Teaching Values and Life Skills) features **Seng** (Chapter 11) and the Teaching and Facilitating Values and Life Skills through PES (T2VLSPES) Framework, a validated dual-cyclical intervention. **Palheta and Milistetd** (Chapter 12) focus on the PES educator and propose enhancements to PES education programmes (i.e., coach education) through a behaviour change model. **Wong, Koh, and Yong** (Chapter 13) explain the two paradoxical goals of athlete development and character building, as well as provide suggestions for programme design in school sports that allows for the integration and synergy of the two goals. **McDonough and Jacobs** (Chapter 14) bring this section to a close by presenting a novel trauma-informed life skill transfer model and outlining practical strategies to intentionally integrate life skills and values into PES activities.

Part 5 (Theory to Practice) beings with **Mar and Koh** (Chapter 15) identifying strategies and methods that facilitate the transfer of values learnt in PES to the classroom and home settings, specifically collaborative efforts between stakeholders in a school setting. **Koh and Salleh** (Chapter 16) explain the "anatomy" of typical PES lessons and activities and provide research-driven strategies that can be incorporated in a practical manner.

Finally, in Part 6 (How We Know It Has Worked), **Koh and Koong** (Chapter 17) explore evaluating the effectiveness of intentionally teaching sports skills, values, and life skills using a free mobile application based on the Arizona State University Observation Instrument. Further, **Tan, Chin, Hisham, Khoo, and Carreres** (Chapter 18) provide strategies to evaluate the intentional teaching of values and life skills in sports using the SportSG's Game for Life framework. **Hodge** (Chapter 19) helps to close this book by discussing PES life skills and values interventions that support psychological needs and promote the well-being of youth.

REFERENCES

Bruner, M., McLaren, C., Sutcliffe, J., Gardner, L., Lubans, D., Smith, J., & Vella, S. (2023). The effect of sport-based interventions on positive youth development: A systematic review and meta-analysis. *International Review of Sport and Exercise Psychology*, 16(1), 368–395. https://doi.org/10.1080/1750984X.2021.1875496

Danish, S., Petitpas, A., & Hale, B. (1993). Life development intervention for athletes: Life skills through sports. *The Counseling Psychologist*, 21(3), 352–385. https://doi.org/10.1177/0011000093213002

Fraser-Thomas, J., Côté, J., & Deakin, J. (2005). Youth sport programs: An avenue to foster positive youth development. *Physical Education & Sport Pedagogy*, 10(1), 19–40. https://doi.org/10.1080/1740898042000334890

Gould, D., & Carson, S. (2008). Life skills development through sport: Current status and future directions. *International Review of Sport and Exercise Psychology*, 1(1), 58–78. https://doi.org/10.1080/17509840701834573

Hellison, D. (2003). *Teaching responsibility through physical activity*. Human Kinetics.

Hodge, K., Danish, S., & Martin, J. (2013). Developing a conceptual framework for life skills interventions. *The Counseling Psychologist*, 41(8), 1125–1152. https://doi.org/10.1177/0011000012462073

Koh, K.T., Komar, J., Newman, T., & Tan, E. (2014).The effects of a Values and Principles in Sports coach education course designed to promote values-driven coaching styles. *International Journal of Sport Science & Coaching*. https://doi.org/10.1177/17479541241266975

Newman, T., Black, S., Santos, F., Jefka, B., & Brennan, N. (2023). Coaching the development and transfer of life skills: A scoping review of facilitative coaching practices in youth sports. *International Review of Sport and Exercise Psychology, 16*(1), 619–656. https://doi.org/10.1080/1750984X.2021.1910977

Qi, S., Hua, F., Zhou, Z., & Shek, D. (2020). Trends of positive youth development publications (1995–2020): A scientometric review. *Applied Research in Quality of Life*, 1–26. https://doi.org/10.1007/s11482-020-09878-3

Vella, S., Braithewaite, R., Gardner, L., & Spray, C. (2016). A systematic review and meta-analysis of implicit theory research in sport, physical activity, and physical education. *International Review of Sport and Exercise Psychology, 9*(1), 191–214. https://doi.org/10.1080/1750984X.2016.1160418

Acknowledgements

We would like to thank all the contributors who accepted our invitation to create this evidence-based resource book and provided valuable insights to further expand our knowledge on coaching values and life skills effectively in physical education and sports settings. We would also like to express our appreciation to Mr. Ng Ser Miang, vice president of the International Olympic Committee; Ms. Liew Wei Li, director-general of education, Singapore; Professor Liu Woon Chia, director, NIE, NTU; Mr. Alan Goh, chief executive officer, Sports Singapore; Chair and Professor Gordon Bloom, Department of Kinesiology and Physical Education, McGill University; and Professor Cliff Mallett, School of Human Movement and Nutrition Sciences, University of Queensland for reviewing and endorsing the relevance, usefulness, and quality of this book, despite their busy schedules.

WHAT ARE VALUES AND LIFE SKILLS?
Part 1

Values and Life Skills: Definition and Importance in Physical Education and Sports

Chapter One

Koon Teck Koh

INTRODUCTION

Values are the principles that serve as guides for desirable behaviours (Halstead & Taylor, 2000, p. 169). They are a set of qualities that enable us to fulfil ourselves and live together in harmony with others in our society. Hence, values serve the welfare of both the self and others. Similarly, life skills "enable individuals to succeed in the different environments in which they live" (Danish et al., 2004, p. 40). Examples of skills that are applicable in various life domains include goal setting, time and stress management, emotional regulation, morals, and teamwork development. Both concepts are similar in that they serve to point individuals in a direction that would prepare them for the future (Danish et al., 2004) and enable them to survive and thrive in society. However, there is a difference between the two concepts. Values are often related to an individual's or a society's beliefs, whereas life skills are actionable behaviours (e.g., communication, social awareness) that an individual possesses. These skills usually facilitate one in navigating through life's challenges to be successful (Camiré et al., 2012; Prajapati et al., 2017).

Values and life skills (VLS) can be integrated into various activities. Particularly, physical education and sports (PES) settings, which refer to the set of planned activities conducted in school under the observation of trained educators, are believed to promote both VLS. PES are mandatory courses for children from a young age, with such lessons continuing throughout adolescence. Physical education teachers and sports coaches (PETSCs) play an important role in providing meaningful learning opportunities in an environment conducive for developing VLS among youth (Li & Ennis, 2017).

An example of how VLS can be integrated in PES would be through team games – such as basketball, netball, and volleyball – where cooperation and communication are needed among team members. Youth learn to respect others and appreciate the diversity of the team, develop effective communication skills, and work together with others to achieve goals through these activities. This facilitates the development of values, allowing youth to establish a sense of belonging and build strong relations with students of different races and social backgrounds (Ministry of Education (MOE), 2018). In addition, PES provides opportunities for children to develop resilience through encountering setbacks and failures, serving as valuable opportunities for growth and learning (Gould & Carson, 2008). Together, such opportunities enhance student learning, allowing students to develop the necessary competencies needed to act for the good of self, others, and society.

The role of PES in promoting VLS has been highlighted by Singapore's deputy prime minister, Mr. Heng Swee Keat, at the opening ceremonies of the 2013 and 2014 National School Games (NSG). He stated, "Sporting excellence and character development are inextricably linked. … Every athlete will face both winning and losing. Our student-athletes must learn to deal with both and learn through them" (Chen, 2013, para. 2) and that

> Sports develop character and values, cultivate positive attitudes and strengthen people skills. … In my view, the most valuable trait that sports develop is grit. Grit is more than resilience. When a student has grit, he is passionate about a long term goal and perseveres towards it.
>
> (Wong, 2014, para. 6)

However, PES, when taught in an unstructured and unintentional way, can also negatively affect children (Koh et al., 2016). This is evident in competitive sports, in which displays of aggression, violence, and conflicts among players arise because of an emphasis on winning (Roberts et al., 2020). Therefore, it is crucial for PETSCs to develop lessons that are suitable, engaging, and impactful for students (Newman & Anderson-Butcher, 2021). The developmental needs and abilities of students need to be considered to develop lessons that are cognitively and affectively beneficial (Nesbitt & Farran, 2021). This requires careful planning, assessment, and reflection.

APPLIED INSIGHTS

To integrate VLS in PES, Brown's (2003) four-stage approach to teaching VLS can be utilised, as it not only aids in the enhancement of the learning experience but leverages technology to ensure that the educational focus extends beyond physical skills to include the development of values. The approach contains the following components. (1) defining: identification and articulation of key values to be taught, (2) modelling: demonstration of proper actions, (3) shaping: correction of negative behaviours while promoting positive ones, and (4) reinforcement: reinforcing positive behaviours through various modalities can be applied.

Defining

First, PETSCs should identify the values they wish to teach. This can be based on the priorities and core values of society and schools. The initial step can involve the thoughtful process where PETSCs consider educational priorities to guide their formation of a value system. The values chosen must be representative of core principles deemed important by society at large. This ensures that the foundational step in VLS is aligned with the desired educational outcomes and societal norms. Furthermore, the values identified should be relevant and meaningful to PES. The values identified should also be practically applicable within the realm of PES so that its integration would be seamless. For example, values such as perseverance and teamwork can be highlighted to facilitate a deeper appreciation of PES by youths during their lessons. In Singapore, MOE places a significant emphasis on nurturing well-rounded individuals who are not only academically proficient but also embody strong moral values. As such, values such as respect, responsibility, resilience, integrity, care, and harmony are prioritised. These values are identified as the basis of personal and societal well-being. The values also align with the national education framework, which is built around the pillars of fostering one's national identity, building resilience, and instilling national core values of meritocracy, integrity, responsibility, and care, which underpins Singapore's social fabric. Furthermore, identification and integration of each school's own core values will also assist teachers in focusing on their efforts and creating learning experiences that are more meaningful and representative of societal values while aligned with each school's educational priorities. Together, the focus ensures coherence and unification in the PES that is taught across all levels and subjects.

The values taught should be observable such that specific behaviours can be identified and reinforced, which also makes it easier for students to understand and apply. Various aspects of VLS learning should be featured regularly within every aspect of teaching and instruction. The following are some examples of values and how they can be taught by PETSCs:

Respect

Defined as the belief in one's "own self-worth and the intrinsic worth of people" (MOE, 2016), when applied in PES, respect can be taught by role-modelling respectful behaviour towards others, encouraging open communication and active listening, and teaching proper etiquette and sportsmanship, such as shaking hands with opponents after a game. It is demonstrated when one shows respect towards others and oneself – for example, by listening attentively to others when they are speaking, valuing the opinions of others, following rules, and giving their best in their assignments (MOE, 2016).

Responsibility

Defined as recognising that one "has a duty to [themselves], [their] family, community, nation, and the world" (MOE, 2016), it can be taught in PES when students are assigned team roles and responsibilities, such as team captain or equipment manager, when they are encouraged to take ownership of their actions and decisions, and when clear expectations are set – for example, punctuality and attendance at practices and games. It is observable when one is accountable for their own actions, learns from mistakes, and does their part in a group setting, even when there is minimal supervision by the teacher (MOE, 2016).

Resilience

Defined as the demonstration of "emotional strength and [perseverance] in the face of challenges" with "courage, optimism, adaptability, and resourcefulness" (MOE, 2016), resilience can be incorporated into PES by setting challenging situations, such as tough opponents or difficult weather conditions, with an emphasis on the importance of perseverance and a growth mindset while celebrating and highlighting successes and progress. It can be observed when one continues to work hard and adapt even after encountering challenges or setbacks (MOE, 2016).

Integrity
Defined as the "[upholding] ethical principles and [having the] moral courage to stand up for what is right" (MOE, 2016), integrity could be modelled and encouraged during PES activities, such as admitting mistakes or taking responsibility for one's actions, emphasising fair play and adherence of game rules, and discussing ethical dilemmas and decision-making in the PES. It is demonstrated when students play by the rules and make ethical decisions during conflict (MOE, 2016).

Care
Defined as acting with "kindness and compassion" to make society a better place (MOE, 2016), care can be integrated into the PES setting by encouraging players to show empathy and compassion towards their teammates and opponents, with an emphasis on self-care and injury prevention, and discussing and modelling healthy and respectful relationships within the team and community. It can be demonstrated when one shows concern, consideration, and empathy for the well-being of their teammates and opponents, and extends their help to someone in need (MOE, 2016).

Harmony
Defined as the "[promotion of] social cohesion" and "[appreciation of] unity and diversity of a multi-cultural society" (MOE, 2016), harmony could be applied in the PES context through the cultivation of a team culture that values diversity and inclusivity, and by encouraging positive communication and conflict resolution skills while emphasising the importance of teamwork in achieving a common goal. It is observable when one cooperates with others in a team, valuing their peers' opinions and encouraging their peers (MOE, 2016).

Modelling

When modelling VLS, a description of the expected action is needed. While it might be tempting to highlight negative examples, it may be more effective to emphasise the positive behaviours and explain what is expected. It is also important for PETSCs to live by and to embody the values and behaviours they teach, setting a good example for their students. PETSCs should be patient, set realistic expectations for their students, be courteous to stakeholders and respect their opinions, have a clear and concise manner of communication, and treat students' mistakes as learning opportunities. Consistency is needed for students to be more receptive towards the intended message.

Additionally, students should practice the modelled behaviours to facilitate transfer out of PES. During the process, PETSCs should adopt a more respectful approach when communicating expectations and use questions to encourage reflection. This can be done during debriefs (Hellison, 1995). Reflection facilitates discussion and verbally addresses the meaning of life skills in PES and how they could be applied in daily life. This would help youths identify important VLS, their strengths in sports, and how these strengths can improve their performance in life. For example, students can realise that through team sports participation, leadership skills are developed. PETSCs can also share their personal attempts, successful and unsuccessful, in VLS transfer during the debriefs.

In this regard, the modelling of behaviours can be executed in various ways, using different mediums. One of which is using videos to facilitate understanding. For example, videos illustrating various VLS in action, such as teamwork, leadership, perseverance, and fair play, can be used as a basis for discussion and analysis. This helps in understanding and internalisation of the VLS and development of critical thinking and communication skills. In addition, videos are helpful for students who learn better through visual or auditory methods, hence providing greater inclusivity in the learning environment.

Students/athletes should be given opportunities to apply and refine their life skills, hence the importance of modelling. Scenarios or case studies are useful to facilitate this. The scenarios can be presented as real-life situations or hypothetical situations designed to encourage critical thinking about the value or skill taught. For example, games requiring teamwork, communication, and problem-solving can be designed to help students/athletes develop skills such as cooperation and leadership (Siedentop, 1994). Additionally, students can be given a chance to apply the VLS learnt in their daily lives, such as in their academic studies, personal relationships, or future careers. This helps reinforce concepts beyond PES (Kolb, 2014). As such, collaboration with other stakeholders and a whole-school approach is important. Through these, students/athletes are encouraged to see the value in action and better understand it through discussion and analysis of the scenarios. Journalling, open-ended questions, or debriefs can be added to help students reflect on the scenarios, during which successes, challenges, and areas for improvement can be discussed. This helps students develop a deeper understanding of themselves, their abilities, and their values.

Shaping

It is important to understand that students are bound to display varying extents of the expected behaviour. Hence, this stage focuses on the correction of negative behaviours while encouraging good ones, especially during lesson time. To shape the VLS taught, persistence and consistency are needed. Positive behaviours should be recognised, credited, and reinforced. However, if negative behaviour is encountered, it should be corrected immediately and consistently. Correction does not necessarily have to be negative or punitive; it can be done in a positive learning environment with genuine care and love. Humour can also be considered to illustrate these DON'Ts. Most importantly, the person exhibiting the negative behaviour has to be corrected in a one-on-one setting or in a small group. The same expectations should be upheld every time, and PETSCs need to understand that not confronting inappropriate behaviour would send a message of acceptance.

Naturally occurring teachable moments can also be seized during the lesson to capitalise on authentic, real-life situations that are relatable to students for them to learn from. This allows students to see the relevance and practicality of the content in the real world. These moments can relate to any topic, including PES values such as sportsmanship, teamwork, and leadership. For example, if a student shows sportsmanship by helping an opponent who has fallen during a game, the coach can use that moment to acknowledge the value of sportsmanship.

Reinforcement

Similar to shaping, reinforcement also serves to promote desired behaviours. However, reinforcement emphasises solely the reinforcement of positive behaviours. This can be done through presenters, spotlighting, or character-related awards. Inviting "guest speakers" combines defining, modelling, and reinforcing in a single session. Speakers could include national youth athletes, national Paralympians, and school team athletes. An overarching theme could be used to facilitate the discussion of the intended learning objective. Spotlighting involves appointing someone to make a positive statement about another member in front of a group. This can be done during or after practice or games. For instance, a student can be identified for something he has done that week which exhibits the qualities of the VLS in focus for the week. Finally, awards can be presented to those who show exceptional sportsmanship and/or those who demonstrate positive values to communicate to students that VLS learning and growth are important.

Teaching at School Level with a Whole-School Approach

Teaching VLS through PES is insufficient. To transfer learning into a non-sports context, other stakeholders, such as Citizenship and Character Education (CCE) teachers and parents, should be involved. In the process, students' interests and abilities should be considered. More support should be given to the students who require more time to learn. Through VLS education, a positive school culture is fostered, and a stronger sense of community can be built which enhances students' holistic development.

Positive Classroom Culture

A positive classroom culture satisfying students' needs is crucial in motivating students to overcome difficulties, challenges, and demands for further growth (Maslow, 1943). The classroom structure should aim to fulfil students' physiological needs, safety, and security, and create a sense of belonging and connection, according to Maslow's Hierarchy of Needs. Lower-Hoppe et al. (2021) found that a safe and supportive environment in which students feel a sense of belonging encourages them to partake in and benefit from VLS in PES. PETSCs should try to be empathetic, warm, caring, and genuine. Only then can conditions supporting athlete learning according to Bloom's taxonomy be created (Bloom et al., 1956; Short & Short, 2005). These conditions are a conducive team environment, positive coach and athlete relationships, modelling positive behaviour, and effectiveness in conducting the programme (Becker, 2009). PETSCs can also refer to Krathwohl's taxonomy of the affective domain when planning their lessons (Krathwohl et al., 1964). The taxonomy highlights the stages of learning through which learning gets internalised and values are formed. Thus, it might be useful for PETSCs to explore ways in which learners can make a progressive commitment towards an intended behavioural outcome. It might help to first concentrate on helping students identify their feelings and/or emotions in a situation before focusing on influencing and modifying students' attitudes, beliefs, and values.

To further encourage participation, a motivational and engaging classroom environment should be created through empowering climates. This includes "task-involved climates" that encourages "effort, learning and skill mastery" and "elements of autonomy supportive climate" informed by the self-determination theory that "recognises athletes' preferences and perspectives and provide meaningful choices and social supports" (Legg et al., 2018, p. 93). Motivation is affected by autonomy, competence, and relatedness (Ryan & Deci, 2017). A mastery-oriented environment facilitates VLS development, and an autonomy-supportive climate was found to be significantly correlated with VLS learning (Federico, 2019). Hence, PETSCs should aim to create a motivational environment by providing an autonomy-supportive climate to improve students' VLS learning of VLS (Newman et al., 2016).

Collaboration with Stakeholders

Collaboration with stakeholders facilitates reinforcement of VLS across contexts (Strachan et al., 2016). Family, school, and community have been indicated as being important in teaching children VLS, according to the former minister of education in Singapore, Mr. Ong Ye Kung (MOE, 2019b), as it allows greater integration of values education and supports students' holistic development through the provision of the necessary skills and qualities needed to thrive in every aspect of life. Thus, it is essential to ensure that all relevant stakeholders, such as CCE teachers and parents, have the same understanding to facilitate students in developing VLS to succeed in life. A set of recommendations guiding the development of positive school-home partnerships has been released, for example, the MOE's Parent Engagement Practices for School-Home-Partnership (MOE, 2019a). These recommendations highlighted the importance of mutual respect and trust between schools and parents to establish a partnership between both parties in creating a positive effect on students' development and well-being (MOE, 2019a).

To achieve the aforementioned goal, clear communication between PETSCs, CCE teachers and parents that highlights the values taught and how it is reinforced during staff and parent-teacher meetings is recommended. This can be achieved by using technology like mobile applications (e.g., WhatsApp or Line) for fast and effective communication once consents are given by various parties. A common set of values and life skills, including meanings and definitions, to be taught can also be established between PETSCs and CCE teachers before VLS teaching and transfer beyond PES. This would ensure reinforcement in non-sports contexts to occur and for students/athletes to develop a better understanding of the importance of VLS and its relevance in their lives. Areas that require more support or intervention can be identified through this process. In addition, as students are most likely to spend a considerable amount of time at home, CCE teachers could provide parents with resources such as worksheets to support them in reinforcing VLS at home.

SUMMARY AND FUTURE DIRECTIONS

In summary, PES provide an opportunity for youth to learn VLS that are valuable in navigating future challenges in life. However, careful planning and implementation of PES lessons are needed to ensure the intended outcomes are maximised. Teaching needs to take students' age and stage of development into consideration, and appropriate strategies must be applied. Additional principles which teachers can note is that the whole-school approach is encouraged, as it involves other key stakeholders, such as CCE teachers and parents, to ensure that the VLS learnt are reinforced in other contexts apart from PES lessons.

Future Directions

Cultural context affects VLS teaching and learning. Research has mainly focused on non-Asian contexts (Dimitrova & Wiium, 2021; Qi et al., 2020). Hence, more needs to be done to investigate VLS in PES in Asia (Ma & Shek, 2019).

In addition, mental well-being is also thought to influence values. Competition in schools can cause stress in students, which might lead to mental health decline that can steer students towards negative tendencies (Camiré et al., 2022). Future research should examine competition in the sporting context and its influence on mental well-being and VLS teaching in students (Seng et al., 2022).

REFERENCES

Becker, A. J. (2009). It's not what they do, it's how they do it: Athlete experiences of great coaching. *International Journal of Sports Science & Coaching*, 4(1), 93–119.

Bloom, B. S., Engelhart, M. D., Furst, E. J., Hill, W. H., & Krathwohl, D. R. (1956). *Taxonomy of educational objectives: The classification of educational goals. Handbook 1: Cognitive domain*. McKay New York.

Brown, B. E. (2003). *Teaching character through sport: Developing a positive coaching legacy*. Coaches Choice.

Camiré, M., Newman, T. J., Bean, C., & Strachan, L. (2022). Reimagining positive youth development and life skills in sport through a social justice lens. *Journal of Applied Sport Psychology*, 34(6), 1058–1076.

Camiré, M., Trudel, P., & Forneris, T. (2012). Coaching and transferring life skills: Philosophies and strategies used by model high school coaches. *The Sport Psychologist*, 26(2), 243–260. https://doi.org/10.1123/tsp.26.2.243

Chen, M. (2013). Education minister reiterates importance of character development through sport. *The Straits Times*. Retrieved from https://www.straitstimes.com/sport/education-minister-reiterates-importance-of-character-development-through-sport

Danish, S., Forneris, T., Hodge, K., & Heke, I. (2004). Enhancing youth development through sport. *World Leisure*, 46(3), 38–49.

Dimitrova, R., & Wiium, N. (2021). *Handbook of positive youth development: Advancing the next generation of research, policy and practice in global contexts*. Springer.

Federico, M. (2019). Does sports build positive youth development? Retrieved from http://hdl.handle.net/20.500.12648/3997

Gould, D., & Carson, S. (2008). Life skills development through sport: Current status and future directions. *International Review of Sport and Exercise Psychology*, 1(1), 58–78.

Halstead, J. M., & Taylor, M. J. (2000). *The development of values, attitudes and personal qualities: A review of recent research*. National Foundation for Educational Research.

Hellison, D. R. (1995). *Teaching responsibility through physical activity*. Human Kinetics.

Koh, K. T., Ong, S. W., & Camiré, M. (2016). Implementation of a values training programme in physical education and sport: Perspectives from teachers, coaches, students, and athletes. *Physical Education and Sport Pedagogy, 21*(3), 295–312.

Kolb, D. (2014). *Experiential learning: Experience as the source of learning and development* (Vol. 1) FT Press.

Krathwohl, D. R., Bloom, B. S., & Masia, B. B. (1964). *Taxonomy of educational objectives, Book II. Affective domain.* David McKay Company.

Legg, E., Newland, A., & Bigelow, R. (2018). Somebody's eyes are watching: The impact of coaching observations on empowering motivational climates and positive youth development. *Journal of Park and Recreation Administration, 36,* 90–106. https://doi.org/10.18666/JPRA-2018-V36-I4-8885

Li, C., & Ennis, C. D. (2017). The teaching of values in physical education: A review. *Physical Education and Sport Pedagogy, 22,* 207–223.

Lower-Hoppe, L., Anderson-Butcher, D., Newman, T., & Logan, J. (2021). The influence of peers on life skill development in a sport-based positive youth development program. *Journal of Sport for Development. 9*(2), 69–85. Retrieved from https://jsfd.org/

Ma, C. M., & Shek, D. T. (2019). Objective outcome evaluation of a positive youth development program: The Project PATHS in Hong Kong. *Research on Social Work Practice, 29*(1), 49–60.

Maslow, A. (1943). A theory of human motivation. *Psychological Review, 50*(4), 370–396.

MOE. (2016). *Physical education teaching & learning syllabus primary, secondary & pre-university.* Ministry of Education, Student Development Curriculum Division. Retrieved from https://www.moe.gov.sg/-/media/files/primary/physical_education_syllabus_2014.pdf

MOE. (2018). Speech by Mr. Ng Chee Meng, Minister for Education (Schools) at the Opening Ceremony of the National School Games 2018. Retrieved from https://www.moe.gov.sg/news/speeches/20180124-speech-by-mr-ng-chee-meng-minister-for-education-schools-at-the-opening-ceremony-of-the-national-school-games-2018

MOE. (2019a). Guidelines for school-home-partnership: Preparing students for the future. Retrieved from https://www.moe.gov.sg/news/press-releases/20190216-guidelines-for-school-home-partnership-preparing-students-for-the-future#:~:text=The%20central%20feature%20of%20the,on%20mutual%20respect%20and%20trust.

MOE. (2019b). Speech by Minister for Education Mr Ong Ye Kung at the National Kindness Awards Ceremony, at D'marquee @ Downtown East. Retrieved from https://www.moe.gov.sg/news/speeches/20191108-speech-by-minister-for-education-mr-ong-ye-kung-at-the-national-kindness-awards-ceremony-at-d-marquee-downtown-east

Nesbitt, K. T., & Farran, D. C. (2021). Effects of prekindergarten curricula: Tools of the mind as a case study. *Monographs of the Society for Research in Child Development, 86*(1), 7–119.

Newman, T. J., & Anderson-Butcher, D. (2021). Mechanisms of life skill development and life skill transfer: Interconnections and distinctions among socially vulnerable youth. *Journal of the Society for Social Work and Research*. https://doi.org/10.1086/715890

Newman, T. J., Ortega, R. M., Lower, L. M., & Paluta, L. M. (2016). Informing priorities for coaching education: Perspectives from youth sport leaders. *International Journal of Sports Science & Coaching*, 11(3), 436–445.

Prajapati, R., Sharma, B., & Sharma, D. (2017). Significance of life skills education. *Contemporary Issues in Education Research*, 10(1), 1–6.

Qi, S., Hua, F., Zhou, Z., & Shek, D. T. (2020). Trends of positive youth development publications (1995–2020): A scientometric review. *Applied Research in Quality of Life*, 17, 421-446.

Roberts, V., Sojo, V., & Grant, F. (2020). Organisational factors and non-accidental violence in sport: A systematic review. *Sport Management Review*, 23(1), 8–27.

Ryan, R. M., & Deci, E. L. (2017). *Self-determination theory: Basic psychological needs in motivation, development, and wellness*. The Guilford Press. https://doi.org/10.1521/978.14625/28806

Seng, Y. B. G., Koh, K. T., & Liem, G. A. D. (2022). *Teaching and facilitating the transference of values and life skills through physical education and sports in Singapore schools [electronic resource]* National Institute of Education, Nanyang Technological University.

Short, S. E., & Short, M. W. (2005). Essay: Role of the coach in the coach-athlete relationship. *The Lancet*, 366, S29–S30.

Siedentop, D. (1994). *Sport education: Quality PE through positive sport experiences*. (No Title).

Strachan, L., MacDonald, D. J., & Côté, J. (2016). Project SCORE! Coaches' perceptions of an online tool to promote positive youth development in sport. *International Journal of Sports Science & Coaching*, 11(1), 108–115.

Wong, A. (2014). Teenager's honesty is what sports can teach, says Heng. *Today*. Retrieved from https://www.todayonline.com/sports/teenagers-honesty-what-sports-can-teach-says-heng

Schools: An Ideal Platform to Teach Values and Life Skills

Chapter Two

Fernando Santos and Marta Ferreira

INTRODUCTION

Considering the current educational landscape, Gandolfi and Mills (2023) acknowledged that "schools are workplaces as well as places of learning [and] young people's human flourishing is dependent upon environments where teachers can develop their capacities too" (p. 584). Such a statement may instigate more questions than answers, including: *Do we want schools to become "workplaces"? Why do we need to reinforce that schools are places where teachers also learn? What does "flourishing" really mean for schools, physical education, and sports?* Based on these questions, understanding and envisioning pathways for how schools can become an ideal platform to teach values and life skills are complex endeavors that require thorough reflection, as well as constructive critique and dialogue. Considering such complexity, posing a central question – *What can this book chapter actually do for scholars, schools, practitioners, and youth?* – may be helpful. However, this is also a conflicting question because there are obviously limitations to what this book chapter and all these actors can, indeed, do. These limitations derive from what schools have become as political, social, and cultural entities in contemporary society (Au, 2016; Clausen, 2015).

Schools serve as spaces of discovery, a laboratory of excellence for youth to learn how to move their bodies, think, experiment, and diverge, as well as to explore their potential (Beni et al., 2023). More so, guided by inclusion, equity, freedom, and acceptance, schools can operate as settings where foundations can be set to create a socially just society (Freire, 1972; Hill et al., 2022). However, schools in contemporary society are built upon neoliberal[1] ideals that highlight the importance of competition, productivity, and economic value (Au, 2016). Indeed, educational content, teaching strategies, and targeted knowledge/skills are often chosen as ways to develop youth into profitable individuals that fit the norm and reinforce the status quo (Bruff & Tansel, 2018; Cobo, 2013; Dede, 2010).

DOI: 10.4324/9781032688657-3

Consequentially, youth are confronted with increased demands across educational systems, such as overwhelming pressures toward academic achievement and school readiness. Such demands are also consequences of "adultification" and "animalization" processes (see Rothwell et al., 2019, for an operationalization of the adultification process in youth sports). *Adultification*[2] reflects the need to prompt youth to perform and follow the standards set by adults (Cooke & Halberstadt, 2021). Furthermore, the process of adultification reduces youth to passive learners who are subject to *normative experiences* (i.e., experiences set by adults who are in control and establish what is deemed acceptable). For example, a teacher may ask students to be effective leaders at all costs without the necessary time and/or support to make mistakes. Thus, adultification has led to deficit-based approaches toward youth, in which youth are considered less human and able, which then justifies depriving them of transformative and emancipatory learning experiences and actual empowerment (Camiré et al., 2023).

Associated with adultification processes comes the notion of *animalization*,[3] which embraces a reductionist approach toward youth. Such an approach highlights the need to control behaviors – what, when, and how youth operate in their lives. Controlling behaviors have become the cornerstone and benchmark for education. Such controlling behaviors require youth to devalue critical thinking and awareness, and simply focus on emergent, concrete, and immediate needs, such as following the curriculum (Cammarota & Fine, 2010). Schools that abide by neoliberal ideals resort to a pedagogy of obedience and manipulation (see Giroux, 2022). Hence, there is a need to carefully reflect on how the neoliberalization of society and, as a consequence, schools impact physical education and sports (PES) programming (Eccles & Gootman, 2002; Lerner, 2021).

To showcase the previous points, two examples are provided. First, PES programs are often used to teach youth life skills and values necessary to thrive in a neoliberal society. These skills are, in some cases, taught without an explicit (and genuine) concern for social justice (see Santos et al., 2022). We should bear in mind that pedagogical models are also permeated by neoliberal values. The fallacy resides in believing that social justice is not an issue that matters in certain fields, areas, and disciplines.

A second example is how PES programs are, in many cases, instrumentalized to develop youth into healthy, functional, and productive individuals who can add value to society (see Malcolm et al., 2023; Edwards et al., 2017; Quennerstedt et al., 2021). The purpose of these PES programs is to develop an adultified and animalized individual who can do good in society, which translates into doing more of the same – ensuring the status quo remains untouched (Camiré 2023; Camiré et al., 2021). Health, life skills, and many other concepts simply become tools to ensure youth are able and willing to satisfy the needs of society and focus on what matters.

Considering the question posed at the onset of this chapter, schools can serve as a crucial setting for the development of critical thinking and reflexive skills that may enable youth to challenge the status quo and foster a more just society (Wilson & Blyth, 2020). Hence, schools can contribute to a society in which capitalism, racism, and mass consumption do not undermine pivotal values for living-doing-(re)doing well, such as equity and inclusiveness. The rest of the chapter aims to provide insights into the need for a post-neoliberal school and provide pedagogical implications for PES programs.

APPLIED INSIGHTS

Making a Case for the Post-Neoliberal School

The post-neoliberal school, as proposed, is a space for questioning taken-for-granted truths and processes. The taken-for-granted truths and processes that are worth questioning refer to what is teachable, how one can teach, and what learning can become. In other words, neoliberal approaches are revisited and deconstructed to create added possibilities for youth development and a better and more just society. Through a post-neoliberal school, we intend to highlight

> the importance of situating innovations alongside local policy mandates and within teachers' local contexts when presenting them to teachers. Further, this holds key implications for policy reform, suggesting that innovative approaches that deal with the how and why of teachers' practice may help teachers understand and (re)interpret the what (i.e. mandated content and assessment) of their physical education teaching in new ways.
>
> (Beni et al., 2023, p. 12)

There are several guiding principles that may need to be considered to appropriately frame the post-neoliberal school. First, learning outcomes and processes can be positioned as one and the same. In this sense, the experience is as valuable as the outcome. Specifically, emphasis is placed on experiences that can (*perhaps should?*) be youth-centric and youth-led, as well as contribute to social justice promotion (Cammarota & Fine, 2010). For example, the experience of teaching another student in a physical education class can be as valuable and (in many cases perhaps more) relevant than what was learned through this experience (e.g., motor skills). The experience of teaching another student can potentially provide new insights into what leadership is, as well as help students envision a life purpose and understand their impact on others. These variables may not translate into immediate learning outcomes. However, if outcomes begin to outweigh the value of experiences in the learning process, neoliberal tendencies tend to emerge. As such, often the quicker outcomes are attained, often the more individualistic and objectified learning may eventually become.

Second, pre-determining what a learning outcome is should not come at the expense of depriving youth of being creative, exploring the unexplored, and leading their own learning processes (Gonzalez et al., 2020; Russell, 2016). If students have limited control over their own experiences, a pedagogy of control may continue to be present across PES programming. Conversely, PES programming may need to embrace a youth-centric approach that instigates youth to become critical thinkers, tolerant, and able to act toward social justice promotion (Kochanek et al., 2022; Mac Intosh et al., 2020; Sakamoto & Pitner, 2005).

Third, we wish to reinforce that schools are not apolitical in nature but there are still many taboo issues that should and must be openly discussed. These issues include discrimination, equity, religion, and politics, among many others (see Brown, 2023, for an example of the need to discuss these topics). Without explicit discussions and consideration for emergent social justice issues, PES programming may inherently contribute to the status quo. It should be noted that neutral political approaches have failed to dismantle systematic oppression (e.g., Robinson et al., 2023). As such, *should we continue to make schools as resources to limit political thinking?* There are possibilities to respectfully and openly discuss all social justice issues with youth. Subsequently, these discussions can help co-construct ideals, premises, and pathways for more socially just ways of living (Camiré, 2022).

Fourth, the post-neoliberal school requires teachers to be differentiated from system enforcers (see Giroux, 2022). Instead, teachers must truly become concerned with social justice and become co-constructors of knowledge. Mimicking social justice discourses, such as presenting a discourse that values social justice without critical action, does not fit these premises and may result in implicit but highly direct forms of oppression (e.g., Walton-Fisette & Sutherland, 2020). These highly direct forms of oppression include limiting what can be subject to discussion in schools and neglecting evidence that supports the need for change to discriminate against minorities. Thus, social justice education should be positioned as a need more than a possibility for some (Bialystok, 2014).

Fifth, research with post-neoliberal schools becomes inquiry and a form of discovery instead of confirmation (Camiré, 2023b). Concepts are constantly revisited and openly questioned to consider the dynamic nature of social justice and society. Discussions held by scholars, physical education teachers, and various actors attempt to engage with concepts and expand their understanding of society and emergent social justice issues to develop meaningful pedagogical practices. Collaborative efforts between all these actors can result in making research meaningful for practice and social justice promotion – finding innovative pedagogies that are social justice-oriented (Sakamoto & Pitner, 2005). In other words, research needs to come together with youth, schools, and communities and realize the complex nature of the social world by attempting to provide voices to all actors (Smith et al., 2023).

Messages for Communities

Based on these guiding principles, we discuss how to foster social justice in and through PES programming. However, before doing so, it becomes important to define social justice in the post-neoliberal school and (re)define life skills.

Concerning a social justice definition within the post-neoliberal school, it is important to highlight that there is not one. This may sound unacceptable for some and understandable for others. Through the tenets of a post-neoliberal school, social justice is incommensurable and can tackle a variety of issues that make the world and communities more just places (Levin, 2020). Therefore, to avoid excluding certain topics, concerns, and approaches, social justice can be operationalized in a multitude of ways so long as such efforts are conducted through contextualized reasoning (Adamson et al., 2022).

However, to potentially operationalize social justice, it may be important to understand that PES have limited powers. Although sports has been granted too much importance in youth's social development (Anderson-Butcher, 2019) and in deconstructing inequities (Trachsler & Handley, 2022), many pitfalls do exist, which creates numerous challenges for practitioners moving forward. Indeed, sports has been considered to have a limited influence in fostering positive youth development outcomes (Bruner et al., 2021). Conversely, sports has been associated with negative outcomes such as discrimination (Baker-Lewton et al., 2017). This is why it becomes relevant to understand how to frame PES programs in ways that enable youth to learn how to foster social justice.

Based on the purpose of the post-neoliberal school, it becomes paramount to acknowledge the several limitations associated with how life skills have been defined and used in past research and practice (see Gould & Carson, 2008, for a life skill definition). Specifically, life skills have served the purpose of preparing youth for the harsh challenges of the neoliberal world, such as being able to persevere, endure, and perform (Pierce et al., 2017). Normative experiences reinforce the values, concerns, objectives, and metrics of the neoliberal society in which we live (Camiré, 2022). Therefore, leadership can also be taught to help youth make others docile, obedient, and easily manipulated individuals. For instance, a teacher may provide a leadership role to students and value their efforts toward making their peers follow orders. The behaviors displayed by the leader may be accepted by the teacher as long as they complete the proposed tasks. Recently, aligned with the need to move toward a post-neoliberal school, researchers have conceptualized the need to include social justice life skills as part of programmatic efforts that aim to better prepare individuals to develop socially just practices (Camiré, 2022; Camiré et al., 2023). Social justice life skills can be defined as life skills that are taught in ways that can serve a social justice mandate. Specifically, they can help youth thrive toward equity, inclusion, and tolerance (Camiré et al., 2021). Examples of social justice life skills include critical thinking, activism, and leadership. Next, we will provide a series of messages for decision-makers to (re)think schools, learning and youth development in contemporary society.

Underpinnings of Social Justice Promotion through Physical Education and Sports

More than teaching social justice life skills in PES programs, efforts may need to be deployed toward social justice education across the school curriculum. The forces of oppression and socialization properties inherent to neoliberal thinking have the necessary power to influence youth. A joint collaborative effort among the school community may be required if youth development is to intersect with social justice. Social justice life skills may serve as a starting point for teachers to develop (novel) pedagogical approaches that can contribute to dismantling inequities and highlight the value of inclusion and antiracist practices, among many other processes outcomes (Lekas et al., 2020).

Social justice experiences (see Newman et al., 2023, for a description of experiential learning processes) also hold important value in helping youth envision the world and prevalent inequities in their context and understand how they can contribute. For instance, youth may need to recognize the numerous inequities, injustices, and maltreatment present in today's society (e.g., Kulick et al., 2019). It is fair to state that youth, in some cases, remain unaware of social injustices and have a limited understanding of what is at stake, as well as who is affected and how. Efforts to refuse to acknowledge the need for social justice promotion have included segregating privileged youth from understanding the social world and desensitizing them toward social injustice issues (i.e., posing a perverse question – *why should they care?*).

Activism and social justice leadership may also need to take center stage in programming (Mac Intosh et al., 2020). Without activism and social justice promotion, youth have no opportunities to become involved in social justice and may simply be victims of a bystander effect. Such bystander effect reflects an awareness that is not followed by critical action, which is why youth need to have opportunities to foster social justice and actively engage with a variety of social justice issues, such as gender equity and LGBTQIAP+ rights. These opportunities may include helping youth identify social justice causes and define a plan of action, openly discuss social injustices particular to their contexts, and create inclusive environments in schools. Such active engagement may involve youth voicing their perspectives, as well as taking action and/or helping others take action toward policy change.

Schools and teachers can act as gatekeepers for shaping priorities in youth development; environments need to be deliberately designed to prompt active engagement. For example, youth can be supported to develop an antiracism campaign for a sports event held at the school. Such antiracism campaigns may help provide voices to athletes who have been victims of racism, as well as create awareness about the need to develop more effective sports policies. Such initiatives can instigate meaningful discussions about racism and discrimination within physical education classes. All youth should be afforded the opportunity to lead in their own way, with their identities and beliefs, as well as according to their interests, agendas, and motivations. Per these premises, social justice leadership (as a social justice life skill) becomes a requirement for social justice promotion. Docile, obedient, and passive individuals who are oppressed by the system most likely cannot act on social justice issues and can develop politically correct discourses that implicitly and covertly reinforce the status quo.

Finally, social justice assessment is a needed step to determine how intentionality translates into practice. Thus, assessment may need to be positioned through a dual-perspective approach. On one hand, schools can engage in process evaluations to determine if and how social justice promotion is permeating teaching and learning processes in PES, as well as across other disciplines. For instance, process evaluations may include peer debriefs, participatory action-research designs, informal reflections, or any resources that enable schools and teachers to understand how social justice is permeating the curriculum in a way that is not superficial, casuistical, and/or propaganda (i.e., careless usage of social justice topics and overall discourse). On the other hand, youth can be assessed in consideration of the guiding principles presented previously in this subsection with particular focus on (a) engagement in social justice experiences, (b) the ability to master social justice life skills, and (c) engagement in activism. An outcome evaluation that is youth-centric may provide insights into the impacts of social justice education on students' behaviors, attitudes and overall learning. Assessment criteria may be tailored to fit the particularities of the sociocultural context and social justice operationalizations.

SUMMARY AND FUTURE DIRECTIONS

Based on the question raised at the onset of this reflexive exercise – *What can this book chapter actually do for schools, scholars, practitioners, and youth?* We have attempted to instigate a reform in the way we think of schools, life skills, as well as PES. Some of the notions advanced may resonate as vague and lack concrete actionable items. However, *should this chapter determine what is best? Or should we try and fail to attempt to understand what is to come for schools?* We have attempted to take on the second question and challenge current approaches toward schools and PES. These reflections have a wider reach than just informing practitioners' efforts to think and do differently. Indeed, researchers have a privileged position and the duty to challenge their own research agendas and routines (i.e., ways to do research and achieve outputs). Without such constructive critique, meaningful change and advances are much more difficult to attain. In fact, PES can be, as it occurs in some sociocultural contexts, a benchmark for neoliberal outputs.

Taking a question-focused approach, it becomes relevant to instigate reflection on how both researchers and practitioners can decide to use the notions advanced in this chapter in their practice. The first imperative question connects to researchers' and practitioners' motivations and values: *can they ignore social justice?* This may seem a rather simple question that entails an obvious answer, but practice tells a different story (i.e., certain practices across educational systems show a complete disregard toward social justice). Thus, there is no space to claim to ignore social justice.

A second set of questions challenges our benefits from the system: *do we really want a post-neoliberal school to emerge? Will a post-neoliberal school completely disregard fast-food research and teaching (producing waste in the process)? What are the costs?* Fast-food research and teaching processes translate into a lack of reflexivity, easily applicable and generalizable practices, as well as make youth achieve neoliberal metrics as quickly as possible, no matter the costs (Koro et al., 2023). Also, depending on how these questions are answered, researchers may need to revisit their research programs and completely reimagine their respective fields. This is a very challenging exercise, but potentially a needed one. Researchers themselves have, in some cases, become docile, obedient, and passive individuals who simply aim to deploy efforts toward superficial metrics such as citation scores (Macdonald, 2022). Finally, one last question may need to be posed: *how can we survive a neoliberal world with a post-neoliberal school?* This is possibly one of the main challenges ahead. Youth need to understand neoliberal thinking and reasoning so they can maneuver the intricacies of attempting change. Well, there are certainly more questions and answers, which creates the necessary rationale to pose the very last question: *do we want to fail doing something different or continue to do the same?* We definitely urge the readers to attempt to do different and fail very well while trying to engage in social justice efforts.

NOTES

1 Neoliberal ideals translate into individualistic ways of thinking and doing instigated by increased and ever-changing competitiveness and need for productivity.
2 Adultification refers to the fact that youth participants are supposed to follow the norms and achieve the performance metrics set for adults.
3 Animalized youth are individuals who have been educated to neglect critical thinking and reflexivity and simply follow and respond to superficial demands and needs set by the neoliberal society we live in.

REFERENCES

Adamson, B., Adamson, M., Clarke, C., Richardson, E., & Sydnor, S. (2022). Social justice through sport and exercise studies: A manifesto. *Journal of Sport and Social Issues*, 46(5), 407–444. https://doi.org/10.1177/01937235221099150

Anderson-Butcher, D. (2019). Youth sport as a vehicle for social development. *Kinesiology Review*, 8(3), 180–187. https://doi.org/10.1123/kr.2019-0029

Au, W. (2016). Meritocracy 2.0: High-Stakes, Standardized Testing as a Racial Project of Neoliberal Multiculturalism. *Educational Policy*, 30(1), 39–62. https://doi.org/10.1177/0895904815614916

Baker-Lewton, A., Sonn, C., Vincent, D., & Curnow, F. (2017). 'I haven't lost hope of reaching out...': Exposing racism in sport by elevating counternarratives. *International Journal of Inclusive Education*, 21(11), 1097–1112. https://doi.org/10.1080/13603116.2017.1350316

Beni, S., Ní Chróinín, D., Fletcher, T., Bailey, J., Cariño Fraisse, L., Down, M., Hamada, M., Riddick, T., Trojanovic, M., & Gross, K. (2023). Teachers' sense-making in implementation of meaningful physical education. *Physical Education and Sport Pedagogy*. Advance online publication. https://doi.org/10.1080/17408989.2023.2260388

Bialystok, L. (2014). Politics without "brainwashing": A philosophical defence of social justice education. *Curriculum Inquiry*, 44, 413–440.

Brown, T. (2023). To be our best selves: Critical dialogue with girls of color about their experiences in a social justice leadership program. *Journal of Curriculum and Pedagogy*, 20(1), 63–89. https://doi.org/10.1080/15505170.2021.1967227

Bruff, I., & Tansel, C. (2018). Authoritarian neoliberalism: Trajectories of knowledge production and praxis. *Globalizations*, 16(3), 233–244. https://doi.org/10.1080/14747731.2018.1502497

Bruner, M., McLaren, C., Sutcliffe, J., Gardner, L., Lubans, D., Smith, J., and Vella, S. (2021). The effect of sport-based interventions on positive youth development: A systematic review and meta-analysis. *International Review of Sport and Exercise Psychology*. Advance online publication. https://doi.org/10.1080/1750984X.2021.1875496

Camiré, M. (2022). The two continua model for life skills teaching. Sport, Education and Society, 28(8), 915–928. https://doi.org/10.1080/13573322.2022.2073438

Camiré, M. (2023). Building a case for infusing posthumanist thinking in the qualitative training of sport and exercise psychology researchers, *International Journal of Sport and Exercise Psychology*. Advance online publication. https://doi.org/10.1080/1612197X.2023.2180072

Camiré, M., Newman, T., Bean, C., & Strachan, L. (2021). Reimagining positive youth development and life skills in sport through a social justice lens. *Journal of Applied Sport Psychology*. Advance online publication. https://doi.org/10.1080/10413200.2021.1958954

Camiré, M., Santos, F., Newman, T., Vella, S., MacDonald, D. J., Milistetd, M., Pierce, S., & Strachan, L. (2023). Positive youth development as a guiding framework in sport research: Is it time to plan for a transition?. *Psychology of Sport and Exercise*, 69, 102505. https://doi.org/10.1016/j.psychsport.2023.102505

Cammarota, J., & Fine, M. (2010). *Revolutionizing education: Youth participatory action research in motion*. Routledge.

Clausen, S. (2015). Schoolification or early years democracy? A cross-curricular perspective from Denmark and England. *Contemporary Issues in Early Childhood*, 16(4), 355–373. https://doi.org/10.1177/1463949115616327

Cobo, C. (2013). Skills for innovation: envisioning an education that prepares for the changing world. *The Curriculum Journal*, 24(1), 67–85. https://doi.org/10.1080/09585176.2012.744330

Cooke, A. N., & Halberstadt, A. G. (2021). Adultification, anger bias, and adults' different perceptions of Black and White children. *Cognition and Emotion*, 35(7), 1416–1422. https://doi.org/10.1080/02699931.2021.1950127

Dede, C. (2010). *Comparing frameworks for 21st century skills*. Solution Tree Press.

Eccles, J., & Gootman, J. (2002). *Community programs that promote youth development*. National Academies Press.

Edwards, L., Bryant, A., Keegan, R., Morgan, K., and Jones, A. (2017). Definitions, foundations and associations of physical literacy: A systematic review. *Sports Medicine*, 47, 113–126. https://doi.org/10.1007/s40279-016-0560-7

Freire, P. (1972). *Pedagogy of the oppressed*. Herder and Herder.

Gandolfi, H. E., & Mills, M. (2023). Teachers for social justice: Exploring the lives and work of teachers committed to social justice in education. *Oxford Review of Education*, 49(5), 569–587. https://doi.org/10.1080/03054985.2022.2105314

Giroux, H. (2022). *Pedagogy of resistance: Against manufactured ignorance*. Bloomsbury Publishing.

Gonzalez, M., Kokozos, M., Byrd, C., & McKee, K. (2020). Critical positive youth development: A framework for centering critical consciousness. *Journal of Youth Development*, 15(6), 24–43. https://doi.org/10.5195/jyd.2020.859

Gould, D., & Carson, S. (2008). Life skills development through sport: Current status and future directions. *International Review of Sport and Exercise Psychology*, 1(1), 58–78. https://doi.org/10.1080/17509840701834573

Hill, J., Walton-Fisette, J. L., Flemons, M., Philpot, R., Sutherland, S., Phillips, S., Flory, S. B., & Ovens, A. (2022). Social justice knowledge construction among physical education teacher educators: The value of personal, professional, and educational experiences. *Physical Education and Sport Pedagogy*. Advance online publication. https://doi.org/10.1080/17408989.2022.2123463

Kochanek, J., Secaras, L., & Erickson, K. (2022). Dialogue in Athletics: An evaluation of a social justice education program in high school sports. *Journal of Applied Sport Psychology*, 35(4), 680–709. https://doi.org/10.1080/10413200.2022.2084181

Koro, M., Wolgemuth, J., & Trinh, E. (2023). Reducing methodological footprints in qualitative research. *Qualitative Inquiry*. Advance online publication. https://doi.org/10.1177/10778004231183944

Kulick, A., Wernick, L., Espinoza, M., Newman, T., & Dessel, A. (2019). Three strikes and you're out: Culture, facilities, and participation among LGBTQ youth in sports. *Sport, Education and Society*, 24(9), 939–953. https://doi.org/10.1080/13573322.2018.532406

Lekas, H., Pahl, K., & Fuller, C. (2020). Rethinking cultural competence: Shifting to cultural humility. *Health services insights*. Advance online publication. https://doi.org/10.1177/1178632920970580

Lerner, R. M. (2021). *Individuals as producers of their own development: The dynamics of person context coactions*. Routledge.

Levin, L. (2020). Rethinking social justice: A contemporary challenge for social good. *Research on Social Work Practice*, 30(2), 186–195. https://doi.org/10.1177/1049731519854161

Mac Intosh, A., Martin, E., & Kluch, Y. (2020). To act or not to act? Student-athlete perceptions of social justice activism. *Psychology of Sport and Exercise*, 51(1), 1–8. https://doi.org/10.1016/j.psychsport.2020.101766

Macdonald, S. (2022). The gaming of citation and authorship in academic journals: A warning from medicine. *Social Science Information*, 61(4), 457–480. https://doi.org/10.1177/05390184221142218

Malcolm, D., Marcén, C., & Pullen, E. (2023). The world health organization, physical activity and the contradictions of neoliberal health promotion. *International Journal of Sport Policy and Politics*. Advance online publication. https://doi.org/10.1080/19406940.2023.2242874

Newman, T., Lee, L., & Stauffer, A. (2023). An experiential approach to understanding PYD from sport-based programs. In N. Holt & M. McDonough (Eds.), *Positive youth development through sport* (3rd ed.). Routledge.

Pierce, S., Gould, D., & Camiré, M. (2017). Definition and model of life skills transfer. *International Review of Sport and Exercise Psychology*, 10(1), 186–211. https://doi.org/10.1080/1750984X.2016.1199727

Quennerstedt, M., McCuaig, L., & Mårdh, A. (2021). The fantasmatic logics of physical literacy. *Sport, Education and Society*, 26(8), 846–861. https://doi.org/10.1080/13573322.2020.1791065

Robinson, E., Newman, T., Scheadler, T., Lower-Hoppe, L., & Baeth, A. (2023). The unique lived experiences of LGBQ athletes: A collegiate women's rugby club team as an inclusive and empowering community. *Journal of Homosexuality*. Advance online publication. https://doi.org/10.1080/00918369.2022.2160684

Rothwell, M., Stone, J., & Davids, K. (2019). Exploring forms of life in player development pathways: The case of British rugby league. *Journal of Motor Learning and Development*, 7(2), 242–260. https://doi.org/10.1123/jmld.2018-0020

Russell, S. T. (2016). Social justice, research, and adolescence. *Journal of Research on Adolescence*, 26(1), 4–15. https://doi.org/10.1111/jora.12249

Sakamoto, I., & Pitner, R. O. (2005). Use of critical consciousness in anti-oppressive social work practice: Disentangling power dynamics at personal and structural levels. *The British Journal of Social Work*, 35(4), 435–452. https://doi.org/10.1093/bjsw/bch190

Santos, F., Newman, T. J., Aytur, S., & Farias, C. (2022). Aligning physical literacy with critical positive youth development and student-centered pedagogy: Implications for today's youth. *Frontiers in Sports and Active Living*, 4, 1–10. https://doi.org/10.3389/fspor.2022.845827

Smith, B., Williams, O., Bone, L., & the Moving Social Work Co-Production Collective. (2023). Co-production: A resource to guide co-producing research in the sport, exercise, and health sciences. *Qualitative Research in Sport, Exercise and Health*, 15(2), 159–187. https://doi.org/10.1080/2159676X.2022.2052946

Trachsler, T., & Handley, M. (2022). Sports, the great equalizer: Influencing future sports professionals view of disabilities: Sports professionals view of disabilities. *Sport Social Work Journal*, 2(1), 49–62. https://doi.org/10.33043/SSWJ.2.1.49-62

Walton-Fisette, J., & Sutherland, S. (2020). Time to SHAPE Up: Developing policies, standards and practices that are socially just. *Physical Education and Sport Pedagogy*, 25(3), 274–287. https://doi.org/10.1080/17408989.2020.1741531

Wilson, C., & Blyth, D. (2020). Race, antiracism, and youth development: From awareness to sustained action. *Journal of Youth Development*, 15(5), 1–15. https://doi.org/10.5195/jyd.2020.1005

Physical Education and School Sports, the Natural Setting for Values and Life Skills

Chapter Three

Scott Pierce, Emily Jones and Andrew Eberline

INTRODUCTION

International tennis icon and social activist Billie Jean King believes that "sports teaches you character, it teaches you to play by the rules, it teaches you to know what it feels like to win and lose – it teaches you about life." This commonly held global belief positions physical education (PE) and sports as contexts that support the personal development of young people. The chapter seeks to promote PE and school-based sports as a natural setting for developing values and life skills for young people.

An ecological systems-based approach provides us with an opportunity to examine the challenges and opportunities for promoting PE and school-based sports as settings for developing values and life skills. A systems-based approach allows us to see a variety of youth experiences, and adult role models play a crucial role in shaping youths' personal development. Pointedly, it recognizes that there is a bidirectional influence between PE and sports settings with societies, communities, organizations, and individual stakeholders (e.g., parents, coaches, teachers), who ultimately influence the youth participants, their values, and their life skills (Dorsch et al., 2022). Personal development can be defined as the growth of personal values – a set of guiding principles and beliefs, and life skills – "internal personal assets, characteristics, and skills such as goal setting, emotional control, self-esteem, and hard work ethic that can be facilitated or developed in sports and are transferred for use in non-sports settings" (Gould & Carson, 2008, p. 60).

This chapter will utilize the authors' experiences as scholar-practitioners in PE, youth sports, and sports psychology domains in the United States to provide applied insights and recommendations for promoting PE and sports as contexts to support the development of values and life skills. Specifically, we will examine the unique contexts of

DOI: 10.4324/9781032688657-4

PE and school-based sports to identify what positions them as settings for developing values and life skills. While these natural settings for personal development exist, we will also explore the complexity and complications in achieving this common mission. This chapter will conclude with a call for collective action for an integrated, systems-based approach to promote values and life skills through PE and sports.

APPLIED INSIGHTS

School-Based Physical Education as a Setting to Promote Values and Life Skills

PE serves as an educational movement to provide physical activity-oriented experiences for school-aged children and youth (typically aged 5–18 years old). While work conditions vary immensely across settings, physical educators are generally tasked with delivering age-appropriate instructional sessions targeting motor skill development and movement competencies, along with lessons associated with life skills and value orientations that transfer beyond the classroom setting.

Quality school-based PE is guided by a curriculum: a written document representing a collection of selected instructional units progressively designed to build upon previous learning and skill/concept mastery. A written PE curriculum also reflects planned formative and summative assessments of learning at critical developmental benchmarks. These benchmarks are established by state and national standards and stated outcomes. In the United States, national standards are developed by professional associations of health and physical educators – namely, the Society of Health and Physical Educators of America (SHAPE America). State-level standards for PE are generally developed by the state-level department of education, or the national standards are adopted. Accountability structures vary for PE professionals across the United States in terms of the how achievement of learning outcomes (e.g., progress toward standards and grade-level benchmarks) is monitored within school-based PE programs.

The current professional standards for K–12 PE, as defined by SHAPE America (2013), reflect two (of five) standards that specifically focus on aspects related to values and life skills. Standard 4 reads, "responsible personal and social behaviors that respect self and others," and Standard 5 states, "value physical activity for health, enjoyment, challenge, self-expression and/or social interaction" (SHAPE

America, 2013). These standards embody fundamental values and life skills that can be mediated by and through sports and physical activity participation, including, but not limited to, self-management, social awareness, goal setting, respecting the rights and feelings of others, teamwork, and effort. The standards provide a guiding framework and rationale for PE practitioners and scholars to figure out how to best create learning environments that introduce, apply, and appropriately evaluate student learning and progress toward these stated learning outcomes.

Programs in Physical Education Embodying Values and Life Skills

In addition to the guiding standards, researchers within the field of PE have established a knowledge base of research-informed curricular models and instructional approaches evidenced to produce values and life skills outcomes for youth. The Teaching Personal and Social Responsibility (TPSR) Model was developed by Don Hellison. TPSR is primarily concerned with developing and fostering life skills in youth – namely problem-solving, autonomy, and a sense of purpose and future (Hellison, 1995). Using physical activity as a medium, TPSR incorporates self-reflection and evaluation of one's level of responsibility, "ranging from a level zero of irresponsibility, through participation and effort under supervision, self-direction, and caring about and helping others, to transference of these skills to life outside the gymnasium" (Casey & Kirk, 2021, p. 56). Originally developed for afterschool physical activity settings for at-risk youth, TPSR is now incorporated into PE class settings with structured learning and instruction to include (1) relational time, (2) awareness talks, (3) physical activity, (4) group meetings as incidents arise, and (5) self-reflection time (Hellison, 2011). Research findings from TPSR implementation in school-based PE settings (Hemphill & Richards, 2016) have provided evidence of positive effects on learner enjoyment, perceived responsibility, and behavioral engagement (Cecchini et al., 2007; Pozo et al., 2018; Simonton & Garn, 2019; Simonton & Shiver, 2021).

Adventure education can also be embedded into PE experiences to influence youth values and life skills. Outward Bound, for example, is an outdoor adventure education course designed to "accelerate the development of independence, initiative, physical fitness, self-reliance, and resourcefulness" of youth participants (Hattie et al., 1997, p. 44). Adventure education has since evolved to education and school-based programs (e.g., challenge ropes courses, backpacking, rock climbing, orienteering) to emphasize the role of character, challenge, and physical endeavor (Boyes, 2000; Prouty et al., 2007). The curricular model involves structured kinesthetic, highly interactive learning experiences designed to provide participants with opportunities to stretch themselves beyond their comfort zone in multiple ways – physically, socially, cognitively, and emotionally (Sutherland & Legge, 2016). As a function of this, a signature feature of adventure education is the elevated holistic learning that is fostered through the *process* of participation (Hastie, 1995; Lugg & Martin, 2001), including (1) experimental learning cycle, (2) full value contract, and (3) challenge by choice. Research findings from adventure education implementation in school-based PE settings related to personal and social skill development have been found to be facilitated through the social experience of participating (Lugg & Martin, 2001) and has assisted in the renegotiation of social hierarchies in PE (Tischler & McCaughtry, 2014).

The Role of Physical Education Teachers in Promoting Values and Life Skills

Within the structure of mandatory PE in the school setting, physical educators are naturally positioned to teach values and life skills through sports and physical activity. They have the daily connection, adult-youth relationships, and activity-based conditions to implicitly and explicitly teach values and life skills. Formal teacher training programs and state-specific licensing policies guide the credentialling requirements for physical educators, in line with these opportunities for supporting youth development. National accrediting bodies (e.g., Council for the Accreditation of Educator Preparation) and discipline-specific professional organizations (e.g., SHAPE America) govern the initial teacher standards that outline skills, knowledge, and dispositions of beginning teachers. Initial teacher standards serve as outcomes accountability metrics and standardized guidelines for formal teacher education programs housed in colleges and universities. These formal teacher education programs espouse the development of the necessary skills, knowledge, and dispositions for effective beginning teachers – including, but not limited to, discipline-specific content knowledge, knowledge of learners, planning and delivery of developmentally appropriate instructional content, assessment of student learning, selection and use of evidence-based curricular models and instructional strategies, and strategies to navigate sociopolitical variables within school-settings. Ultimately, physical educators are trained to understand and support the development of youth and life skills through physical activity.

In this crucial role, the identities and ideologies of educators must be considered. In the United States, the racial, ethnic, and cultural diversity represented in the PE teacher workforce is not matched to the demographics of the learners within their care. In 2019, less than 50% of school-aged children in the United States identified as white, in contrast to 79% of public school educators (National Center for Educational Statistics, 2019). Within PE, these numbers are similar, with only a small percentage of teachers, coaches, and sports administrators representing persons of color (Hodge et al., 2008). Establishing safe and inclusive environments for all learners is essential and is reinforced by the formal training and credentialling experience for educators. To continue to enhance the capacity of PE as a setting to teach values and lie skills, we must promote cultural humility (i.e., self-exploration and self-critique combined with a willingness to learn from others) and cultural competence (i.e., understand and respect values, attitudes, beliefs, and mores that differ across cultures) in physical educators. Doing so will help to support culturally appropriate values and life skills rather than those driven solely by an educator's personal background and experience (Newman et al., in press).

School-Based Sports as a Natural Setting for Values and Life Skills

In many countries, sports is one of the most popular extracurricular activities for school students (Turgeon et al., 2019). School sport represents a developmental context characterized by team selections based on tryouts, a strong commitment from youth to practice outside of regular class hours, and structured competition with other schools (Camiré & Kendellen, 2016). This competitive, interscholastic nature is what differentiates school sport from PE. Subsequently, school sports is also positioned as a natural setting for youth participants to promote values and life skills.

While having an indirect influence on youth participants, organizations in the environmental subsystem serve a pivotal role in setting the mission and standards for what sports can and should be (Dorsch et al., 2022). In the United States, the National Federation of High School State Associations (NFHS) serves as the governing organization for high school sports and "serves as the national authority that promotes and protects the defining values of education-based high school athletics" (NFHS, 2023a). In this role, the promotion of values and life skills in sports participants is often an explicit priority in the mission of school sports. Specifically, the NFHS believes that student participation in interscholastic sports "enriches the educational experience… promotes respect, integrity, and sportsmanship…and develops leadership and life skills" (NFHS, 2023b). With this aspirational focus on developing values and life skills in youth participants in school sports, it is necessary to first define the structure and design of school sports and identify if and how values and life skills are developed.

How the Structure of School Sports Supports Values and Life Skills
Each year, over eight million youth participate in high school sports in the United States (NFHS, 2023a). Students between 13 and 18 years of age are presented with a variety of opportunities to participate in individual and team high school sports. The average season for a high school sports is three months, allowing students opportunities to participate in multiple sports during an academic year. However, due to geographic locations, student populations, and financial resources and access, there can be great variation in the number of sports opportunities available.

There is extensive research that supports the contention that the natural setting of school sports is inherently positioned to support the development of values and life skills for those who participate. Turgeon et al. (2019) conducted a literature review to examine psychosocial outcomes associated with high school sports participation. The findings from the review revealed that youth participating in school sports reported higher positive values, social competencies, cognitive skills, and identity than peers not participating in sports. Sports participation has also been associated with positive mental health outcomes such as higher self-esteem and fewer panic disorders. Finally, student-athletes have reported increased school engagement and grade averages and believe that they develop life skills through their sports experience and transfer them to other areas of life. Conversely, negative outcomes from school sports were also identified. For example, increased stress, burnout, racism, and discrimination have also been associated with school sports participation (see Turgeon et al., 2019, for a full review). Subsequently, school sports can, but does not guarantee, the development of positive psychological, academic, and behavioral outcomes for youth participants.

The Role of School Sports Coaches in Promoting Values and Life Skills

The depth and quality of this development are dependent on how coaches structure the sports environment and deliberately teach the development and transfer values and life skills (Bean et al., 2018). To directly speak to coaches, Carson-Sackett and Gano-Overway (2017) identified five best practices for effective teaching of values and life skills in high school sports. They encouraged coaches to (1) plan for life skills development, (2) use effective strategies for teaching life skills, (3) create an optimal sports climate, (4) build relationships, and (5) promote life skills transfer.

To position the role of coaches in supporting the development of life skills more conceptually, the implicit and explicit framework can be used (Turnnidge et al., 2014). Implicitly, coaches can lean on the inherent features of school sport (i.e., competition, relationships) to create positive experiences that lead to life skills development and transfer. Explicitly, coaches can intentionally discuss and practice life skills with youth in sport and in other life domains. While empirical evidence exists to support each approach independently, scholars have come to a consensus that coaches should integrate both approaches to maximize life skills outcomes for youth participants (Holt et al., 2017). Based on this notion, Bean et al. (2018) proposed the implicit to explicit continuum for coaching life skills that delineates the teaching of life skills along six levels of intentionality. Levels 1 and 2 represent implicit approaches for life skills development whereby coaches work to structure the sport context (e.g., designing the program) and facilitate a positive climate (e.g., fostering positive relationships). Levels 3 to 6 represent explicit approaches whereby coaches deliberately discuss (i.e., level 3) and help athletes practice (i.e., level 4) life skills in sport and discuss (i.e., level 5) and facilitate practice (i.e., level 6) of life skills transfer beyond sports.

Efforts have been made to formalize life skills coaching education to help high school coaches move toward implementing explicit approaches (Camiré et al., 2020). Yet, Pierce and colleagues (2024) found that high school participants believed that the most significant predictor of life skill development outcomes was implicit coaching approaches (i.e., structuring and facilitating a positive climate) more so than explicit coaching approaches (i.e., discussing and practicing life skills). These findings raise the question of how prepared they are to explicitly support the development of values and life skills.

In the United States, approximately 50% of high school coaches are teachers in the school system, and 50% are noneducators with no educational background in child development (Anderson-Butcher & Bates, 2022). While the NFHS "develops and delivers impactful, innovative and engaging educational programs" (NFHS, 2023b), coach-specific training and training topics vary significantly by state. While most states require training for coaches, there is great variation and limitations in the requirements and opportunities for education around life skills or positive youth development in sports (Atkinson et al., 2022). Coach education could act as a catalyst in making high school sports impactful (Turgeon et al., 2019), yet this case analysis of the United States indicates that much work is still needed for us to have full confidence in school-based sports to fulfill its inherent potential for supporting values and life skills. It is necessary that coaches are intentionally supported and trained to implicitly and explicitly coach values and life skills.

PHYSICAL EDUCATION AND SCHOOL SPORTS: ATTEMPTING TO ACHIEVE A COMMON MISSION

Both school-based sports and PE strive to help develop students' motor and life skills through their respective entities. Collectively, having school-based sports and PE together in the educational setting for youth provides the opportunity for positive additive effects on values and life skills. While the overarching missions are in place, how individuals in both areas attempt to reach their goals varies widely. Currently, PE is guided by professional organizations, such as SHAPE America, while school-based sports is often limited to state association requirements. While the governing bodies (e.g., NFHS) attempt to govern sports, ensuring quality control can be difficult. Implementation of ideals in

PE and sports are delivered by individuals, influenced by their experiences and philosophies. Schools have various agendas, and reaching a consensus can be challenging (Danish et al., 2005). Ultimately, the potential of PE and sports to support the development of values and life skills in youth participants has not been maximized.

At the macro-level related to training, PE, by and large, requires specialization (state teaching licensure) to be taught in a PreK–12 setting. In contrast, coaching often relies on limited requirements (often a single coaching authorization course). In some cases, PE teachers also coach, which can add role conflict based on time constraints, role requirements, and rewards (Richards & Templin, 2012). Both professions can create positive experiences related to increased physical literacy and transferable life skills or provide negative enduring memories related to activity (Strean, 2009). In fact, high school teacher-coaches have suggested that greater congruence in philosophies and messages from teachers and coaches would enhance life skills learning for youth (Pierce et al., 2019). With the overlap in knowledge specialization, along with similar missions, goals, and interests, school-based sports and PE can take a more harmonious approach to accomplish similar goals in student life skills development.

At the micro-level, it is critical to examine *whose values* are being conveyed and *whose ideologies* are perpetuated through formal educational curricula and the impact on life skills learning and transfer. Educators (both teachers and coaches) should place careful consideration on these questions at the forefront of their work (Boyd et al., 2021). Culturally responsive pedagogy and teaching practices must address the inherent and value-added diversity observed across racial and ethnic groups, regional and geographic settings, as well as differences in religion, politics, language, and generations. Life skills and values related to social justice and equity can and should be a priority for teachers and coaches in the school setting (Newman et al., 2022). Yet, it is notable that some high school coaches, for example, have shared a reluctance of lack of confidence in teaching social justice life skills through sports (Newman et al., in press).

Educators occupy a privileged position within US public schools; they are traditionally regarded as authority figures with a degree of power. The codes of conduct and ethical principles inherent to the teaching profession are woven into the fabric of policies, procedures, and outcomes accountability structures mentioned earlier. When considering the task of imparting values and life skills to school-aged children and youth through formal education settings for teachers and coaches, it is crucial to engage in discourse on how to respect and uphold the values and beliefs of the population being taught. This should prioritize honoring the diverse perspectives of those being educated rather than imposing the values of an individual or conforming solely to contemporary social norms.

SUMMARY AND FUTURE DIRECTIONS

Together, schools and educators (both physical educators and sports coaches) possess great potential to impart and reinforce life skills to children and youth. However, to see that potential fully realized, there must be greater coordination across system components, including teacher and coach education, professional organizations, policy, and legislation. Any attempt to foster collaboration among these components will be incomplete if it does not explicitly address the pressing and contemporary issues of diversity, equity, inclusion, and access. These issues significantly influence both the teacher and coach workforce and the students/athletes they serve. Furthermore, there is a need for concerted efforts to ensure the skills and competencies emphasized in teacher and coach education, as well as professional development initiatives, align most accurately with those needed to effectively address the diverse needs of 21st-century students/athletes.

Currently, both school-based sports and PE operate in separate siloed approaches, especially in a higher education capacity. The two entities could work together to strengthen student and athlete interactions and life skills. Developing life skills can be accomplished through implicit coaching approaches, such as structuring and facilitating positive learning environments, and aligns with PE. Quality work occurs throughout programs and athletics, but bringing entities together could benefit students, which is, or should be, the goal for each group. Working together could help co-design instruction and professional development opportunities to teach life skills and values in PE and sports.

One potential solution would be to promote the systematic integration of coaching and PE governing bodies. Finding common goals and messaging could enhance the cross-pollination of ideas to support teacher and coach education and provide a more robust approach to help deliver life skills. In the United States, folding into a unified approach between SHAPE, the NFHS, and state athletic and teacher associations could also help strengthen education for the 50% of coaches who teach while also providing opportunities for those outside education to learn and grow in their coaching abilities. Governance could help ensure quality control to a certain degree and help unify organizations across the United States.

Another consideration could be the development of alternative routes to certification and licensure. Atkinson et al. (2022) found that coaching licensure processes can be expensive and laborious while also primarily focusing more on the physical component compared to the social-emotional element. PE and sports could co-design instruction and professional development opportunities to emphasize and teach life skills in addition to the respective sport(s) content. Additionally, PE and sports must value equity, access, and opportunity for its changing target audience. Inclusive governing bodies could help provide opportunities for individuals with varying backgrounds to have a seat at the table, which would, in turn, help provide equitable access to influencing the directions and help set students up for success.

REFERENCES

Anderson-Butcher, D., & Bates, S. (2022). *National Coach Survey final report*. The Ohio State University Initiative, Columbus, OH.

Atkinson, O., Bates, S., Anderson-Butcher, D., Mack, S., & Goodway, J. (2022). Mapping school-based coach education requirements in the United States. *International Sport Coaching Journal*, 10(2), 276–288.

Bean, C., Kramers, S., Forneris, T., & Camiré, M. (2018). The implicit/explicit continuum of life skills development and transfer. *Quest*, 70(4), 456–470.

Boyd, K. L., Simon, M., & Dixon, C. E. (2021). Culturally relevant and sustaining pedagogies for and by Black and Latinx preservice physical education teachers. *Journal of Teaching in Physical Education*, 41(2), 212–222.

Boyes, M. (2000). The place of outdoor education in the health and physical education curriculum. *Journal of Physical Education New Zealand*, 33(2), 75–88.

Camiré, M., & Kendellen, K. (2016). Coaching for positive youth development in high school sport. In *Positive youth development through sport* (pp. 126–136). Routledge: Taylor and Francis Group.

Camiré, M., Kendellen, K., Rathwell, S., & Turgeon, S. (2020). Evaluating the coaching for life skills online training program: A randomised controlled trial. *Psychology of Sport and Exercise*, 48, 101649.

Carson-Sackett, S., & Gano-Overway, L. A. (2017). Coaching life skills development: Best practices and high school tennis coach exemplar. *International Sport Coaching Journal*, 4(2), 206–219.

Casey, A., & Kirk, D. (2021). *Models-based practice in physical education*. Routledge.

Cecchini, J.A., Montero, J., Alonso, A., Izquierdo, M., & Contreras, O. (2007). Effects of personal and social responsibility on fair play in sports and self-control in school-aged youths. *European Journal of Sport Science*, 7, 203–211.

Danish, S. J., Forneris, T., & Wallace, I. (2005). Sport-based life skills programming in the schools. *Journal of Applied School Psychology*, 21(2), 41–62.

Dorsch, T. E., Smith, A. L., Blazo, J. A., Coakley, J., Côté, J., Wagstaff, C. R., Warner, S., & King, M. Q. (2022). Toward an integrated understanding of the youth sport system. *Research Quarterly for Exercise and Sport*, 93(1), 105–119.

Gould, D., & Carson, S. (2008). Life skills development through sport: Current status and future directions. *International Review of Sport and Exercise Psychology*, 1(1), 58–78.

Hastie, P. (1995). Ecology of a secondary school outdoor adventure camp. *Journal of Teaching in Physical Education*, 15, 79–97.

Hattie, J., Marsh, H. W., Neill, J. T., & Richards, G. E. (1997). Adventure Education and Outward Bound: Out of class experiences that make a lasting difference. *Review of Educational Research*, 67(1), 43–87.

Hellison, D. (1995). *Teaching responsibility through physical activity*. Human Kinetics.

Hellison, D. (2011). *Teaching responsibility through physical activity* (3rd ed.). Human Kinetics.

Hemphill, M. A., & Richards, K. A. R. (2016). "Without the academic part, it wouldn't be squash": Youth development in an urban squash program. *Journal of Teaching in Physical Education*, 35, 263–276.

Hodge, S. R., Dixson, A. D., Harrison Jr., L., & Burden Jr., J. W. (2008). Brown in black and white-then and now: A question of educating or sporting African American males in America. *American Behavioral Scientist*, 51(7), 928–952. https://doi.org/10.1177/0002764207311998

Holt, N. L., Neely, K. C., Slater, L. G., Camiré, M., Côté, J., Fraser-Thomas, J., MacDonald, D., Strachan, L., & Tamminen, K. A. (2017). A grounded theory of positive youth development through sport based on results from a qualitative meta-study. *International Review of Sport and Exercise Psychology*, 10(1), 1–49.

Lugg, A., & Martin, P. (2001). The nature and scope of outdoor education in Victorian schools. *Australian Journal of Outdoor Education*, 5(2), 42–48.

National Center for Educational Statistics. (2019). *Back to school statistics*. U.S. Department of Education. Retrieved from https://nces.ed.gov/fastfacts/display.asp?id=372

National Federation of State High School Associations. (2023a, November 1). *Mission Statement*. Retrieved from https://www.nfhs.org/who-we-are/missionstatement

National Federation of State High School Associations. (2023b, November 1). *High school participation archive*. Retrieved from https://www.nfhs.org/sports-resource-content/high-school-participation-survey-archive/

Newman, T. J., Santos, F., Collins, K., Pierce, S., Kochanek, J., Mercier, V., & Lee, L. (2024). Social justice promotion in youth sport: insights from current high school coaches. *Sports Coaching Review*, Advanced online publication, 1–28.

Newman, T. J., Santos, F., Pierce, S., Collins, K., & Mercier, V. (2022). Coach education and coach development within a contemporary social justice society: Implications for future research and potential pitfalls. *Quest, 74*(3), 234–250.

Pierce, S., Erickson, K., & Dinu, R. (2019). Teacher-coaches' perceptions of life skills transfer from high school sport to the classroom. *Journal of Applied Sport Psychology, 31*(4), 451–473.

Pierce, S., O'Neil, L., Camiré, M., Bean, C., & Rathwell, S. (2024). Examining the relationship between coaching approaches for life skills development and life skills outcomes for high school student-athletes. *International Sport Coaching Journal*, Advanced online publication, 1–12.

Pozo, P., Grao-Cruces, A,. & Pérez-Ordás, R. (2018). Teaching personal and social responsibility model-based programmes in physical education: A systematic review. *European Physical Education Review, 24*, 56–75.

Prouty, D., Panicucci, J., & Collinson, R. (2007). *Adventure education: Theory and practice.* Human Kinetics.

Richards, K. A. R., & Templin, T. J. (2012). Toward a multidimensional perspective on teacher-coach role conflict. *Quest, 64*(3), 164–176.

SHAPE America – Society of Health and Physical Educators. (2013). National standards for K–12 physical education. Retrieved from www.shapeamerica.org

Simonton, K. L., & Garn, A. C. (2019). Exploring achievement emotions in physical education: The potential for the control-value theory of achievement emotions. *Quest, 71*, 434–446.

Simonton, K. L., & Shiver, V. N. (2021). Examination of elementary students' emotions and personal and social responsibility in physical education. *European Physical Education Review, 27*(4). https://doi.org/10.1177/1356336X211001398

Strean, W. B. (2009). Remembering instructors: Play, pain and pedagogy. *Qualitative Research in Sport and Exercise, 1*(3), 210–220.

Sutherland, S., & Legge, M. (2016). The possibilities of "doing" outdoor and/or adventure education in physical education/teacher education. *Journal of Teaching in Physical Education, 35*, 299–312.

Tischler, A., & McCaughtry, N. (2014). Shifting and narrowing masculinity hierarchies in physical education: Status matters. *Journal of Teaching in Physical Education, 33*, 342–362.

Turgeon, S., Kendellen, K., Kramers, S., Rathwell, S., & Camiré, M. (2019). Making high school sport impactful. *Kinesiology Review, 8*(3), 188–194.

Turnnidge, J., Côté, J., & Hancock, D. J. (2014). Positive youth development from sport to life: Explicit or implicit transfer? *Quest, 66*(2), 203–217.

Science of Learning
Part 2

Understanding Youth Sports through
Experiential Learning

Chapter Four

Levone Lee, Anne Stauffer, Sandy Nino, Ellison Blumenthal and Tarkington J Newman

INTRODUCTION

One of the most persistent challenges for youth coaches, sports programs, and researchers alike centers on how youth sports coaches effectively promote the development and transfer of positive youth development (PYD) outcomes, such as life skills and values. From a PYD perspective, life skills and values are traditionally positioned as key outcomes that equip youth to handle the challenges and stressors of life (Gould & Carson, 2008; Holt et al., 2017). Research indicates that youth develop life skills (e.g., Newman, 2020) and learn values (e.g., Koh et al., 2016) through their participation in sports. For instance, Kendellen and Camiré (2017) demonstrated youth learn traditional life skills, including interpersonal communication skills and self-regulation skills, through participation in high school sports and subsequently apply these skills in other domains of their lives (e.g., school, academics). More recently, scholars advocated for the need to teach *social justice life skills* through youth sports participation (e.g., Camiré et al., 2022, 2023; Newman, Black et al., 2023). Indeed, research has demonstrated that youth sports can serve as a context to learn social justice life skills, such as healthy masculinity (Newman et al., 2022) and LGBTQ+ allyship (Robinson et al., 2023).

However, although much is known about PYD outcomes and (to some extent) how coaches can promote the development and transfer of such outcomes (Newman, Santos et al., 2023), less is known about the holistic learning process that occurs within youth sports as a learning environment. This lack of understanding is especially troubling considering the sociopolitical influences (i.e., systemic inequality and discrimination) that affect athletes and coaches in youth sports systems. One holistic perspective of the learning process, known as *facilitated experiential learning* – which centers on the dynamic relationship between youth athletes and coaches within socially constructed

DOI: 10.4324/9781032688657-6

learning environments – may provide critical insights for coaches who seek to promote traditional life skills, social justice life skills, and values. Expanding on previous theoretical scholarship (e.g., Newman & Alvarez, 2015; Newman & Lower 2019; Newman et al., 2024), the current chapter advances the *Critical* Coaching on the Wave (Critical CotW) Model, which is grounded in the process of experiential learning. Specifically, the current chapter illustrates how coaches can engage in social justice promotion by leveraging their unique positionality within youth sports systems as they seek to maximize youth learning opportunities.

THEORETICAL UNDERSTANDING OF EXPERIENTIAL LEARNING

Experiential learning theory (ELT) describes the change process of knowledge and skill acquisition that occurs through firsthand experiences (Dewey, 1916; Kolb, 1984). As the founder of ELT, Dewey (1938) advocated for a dynamic and interactive approach to educational pedagogy in which learners actively participate in experiences, reflect upon those experiences, and incorporate novel insights into their understanding of the world. Since Dewey's original work, several ELT models have been proposed. For example, Kolb's (1984) four-stage learning cycle and Joplin's (1981) five-stage model of experiential learning underscore two divergent perspectives of ELT. Both ELT models emphasize the action-reflection process, but they differ in their views on the external role of the facilitator in the learning process.

Kolb's (1984) and Kolb et al. (2014) intrapersonal model of ELT consists of a four-stage learning cycle that focuses on the learner's internal cognitive processes. Specifically, Kolb's iteration of ELT underscores that learning, which is driven by new experiences, involves developing abstract concepts that are adaptable to a variety of situations. The four-stage learning cycle includes (1) concrete experience, (2) reflective observation, (3) abstract conceptualization, and (4) active experimentation. Concrete experiences (e.g., feelings) occur when a learner encounters new experiences or reinterprets prior experiences from a new perspective. During reflective observation (e.g., watching), the learner reflects on these new experiences, particularly noting inconsistencies between these experiences and their preexisting understanding. The stage of abstract conceptualization (e.g., thinking) occurs when the learner translates reflection into new ideas or modifies existing abstract concepts based on new experiences. Finally, active experimentation (e.g., doing) denotes when the learner applies newly developed or modified concepts to real-world situations. Kolb (1984) emphasized that learning is an integrated process, with each stage mutually reinforcing the next. Although this learning cycle can begin at any of the stages, effective learning only occurs when all four stages are completed; therefore, no single stage is effective as a stand-alone learning procedure. In the end, Kolb's (1984) model asserts that the learner should take center stage in the learning process without regard to the external role of the facilitator.

In contrast to Kolb's iteration of ELT, which focuses on an internal learning cycle, Joplin's (1981) five-stage model highlights a two-phase learning process that emphasizes an experience (i.e., learning) and reflection (i.e., learning experiences constructed by trained facilitators). Joplin's (1981) model is structured around a central hurricane-like cycle in which the hurricane represents a challenging action and includes the stages of (1) focus, (2) action, (3) support, (4) feedback, and (5) debriefing. Focus refers to a learner's directed attention toward new tasks, which is carefully shaped to include specific guidance without overwhelming detail, allowing room for unplanned learning. Action involves accomplishing tasks (e.g., solving problems and assuming responsibilities) in unfamiliar situations and allows the development of new skills. To demonstrate support, trained facilitators establish a safe environment and express care (i.e., showing genuine interest, offering assistance), which, in turn, encourages a learner to take risks and experiment through various means. Regarding feedback, facilitators provide specific feedback on a learner's actions (e.g., working style, interactions) and concrete examples to enhance the internalization of learning. Finally, during the debriefing stage, a learner reflects on past experiences through group discussions, thematic papers, or presentations to inform future decisions, facilitate knowledge transfer, and turn insights into focal points for the next cycle of the five-stage process. The hurricane-like cyclical process starts with a directed focus and concludes with the emergence of new insights. These insights can then be turned into new focal points for the subsequent cycle, perpetuating a continuous cycle of knowledge development. Thus, converging from Kolb's iteration of ELT, Joplin (1981) underscored the learning process for learners and specified the general responsibilities of facilitators in the experiential learning process.

THE CRITICAL COACHING ON THE WAVE MODEL

Within sports-based PYD scholarship, Newman, Black et al. (2023) proposed the concept of *facilitated experiential learning*. Building upon the foundations of Joplin (1981) and Roberts (2006), facilitated experiential learning underscores the reflective and reflexive interactions between the facilitator (e.g., coach) and the learner (e.g., youth athlete) throughout the experiential learning process. In this way, learning is understood as a transformative process that takes place between a learner and trained facilitator (Thomas, 2008) – and suggests that real-world experiences are reflected upon and internalized to shape the learner's future emotions, behaviors, and cognitions (e.g., Gass et al., 2020). Therefore, within facilitated experiential learning, the facilitator – in collaboration with the learner – is positioned as a pivotal change agent that shapes the socially constructed learning environment of youth sports. Consequently, the coach is uniquely situated to leverage their positionality and optimize learning opportunities that occur within sports. Learning opportunities may manifest organically – during sports drills and competitions as teachable moments – or they can be intentionally designed, often through sequenced sports-based activities meant to directly teach a desired skill. Further, these dynamic interactions that occur between the coach and athlete unfold within a socially constructed environment, which is shaped by historical elements (e.g., traditions) and contemporary sociopolitical influences (e.g., norms). Thus, it is imperative to acknowledge that facilitated experiential learning is continually (re)shaped by the interplay of historical systems of privilege-power-oppression, contemporary sociopolitical climate, and youth sports culture.

The Critical CotW Model is a theoretically derived framework designed to guide youth sports coaches (and other youth sports leaders, e.g., physical education teachers, recreational counselors) through the facilitated experiential learning process. Originally developed by adapting the *Facilitated Wave Model* used for adventure therapy (Alvarez & Stauffer, 2001; Alvarez et al., 2020), the current iteration of the model illustrates the dynamic process of learning that occurs between a coach and athlete within the socially constructed learning environment of youth sports (Newman et al., 2017). As such, the *wave* is used as a metaphor that represents the spontaneous ups and downs that occur within both sports (e.g., winning, losing) and life (e.g., successes, challenges). Further, the current iteration of the Critical CotW Model is grounded in notions of critical PYD (CPYD), which seeks to promote the development of critical consciousness (Gonzalez et al., 2020). The development of critical consciousness is essential for both the learning process and the holistic development of youth. By achieving critical consciousness, the learner actively engages in critical reflection (i.e., understanding systems of privilege-power-oppression), cultivates political efficacy (i.e., belief in one's capacity to effect social change), and engages in critical action (i.e., social justice life skills). Examples of social justice life skills include antiracism, LGBTQ+ allyship, healthy masculinity, and mental health literacy – and may take the form of athlete activism (Kluch, 2020).

APPLIED INSIGHTS

Ultimately, the Critical CotW Model positions the coach as an active agent of change within the learning process and is composed of six interrelated processes meant to help coaches navigate the learning process and facilitate PYD outcomes. The six steps of the Critical CotW Model include (1) assessing "Point A," (2) fostering a supportive team culture, (3) intentionally designing the learning experience, (4) facilitating the learning experience, (5) debriefing the learning experience, and (6) reflecting on the learning process. Much like other conceptualizations of ELT (e.g., Joplin, 1981; Kolb, 1984), the distinct processes of the Critical CotW Model are dynamic and interrelated in nature. In other words, to appropriately meet the needs of youth athletes, the processes of the model may need to occur simultaneously and iteratively. Nonetheless, the Critical CotW Model is meant to empower youth sports coaches by providing tangible implicit and explicit (see Bean et al., 2018) *facilitative coaching practices* meant to teach traditional life skills, social justice life skills, and values alike.

ASSESS "POINT A"

Assessing Point A entails understanding (i.e., assessing) and challenging one's own coaching philosophy, as well as the identities, values, and passions of the youth athletes they coach. In doing so, coaches must develop a social justice–oriented coaching philosophy in which they strive to understand their unique positionality (e.g., intersectional identity, power privilege), both within their immediate sports environment and the broader sociopolitical sports context. Coaches understanding their unique positionality is crucial because such an awareness affects their cultural competence and cultural humility, as well as their ability to be cognizant of any implicit biases they may hold (particularly related to the youth they coach). Such insights may be achieved through constant self-questioning of the power privilege that they may embody (e.g., being an adult) and the systems that are common throughout youth sports (e.g., pay-to-play programs). Coaches should critically self-reflect on how their core values are reflected in their coaching, as well as how their holistic identity interacts with power-privilege-oppression dynamics, both in and out of sports. Once a social justice–oriented coaching philosophy is developed, coaches must consider how they can best leverage their power privilege to engage in social justice promotion and disrupt systems of oppression. In doing so, coaches must reflect on how they are positioned to serve not only their team but also the broader sports and community cultures.

In addition to understanding their own coaching philosophy, coaches must seek to learn about each athlete's holistic and intersectional identity. Getting to know individual athletes by listening and learning about their individual experiences, knowledge, and values helps coaches more effectively meet athletes "where they are" (e.g., developmentally, culturally) and can lead to the development of positive coach-athlete relationships. To learn about the holistic and intersectional identities of the athletes, coaches should use open-ended questions and practice intentional listening skills. Additionally, coaches can learn about athletes by paying attention to the way athletes communicate and interact with their teammates, friends, and parents. Ultimately, coaches must view athletes through a person-in-environment lens, which recognizes that one's lived experiences and well-being are directly influenced by social, cultural, economic, and environmental factors. This approach allows coaches to view athletes as whole people and, in turn, may help coaches understand how a diversity of factors can affect both the learning and performance of youth athletes.

FOSTER A SUPPORTIVE TEAM CULTURE

Fostering a supportive team culture is a critical and foundational component of a positive team climate (i.e., environment), which is inclusive of positive coach-athlete relationships and prosocial intra-team dynamics. Coaches – as the primary adults – are expected to create a safe learning environment that allows youth to practice new skills, make mistakes, and learn without fear of retribution. Further, coaches can foster a supportive team climate by providing athletes with the space to freely share their viewpoints and express their thoughts. For example, coaches should ask open-ended questions and listen intentionally when introducing new concepts and creating new strategies.

This willingness to work collaboratively with athletes should also be demonstrated when determining team goals – whether it be for advocacy efforts or wins/losses. Collaboration can be actualized by simply asking athletes their thoughts and integrating their viewpoints into the team's goals. From a social justice perspective, coaches and athletes should collaboratively identify inequities in their sports setting (e.g., safety concerns for LGBTQ+ athletes) and the social justice life skills needed to address such disparities (e.g., LGBTQ+ allyship). Ultimately, such a collaborative and supportive approach provides a sense of autonomy in the learning process and empowers athletes to take ownership of their actions and behaviors.

INTENTIONALLY DESIGN THE EXPERIENCE

Intentionally designing the learning experience requires coaches to create sports activities that allow athletes to learn new knowledge and practice new skills. One strategy for intentionally designing learning experiences is to progressively sequence challenging activities that continuously build upon each other. In this way, coaches must ensure that athletes have demonstrated competence in fundamental skills before advancing to mastery of complex skills. As an example, in the context of basketball, it is advisable for an athlete to master the technique of shooting a layup before venturing into attempting shots from the three-point line. From a social justice perspective, athletes should learn the value of communication and teamwork before engaging in social protests.

Additionally, to maximize the learning experience, sports activities should be designed to teach sports skills and life skills simultaneously. In this process, it is crucial for coaches to further demonstrate the connection between sports skills, traditional life skills, and social justice life skills. For instance, coaches should explore the incorporation of activities that promote important life skills (e.g., teamwork) both on (e.g., teamwork in practicing new gameplay) and off the field (e.g., teamwork in community services/advocacy) for sports programming. This design of sports program intentionally aims to immerse athletes in real-world experiences they encounter during practices and in daily life. In this intentionally facilitated, low-stakes, experiential learning environment, coaches should encourage athletes to (re)act to dynamic situations. More importantly, coaches need to demonstrate social justice life skills (e.g., communicational skills, advocacy skills) intentionally and consciously. In all, coaches should utilize this intentional design of experience as a unique learning environment for athletes navigating uncertain situations. This aids athletes in establishing connections between their personal values, social justice values, and the values inherent in sports, thereby empowering them to take charge of their positive developmental outcomes.

FACILITATE THE LEARNING

Within the facilitating the learning process, the coach is recognized as a key changing agent within the reflective and reflexive learning process. As such, intentional facilitative coaching employs practices that optimize learning opportunities. In youth sports, such intentional interactions are referred to as being either indirect or direct (Gould & Carson, 2008) or – more commonly – explicit and implicit in nature (Bean et al., 2018). These deliberate coaching approaches are known to be associated with the cultivation and transfer of life skills. Facilitative coaching practices (see Newman, Santos et al., 2023) include adopting a strengths-based approach, individualizing feedback, and identifying teachable moments.

For instance, by adopting a strengths-based approach, coaches acknowledge positive social justice behaviors by providing individualized feedback when athletes demonstrate social justice life skills. Such feedback is instrumental in promoting an optimal learning environment, highlighting comprehension, motivation, and continuous improvement. This individualized feedback also facilitates timely corrections, identifies strengths and weaknesses, and nurtures a growth mindset. Further, teachable moments are recognized as learning opportunities that naturally occur within sports. These teachable moments may include winning, losing, injuries, and playing time concerns. Thus, both positive experiences (e.g., winning) and problems athletes face (e.g., injuries and playing time) are opportunities for learning that coaches can teach players about reframing. Helping athletes reframe their thoughts in a more positive, prosocial way implores them to think critically about their role in the process of learning. For instance, coaches can use these moments to facilitate individual and team discussions to promote emotional regulation through sportspersonship.

DEBRIEF THE EXPERIENCE

Debriefing the experience serves as a crucial strategy to amplify the transfer of skills acquired within the sporting context to real-life situations. Coaches can facilitate the transfer of knowledge by linking teachable moments that occur within sports to other situations in their lives (e.g., at home, in school). Moreover, coaches need to highlight these moments to encourage athletes to consider their choices and actions carefully by posing open-ended questions that require reflection. Some examples of open-ended questions could include, "What could have been done differently?" and "How can we approach this situation more effectively next time?" Further, debriefing involves providing deliberate opportunities for athletes to apply and transfer these life skills beyond the confines of the sports context. By encouraging athletes to apply the skills learned in sports to other domains, such as at school or in relationships, individuals can enhance their understanding of these new skills.

One strategy that coaches can use to enhance the transfer process is known as the *What? So What? Now What?* Approach. In the initial "what" stage, open-ended questions and observations are often utilized to initiate a conversation regarding the activity. Coaches should create a safe space to encourage athletes to share their observations, actions, and feelings related to the experience. Coaches can offer specifics (e.g., whether the activity was easy or challenging, whether the objectives were achieved) to prompt engagement. Transitioning to the "so what" stage, the focus broadens to generalize the experience and contemplate the underlying factors that influenced thoughts and behaviors. Coaches should encourage athletes to abstractly consider the broader significance of the experience, emphasizing skills learned and the transferability of skills to other contexts. The final stage, "now what," is the phase that facilitates intentional transference. Youth are prompted to think concretely about how to apply skills (e.g., teamwork, communication) developed in sports in various life situations (e.g., school, workplace). For instance, an athlete who has developed strong teamwork skills on the field may exhibit effective collaboration in a professional setting, contributing positively to group projects, fostering a cooperative work environment, and enhancing overall productivity. These critical teamwork skills can further be extended to social justice actions (e.g., allyship building, antiracism advocacy). The ability to work harmoniously with others, honed through sports, is a valuable life skill that transcends athletic endeavors and finds practical application in various aspects of life.

REFLECT ON THE PROCESS

The willingness to reflect on one's positionality as a key facilitator in the learning process is important. Thus, to ensure that they maximize their own positionality within the sports environment and to contribute to their own learning, coaches must evaluate how they facilitated each process of the Critical CotW Model. For instance, coaches should engage in critical self-reflection by examining their privilege and power within the learning process and how their positionality impacted their decision-making processes. To do so, coaches may choose to keep a coaching journal to write and reflect on not only their behaviors and decisions but also on the rationale and thought behind their actions. Further, coaches must consider if/how their choices supported the healthy development of athletes and targeted goals. Coaches should also seek continuous feedback from others (e.g., other coaches, athletes, parents). Seeking feedback from various sources is a valuable practice for coaches, as it promotes inclusivity through a diversity of thought, as well as contributes to their own continuous development effectiveness of using facilitative coaching practices.

SUMMARY AND FUTURE DIRECTIONS

This chapter highlights the critical role that youth sports coaches play in facilitating an experiential learning environment for youth athletes. The Critical CotW Model helps to assuage several issues that exist within youth sports scholarship. For instance, although many models are ecological in nature, such models often focus on heuristic conceptualizations of life skill development or transfer (e.g., Gould & Carson, 2008; Pierce et al., 2017) and are not designed to provide intentional facilitative coaching practices that can be used by youth sports coaches

(Jacobs & Wright, 2018). Indeed, the Critical CotW Model – which is grounded in ELT – has been constructed to assist coaches in intentional efforts to engage in social justice promotion (by teaching social justice life skills). Our contemporary sociopolitical culture is marked by persistent power-privilege-oppression inequities and injustices; thus, youth sports coaches must begin to critically consider their unique positionality as they seek to maximize youth learning opportunities.

REFERENCES

Alvarez, A., & Stauffer, G. (2001). Musings on adventure therapy. *Journal of Experiential Education*, 24(2), 85–91. https://doi.org/10.1177/105382590102400205

Alvarez, A., Stauffer, G., Lung, M., Sacksteder, K., Beale, B., & Tucker, A. (2020). *Adventure group psychotherapy: An experiential approach to treatment*. Routledge. https://doi.org/10.4324/9781003103103.

Bean, C., Kramers, S., Forneris, T., & Camiré, M. (2018). The implicit/explicit continuum of life skills development and transfer. *Quest*, 70(4), 456–470. https://doi.org/10.1080/00336297.2018.1451348

Camiré, M., Newman, T., Bean, C., & Strachan, L. (2022). Reimagining positive youth development and life skills in sport through a social justice lens. *Journal of Applied Sport Psychology*, 34(6), 1058–1076. https://doi.org/10.1080/10413200.2021.1958954

Camiré, M., Santos, F., Newman, T., Vella, S., MacDonald, D., Milistetd, M., Pierce, S., & Strachan, L. (2023). Positive youth development as a guiding framework in sport Research: Is it time to plan for a transition? *Psychology of Sport and Exercise*, 2023, 102505. https://doi.org/10.1016/j.psychsport.2023.102505

Dewey, J. (1916). Democracy and education. In J. Boydston (Ed.), *The middle works, 1899–1924* (Vol. 9, pp. 4–370). SIU Press.

Dewey, J. (1938). *Experience and education*. Simon & Schuster.

Gass, M., Gillis, L., & Russell, K. (2020). *Adventure therapy: Theory, research, and practice* (2nd ed.). Routledge. https://doi.org/10.4324/9781003016618

Gonzalez, M., Kokozos, M., Byrd, C., & McKee, K. (2020). Critical positive youth development: A framework for centering critical consciousness. *Journal of Youth Development*, 15(6), 24–43. https://doi.org/10.5195/jyd.2020.859

Gould, D., & Carson, S. (2008). Life skills development through sport: Current status and future directions. *International Review of Sport and Exercise Psychology*, 1(1), 58–78. https://doi.org/10.1080/17509840701834573

Holt, N., Neely, K., Slater, L., Camiré, M., Côté, J., Fraser-Thomas, J., MacDonald, D., Strachan, L., & Tamminen, K. (2017). A grounded theory of positive youth development through sport based on results from a qualitative meta-study. *International Review of Sport and Exercise Psychology*, 10(1), 1–49. https://doi.org/10.1080/1750984X.2016.1180704

Jacobs, J., & Wright, P. (2018). Transfer of life skills in sport-based youth development programs: A conceptual framework bridging learning to application. *Quest*, 70(1), 81–99. https://doi.org/10.1080/00336297.2017.1348304

Joplin, L. (1981). On defining experiential education. *Journal of Experiential Education*, 4(1), 17–20. https://doi.org/10.1177/105382598100400104

Kendellen, K., & Camiré, M. (2017). Examining the life skill development and transfer experiences of former high school athletes. *International Journal of Sport and Exercise Psychology*, 15(4), 395–408. https://doi.org/10.1080/1612197X.2015.1114502

Kluch, Y. (2020). "My story is my activism!": (Re-)definitions of social justice activism among collegiate athlete activists. *Communication & Sport*, 8(4–5), 566–590. https://doi.org/10.1177/2167479519897288

Koh, K., Ong, S., & Camiré, M. (2016). Implementation of a values training program in physical education and sport: Perspectives from teachers, coaches, students, and athletes. *Physical Education and Sport Pedagogy*, 21(3), 295–312. https://doi.org/10.1080/17408989.2014.990369

Kolb, D. (1984). *Experiential learning: Experience as the source of learning and development*. Prentice-Hall.

Kolb, D., Boyatzis, R., & Mainemelis, C. (2014). Experiential learning theory: Previous research and new directions. In R. J. Sternberg & L. Zhang (Eds.), *Perspectives on thinking, learning, and cognitive styles* (0 ed., pp. 227–248). Routledge. https://doi.org/10.4324/9781410605986-9

Newman, T. (2020). Life skill development and transfer: "They're not just meant for playing sports". *Research on Social Work Practice*, 30(6), 643–657. https://doi.org/10.1177/1049731520903427

Newman, T., & Alvarez, A. (2015). Coaching on the wave: An integrative approach to facilitating youth development. *Journal of Sport Psychology in Action*, 6(3), 127–140. https://doi.org/10.1080/21520704.2015.1073203

Newman, T., Alvarez, M., & Kim, M. (2017). An experiential approach to sport for youth development. *Journal of Experiential Education*, 40(3), 308–322. https://doi.org/10.1177/1053825917696833

Newman, T., Black, S., Santos, F., Jefka, B., & Brennan, N. (2023). Coaching the development and transfer of life skills: A scoping review of facilitative coaching practices in youth sports. *International Review of Sport and Exercise Psychology*, 16(1), 619–656. https://doi.org/10.1080/1750984X.2021.1910977

Newman, T., Lee, L., & Stauffer, A. (2024) An experiential approach to facilitative coaching and teaching social justice life skills. In N. Holt & M. McDonoug (Eds.), *Positive youth development through sport* (4th ed., pp. 237–250). Routledge.

Newman, T., & Lower, L. (2019). Coaching the youth sport coach: Integrating theory and pedagogy through adventure-based experience. In F. Santos, L. Strachan, P. Pereira, & D. MacDonald (Eds.), *Coaching positive development: Implications and practices from around the world* (pp. 187–204). Omniserviços.

Newman, T., McCray, K., Lower-Hoppe, L., Rockhill, C., Ingram, D., Ohanasian, J., & Simmons-Horton, S. (2022). Healthy masculinity construction: The influence of race, faith and athletics. *Children & Society*, 37(3), 854–874.

Newman, T., Santos, F., Pierce, S., Collins, K., & Mercier, V. (2023). Coach education and development within a contemporary social justice society: Implications for future research and potential pitfalls. *Quest*, 1–17. https://doi.org/10.1080/00336297.2022.2080082

Pierce, S., Gould, D., & Camiré, M. (2017). Definition and model of life skills transfer. *International Review of Sport and Exercise Psychology*, 10(1), 186–211. https://doi.org/10.1080/1750984X.2016.1199727

Roberts, G. (2006). A philosophical examination of experiential learning theory for agricultural educators. *Journal of Agricultural Education*, 47(1), 17–29. https://doi.org/10.5032/jae.2006.01017

Robinson, E., Newman, T., Scheadler, T., Lower-Hoppe, L., & Baeth, A. (2023). The unique lived experiences of LGBQ athletes: A collegiate women's rugby club team as an inclusive & empowering community. *Journal of Homosexuality*, 1–27. https://doi.org/10.1080/00918369.2022.2160684

Thomas, G. (2008). Preparing facilitators for experiential education: The role of intentionality and intuition. *Journal of Adventure Education and Outdoor Learning*, 8(1), 3–20. doi:10.1080/14729670701573835

The Development of Life Skills through Sports from the Bioecological Theory Lens

Chapter Five

Vitor Ciampolini, Juarez Vieira do Nascimento and Michel Milistetd

INTRODUCTION

In the last several decades, many researchers in sports psychology throughout the world have focused their efforts on better understanding the educational and socio-emotional contributions of sports (Danish, 1983; Qi et al., 2020). Scholars have attempted to understand why certain contextual conditions, such as meaningful experiences and interpersonal relationships with teammates and coaches, can enable sports practitioners to foster particular developmental outcomes (Coakley, 2011; Gould & Carson, 2008). Some researchers have delineated such outcomes as life skills, which are "those internal personal assets, characteristics and skills such as goal setting, emotional control, self-esteem, and hard work ethic that can be facilitated or developed in sports and are transferred for use in non-sports settings" (Gould & Carson, 2008, p. 60).

Life skills development is one of the goals of the positive youth development (PYD) perspective (Silbereisen & Lerner, 2007). In contrast to previous views of youth as "problems to be managed" that dominated in the 20th century, from a PYD point of view, young people are envisioned as "resources to be developed" that have the potential for a bright future (Damon, 2004; Lerner et al., 2005). PYD is anchored in relational developmental systems metatheory, a set of theories from several research areas that highlight how human development involves mutually influential relations between the person and the constantly changing contexts around them (Geldhof et al., 2013; Lerner et al., 2019). Amongst these theories is the work of Urie Bronfenbrenner, who conducted internationally recognised research on human development starting in the 1970s (Bronfenbrenner, 1979).

Throughout his journey, Bronfenbrenner's reflections and self-criticisms made his work evolve to provide further details on the dimensions and factors present in human development (Lerner,

DOI: 10.4324/9781032688657-7

2005; Rosa & Tudge, 2013). His first studies started with the interplay between multiple contexts and children's development, and his work later progressed from an ecological to a bioecological theory (Bronfenbrenner, 1979, 2005). Including the "bio" in the theory shifts the focus from the context to the person and its particular characteristics that highly influence human development (Rosa & Tudge, 2013). Within Bronfenbrenner's bioecological theory, a Process-Person-Context-Time (PPCT) Model suggests that human development occurs through *processes* (e.g., experiences, relationships, engagement in activities) in the *person's* immediate contexts (e.g., school, home), which in turn is influenced by (and also influences) other proximal and distal *contexts* (e.g., parents work, culture system) across *time* (Bronfenbrenner & Morris, 1998, 2006). With its anchors in psychology, sociology, and biology, bioecological theory offers a plethora of details and conceptual structures that have contributed for decades to the investigation of human development through sports (Dorsch et al., 2020; Pierce et al., 2017).

Although bioecological theory offers a multifaceted understanding of human development in developmental psychology, the number of empirical studies adequately anchored in the theory remains limited amongst youth sports research. Pierce et al. (2017) used some principles and the dimensions of bioecological theory to develop a theoretical model intended to frame the development and transfer of life skills through sports. Holt et al. (2008) used ecological theory to investigate the development of life skills in Canadian high school sports. On many occasions, empirical studies on life skills development have cited Bronfenbrenner's work but do not explicitly articulate his concepts as the primary guiding framework (e.g., Newman et al., 2021; Pierce et al., 2019; Subijana et al., 2022). As researchers in the last few years have continuously highlighted the complexity inherent to the process of life skills development (e.g., Jacobs & Wright, 2018; Pierce et al., 2017; Ronkainen et al., 2020), connecting the bioecological theory principles to research on life skills development may contribute to encapsulating its complexity.

With the continued global expansion of PYD (Qi et al., 2020) and life skills (McLaren et al., 2021) publications in recent years, it seems timely to reinforce the importance of investigating life skills development through sports from a properly articulated rendering of bioecological theory. Thus, by connecting the tenets of bioecological theory to previous studies on life skills, this chapter aims to propose a model to frame life skills development through sports. This chapter intends to guide scholars, coaches, and sports stakeholders in the future development of practices and research by approaching the development of life skills through bioecological theory.

A BIOECOLOGICAL MODEL FOR FRAMING LIFE SKILLS DEVELOPMENT IN SPORTS

In the past years, scholars from different research fields have made efforts to frame Bronfenbrenner's theories in illustrative models (e.g., Bond, 2019; Bone, 2015; Dorsch et al., 2020). In general, the models are similar in structure as they use several circles, one inside the other, to represent the influence among the systems and elements proposed in bioecological theory. This similarity is probably due to Bronfenbrenner's analogy that "the ecological environment is conceived as a set of nested structures, each inside the next, like a set of Russian dolls" (Bronfenbrenner, 1979, p. 3). Based on the same principle, our model also uses a set of integrated circles to illustrate the ecological systems. Yet, we believe our model innovates by being the first (as far as we know) to include the proximal processes and to propose an interactive strategy for visualising the influence of several elements necessary for human development to occur. However, it is essential to reflect on the extent to which this model progresses compared to those from other fields (e.g., Bond, 2019; Bone, 2015), as well as the model proposed by Pierce et al. (2017) for life skills transfer.

When writing this chapter, we constantly asked ourselves: "to what extent is this model helping researchers move forward?" This is a common question in the research community, given that one of the goals of research is to improve on what we know about how the "world works" (Neuman, 2014). In our case, one of the main reasons for such questioning lies in the seminal work of Pierce et al. (2017) in elaborating a model for life skills transfer based on the work of Urie Bronfenbrenner. After continuous reflections, we recognised that our model does not aim to improve the conceptualisation proposed by Pierce et al. (2017) and provide more details on the elements and concepts of their model. Instead, we intend to provide a broader view and illustrate the relationship among the four dimensions of

Bronfenbrenner's PPCT Model in influencing life skills development. Through an interactive and easy-to-understand figure, this model does not aim to help researchers move forward but to figuratively "move backwards" to observe and broadly understand how life skills development occurs as a complex bioecological process of human development. In short, we aim to help readers take a step back to be able to take two steps forward.

OVERVIEW OF THE MODEL

The Biological Model of Life Skills Development (BMLSD; Figure 5.1) aims to illustrate how the four dimensions of the PPCT Model influence life skills development. The gears inside the microsystems represent the process dimension. The person is represented by the inner gear at the figure. The four contexts (i.e., micro, meso, exo, and

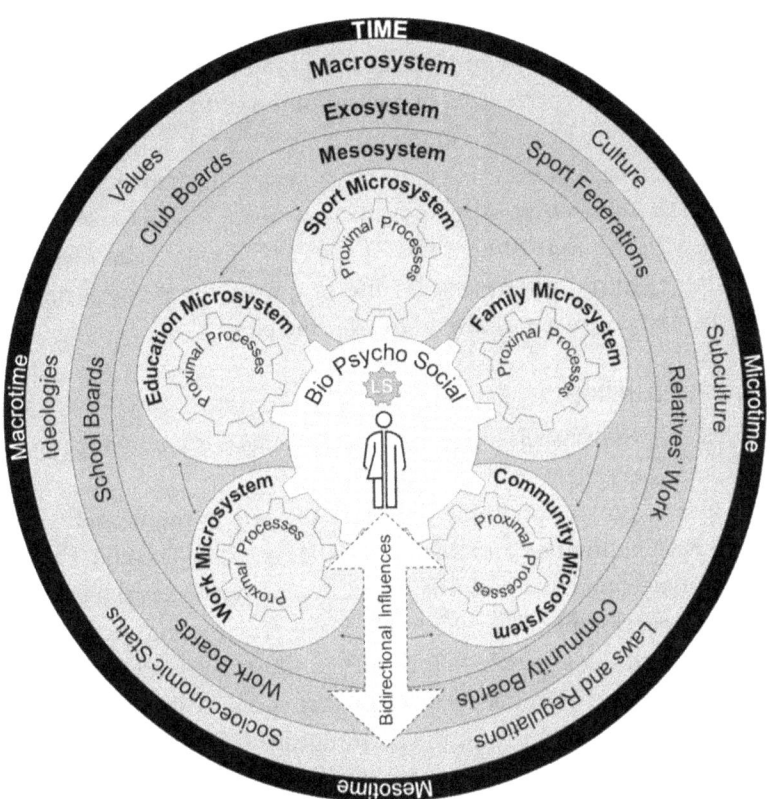

Figure 5.1 The BMLSD

macrosystems[1]) are portrayed around the person, and time encompasses all the elements together. At the bottom, the two-way arrow represents the reciprocal forces of influence (i.e., between the outer and inner elements). Although this chapter focuses on sports, the model elucidates other microsystems, processes, and elements that scholars, coaches, and sports stakeholders should consider when conceptualising life skills development.

In the BMLSD, the small gear with the initials "LS" inside the bigger gear represents the concept of life skills. Although life skills is a broad concept that includes other terms (e.g., psychosocial skills, knowledge, values) and is the focus of this model, one should recognise that this is only *one* of the *multiple* concepts related to the person's biopsychosocial development (Ronkainen et al., 2022), such as personal assets (Benson, 2003), social skills, and mental toughness. Indeed, Ronkainen et al. (2020) raised relevant questions about investigating life skills as a standardised "list" of measurable values and attitudes that the person develops in sports and how such an approach can lead to a false perception of control of the complex and multifaceted process of human development.

This section focuses on promoting a better understanding of the BMLSD by connecting insights from previous life skills research in sports with the four dimensions of the PPCT model. The life skills research cited did not necessarily use or quote bioecological theory, but their results relate to several of its principles.

APPLIED INSIGHTS

Process: Relationships and Activities as Proximal Processes for Life Skills Development

The idea to portray proximal processes as gears in the model comes from Bronfenbrenner and Morris' (2006, p. 798) account that in human development, "proximal processes are posited as the primary *engines* of development." In the BMSLD, the proximal processes' gears connect with the person's yellow gear to illustrate the reciprocity in which the other is influenced when one spins. Also, the spinning force could start either from the person gear or the proximal process gear. That is, the person's biopsychosocial characteristics can influence the engagement with a proximal process, such as an introverted youth who hesitates to talk to peers when warming up before a match (e.g., Jones & Lavallee, 2009) or engagement in the proximal process can influence the person, like developing a life skill as an outcome of participating in a sports activity (e.g., Jacobs & Wright, 2019; Weiss et al., 2013; Wright et al., 2020).

In terms of proximal processes in the sports context, several scholars have highlighted the important role played by sports coaches in the development of life skills through the modelling of appropriate behaviours and the establishment of nurturing relationships (e.g., Gould & Carson, 2008; Hemphill et al., 2019; Nunes et al., 2021; Wright et al., 2020). Under the lens of bioecological theory, Bronfenbrenner (2005) reports the importance of the presence of a third party who offers assistance, encouragement, and affection, and spends long periods in joint activities. The developmental outcomes (e.g., life skills) that can derive from the nurturing relationships established between coaches and athletes can be understood through the concept of "dyad," known as a system of two individuals. The potential for life skills development increases when coaches and athletes establish what Bronfenbrenner (1979) calls a primary dyad, exemplified by a strong emotional connection, whereby even when physically distant, both parties can still influence each other's thoughts and actions.

The activities in sports practices are another example of meaningful proximal processes in the sports microsystem. As it pertains to life skills development, a debate that continues today relates to the extent to which sports practices should be intentionally structured to promote life skills development. Thus far, the empirical evidence tends to indicate that the development of life skills can occur through explicit (Bean & Forneris, 2016; Hemphill et al., 2019) and implicit (Jones & Lavallee, 2009; Nunes et al., 2021) processes. Nevertheless, the intentional structuring of the sports context is generally deemed to be further conducive to the development of life skills (e.g., Bean & Forneris, 2016; Hemphill et al., 2019; Kendellen et al., 2017), mainly because coaches adopting explicit approaches provide athletes with opportunities to "experience" life skills and discuss how life skills can be applied in sports and transferred to other contexts of life (Bean & Forneris, 2016; Kendellen et al., 2017).

Person: The Active Role Played by the Person's Characteristics in the Development of Life Skills

When using the concept of life skills, empirical studies tend to focus on programme characteristics, with less attention usually paid to people's biopsychosocial characteristics (e.g., Bean & Forneris, 2016; Wright et al., 2020). However, when Jones and Lavallee (2009) identified that a tennis athlete realised her perfectionist and dedicated personality helped her develop life skills through sports, they highlighted the person's active role in the human development process. The athlete described her psychological dispositions, which in bioecological theory refer to the characteristics that can activate proximal processes in a particular context, in this case, her interactions with the properties, agents, and experiences within the sports context. Accordingly, life skills development is not necessarily a process that always initiates when the person enters the sports context. As Gould and Carson (2008) and Pierce et al. (2017) previously suggested, individuals do not enter the sports system devoid of previous autobiographical experiences, competencies, and life skills. Some life skills could be part of one's personality traits (e.g., communication and leadership) or have been developed in other contexts before entering sports (e.g., family and community) and should be acknowledged by researchers, coaches, and sports stakeholders.

Even though one could claim to have developed a life skill, its transfer to another context still depends on the features of the application context and one's conscious decision to use the life skill. In Kendellen and Camiré's (2019) study, one of the participants mentioned how he decided to transfer the communication skills he learned in sports because he gained personal satisfaction from helping others, and his classmate was a good friend. Conversely, Jacobs and Wright (2018) advocated that youth may decide not to transfer a life skill if they fear looking "uncool" in front of their friends – for example, when reprimanding a friend for swearing in front of a younger child. These findings imply that although several proximal processes in different microsystems could serve as powerful influences for life skills development, the person is still the main entity responsible for taking the last (and most important) step: transferring life skills to other contexts (Jacobs & Wright, 2018; Kendellen & Camiré, 2019).

Due to the person's biopsychosocial characteristics and experiential subjectivity, researchers have identified that the same stimuli offered in sports programmes result in different developmental outcomes for youth participants (Jacobs & Wright, 2019; Martinek et al., 2001). In elite sports, athletes reported the development of life skills even during negative career experiences, such as injuries, periods without contracts, homesickness, and limited social interactions (Nunes et al., 2021). Therefore, when considering life skills development, thorough attention should be paid to the person's biopsychosocial characteristics and how they attribute meaning to the proximal processes they engage in.

Context: The Multiple Systems Influencing Life Skills Development

Despite the focus of this chapter on the context of sports, it is essential to recognise the role played by educational (i.e., early, primary, secondary, and tertiary levels), family, work, and community microsystems to life skills development. This notion comes from Bronfenbrenner's (1979) early formulations regarding the influence of multiple and nested structures on human development. In sports-related research, Pierce et al. (2017) previously acknowledged the influence of several contexts on life skills development by indicating the school, family, vocational, and extracurricular contexts in addition to sports. Nevertheless, the influence of these microsystems differs for each person due to internal (i.e., biopsychosocial characteristics, age, interests) and external factors (i.e., place of residence, culture, socioeconomic status). Taking age as an example, one could be more influenced by the education, family, sports, and community microsystems during childhood and more influenced by the work microsystem during adulthood due to time spent and daily relevance reasons.

When it comes to the influence of sports as a microsystem, the belief and discourse about its potential for human development (and for life skills development) have spread for many decades due to the wealth of positive values and meanings attributed to this environment, such as overcoming obstacles and working as a team (Coakley, 2011). However, researchers have challenged this premise by recognising that sports has also contributed to practitioners being aggressive and disrespectful (Kavussanu, 2008), taking drugs and engaging in violence (Cowan & Taylor, 2016), and being encouraged by coaches to cheat during games and competitions (Romand & Pantaléon, 2007). Therefore, a more pragmatic view is currently adopted that the sports microsystem may be conducive to development when it fosters positive relationships, norms, and moral conduct guided by ethical principles (Coakley, 2011).

When investigating human development based on the person's involvement in the sports mesosystem (i.e., school-family or school-sports), it is essential to align values, discourses, and appropriate practices to leverage the development of life skills (Pierce et al., 2017). For Bronfenbrenner (1979), the potential for development in a context is dependent on the quality of the existing connections in a mesosystem, especially when the person develops primary dyads in both contexts. In the case of the high school teacher-coach in the Martin, Camiré, and Kramers (2021) study, the transfer of life skills was facilitated due to his relationship with student-athletes and explicit strategies in both contexts. When social agents are not present in two (or more) contexts, transfer can be supported or hindered by parents, teachers, coaches, peers, teammates, and siblings (Pierce et al., 2020).

Above the mesosystem is the exosystem. For Bronfenbrenner (1979), even if the person is not in direct contact with the exosystem, the actions and decisions of one reverberate in the other. In sports, the exosystem can be represented by the boards of clubs and sports federations seeking to structure their programmes to enhance the development of life skills, for example (Hemphill et al., 2019; Kendellen et al., 2017). One of the main strategies used by organisations has been the selection of specific life skills that exemplify organisational objectives for athlete development (Hemphill et al., 2019; Kendellen et al., 2017). Also, organisations have offered coach education programmes to help coaches visualise concrete strategies to implement on the ground (Falcão et al., 2017; Weiss et al., 2013). As a result of the decisions and training occurring in the exosystem, youth participants are engaging in practices (i.e., proximal processes) explicitly structured to support life skills development and learn how to respect others, manage emotions, be responsible, and be a good leader (Jacobs & Wright, 2019; Weiss et al., 2013).

Considering that the macrosystem comprises the overarching patterns of a particular group of locations, a study with New Zealand rugby coaches appears to illustrate one example. Hassanin et al. (2018) indicated that the rugby coaches interviewed felt that the Māori[2] cultural values, principles, and rituals highly influenced how they approached rugby. This influence makes them place more importance on personal and moral development to maintain what they believe to be the traditional values and the role of rugby in New Zealand. Thus, these rugby coaches seemed to adopt a more humanistic coaching approach (Hassanin et al., 2018), which has been identified as a valuable path for promoting the development of life skills, such as communicating better, willingness to help teammates, and respect for others (Falcão et al., 2017).

Time: The Influence of Micro-, Meso-, and Macrotime on Life Skills Development

In the BMLSD, the time dimension is responsible for putting all the elements in motion, allowing the gears to spin and human development to occur. To help readers visualise the effect of time on the model, we created an animated version of the BMLSD that can be found by scanning the QR code in Figure 5.2.

In the time dimension, macrotime stands as the overarching concept that account for the changes in society from time to time (i.e., years, decades, and centuries) that lead to different stimuli for human development (Bronfenbrenner, 2005). For example, it is due to macrotime that in the past decades, a significant shift occurred where both adults of the household embarked on full-time work journeys, which led to the responsibility for the education of their children to be transferred from the family to other contexts (Bronfenbrenner, 2005). In the sports context, Gould et al. (2019) identified that changes in society have led the generation of athletes born after 1996 (called Generation Z) to present difficulties in communicating effectively, dealing with adversities, and setting long-term goals while being more curious,

Figure 5.2 QR code to access the animated version of the BMLSD

open to learning, and displaying better technology skills. As the process of human development is bidirectional (Bronfenbrenner, 1979, 2005), different characteristics across the generations lead to the need for different approaches to coaching and teaching life skills. Tennis coaches in Gould et al.'s (2019) study reported using open-ended questions in feedback to encourage communication, creating stressful and challenging situations in practice to help them cope with adversity, and setting daily goals to keep athletes focused and motivated on skills improvement

In their conceptual model for life skills transfer, Pierce et al. (2017) recognised that in addition to influencing development, time is an element that can prevent or enhance the transfer of life skills to contexts other than sports. Freire et al. (2020) and Subijana et al. (2022) identified that older individuals who got involved in sports for longer scored higher in life skill development questionnaires than younger peers. These findings illustrate the concepts of microtime and mesotime (Bronfenbrenner & Morris, 1998, 2006). That is, for proximal processes to be effective, they must occur "on a fairly regular basis over extended periods of time" (Bronfenbrenner & Morris, 2006, p. 797). In the BMLSD, microtime and mesotime would be represented by the spin continuity of the proximal processes gears. Thus, the more the person engages in proximal processes in the microsystems in which they participate, the more the gear spins and the higher the potential for life skills development.

SUMMARY AND FUTURE DIRECTIONS

For understanding the central tenets of the BMSLD, it is critical to emphasise the need for coaches and sports stakeholders to recognise the bidirectional nature of human development and understand that coaches' teaching of life skills should not be considered a standardised and one-sided process – from coaches to athletes. First, coaches should acknowledge that they also develop by interacting with athletes. Second, athletes' biopsychosocial characteristics should guide the selection of life skills and how they will be addressed in practice. In the case of sports programmes with a pre-defined set of life skills to be developed, coaches can promote the development of other life skills based on modelling behaviour, meaningful relationships, and conversations about teachable moments without changing pre-established plans. Moreover, it is important that planning be flexible by allowing activities to change throughout the season through the recognition of the biopsychosocial characteristics of the athletes and the professional development of coaches and sports stakeholders.

As aforementioned, one should also consider that athletes' characteristics directly influence their interaction with the proximal process and its developmental outcomes. For example, a shorter person who practices a sports where height is an advantage may face more challenges than taller people, such as grabbing a rebound in basketball and blocking a spike in volleyball. As a result of constant frustration and dedication to improve their athletic performance and overcome these challenges, the person may develop life skills like perseverance and resilience. Therefore, coaches and sports stakeholders need to identify their athletes' biopsychosocial characteristics (e.g., motor skills, body composition, personality, background), be aware of potential challenges they may face in sports participation, and work on a personal level to facilitate life skills development and transfer.

For Bronfenbrenner (2005, p. 3), development is a "phenomenon of continuity and change in the biopsychological characteristics of human beings." Hence, life skills development is highly influenced by experiences in competitions, relationships with referees and opponents, as well as the rules and subculture of each sports (Dorsch et al., 2020). The potential for life skills development increases when the person finds in sports an alignment between the different contexts (i.e., sports, school, family, and community) and agents (i.e., parents, siblings, coaches, schoolteachers, and peers), creating a whole system that catalyses the developmental outcomes of the sports experience.

NOTES

1 Microsystem: context in which the person participates directly, such as family, school, and sports; mesosystem: interrelationships between two or more microsystems; exosystem: contexts in which the person does not directly participate but which influences and can be influenced by the person; macrosystem: system of cultures, subcultures, values, and ideologies of certain groups, locations, or countries.
2 The Māori are the *tangata whenua*, the Indigenous people of Aoteaora New Zealand.

REFERENCES

Bean, C., & Forneris, T. (2016). Examining the importance of intentionally structuring the youth sport context to facilitate positive youth development. *Journal of Applied Sport Psychology*, 28(4), 410–425. https://doi.org/10.1080/10413200.2016.1164764

Benson, P. L. (2003). Developmental assets and asset-building communities: Conceptual and empirical foundations. In R. M. Lerner & P. L. Benson (Eds.), *Developmental assets and asset building communities: Implications for research, policy and practice* (pp. 19–43). Kluwer.

Bond, M. (2019). Flipped learning and parent engagement in secondary schools: A South Australian case study. *British Journal of Educational Technology*, 50(3), 1294–1319. https://doi.org/10.1111/bjet.12765

Bone, K. D. (2015). The bioecological model: Applications in holistic workplace well-being management. *International Journal of Workplace Health Management*, 8(4), 256–271. https://doi.org/10.1108/IJWHM-04-2014-0010

Bronfenbrenner, U. (1979). *The ecology of human development: Experiments by nature and design*. Harvard University Press.

Bronfenbrenner, U. (Ed.). (2005). *Making human beings human: Bioecological perspectives on human development*. Sage Publications.

Bronfenbrenner, U., & Morris, P. A. (1998). The ecology of developmental process. In W. Damon & R. M. Lerner (Eds.), *Handbook of child psychology: Volume 1. Theoretical models of human development* (5th ed., pp. 993–1028). John Wiley.

Bronfenbrenner, U., & Morris, P. A. (2006). The bioecological model of human development. In W. Damon & R. M. Lerner (Eds.), *Handbook of child psychology: Volume 1. Theoretical models of human development* (6th ed., pp. 793–828). John Wiley.

Coakley, J. (2011). Youth sports: What counts as "positive development?". *Journal of Sport and Social Issues*, 35(3), 306–324. https://doi.org/10.1177/0193723511417311

Cowan, D., & Taylor, I. M. (2016). 'I'm proud of what I achieved; I'm also ashamed of what I done': A soccer coach's tale of sport, status, and criminal behaviour. *Qualitative Research in Sport, Exercise and Health*, 8(5), 505–518. https://doi.org/10.1080/2159676X.2016.1206608

Damon, W. (2004). What is positive youth development? *The ANNALS of the American Academy of Political and Social Science*, 59(1), 13–24. https://doi.org/10.1177/0002716203260092

Danish, S. (1983). Musings about personal competence: The contributions of sport, health, and fitness. *American Journal of Community Psychology*, 11(3), 221–240. https://doi.org/10.1007/BF00893365

Dorsch, T. E., Smith, A. L., Blazo, J. A., Coakley, J., Côté, J., Wagstaff, C. R., Warner, S., & King, M. Q. (2020). Toward an integrated understanding of the youth sport system. *Research Quarterly for Exercise and Sport*, 93(1), 105–119. https://doi.org/10.1080/02701367.2020.1810847

Falcão, W. R., Bloom, G. A., & Bennie, A. (2017). Coaches' experiences learning and applying the content of a humanistic coaching workshop in youth sport settings. *International Sport Coaching Journal*, 4(3), 279–290. https://doi.org/10.1123/iscj.2017-0027

Freire, G. L. M., da Silva, A. A., de Moraes, J. F. V. N., Costa, N. L. G., de Oliveira, D. V., & do Nascimento Junior, J. R. A. (2020). Do age and time of practice predict the development of life skills among youth futsal practitioners? *Cuadernos de Psicología del Deporte*, 21(1), 135–145. https://doi.org/10.6018/cpd.419151

Geldhof, G. J., Bowers, E. P., Johnson, S. K., Hershberg, R., Hilliard, L., Lerner, J. V., & Lerner, R. M. (2013). Relational developmental systems theories of positive youth development: Methodological issues and implications. In P. C. M. Molenaar, R. M. Lerner, & K. M. Newell (Eds.), *Handbook of developmental systems theory and methodology* (pp. 66–94). The Guilford Press.

Gould, D., & Carson, S. (2008). Life skills development through sport: Current status and future directions. *International Review of Sport and Exercise Psychology*, 1(1), 58–78. https://doi.org/10.1080/17509840701834573

Gould, D., Nalepa, J., & Mignano, M. (2019). Coaching generation Z athletes. *Journal of Applied Sport Psychology*, 32(1), 104–120. https://doi.org/10.1080/10413200.2019.1581856

Hassanin, R., Light, R. L., & Macfarlane, A. (2018). Developing 'good buggers': Global implications of the influence of culture on New Zealand club rugby coaches' beliefs and practice. *Sport in Society*, 21(8), 1223–1235. https://doi.org/10.1080/17430437.2018.1443598

Hemphill, M. A., Gordon, B., & Wright, P. M. (2019). Sports as a passport to success: Life skill integration in a positive youth development program. *Physical Education & Sport Pedagogy*, 24(4), 390–401. https://doi.org/10.1080/17408989.2019.1606901

Holt, N. L., Tink, L. N., Mandigo, J. L., & Fox, K. R. (2008). Do youth learn life skills through their involvement in high school sport? A case study. *Canadian Journal of Education*, 31, 281–304. https://doi.org/10.2307/20466702

Jacobs, J., & Wright, P. (2018). Transfer of life skills in sport-based youth development programs: A conceptual framework bridging learning to application. *Quest*, 70(1), 81–99. https://doi.org/10.1080/00336297.2017.1348304

Jacobs, J., & Wright, P. M. (2019). Thinking about the transfer of life skills: Reflections from youth in a community-based sport programme in an underserved urban setting. *International Journal of Sport and Exercise Psychology*, 19(3), 380–394. https://doi.org/10.1080/1612197X.2019.1655776

Jones, M., & Lavallee, D. (2009). Exploring perceived life skills development and participation in sport. *Qualitative Research in Sport and Exercise*, 1(1), 36–50. https://doi.org/10.1080/19398440802567931

Kavussanu, M. (2008). Moral behaviour in sport: A critical review of the literature. *International Review of Sport and Exercise Psychology*, 1(2), 124–138. https://doi.org/10.1080/17509840802277417

Kendellen, K., & Camiré, M. (2019). Applying in life the skills learned in sport: A grounded theory. *Psychology of Sport and Exercise*, 40, 23–32. https://doi.org/10.1016/j.psychsport.2018.09.002

Kendellen, K., Camiré, M., Bean, C. N., Forneris, T., & Thompson, J. (2017). Integrating life skills into Golf Canada's youth programs: Insights into a successful research to practice partnership. *Journal of Sport Psychology in Action*, 8(1), 34–46. https://doi.org/10.1080/21520704.2016.1205699

Lerner, R. M. (2005). Foreword – Urie Bronfenbrenner: career contributions of the consummate developmental scientist. In U. Bronfenbrenner (Ed.), *Making human beings human* (pp. IX–XXIX). Sage Publications.

Lerner, R. M., Almerigi, J. B., Theokas, C., & Lerner, J. V. (2005). Positive youth development: A view of the issues. *Journal of Early Adolescence*, 25(1), 10–16. https://doi.org/10.1177/0272431604273211

Lerner, R. M., Tirrell, J. M., Dowling, E. M., Geldhof, G. J., Gestsdóttir, S., Lerner, J. V., King, P. E., Williams, K., Iraheta, G., & Sim, A. T. (2019). The end of the beginning: Evidence and absences studying positive youth development in a global context. *Adolescent Research Review*, 4(1), 1–14. https://doi.org/10.1007/s40894-018-0093-4

Martin, N., Camiré, M., & Kramers, S. (2021). Facilitating life skills transfer from sport to the classroom: An intervention assisting a high school teacher-coach. *Journal of Applied Sport Psychology*, 1077–1101. https://doi.org/10.1080/10413200.2021.1917016

Martinek, T., Schilling, T., & Johnson, D. (2001). Transferring personal and social responsibility of underserved youth to the classroom. *The Urban Review*, 33(1), 29–45. https://doi.org/10.1023/A:1010332812171

McLaren, C. D., Sutcliffe, J. T., Gardner, L. A., Vella, S. A., & Bruner, M. W. (2021). Mapping the scientific structure of positive youth development research in sport. *International Review of Sport and Exercise Psychology*, 1–22. https://doi.org/10.1080/1750984X.2021.1969675

Neuman, L. W. (2014). *Social research methods: Qualitative and quantitative approaches* (7th ed.). Pearson Education Limited.

Newman, T. J., Santos, F., Black, S., & Bostick, K. (2021). Learning life skills through challenging and negative experiences. *Child and Adolescent Social Work Journal*, 1–15. https://doi.org/10.1007/s10560-021-00739-y

Nunes, E. L. G., Ciampolini, V., Santos, F., Palheta, C. E., Nascimento, J. V., & Milistetd, M. (2021). Composite vignettes of former Brazilian high-performance volleyball athletes' perspective on life skills learning and transfer. *Journal of Sports Sciences*, 39(23), 2674–2682. https://doi.org/10.1080/02640414.2021.1951054

Pierce, S., Erickson, K., & Dinu, R. (2019). Teacher-coaches' perceptions of life skills transfer from high school sport to the classroom. *Journal of Applied Sport Psychology*, 31(4), 451–473. https://doi.org/10.1080/10413200.2018.1500402

Pierce, S., Erickson, K., & Sarkar, M. (2020). High school student-athletes' perceptions and experiences of leadership as a life skill. *Psychology of Sport and Exercise*, 51, 1–10. https://doi.org/10.1016/j.psychsport.2020.101716

Pierce, S., Gould, D., & Camiré, M. (2017). Definition and model of life skills transfer. *International Review of Sport and Exercise Psychology*, 10(1), 186–211. https://doi.org/10.1080/1750984X.2016.1199727

Qi, S., Hua, F., Zhou, Z., & Shek, D. T. (2020). Trends of positive youth development publications (1995–2020): A scientometric review. *Applied Research in Quality of Life*, 17, 421–446. https://doi.org/10.1007/s11482-020-09878-3

Romand, P., & Pantaléon, N. (2007). A qualitative study of rugby coaches' opinions about the display of moral character. *The Sport Psychologist*, 21(1), 58–77. https://doi.org/10.1123/tsp.21.1.58

Ronkainen, N., Aggerholm, K., Allen-Collinson, J., & Ryba, T. V. (2022). Beyond life-skills: Talented athletes, existential learning and (Un)learning the life of an athlete. *Qualitative Research in Sport, Exercise and Health*, 1–15. https://doi.org/10.1080/2159676X.2022.2037694

Ronkainen, N., Aggerholm, K., Ryba, T. V., & Allen-Collinson, J. (2020). Learning in sport: from life skills to existential learning. *Sport, Education and Society*, 26(2), 214–227. https://doi.org/10.1080/13573322.2020.1712655

Rosa, E. M., & Tudge, J. (2013). Urie Bronfenbrenner's theory of human development: Its evolution from ecology to bioecology. *Journal of Family Theory & Review*, 5(4), 243–258. https://doi.org/10.1111/jftr.12022

Silbereisen, R. K., & Lerner, R. M. (2007). Approaches to positive youth development: A view of the issues. In R. K. Silbereisen & R. M. Lerner (Eds.), *Approaches to positive youth development* (pp. 3–30). Sage Publications.

Subijana, C. L., Ramos, J., Harrison, C. K., & Lupo, C. (2022). Life skills from sport: The former elite athlete's perception. *Sport in Society*, 25(5), 1051–1064. https://doi.org/10.1080/17430437.2020.1820991

Weiss, M. R., Stuntz, C. P., Bhalla, J. A., Bolter, N. D., & Price, M. S. (2013). 'More than a game': Impact of The First Tee life skills programme on positive youth development: project introduction and year 1 findings. *Qualitative Research in Sport, Exercise and Health*, 5(2), 214–244. https://doi.org/10.1080/2159676X.2012.712997

Wright, P. M., Howell, S., Jacobs, J., & McLoughlin, G. (2020). Implementation and perceived benefits of an after-school soccer program designed to promote social and emotional learning. *Journal of Amateur Sport*, 6(1), 125–145. https://doi.org/10.17161/jas.v6i1.8635

Practical Approaches to Teaching Values and Life Skills

Chapter Six

Samantha Bates, Dawn Anderson-Butcher
and Kylee Ault-Baker

INTRODUCTION

Imagine cutting a lap on the track while conditioning weekly when the coach is not watching and feeling winded in the first game. How does cutting the lap relate to not finishing a training your boss asked you to complete and then feeling unprepared in a meeting? *Imagine learning how to ski.* How does practicing, seeing improvements over time, figuring out how to avoid falling, or committing to more challenging slopes relate to starting a new job? *Imagine hearing the play called and running to the left side of the field, but then the goaltender throws the ball to the middle of the field.* How does not studying the playbook relate to doing poorly on a math test? How does this example relate to you and your spouse forgetting to pick up your youngest child from school?

No surprise to those reading this chapter that physical education and sports (PES) can enhance notable domains of health, including physical fitness, physical activity, motor skills, and mental health. These settings also can facilitate the development of values and life skills that extend far beyond the gym, court, or field. Values are principles and convictions that guide behavior, including standards deemed good or desirable (Halstead & Taylor, 2000, p. 169). In the example where you imagined cutting a lap during training when no one was watching, values of *integrity*, *honesty*, and *responsibility* were connected to PE activities, sports practices, and athletic competitions and games. Meanwhile, life skills "encompass a range of personal assets including psychosocial skills, knowledge, dispositions, and identify constructions and transformation (Pierce et al., 2017, p. 195)." In short, life skills can be intrapersonal (e.g., time management) and interpersonal (e.g., communication). Learning to ski teaches intrapersonal skills related to one's mind, thoughts, and emotions, such as *commitment*, *perseverance*, *adaptability*, *effort*, and *discipline*. Meanwhile, the miscommunication between an athlete and the quarterback teaches interpersonal

DOI: 10.4324/9781032688657-8

skills related to interactions among individuals or groups, such as *communication*, *teamwork*, and *conflict resolution*, as well as intrapersonal skills that transcend sports, including *planning*, *preparation*, *problem-solving*, and *decision-making*.

As evidenced by the previous examples, PE and sports are highly accessible contexts for promoting positive youth development (PYD) and the development of life skills and values. This is especially relevant given mandates for PE curricula exist in most countries worldwide (UNESCO, 2013), and over 50% of children in some developed countries participate in organized sports (Black et al., 2022; Project Play, 2023). In the United States, the National Recreation and Park Association (2023) reports that five in six agencies provide or facilitate local sports programming. Moreover, 29% of US youth played travel sports in 2022 (Project Play, 2023). Given high levels of participation, PE and sports have the immense potential to provide young people with ready-made peer groups to practice building relationships, challenges that teach persistence in the face of adversity, and activities that simulate real-world tasks that require teamwork, communication, and self-evaluation. These skills, in turn, can facilitate future successes and resilience in school, work, relationships, and life.

While sports is a context ripe for teaching values and life skills, recent US National Coach Survey data indicate that only 47% of coaches and PE educators feel confident in their ability to teach life skills through sports (Anderson-Butcher & Bates, 2022). Alternatively, when coaches report a high valuation of integrating life skills into sports practices and lessons, they also are more likely to report having a significant impact on the young people they coach and to be satisfied in their role, and are more likely to be retained as coaches (Anderson-Butcher & Bates, 2022; Bates & Anderson-Butcher, 2023). As evidenced by these findings, there is a need to provide PE educators and coaches with practical strategies regarding *how* to teach values and life skills to impact students and athletes participating in PE and sports positively, but also to help them be more successful in their traditional instructional and coaching roles (Anderson-Butcher & Bates, 2022; Koh et al., 2016).

Approaches to Teaching Values and Life Skills

Teaching values and life skills through PE and sports are often discussed within two frames: *sports plus* and *plus sports* (Coalter, 2007). Objectives of sports plus approaches are increased participation in sports and improved performance, both of which are achieved through providing quality instruction, equipment, and other resources. The primary benefits of sports plus approaches include general fitness and sports skill development, and secondary benefits inclusive of life skill development. In short, sports plus approaches encompass traditional sports contexts (e.g., school, recreational, and competitive settings) predominantly focused on the "X's and O's," which then add in elements of PYD as a bonus. Alternatively, plus sports approaches emphasize sports as the tool to help forge PYD and social change. Plus sports approaches focus on nonsport outcomes, ones such as improving life skills, providing mentorship and guidance, promoting social capital and a sense of belonging, and/or reducing violence. Plus sports often aligns with prevention and PYD priorities by helping young people develop skills and values that extend beyond PES and sports to promote positive social change and other healthy youth outcomes.

Historically, PES and sports programs are often situated within contexts prioritizing skill development and physical activity (e.g., sports plus). However, coaches and PES educators can intentionally leverage PES to teach values and life skills and build programs that draw upon practical approaches across these two frames (e.g., plus sports). At the intersection of these two approaches is a common misconception that values and life skills are often "caught." Values and life skills need to be intentionally "taught." Specifically, Bean et al. (2018) and Turnnidge et al. (2014) proposed life skills are intentionally taught on a continuum ranging from implicit (e.g., structure of the environment and team environments) to explicit (e.g., discussion and practice of life skills) practices. Similarly, Pierce et al.'s (2017) model of life skill transfer contends that the learning context directly influences life skill development, and intentional coaching practices can facilitate transfer.

Using this continuum as a guide, effective coaches and PES educators weave teaching values and life skills into their pedagogy and embed implicit and explicit activities into their instructional designs. In these contexts, PYD outcomes parallel those focused on physical competencies and are not seen as "extra." Next, our applied insights section demonstrates how sports coaches and PES educators can intentionally integrate values and life skills into lessons.

APPLIED INSIGHTS

In this section, we share strategies utilized by researchers and practitioners with a collective 50 years of experience in sports-based PYD, coach education and training, and out-of-school time programming. In addition to serving in traditional coaching roles, the authors of this chapter have co-led the development and implementation of LiFEsports at The Ohio State University (OSU; www.lifesports.osu.edu), a nationally recognized model of sports-based PYD, and Coach Beyond, a training and education program designed to promote athlete mental health and support whole child development. For context, LiFEsports traditionally acts as a plus sports model, engaging over 900 youth experiencing social vulnerabilities in sports-based PYD programming during summer and out-of-school time. LiFEsports is a proven model, with over 30 peer-reviewed articles demonstrating outcomes and crucial evidence-based practices that serve as effective program mechanisms for promoting life skill development (Anderson-Butcher et al., 2024). Meanwhile, Coach Beyond is a training and education program designed to help coaches go beyond the "X's and O's" and incorporate important topics in their coaching practices, such as supporting mental health, developing leaders, and cultivating positive team environments (Bates et al., 2023). To situate our approaches, we often ground our examples around life skills intentionally taught via our LiFEsports summer camps, including Self-Control, Effort, Teamwork, and Social Responsibility (SETS). Implicit and explicit strategies and evidence-based practices known to work in our research and practice are further shared here.

Implicit Approaches

Before teaching values and life skills, coaches and PES educators must intentionally cultivate psychologically and physically safe and structured environments that support learning and engagement (Gould & Carson, 2008; Newman & Anderson-Butcher, 2021; Newman et al., 2023). Newman and colleagues (2023) found these implicit approaches often involve developing a PYD-focused coaching philosophy, using a strength-based approach, establishing a prosocial culture, fostering positive relationships, and supporting youth autonomy. Next, we offer practical examples of these concepts for use in the gym or at practice.

Preparation, Greetings, and Routines

Implicit instruction begins with preparing for your lesson or practice before students and/or athletes arrive, having a plan with clear learning objectives, and setting up equipment and activities beforehand to optimize time on task and opportunities for instruction (Anderson-Butcher et al., 2018). Additionally, to foster positive relationships, coaches and PES educators need to know every child's name and greet them when they arrive. A warm tone of voice, open body language, and encouragement to engage in a routine at the beginning of every lesson, practice, or competition can facilitate a sense of safety, structure, and belonging. One practical approach related to supporting youth autonomy is having students find a spot or line on the floor, court, or field and implementing a warm-up routine such as stretching with music or creating a circuit where students move through multiple stations for a set amount of time (e.g., five minutes stretching at first rotation, five minutes jogging around the gym). Coaches can also foster initiative while encouraging engagement before a lesson begins by allowing for choice and leadership in keeping track of when it is time to switch rotations.

Check-in Activities

To cultivate a prosocial culture, we recommend starting each lesson or practice with a pair and share activity (i.e., "check-in") designed to strengthen relationships and empathy (Bates et al., 2023). For example, at LiFEsports and in our coach education lessons, we model how a coach or instructor would say, "Let's count off and get with a partner. Take three minutes to share how you are feeling today using a weather report. For instance, are you 75 and sunny, and why? Is a storm expected? If so, why?" Other examples include questions like: "How charged is your battery today and why?," or "Describe how you feel today using an emoji. Why does that emoji describe how you are feeling?" Sports coaches can even use sports-specific examples, such as, "If you had to say how you are feeling today in yards and downs, what would you say? 1st and long? 3rd and short?" or "What kind of volleyball serve did today feel like, and why? Hit the net? Barely go over the net? Soar over the net?" Check-ins can help cultivate a positive, youth-centered environment that encourages emotional safety; gauge a young person's overall well-being; and allow coaches and PES educators to follow up with them if anything concerning is shared or voiced consistently over time (Bates et al., 2023). They also destigmatize mental health and create safe spaces for conversations about feelings and help-seeking.

Safety, Structure, and the "Why"

Next, coaches and PES educators can describe the lesson's structure, objectives, and expectations (also called an "anticipatory set"). Outlining a lesson and explaining what will happen first, second, and third, and how the lesson will commence with a debrief, can help students and athletes, especially those with trauma or attention issues, anticipate changes and understand the flow of the session (Anderson-Butcher et al., 2018). Also, remember to share the "why" behind implementing certain activities by explicitly articulating the hope that participants will make mistakes, take risks, and try new things, as these will ultimately promote learning, tenacity, and resilience. In *sports plus* settings, coaches can outline their practice plan and describe how the activities will help the athletes or team progress toward their goals. Doing so intentionally models the following life skills: organization, planning, preparation, commitment, goal-setting, and decision-making.

In *plus sports* settings, coaches and PES educators can emphasize the importance of having a safe space and allow for explicit goals related to fun and enjoyment. Furthermore, safety in *plus sports* settings is important and is often tied to teaching fundamental skills that prevent injuries and promote participation. For example, before every LiFEsports lesson, participants are cued to use three to four key sports skills to keep their bodies and one another safe. In soccer lessons focused on passing, cues include using the inside of one's foot, keeping one's eyes up, planting the other foot in the direction one wants the ball to go, and communicating with one's partner (Anderson-Butcher et al., 2018). Safety is also taught and reinforced by cues related to the environment, such as asking everyone to keep the balls on the floor (e.g., assessing one's strength), maintaining distance from peers, and keeping voices on a scale of four out of ten (e.g., coaches can model voice level). Coaches and PES educators can also ask participants to add other ideas about keeping one another safe and having fun during the lesson and probe for examples of unsafe behaviors (e.g., kicking the ball too high might hit someone in the head). These implicit strategies model and facilitate open communication, encourage collaboration, and cultivate a safe and supportive environment.

Explicit Approaches

Next, we discuss more explicit approaches, including direct strategies to facilitate life skill transfer that accompany the development of a safe and supportive climate, positive coach-athlete relationships, and a well-structured environment. Newman and colleagues (2023) found explicit approaches often include discussing and teaching life skills, creating opportunities to practice life skills in sports, supplying direct feedback, debriefing sports experiences to enhance life skill transfer, and providing opportunities to transfer outside of sports. At LiFEsports and during our Coach Beyond trainings, we encourage coaches and PES educators to also identify values or life skills they want their students or athletes to develop. This can be a core set of life skills such as the SETS taught at LiFEsports or expectations regarding behaviors or attitudes for teams, athletic programs, or classrooms. Teams or programs may develop acronyms to define specific life skills, such as "SOAR" (Safety, Ownership, Achievement, Respect) to help them move through a season. Similarly, PES educators may utilize language in alignment with their school's positive behavioral intervention and supports and use value statements to define expected behaviors, such as "Be safe. Be respectful. Be responsible." Once identified, coaches and PES educators can use several evidence-based instructional strategies, such as framing, modeling, providing feedback, and implementing reinforcements to support learning and application of these life skills and values to sports and other contexts.

Frame and Model

Once students or athletes are ready to engage in a lesson, first frame the lesson by discussing at least one life skill or value that is the focus for that day. Bodey et al. (2009) encouraged coaches and PES educators to keep it simple by only including one life skill per practice or lesson and to ensure the life skills or values taught match the developmental age of the participants (Anderson-Butcher et al., 2018). Using an example from LiFEsports, coaches would start a soccer or lacrosse lesson by saying,

Today, we will focus on *effort* while passing Effort is the energy and hard work you put into something to help you reach your goals. Effort also is shown when you make a mistake, then a correction, and then master the skill.

Then, an essential next step is to model both the sports skills being taught (e.g., passing) *and* the life skill or value. Building on the previous example, a coach or educator can demonstrate the behaviors they hope to see by going through an activity step by step. As they model the drill or activity, they can integrate the life skill into the simulation by saying, "See, I'm using *effort* to keep the ball close to my body as I move through the cones." After a coach models a drill, ask the participants to reflect on other ways the life skill or value was modeled: "How else did you see me use *effort* just then and in what ways did you use *effort* as you were learning."

Provide Feedback and Praise

Coaches and PES educators then want to provide feedback and verbal praise as lessons progress. Effective feedback is notably individualized, specific, congruent (e.g., matches), and timely (close to the timing of the behavior or opportunity for improvement). An example of effective feedback immediately after practice is a coach saying, "Sean, you put in great effort today when you saved the ball from going out of bounds and resulting in a corner kick. Great job!" The verbal message (praising effort and providing specific feedback on the tactic) is congruent if matched with positive nonverbal cues, such as a smiling face and enthusiastic tone. Specific examples of how the participant demonstrated the life skill or value should be delivered as close to the timing of the behavior to ensure the intended message is understood as something they should replicate or adapt in the future. Coaches also can go one step further by connecting the praise to ways behaviors seen in sports are connected to school or life. For example, a coach can add the following to the end of Sean's feedback: "I want to see that same level of effort when you study for your math test!"

Leverage Teachable Moments

Play, recreation, and sports activities also provide ample opportunities to build upon teachable moments where coaches and PES educators can act as role models (Pierce et al., 2018) and cultivate cultures in which it is safe to take risks, make mistakes, and continue learning. For example, a coach can use the loss of a game to teach values of honesty and perseverance by sharing how they felt (e.g., frustrated, proud), what they did to process the emotion (e.g., went for a run, called a friend, celebrated by getting ice cream), and how they want to continue to improve and show up as a dedicated member of the team. In our Coach Beyond programming, we teach coaches to use the acronym "WIN," which stands for *"What's Important Now?"* This language can teach students and athletes how to refocus their attention after a win or a challenging moment in the gym or after a game. It can also turn challenging moments into valuable learning experiences and foster learning environments that normalize feedback and continued growth as you stop practice to provide specific feedback or demonstrate proper techniques. Many of our Coach Beyond participants like integrating the following phases into their coaching practices: "Let's get one percent better today" or framing wins and losses as "wins and lessons." Coaches and PES educators can empower social cohesion by asking, "How did you help someone else get better today?" Together, these approaches promote life skills and values and avoid the emergence of shame- or blame-based team cultures.

Implement Behavioral Reinforcements

A critical component of the LiFEsports model is using behavioral tokens, or LiFEsports branded buttons with OSU Buckeye leaves on them that participants pin to their shirts or bags. The OSU Buckeye leaves align with the school's mascot and signature tree in the state – the buckeye tree. When athletes perform well on and off the field at OSU, they get buckeye stickers on their helmets. At LiFEsports, these buttons act as a token economy system typically found in traditional social skills interventions and are used to recognize participants who demonstrate specific life skills desired by the program (i.e., SETS). Each LiFEsports staff member receives eight tokens (two tokens per curricular session) at the beginning of each day to use as behavioral reinforcements during camp. LiFEsports staff leading the play-based social skills curriculum, Chalk Talk, or sports sessions intentionally distribute tokens during the debriefing process at the end of each curricular session.

Staff are instructed to communicate the specific youth behavior the token reinforces (i.e., one of the SETS). Based on our research, youth participants learned more about SETS when they valued and received verbal reinforcements about the life skills being taught rather than being the recipient of a button (Anderson-Butcher et al., 2021). Other reinforcements, such as mystery motivators, can also be integrated into gym lessons. This reinforcement is implemented by letting students know the coach or PES educator is looking for students who demonstrate teamwork during the activity. Then, at the end of the lesson, specific and individualized feedback is provided to those who demonstrated a life skill such as teamwork, and they get to draw a mystery prize out of a bag (e.g., first in line or captain for the next game).

Practice and Transfer

Students and athletes also need opportunities to practice the life skills and values taught through sports (Ault et al., 2023), just as they might practice foul shots and penalty kicks. At LiFEsports, participants learn about SETS through our play-based educational social skills lessons, called Chalk Talk. Then, participants get opportunities to practice their life skills in eight different sports and at the end of the summer at the LiFEsports Games (e.g., final competitions modeled after the Olympics with team flags, metals). Additionally, our team incrementally increases the level of challenge during practice, creating an environment where participants must apply life skills and values to new challenges (demonstrating effort, persistence, and ultimately mastery). Increasing task intensity helps push learners into their zone of proximal development. Greater intensity and varied tasks can lead to better retention of skills and build confidence as one tries, learns, and sees links between behaviors and accomplishing new things. Further, LiFEsports participants attend booster sports clinics throughout the year where the skills are taught and practiced again. Our research shows participants are more likely to transfer and apply SETS outside of our program when they attend boosters, and those attending at least one booster sports clinic annually were more likely to return to the program the following year, further denoting the importance of extending learning opportunities to facilitate long-term engagement in sports.

Debrief

Debriefing a lesson is one of the most critical aspects of teaching life skills and values through sports and involves reflecting on experiences to process learning and foster application (Newman et al., 2023; Pierce et al., 2017). Debriefs are most effective when framed using the "What? So What? Now What?" framework (Borton, 1970). Using this framework, the "What?" question helps the learner return to the original goal or objective and make the link between the life skill and value and the sports or play activities. The "So What?" question prompts the learner to reflect on the experience and information. This question helps students and athletes consider why this life skill or value matters. The "Now What" question orients the learner toward transferring the skill to other contexts or scenarios. Building upon past examples using effort, a coach or educator might say the following as an example: (a) What was the life skill we focused on today? What did effort look like during our activities? (b) What is the importance of effort? (c) What are ways we can use effort in the future (e.g., in school, relationships, community)? Coaches and PES educators can then add questions to keep the discussion going, ask clarifying questions, and redirect questions to other students to elevate different viewpoints. Alternatively, another effective facilitation skill for debriefing is allowing for silence, as this is usually when students or athletes think and organize their thoughts.

Encourage Reflection

Finally, provide ample opportunities for reflection and processing to further learning and transfer beyond the gym, court, mat, or field into school and life. Self-reflection plays a vital role in developing critical thinking and problem-solving skills (Colley et al., 2012) and allows young people to create meaning and conceptualization from their experiences (Brockbank & McGill, 1998). Reflection is often a missed component in the planning of PE or sports lessons that use experiential learning (i.e., transforming experiences into learning via the facilitator's instruction, cues, and intentionality). Duley (1981, p. 611) points out, "The skill of experiential learning in which people tend to be the most deficient in is reflection." Others have referred to reflection as a neglected area in learning

(Boud et al., 1985). From a practical perspective, we teach our Coach Beyond participants to use sports-focused language to help athletes engage in reflection, whether about a poor performance or a negative interpersonal interaction. Coaches and athletes are encouraged to metaphorically go back and "watch the film" together to examine past behaviors and use them to identify opportunities to handle a future situation. Probing athletes to think about multiple alternatives can enhance their problem-solving and decision-making skills and provide insight into how they can improve over time. When debriefing at LiFEsports, participants are asked to think about the life or social skill of the day, when they used the skill or saw others emulating the skill. Then, the reflection advances to questions about why this life or skill is important and how you can use it beyond the court, mat, field, etc.

For PES educators, reflective writing can facilitate student engagement in learning and help push the learner to reflect on how they learned the skills (Colley et al., 2012; Mezirow, 1990). Using LiFEsports as an example, participants are asked weekly to utilize journals to reflect on the life skills taught through the Chalk Talk and sports sessions (see Figure 6.1). In addition, participants are asked to draw and reflect upon how the life skill could be used at home or school. Journals include prompts such as, "Draw a picture of you having self-control at home or school." By thinking about lessons and behaviors, participants can better connect play, recreation, and sports activities to life skills and to life outside of camp.

Figure 6.1 LiFE *sports* journal reflection example

SUMMARY AND FUTURE DIRECTIONS

In summary, teaching life skills and values requires integrating implicit and explicit approaches into one's pedagogical practice. This chapter provided several practical and translational ways to go beyond the "X's and O's" to facilitate learning. Key explicit strategies include framing and modeling life skills and values, leveraging teachable moments, providing opportunities to practice and transfer skills, and encouraging reflection. Using these strategies and others, coaches and PES educators can make sports, recreation, and play activities more holistic and experiential but also more enjoyable and beneficial for students and athletes.

As we look toward the future, coaches and PES educators will be called upon to adapt to educational, technological, societal, and historic shifts and innovations. Already, sports and PES were adapted during the COVID-19 pandemic to facilitate lessons on life skills and values in blended, online, or hybrid learning environments (Bates et al., 2021). Undoubtedly, trends may continue and require us to think about how to integrate life skills and values into virtual or augmented reality, fitness apps, and wearable devices. Such innovations, including ones using sports plus and plus sports approaches, may require us to simultaneously engage young people in positive physical health behaviors and promote social learning, especially as screen time increases among children and adolescents globally. Further, the emergent youth mental health crisis has and will continue to require coaches and PES educators to facilitate lessons on wellness, including instruction on mindfulness, self-talk, stress management, coping, etc., to prevent crises and promote resilience in schools and communities worldwide. As the landscape of education and sports evolves, coaches and PES educators will be dynamic vehicles in not only shaping *how* students and athletes learn but also informing *what* they learn to become well-rounded, resilient, socially responsible, and engaged citizens.

REFERENCES

Anderson-Butcher, D., Bates, S., Wade-Mdivianian, R., & Mack, S. (2024). Positive youth development in community sport settings. In N. Holt & M. McDonough (Eds.), *Positive youth development through sport* (3rd ed.). Routledge. https://doi.org/10.4324/9781003395867-25

Anderson-Butcher, D., & Bates, S. (2022). National Coach Survey final report. The Ohio State University Initiative, Columbus, OH. Retrieved from https://www.aspeninstitute.org/wp-content/uploads/2022/11/national-coach-survey-report-preliminary-analysis.pdf

Anderson-Butcher, D., Bates, S., Wade-Mdivanian, R., & Mack, S. (2021). Community sport as a context for positive youth development. In N. Holt & M. McDonough (Eds.), *Positive youth development through sport* (3rd ed.) (pp. 269–287). Routledge.

Anderson-Butcher, D., Wade-Mdivanian, R., & Davis, J. (2018). *Social/life skill intervention and sport intervention curriculum.* LiFEsports Initiative, The Ohio State University.

Ault, K. J., Blanton, J. E., & Pierce, S. (2023). Student-athletes' perceptions of relationship quality and life skills development. *Journal of Applied Sport Psychology*, 1–22. https://doi.org/10.1080/10413200.2023.2197970

Bates, S., & Anderson-Butcher, D. (2023). Leveraging sport as a context for character development: The benefit for coaches. *Journal of Character Education*, 19 (45293), 1–15.

Bates, S., Anderson-Butcher, D., Ute, D., McVey, D., Mack, S. Nothnagle, E., Wade-Mdivanian, R., Davis, J., DeVoll, J., Vassaloti, J., Hix, J., Pata, K., Bobek, N., Ludban, C., Myers, K., Porter, K., Quackenbush, J., Roberts, J., Hajjar, N., Durbin, P., Wolfe, T., & Magistrale, N. (2023). Mental health training for high school coaches and athletic directors: Community-based participatory research to Coach Beyond. *International Journal of Sport Science & Coaching*. https://doi.org/10.1177/17479541231201257

Bates, S., Greene, D., & O'Quinn, L. (2021). Virtual sport-based positive youth development during the COVID-19 pandemic. *Child and Adolescent Social Work Journal*, 38(4), 437–448.

Bean, C., Kramers, S., Forneris, T., & Camiré, M. (2018). The implicit/explicit continuum of life skills development and transfer. *Quest*, 70(4), 456–470. https://doi.org/10.1080/00336297.2018.1451348

Black, L., Terlizzi, E., & Vahratian, A. (2022). Organized sports participation among children aged 6-17 years: United States, 2020. Retrieved from https://www.cdc.gov/nchs/data/databriefs/db441.pdf

Bodey, K. J., Schaumleffel, N. A., Zakrajsek, R., & Joseph, S. (2009). A strategy for coaches to develop life skills in youth sport. *Journal of Youth Sports*, 4(2), 16–20.

Borton, T. (1970). *Reach, touch, and teach: Student concerns and process education.* McGraw Hill.

Boud, D., Keogh, R., & Walker, D. (1985). *What is reflection in learning? Reflection: Turning experience into learning* (pp. 7–17). Routledge Falmer: Taylor & Francis Group.

Brockbank, A., & McGill, I. (1998). *Facilitating reflective learning in higher education.* Society for Research into Higher Education, Open University Press.

Coalter, F. (2007). **Wider social role for sport**: *Who's keeping the score?* Routledge.

Colley, B. M., Bilics, A. R., & Lerch, C. M. (2012). Reflection: A Key Component to Thinking Critically. *The Canadian Journal for the Scholarship of Teaching and Learning*, 3(1), 1–19.

Duley, J. S. (1981). Field experience education. In Chickering, A. W. (Ed) *The Modern American College: Responding to the New Realities of Diverse Students and a Changing Society* (pp. 600–613). San Francisco: Jossey-Bass.

Gould, D., & Carson, S. (2008). Life skills development through sport: Current status and future directions. *International Review of Sport and Exercise Psychology*, 1(1), 58–78. https://doi.org/10.1080/17509840701834573

Halstead, J. M., & M. J. Taylor. (2000). Learning and teaching about values: A review of recent research. *Cambridge Journal of Education*, 30(2), 169–202.

Koh, K. T., Ong, S. W., & Camiré, M. (2016). Implementation of a values training program in physical education and sport: perspectives from teachers, coaches, students, and athletes. *Physical Education and Sport Pedagogy*, 21(3), 295–312.

Mezirow, J. (1990). *Fostering critical reflection in adulthood* (pp. 1–18). Jossey-Bass Publishers.

National Recreation and Parks Association. (2023). Access to youth sports. Retrieved from https://www.nrpa.org/our-work/partnerships/initiatives/park-access/access-to-youth-sports/

Newman, T. J., & Anderson-Butcher, D. (2021). Mechanisms of life skill development and life skill transfer: Interconnections and distinctions among socially vulnerable youth. *Journal of the Society for Social Work and Research*, 12(3), 489–519.

Newman, T. J., Black, S., Santos, F., Jefka, B., & Brennan, N. (2023). Coaching the development and transfer of life skills: A scoping review of facilitative coaching practices in youth sports. *International Review of Sport and Exercise Psychology*, 16(1), 619–656.

Pierce, S., Gould, D., & Camiré, M. (2017). Definition and model of life skills transfer. *International Review of Sport and Exercise Psychology*, 10(1), 186–211.

Pierce, S., Kendellen, K., Camiré, M., & Gould, D. (2018). Strategies for coaching for life skills transfer. *Journal of Sport Psychology in Action*, 9(1), 11–20. https://doi.org/10.1080/21520704.2016.1263982

Project Play. (2023). Youth sport facts: Participation rates. Retrieved from https://projectplay.org/youth-sports/facts/participation-rates

Turnnidge, J., Côté, J., & Hancock, D. J. (2014). Positive youth development from sport to life: Explicit or implicit transfer? *Quest*, 66, 203–217. https://doi.org/10.1080/00336297.2013.867275

United Nations Educational, Scientific, and Cultural Organization [UNESCO]. (2013). World-wide survey of school physical education. Retrieved from https://en.unesco.org/inclusivepolicylab/e-teams/quality-physical-education-qpe-policy-project/documents/world-wide-survey-school-physical

Myth of Character Education
Part 3

Values and Life Skills Are Learnt When Participating in PES (Physical Education and Sports) Context

Chapter Seven

Zhihua Yin and Yue Xu

INTRODUCTION

Character education equips students with skills to protect themselves from abuse, exploitation, and risky behaviours by making informed decisions (Abdullah et al., 2019; Berkowitz & Bier, 2005). In PE class, life skills encompass personal assets like goal setting, emotional control, and self-esteem, which are transferable to non-sport settings (Gould & Carson, 2008). These skills, including communication and problem-solving, enhance behavioural, cognitive, and interpersonal abilities for success in society (Kawabata, 1994). Transferable beyond school, they are developed through modelling and feedback (Danish & Nellen, 1997; Gould & Carson, 2008), fostering positive behaviour and lifelong learning as students transition to adulthood (Bancin & Ambarita, 2019; Nasheeda et al., 2019). This promotes positive values, dispels misconceptions, and guides individuals towards fulfilling lives.

PE plays a crucial role in developing values and life skills (Burhaein et al., 2018), starting from a young age, enabling individuals to become active, independent, and responsible members of society (Chen & Tsuchiya, 2016; Ueno, 2012). However, effective guidance is essential for intended learning outcomes. Mere participation in PE or sports activities does not guarantee character development or the acquisition of life skills. Effective guidance in sports education aligns with character-building (Bialik et al., 2015), offering teachable moments for educators to impart concrete life lessons. This hands-on approach allows students to develop core values and practice essential life skills (Hellison, 1987), including emotional intelligence and effective communication. They learn to navigate setbacks with confidence and resilience, fostering positive mental health (Darlington-Bernard et al., 2023; Savoji & Ganji, 2013). For students with disabilities, sports provide a platform for advocacy and positive change (Nasheeda et al.,

DOI: 10.4324/9781032688657-10

2019), enhancing physical, psychological, and social development, promoting inclusion, and reducing isolation (Abu Altaieb et al., 2017).

Personal assets and life experiences are crucial for students' development of life skills, underscoring the need for tailored teaching content that aligns with diverse cultural contexts (Pierce et al., 2017). In China, ongoing educational reforms aim to promote students' overall development and health, with the PE curriculum revised to include life skills development as a key objective (Zheng et al., 2023). A study adapted the Life Skills Scale for PE (LSSPE) into the physical education and sports (PES) context, providing evidence of its validity and reliability (Ji et al., 2022). Thus, exploring life skills teaching with consideration for national characteristics is valuable.

Despite PE teachers' potential to impart life skills(Cronin et al., 2020; Cronin et al., 2018; Hayden et al., 2015; Johnson et al., 2011), several barriers hinder their effectiveness. Many North American PE classrooms may not foster such learning environments (Goudas et al., 2006), while teachers may lack proper training in life skills education, revealing a critical gap in their preparedness for this role (Wangchuk et al., 2019). A shortage of material resources due to limited financial support often restricts schools from acquiring necessary teaching materials, impacting life skills education implementation (Wangchuk et al., 2019). This underscores the urgent need for guidance and support to enable PE teachers to effectively incorporate life skills education.

In this chapter, PE teachers are presented with a rationale for teaching values and life skills, an outline of the skills required, and practical suggestions for how to implement these concepts. The insights provided here provide theoretical and practical guidance for PE teachers aiming to instil values and life skills in their students. As a means of enhancing the quality of learning, this chapter emphasises the importance of supporting PE teachers and coaches through professional development.

APPLIED INSIGHTS

Part I emphasises the importance of committing to teaching values and life skills in PES context. This encompasses an understanding of the responsibilities involved, ensuring students' safety, demonstrating appropriate movements and standards, and guiding and motivating them towards their goals. The aim is to instil positive outcomes that enables youth's success in various contexts through living meaningful lives and helping them navigate everyday challenges. Part II delves into learning from successful programmes that focus on imparting values and life skills through PES context. It highlights specific programmes like Petitpas' Play It Smart Programme, Lee's Project Effort Programme, Walsh's Career Club Programme, Nick Beamish's "Daily" programme, and Weiss' the First Tee Programme. These programmes have unique structures tailored to their respective target audiences and objectives. To ensure that the teaching of life skills is culturally sensitive, we have incorporated studies and research on life skills from diverse countries, including Chinese wisdom.

Making a Commitment to Teach Values and Life Skills through PES Context

Understanding the Responsibilities When Teaching Values and Life Skills in PES Context

- Help and protect students to avoid unnecessary injuries
  An important issue is the protection of life from dangers of various origins (e.g., at home, street, water, ice, playground, sports grounds) (Lenzen et al., 2023). Thus, creating a safer learning environment for teaching values and life skills through sports involves prioritising safety to prevent injuries. This not only ensures participants' well-being but also fosters a positive atmosphere for personal growth. The goal of life skills education is to enhance well-being and empower students to navigate challenges independently. Therefore, maintaining a vigilant approach to safety is crucial. Teachers should educate students about potential risks in sports, emphasising correct techniques, equipment use, and safety protocols. For example, in China, the First Aid for Sports Training Course teaches life-saving skills for both children and adults, covering common injuries like nosebleeds, fainting, and head injuries.
- Demonstrate relevant movements and set proper standards
  Physical (e.g., taking a right posture) is one of the dimensions of teaching life skills in PES context (Darlington-Bernard et al., 2023). Teaching life skills to students presents challenges due to their diverse needs. Clear standards are set through relevant movement demonstrations, which is crucial for beginners who

rely on observation to grasp skills visually. Expectations must be realistic, considering safety, technique, and individual abilities. Demonstrations should explain the purpose, emphasise key elements, and break down movements step by step, accommodating various skill levels. Effective demonstration, an art requiring practice, enhances learning and safety, and equips students with vital life skills. It's not solely about demonstrating movements; it's about how individuals learn from experiences. For instance, correcting a student's basketball jump shot may not directly develop a life skill, but the focus on consistent practice could.

- Guide and motivate students to achieve every single goal
Guidance and motivation play vital roles in learning life skills. According to a life skills intervention model, meeting and internalising basic needs increase the likelihood of developing life skills (Hodge et al., 2012). Creating a supportive learning environment is essential for fostering growth, resilience, and purpose. In PES, teachers serve as guides and motivators to keep students engaged in learning values and life skills (Lenzen et al., 2023). It's crucial to tailor teaching styles to the PES context, offering clear guidance on techniques, safety, and movement. Encouraging questions promotes a growth mindset, empowering students to overcome obstacles and acquire invaluable life skills. Personalised goal setting and progress monitoring track students' advancement, while regular follow-ups and positive reinforcement foster a sense of accomplishment and self-improvement.

Believe Ideological Outcomes of Teaching Values and Life Skills in PES Context

- Enable youth to succeed in the different contexts
Life skills are important in allowing individuals to adapt to different situations (Burhaein et al., 2018). Youth mentoring encourages skill development when students encounter novel challenges, thus fostering positive and supportive relationships conducive to learning life skills (DuBois et al., 2002; Rhodes et al., 2006). Skills important in the real world, such as decision-making, problem-solving, communication, and interpersonal skills, should be emphasised to equip students with the necessary skill sets to excel in various environments, including personal relationships, academic pursuits, and future careers. In light of current curriculum reforms in Hong

Kong, schools are required to provide career-related experiences for all high school students. As a result of the "individual student planning" component of comprehensive counselling programmes, the Hong Kong Association of Careers Masters and Guidance Masters has initiated a project aimed at developing curriculum resources for career education for high school students (Yuen et al., 2010).

- Manage various problems arising in daily life
China exhibits significant variation among its provinces and regions, offering valuable insights for identifying specific content for teaching life skills. Set an example from rural areas; although parents and youth express high aspirations for education, secondary students are beginning to believe that attending school is useless. Out-of-school sources appeared to be more important than school sources and associated with perceived career development competence in many countries (Lee, 2017). Ideally, a practical illustration from a swimming course demonstrates how PE teachers can address this. By exposing students to different water environments – from calm to wavy waters – instructors prompt them to adapt their strokes and techniques accordingly. This exercise fosters adaptability and flexibility, crucial attributes in effectively managing change. These skills are transferable to real-life situations where adaptability is needed. Additionally, unexpected scenarios can be introduced, such as abrupt changes in water depth or emergency situations to sharpen adaptability and instil confidence and preparedness in students, proving invaluable in facing unforeseen challenges in life.

Examples of Successful Programmes about Values and Life Skills in PES Contexts

Unique Structure of Each Programme

- Play It Smart Programme (2004) for high school student-athletes
The Play It Smart programme is designed to meet the specific needs of high school students by leveraging the motivating environment of sports participation (Larson, 2000). Research highlights the importance of sports achievements for adolescents, often surpassing academic success (Weiss, 1995). The programme aims to facilitate psychosocial development in youth through sports-based activities by providing a framework emphasising self-discovery, positive external and internal assets, and ongoing evaluation (Petitpas et al., 2004).

High school athletes often attribute their behaviour to external influences, with coaches being the most influential adults (Leunes & Nation, 1982). Play It Smart forms partnerships between academia and coaches to create an environment conducive to positive growth for high school students. Additionally, studies show that high school athletes in leadership roles outside sports demonstrate high levels of career and personal maturity (Danish et al., 1996). Hence, the programme emphasises community service projects to instil civic responsibility and maturity. By targeting high school students, Play It Smart aligns its strategies with their developmental needs, fostering athletic growth and life skills essential for success beyond sports (Petitpas et al., 2004).

Similarly, a study on female soccer team members revealed that they acquire life skills primarily from the sports context, including teammates, coaches, and competitive settings. Family plays a significant role, while school and work are less prominent (Shek et al., 2020). This suggests that adapting the 4Cs are explained, the dimensions include character, competence, confidence, and connection to Chinese contexts is suitable for athletes, reflecting the intense training demands associated with national teams (Zhu et al., 2023).

- Project Effort Programme (2009) across two different cultures
Lee's study compared the cultural influences on life skills learning between two distinct settings: Project Effort and conventional school environments. Project Effort seamlessly integrated learning with physical education (PE), fostering a value-based understanding of activity akin to the Personal and Social Responsibility Model (Hellison & Cutforth, 2003). Participants formed meaningful relationships, echoing positive youth development programmes.

In contrast, the school environment was marked by boredom and safety concerns like weapons possession and violence. This disparity underscores the impact of school settings on life skills acquisition and application. Project Effort's emphasis on values and safety starkly contrasted with the challenges in schools, highlighting the need for tailored approaches (Lee & Martinek, 2009).

Additionally, a study comparing vocational education between Mainland China and Hong Kong revealed differences in career and life planning education. Certain interventions, like connecting study opportunities to careers and enhancing work-related learning, were lacking in Hong Kong secondary schools (Lee, 2017). These findings emphasise the importance of adapting life skills education to diverse educational contexts.

- Career Club Programme (2008) focusing on future decisions
Walsh's Career Club Programme (2008) guides students in making informed decisions about their future paths, a crucial aspect of life skills education. Through mentoring experiences, it encourages reflective discussions about career ambitions (Walsh, 2008). The programme emphasises traits essential for success, integrating resiliency, social competence, problem-solving, autonomy, and purpose. Initial results show effectiveness in exploring coaching as a potential career path. Refinements aim to deepen participants' career explorations, guided by a strong theoretical foundation adaptable to various educational initiatives (Walsh, 2008).

  In Hong Kong, students demonstrate lower proficiency in job search and interview preparation skills. In response, the Education Bureau released "The Guide on Life Planning Education and Career Guidance for Secondary Schools," outlining seven dimensions of career intervention, including life planning education, career guidance framework, study-career linkage, schoolwide activities, work-related learning, individual planning, and responsive services (Lee, 2017).

- "Daily" Programme (2010) based on the Teaching Personal and Social Responsibility (TPSR) Model
Nick Beamish's "Daily" Programme (2010) is a successful model for teaching life skills through PES context. It was developed based on the TPSR model. It focuses on an after-school physical activity curriculum designed to instil positive life skills in youth for eight months (Beamish, 2012).

  A study revealed that the "Daily" Programme creates a conducive learning environment which significantly influences the development of life skills. Emphasis is placed on fundamental skills like responsibility, respect, communication, effort, teamwork, self-awareness, and leadership, which are strategically integrated into the programme's activities, allowing students to gradually cultivate these skills over time.

  Notably, the programme has been successful in fostering a sense of ownership and responsibility among participants. Accountability is instilled by getting the group to define "responsibility" together. Tasks increase in complexity over time as students begin to take charge of their own fitness and take on leadership positions. Additionally, the programme effectively incorporates the value of respect by getting participants to define respectful and disrespectful behaviour. The definition serves as a clear reference for appropriate conduct in various scenarios, contributing to a positive and respectful learning environment.

- The First Tee Programme (2012) highlights interpersonal and self-management skills

Weiss' First Tee Programme (2012) follows a tailored framework by Petitpas et al. (2004) to empower young individuals. The First Tee aims to shape the lives of youth through educational initiatives involving golf that instil values, build character, and foster healthy choices (Weiss et al., 2013).

At the heart of the First Tee's approach is interpersonal and self-management skills. The programme employs a systematic and progressive teaching approach that includes goal-setting and advanced personal development. Coaches undergo comprehensive training to get certified and effectively deliver the life skills curriculum.

The programmes have successfully integrated life skills with golf activities seamlessly. A variety of teaching methods that align with the First Tee Coach Philosophy emphasising activity-based, mastery-driven, youth-empowering, and continuous learning strategies are used. Additionally, a positive and trusting atmosphere is created through supportive relationships. This aligns with the positive youth development framework that underscores the importance of positive interactions between adults and youth participants.

Common Elements in These Programmes

- Youth are treated as resources to be developed – building on their strengths and focusing on holistic development

These programmes view youth as valuable resources for development, emphasising strengths and holistic growth. They focus on nurturing strengths alongside addressing weaknesses, recognising that a well-rounded individual is better equipped for life's challenges.

- Respect the individuality of each youth
  These programmes aim to cater to each unique individual, tailoring their strategies to meet individuals' specific needs and preferences.
- Empower youth
  The programmes actively involve youth in decision-making and goal-setting processes. In the process, this empowers youth by instilling a sense of ownership and responsibility in their personal development journeys.
- Establish clear expectations based on a strong set of values
  The programmes establish clear expectations grounded in a set of core values. This framework provides a moral compass for youth that guides their behaviour and decisions.
- Help youth think ahead
  The programmes encourage youth to think about and plan for their future. This forward-looking approach helps in goal setting and working towards realising their aspirations.
- Provide a physically and emotionally safe environment
  These programmes acknowledge the importance of creating a physically and emotionally safe environment where youth can feel secure to express themselves.
- Prolonged engagement in a compact community setting
  Small numbers and long-term participation foster a sense of belonging and membership which provides a supportive network for youth.
- Maintain a local connection in the community
  Maintaining a strong connection to the local community allows youth to cultivate a sense of belonging to the society which provides a sense of identity and purpose.
- Resilience and leadership when facing obstacles
  In the face of challenges, these programmes encourage resilience and leadership. This imbues a sense of determination to overcome challenges, fulfilling the aims of the programme.
- Mentorship opportunities
  An important highlight of these programmes is the opportunity to work with a mentor. Mentorship offers guidance, support, and positive role modelling, which are vital for youth development.

SUMMARY AND FUTURE DIRECTIONS

Summary

The guide stresses the importance of commitment in teaching values and life skills through sports, as mere participation doesn't ensure learning. Responsibilities include ensuring safety, demonstrating movements, and understanding learning styles to motivate students towards future goals, fostering positive outcomes like thriving in diverse contexts and overcoming challenges. Teaching life skills in PES is vital, covering behavioural, cognitive, and interpersonal capacities. It equips individuals with essential skills for safety and decision-making, such as communication, problem-solving, and critical thinking. Global programmes like Play It Smart, Project Effort, and Career Club instil values and life skills through PES, recognising youths' potential and empowering them to plan for their future in a safe environment, fostering belonging, resilience, and leadership with mentorship guidance.

Future Directions: Suggestions for Teaching Values and Life Skills in PES Context

Teaching Context

- PE classrooms

  In PE classrooms, the structured curriculum provides educators with a unique platform to teach students the significance of rules and regulations. This environment fosters a sense of community and shared purpose among students, highlighting the benefits of adherence to rules while promoting mutual support. Teachers can facilitate various activities such as providing feedback, discussing life skill applications, assisting in action plans, and offering skill practice opportunities (Bean et al., 2018).

- After-school physical activities

  After-school programmes reinforce values and life skills in addition to formal education. As students engage in diverse physical activities, they learn important life lessons and gain meaningful insight. As a result of these extracurricular pursuits, students develop essential life skills such as teamwork, resilience, and leadership. Hence, students can acquire a holistic skill set by integrating formal and informal education.

- Homework assignment

  Assigning homework on values and life skills promotes independent reflection and application, extending learning beyond the

classroom. This allows students to delve into these concepts personally, fostering practical skills and deeper understanding. Such assignments reinforce classroom teachings and empower students to apply these lessons in real-life situations.
- Physical fitness assessments
Physical fitness assessments provide an ideal opportunity to underscore the significance of values and life skills within PE. Integrating these concepts into assessments helps students recognise the holistic nature of personal development. A study assessing the effectiveness of a life skills programme in PE found that participants in the experimental group showed greater improvement compared to the control group (Goudas et al., 2006). Striving for better assessment results not only enhances physical abilities but also strengthens students' resilience in facing life's challenges.

Teaching Content and Approach
- Traditional sports activities
Integrating values and life skills within traditional sports activities provides a dynamic platform for experiential learning. Students can directly apply these principles in competitive and cooperative settings, fostering a well-rounded understanding of their significance. For example, utilising tai chi as a means to learn stress management (Robins et al., 2012) and leveraging rugby to enhance empowerment among minority groups (Robinson et al., 2024).
- Pop sports among youth
Pop sports, or popular sports among youth, attract a diverse range of participants, fostering inclusivity and appreciation for diversity. With a wide variety of backgrounds represented, students involved in these sports develop an inclusive mindset and easily integrate into diverse environments. They embrace different cultures through the game, finding a strong sense of belonging within society.
- Physical fitness training
Physical fitness training is a character-building platform instilling self-discipline, goal orientation, and essential life competencies. Whether in the gym or elsewhere, setting goals and managing time and energy effectively prepare students for life's challenges.

- Outdoor activities

  Outdoor activities uniquely teach values and life skills by fostering adaptability, resilience, teamwork, and problem-solving in unpredictable environments. By encouraging students to step out of their comfort zones, they apply these skills authentically.

REFERENCES

Abdullah, I., Hudayana, B., Kutanegara, P. M., & Indiyanto, A. (2019). Beyond school reach: Character education in three schools in Yogyakarta, Indonesia. *Journal of Educational and Social Research*, 9(3), 145.

Abu Altaieb, M. H., Mousa Ay, K., Al Dababseh, M. F., Bataineh, M., Al-Nawaiseh, A. M., & Taifour, A. (2017). The impact of an educational course for swimming on free style swimming performance and life skills for deaf students. *Journal of Human Sport and Exercise*, 12(4), 1265–1277. https://doi.org/10.14198/jhse.2017.124.13

Bancin, A., & Ambarita, B. (2019). Education Model Based on Life Skill (a Meta-Synthesis). 4th Annual International Seminar on Transformative Education and Educational Leadership (AISTEEL 2019),

Beamish, N. (2012). *Developing life skills through physical activity: A teaching personal and social responsibility model approach.* Brock University

Bean, C., Kramers, S., Forneris, T., & Camiré, M. (2018). The implicit/explicit continuum of life skills development and transfer. *Quest*, 70(4), 456–470. https://doi.org/10.1080/00336297.2018.1451348

Berkowitz, M. W., & Bier, M. C. (2005). *What works in character education: A research-driven guide for educators.* Character Education Partnership.

Bialik, M., Bogan, M., Fadel, C., & Horvathova, M. (2015). Character education for the 21st century: What should students learn. *Center for Curriculum Redesign*, 1–35, 3.

Burhaein, E., Phytanza, D. T. P., & Ghautama, W. S. (2018). Life skill dimension based on unified sports soccer program in physical education of intellectual disability. *YBPD Yaşam Becerileri Psikoloji Dergisi*, 2(4), 199–205. https://doi.org/10.31461/ybpd.453865

Chen, Y., & Tsuchiya, H. (2016). The relationship between the motivation for physical activity and life skills among Chinese and Japanese college students. *Advances in Physical Education*, 6(4), 283–291. https://doi.org/10.4236/ape.2016.64029

Cronin, L. D., Allen, J., Mulvenna, C., & Russell, P. (2018). An investigation of the relationships between the teaching climate, students' perceived life skills development and well-being within physical education. *Physical Education and Sport Pedagogy*, 23(2), 181–196. https://doi.org/10.1080/17408989.2017.1371684

Cronin, L. D., Marchant, D., Johnson, L., Huntley, E., Kosteli, M. C., Varga, J., & Ellison, P. (2020). Life skills development in physical education: A self-determination theory-based investigation across the school term. *Psychology of Sport and Exercise*, 49, 101711. https://doi.org/10.1016/j.psychsport.2020.101711

Danish, S. J., & Nellen, V. C. (1997). New roles for sport psychologists: Teaching life skills through sport to at-risk youth. *Quest*, 49(1), 100–113.

Danish, S. J., Nellen, V. C., & Owens, S. S. (1996). *Teaching life skills through sport: Community-based programs for adolescents*. Exploring sport and exercise psychology (pp. 205–225). American Psychological Association.

Darlington-Bernard, A., Salque, C., Masson, J., Darlington, E., Carvalho, G. S., & Carrouel, F. (2023). Defining life skills in health promotion at school: A scoping review [Review]. *Frontiers in Public Health*, 11. https://doi.org/10.3389/fpubh.2023.1296609

DuBois, D. L., Holloway, B. E., Valentine, J. C., & Cooper, H. (2002). Effectiveness of mentoring programs for youth: A meta-analytic review. *American Journal of Community Psychology*, 30(2), 157–197. https://doi.org/10.1023/a:1014628810714

Goudas, M., Dermitzaki, I., Leondari, A., & Danish, S. (2006). The effectiveness of teaching a life skills program in a physical education context. *European Journal of Psychology of Education*, 21(4), 429–438. https://doi.org/10.1007/BF03173512

Gould, D., & Carson, S. (2008). Life skills development through sport: Current status and future directions. *International Review of Sport and Exercise Psychology*, 1(1), 58–78. https://doi.org/10.1080/17509840701834573

Hayden, L. A., Whitley, M. A., Cook, A. L., Dumais, A., Silva, M., & Scherer, A. (2015). An exploration of life skill development through sport in three international high schools. *Qualitative Research in Sport, Exercise and Health*, 7(5), 759–775.

Hellison, D. (1987). The affective domain in physical education: Let's do some housecleaning. *Journal of Physical Education, Recreation & Dance*, 58(6), 41–43.

Hellison, D., & Cutforth, N. (2003). *Youth development and physical activity: Linking universities and communities*. Human Kinetics.

Hodge, K., Danish, S., & Martin, J. (2012). Developing a conceptual framework for life skills interventions. *The Counseling Psychologist*, 41(8), 1125–1152. https://doi.org/10.1177/0011000012462073

Ji, X., Zheng, S., Cheng, C., Cheng, L., & Cronin, L. (2022). Development and psychometric evaluation of the Chinese version of the life skills scale for physical education. *International Journal of Environmental Research and Public Health*, 19(9), 5324. https://doi.org/10.3390/ijerph19095324

Johnson, A., Angra, I., Dewar, B., Weir, J., McIntyre, R., Jedraszczyk, R., & Iannucci, C. (2011). Using physical activity to develop life skills: The Manchester example. *Physical & Health Education Journal*, 77(1), 22.

Kawabata, T. (1994). *World Health Organization world life skills education*. Taishukan-Shoten.

Larson, R. W. (2000). Toward a psychology of positive youth development. *American Psychology*, 55(1), 170–183. https://doi.org/10.1037//0003-066x.55.1.170

Lee, J. C.-K. (2017). Curriculum reform and supporting structures at schools: challenges for life skills planning for secondary school students in China (with particular reference to Hong Kong). *Educational Research for Policy and Practice*, 16(1), 61–75. https://doi.org/10.1007/s10671-016-9202-y

Lee, O., & Martinek, T. (2009). Navigating two cultures: An investigation of cultures of a responsibility-based physical activity program and school. *Research Quarterly for Exercise and Sport*, 80(2), 230–240. https://doi.org/10.1080/02701367.2009.10599557

Lenzen, B., Buyck, Y., & Bouvier, A. (2023). Teaching life skills in physical education within different teaching traditions: A narrative review. *Education Sciences*, 13(6), 605. https://www.mdpi.com/2227-7102/13/6/605

Leunes, A., & Nation, J. R. (1982). Saturday's heroes: A psychological portrait of college football players. *Journal of Sport Behavior*, 5(3), 139–149.

Nasheeda, A., Abdullah, H. B., Krauss, S. E., & Ahmed, N. B. (2019). A narrative systematic review of life skills education: Effectiveness, research gaps and priorities. *International Journal of Adolescence and Youth*, 24(3), 362–379. https://doi.org/10.1080/02673843.2018.1479278

Petitpas, A. J., Van Raalte, J. L., Cornelius, A. E., & Presbrey, J. (2004). A life skills development program for high school student-athletes. *The Journal of Primary Prevention*, 24(3), 325–334. https://doi.org/10.1023/B:JOPP.0000018053.94080.f3

Pierce, S., Gould, D., & Camiré, M. (2017). Definition and model of life skills transfer. *International Review of Sport and Exercise Psychology*, 10(1), 186–211. https://doi.org/10.1080/1750984X.2016.1199727

Rhodes, J. E., Spencer, R., Keller, T. E., Liang, B., & Noam, G. (2006). A model for the influence of mentoring relationships on youth development. *Journal of Community Psychology*, 34(6), 691–707. https://doi.org/10.1002/jcop.20124

Robins, J. L. W., Elswick, R. K., & McCain, N. L. (2012). The story of the evolution of a unique Tai Chi Form: Origins, philosophy, and research. *Journal of Holistic Nursing*, 30(3), 134–146. https://doi.org/10.1177/0898010111429850

Robinson, E., Newman, T. J., Scheadler, T. R., Lower-Hoppe, L. M., & Baeth, A. (2024). The unique lived experiences of LGBQ athletes: A collegiate women's Rugby Club team as an inclusive & empowering community. *Journal of Homosexuality*, 71(4), 1003–1029. https://doi.org/10.1080/00918369.2022.2160684

Savoji, A. P., & Ganji, K. (2013). Increasing mental health of university students through life skills training (LST). *Procedia, Social and Behavioral Sciences*, 84, 1255–1259. https://doi.org/10.1016/j.sbspro.2013.06.739

Shek, D., Lin, L., Ma, C., Yu, L., Leung, J., Wu, F., Leung, H., & Dou, D. (2020). Perceptions of adolescents, teachers and parents of life skills education and life skills in high school students in Hong Kong. *Applied Research in Quality of Life*, 16. https://doi.org/10.1007/s11482-020-09848-9

Ueno, K. (2012). Relationship between adoption of a belief in life skills and acquisition of time perspective through participation in athletic clubs. *International Journal of Sport and Health Science*, 10, 71–81.

Walsh, D. (2008). Helping youth in underserved communities envision possible futures: An extension of the teaching personal and social responsibility model. *Research Quarterly for Exercise and Sport*, 79(2), 209–221. https://doi.org/10.5641/193250308X13086753543572

Wangchuk, C., Wangchuk, C., Choki, K., & Drakpa, D. (2019). Challenges of implementing life skills education in schools in Punakha: A qualitative research. *Rabsel – the CERD Educational Journal*, 20, 35–51.

Weiss, M. R. (1995). *Children in sport: An educational model*. Human Kinetics.

Weiss, M. R., Stuntz, C. P., Bhalla, J. A., Bolter, N. D., & Price, M. S. (2013). 'More than a game': Impact of The First Tee life skills programme on positive youth development: Project introduction and Year 1 findings. *Qualitative Research in Sport, Exercise and Health*, 5(2), 214–244. https://doi.org/10.1080/2159676X.2012.712997

Yuen, M., Chan, R. M. C., Gysbers, N. C., Lau, P. S. Y., Lee, Q., Shea, P. M. K., Fong, R. W., & Chung, Y. B. (2010). Enhancing life skills development: Chinese adolescents' perceptions. *Pastoral Care in Education*, 28(4), 295–310. https://doi.org/10.1080/02643944.2010.528015

Zheng, S., Ji, X., Cheng, L., Xu, J., & Cronin, L. D. (2023). Perceptions of the motivational climate, basic psychological needs, and life skills development in Chinese physical education students. *Frontier in Psychology*, 14, 1232849. https://doi.org/10.3389/fpsyg.2023.1232849

Zhu, Q., Pynn, S. R., Holt, N. L., Huang, Z., & Jørgensen, H. (2023). Life skills development and learning contexts among members of China women's national soccer teams. *International Journal of Sport & Exercise Psychology*, 21(1), 15–32. https://search.ebscohost.com/login.aspx?direct=true&db=s3h&AN=161082764&site=ehost-live&scope=site

Values and Life Skills Are Learnt When Participating in Activities

Chapter Eight

Zarizi Ab Rahman

INTRODUCTION

Since UNESCO declared 2015 the "UN International Year of Sports and Physical Education (PE)," governments worldwide have recognised PE as a comprehensive subject. In Malaysia, physical education (PE) is a compulsory and core subject for all school students aged 7–17. PE is a subject that emphasises human movement, knowledge, social and life skills, and values. It uses educational activities to promote human well-being, character building, and the development of individuals with a solid national identity characterised by a collective spirit and outstanding behaviour. PE is a significant subject that helps students develop essential motor skills, health knowledge, life skills, and values necessary for various aspects of their lives. Introducing life skills and values to children is crucial for personal growth and development.

In this regard, PE is vital in building and reinforcing life skills and values through activities such as movement, games, and sports. Children's experiences may provide positive development – for example, participation in physical activity and Sports may enhance interpersonal relationships, communication, emotional control, self-esteem, self-confidence, demonstrated sportsmanship, and respect for people that can be considered as life skills and values. Therefore, the quality of teaching PE plays an important role in ensuring that life skills and values can be embedded in the process of teaching and learning. However, PE has faced several challenges globally, including ineffective delivery, insufficient time allocation, lack of qualified teachers, and inadequate facilities. PE classes are often shortened or replaced, leading to decreased physical activity and a lack of parental involvement (Swamy, 2022; Osborne et al., 2016; Wintle, 2022; Arockiaraj, 2017). In Malaysia, PE is often seen as unimportant compared to other subjects. Despite the Ministry of Education acknowledging PE's importance to children, it remains unrecognised for academic

DOI: 10.4324/9781032688657-11

improvement. To ensure its integration into the education system, the ministry has mandated PE as a core subject at all levels of schooling, as stated in the Education Act 1996 (Act 550).

Studies in Malaysia have highlighted challenges in implementing high-quality PE. It was found that administrative issues, lack of supervision, course availability, staff training, and facility insufficiency have affected PE implementation (Wee, 2017). PE administrative issues stem from inadequate teacher monitoring, replacement of PE classes for other subjects, and inadequate staff training programmes organised by most administrators (Wee, 2017). These issues arise from misconceptions and myths about PE, as mentioned earlier. Moreover, while formal evaluation is done through "school evaluation" for various components (Eng Hoe, 2013a), the lack of supervision in PE (Wee et al., 2021) and the tendency to replace it with other subjects demonstrate that PE is not important to related parties. Previous studies have indicated that principals regularly allow PE to be replaced by other subjects (Eng Hoe, 2009, 2013b) to help teachers finish the syllabus (Ai Ling & Salamuddin, 2010). The scenario is similar to other countries where PE experienced a lack of federal support, resulting in decreased physical activity (PA) programmes and resources (McMurrer, 2008) because of the focus on academic achievement and accountability in core subjects (McKenzie & Lounsbery, 2009). Meanwhile, Osborne et al. (2016) found that PE teachers feel devalued in Brazil and receive less support from school administration since PE is regarded as a marginalised subject. Alharbi (2020) also revealed that the issue of PE is a worldwide issue, including the United States of America, Canada, the United Kingdom, China, Africa, and the Middle East. This problem results from the focus on academic success, leading to a neglect of PE.

Fonyi and Soon (2021) revealed that administrators have a less-than-positive attitude towards the implementation of PE. Similarly, other recent findings stated that the administrators did not consult and observe PE teachers related to teaching and learning (Wee et al., 2021). Mohd Nasiruddin (2020) indicated that most principals did not understand and value the role of PE as the core subject in shaping students' awareness of the importance of a healthy lifestyle. Furthermore, several concerns related to PE, such as unqualified teachers (Aboshkair et al., 2012; Ai Ling & Salamuddin, 2010; Wee, 2017), inadequate facilities and equipment (Wee et al., 2021; Syed Ali et al., 2014), and insufficient staff training programmes (Ai Ling & Salamuddin 2010) have been observed.

These issues surfaced due to school administrators' inability to demonstrate quality PE implementation (Fonyi & Soon, 2021) and the misconception that PE is a subject of little significance with no academic value. In Malaysia, the PE curriculum is known as the Standard Curriculum for Primary Schools and Secondary Schools, which clearly outlines the learning domains teachers must cover. The PE curriculum is designed to promote personal growth and development, aiming to foster a dynamic, prosperous, and productive society. The programme is structured around several key components, including fitness, skills, games, and athletics. These pillars facilitate the attainment of PE goals. PE teachers must adhere to content and learning standards, covering three learning domains.

Based on the curriculum, the PE teacher should deliver a learning experience that places equal emphasis on the development of the psychomotor, cognitive, and affective domains. Using appropriate methods will enable children to develop positively, eventually equipping them to face the complexities of today's world. Furthermore, incorporating fun, creativity, and interactivity in PE fosters children's cognitive ability development, hence aiding students in subjects that place greater emphasis on public assessment. Nevertheless, PE has the potential to cover various aspects, but the issues mentioned earlier often hinder its implementation. Most of the issues in PE resulted from myths and misconceptions about this subject. A common misconception is that engaging in sports can negatively impact academic performance. However, several studies have shown that participating in sports enhances academic achievement and cognitive development (Burns et al., 2020; Juliana & Afrianti, 2020; Walsh et al., 2020; Ahmad et al., 2019; Valkenborghs et al., 2019) among students.

Moreover, PE is often misunderstood by teachers who believe that it is only meant to produce athletes. As a result, they tend to focus solely on developing students' sports skills in their lessons. The psychomotor domain typically receives the most attention, while the other domains are perceived to develop spontaneously. PE teachers who do not understand the actual purpose of PE mainly emphasise team sports and game-based models, often neglecting to equip students with the essential skills to cultivate healthy living habits and develop positive attitudes towards health, fitness, and PA (Ferkel et al., 2019). The mechanism is incorrect because students may not be aware of the life skills and values that consist of PA. The PE teacher should follow the syllabus to cover psychomotor, cognitive, and affective domains. This enables effective teaching of life skills and values to students. A study by Hashim (2000) found that even though PE teachers know the importance of instilling values while teaching PE, most lack clarity on the suitable approach to instil the values during teaching activities. Issues and misconceptions in PE negatively impact teaching quality in three learning domains. While PE has the potential to develop life skills and values, it fails to focus on cognitive and affective domains, hindering educational objectives.

APPLIED INSIGHTS

PE instruction requires cognitive, affective, and psychomotor domains, with at least three teaching objectives covering all three areas. Teaching activities should cover all domains to achieve objectives. Scholars have asked PE teachers to incorporate social and emotional learning (SEL) into their instruction. SEL encompasses cognitive and affective domains (Mahoney et al., 2018; Taylor et al., 2017). Engaging children in PA fosters positive growth and development, with a growing recognition of the importance of cultivating life skills and values through sports and PA (Cronin et al., 2020; Edivaldo Góis Junior, 2014; Bailey, 2006; Danish et al., 2004).

The World Health Organisation (1994) defines life skills as the adaptable and constructive behaviours that enable individuals to effectively manage daily life's demands and obstacles, ensuring they live and perform effectively in their surroundings. Hendricks (1998) refers to life skills as "skills that help an individual to be successful in living a productive and satisfying life." Meanwhile, values are fundamental principles that reflect what is essential to a person or group (Madrona et al., 2017). They are a guiding force for behaviour and decision-making and are shaped by various factors such as culture, religion, and personal experiences. According to the PE syllabus in Malaysia settings, several values have been incorporated, such as compliance with the rules and regulations, demonstrating ethics and sportsmanship, teamwork, and others. In addition, the Malaysian curriculum requires that teaching and learning incorporate values that include spirituality, humanity, and citizenship, which are to be applied in daily life. That strategy is compulsory for each lesson and is known as cross-curricular elements (Ministry of Education 2016).

Psychosocial competencies and interpersonal skills are crucial for effective problem-solving, decision-making, communication, positive relationships, empathy, and healthy, productive living in today's world. (Amulya, 2020). According to Malaysia's primary and secondary school PE syllabus (Ministry of Education 2016), there is a notable focus on fostering 21st-century competencies such as critical thinking, effective communication, collaboration, knowledge acquisition, curiosity, empathy, and a sense of national identity. These proficiencies are strongly linked to values and life skills, emphasising the significance of PE teachers integrating PA that fosters the growth of these qualities. Furthermore, the syllabus contains content and learning standards that specify the requirements for students to explain, identify, apply, analyse, make wise decisions, formulate strategies, resolve issues, exhibit sportsmanship, collaborate in teams, and develop other values and life skills. Moreover, prior research has also emphasised PE as a setting that may enhance students' life skills (Goudas, 2010; Holt et al., 2012; Jenny & Rhodes, 2017).There are several strategies to instil life skills and values through PA in PE lessons.

The PE teacher should carefully design the lesson and set the learning objectives based on the PE syllabus to help students learn values and life skills through PA. Therefore, the activities in the class should be following the learning objectives. For example, the teacher chooses the topic of passing in football and creates mini-games to ensure that the students apply the passing techniques. The teacher may request the students to analyse the application of force in the mini-games, their role as team members, and their ability to show respect towards their teammates and demonstrate sportsmanship, leadership, strategies planning, and other life skills and values. Consequently, students have been indirectly exposed to the ability to analyse and understand values. Additionally, mini-games can enhance students' life skills and values, such as fair play, adherence to rules, emotional regulation, and social interactions. A reflection session following the activity could help students learn how mini-games can impart lessons in leadership, sportsmanship, strategy planning, and other areas. Teachers should engage students by providing inquiries or scenarios that allow for developing leadership and other life skills through mini-games. Therefore, it is the teacher's role to ensure that students learn about life skills and values, not just psychomotor skills.

Employing appropriate pedagogical approaches in PE can provide students the chance to cultivate life skills and values. Reciprocal and self-check teaching methods in performed PA can improve social skills (Muska & Ashworth, 2002), including students' ability to work together, increase self-confidence, promote self-independence, and communicate effectively. Furthermore, when conducting a motor skills demonstration, it is imperative that students actively participate in the demonstration rather than relying solely on the teacher. Even though some teachers argue that students may perform incorrectly in motor skills, the teacher must be aware that their role in teaching and learning is more to facilitate students. In the context of performing the demonstration of motor skills by the students, the teacher must observe and correct if necessary. Mitchell and Walton-Fisette (2016) suggest that having students demonstrate a task can be more effective than using an adult model, as it allows their peers to observe and learn from the process. Student demonstration of motor skills improves self-confidence, motivation, communication, self-esteem, and courage, which are life skills and values.

Student-centred instruction may also foster life skills and values. Studies have found that student-centred approaches, particularly problem-based learning (PBL), can improve team player development in youth football by actively involving students in problem-solving activities (Hubball & Robertson, 2004). Hence, PE teachers could implement PBL to foster the development of life skills and values in students. An example of how PBL can be applied in PA is by assigning a task to a group of students and instructing them to complete it. For instance, the teacher might instruct students to design a circuit training that explicitly targets improving muscle endurance. It will allow students to collaborate, engage in problem-solving, utilise communication skills, demonstrate leadership skills, employ critical and creative thinking, foster relationships, show respect for team members, and engage in teamwork. The 21st century demands students to do more than memorise information due to rapid technological progress. Accordingly, the students must have life skills and values such as creativity, adaptability, effective communication, collaborating with varied groups, courage, self-independence, and others. Hence, a student-centred approach cultivates these abilities by encouraging progress and empowering students to perform class activities. Furthermore, this technique is significant, as it enhances the ability for critical thinking. When students take complete ownership of their learning, they acquire the skills to analyse information, assess sources, and think critically about intricate matters.

Encouraging students to engage in reflective thinking after each PA session can effectively foster the development of life skills and values. By reflecting on their experiences, students can identify the knowledge they have gained and integrate it with their existing knowledge (Jha & Shah, 2018). It's important to note that reflective thinking is an active and ongoing process that draws upon past experiences to inform future decision-making. The PE teacher should engage students with relevant inquiries to ensure that they can explain the life skills and values they have acquired via PA. Consider asking students questions such as: *"How does the mini-game demonstrate teamwork?"* *"Why is communication important for achieving goals in your team?"* *"What is the significance of adhering to the rules in the mini-game?"* These questions can start student discussions to ensure they know about the life skills and values in the mini-game. Through reflective thinking, students can understand the importance of these skills, such as teamwork, and values, such as adherence to the rules in dealing with real-life situations effectively.

PE teachers must integrate creative and interactive components into their teaching to cultivate enjoyment among students. Chen (1998) pointed out that students might get bored if PA focuses more on competitive sports events than on teaching individuals motor abilities. Research has also discovered that boredom during PE classes may negatively impact students' desire to engage in physical activities (Cuevas-Campos et al., 2020; Simonton & Garn, 2019). Moreover, collaborative learning activities, as opposed to competitive ones, are essential for students' engagement and social success in PE, as similarly found in Garn et al. (2011). Collaborative learning involves students working together in groups. The teacher assigns a task, such as having a group of students discuss, plan, and perform a creative movement. This activity helps students improve their decision-making abilities, teamwork, respect for others, creative thinking, and interpersonal skills.

Thus, engaging in collaborative activities can effectively encourage maximum student engagement in PE lessons. Active participation in PA will allow teachers to emphasise the learning of life skills and values to their students.

Although the aforementioned strategies effectively develop essential skills, it is important to recognise the significant role teachers play. This is because just incorporating these strategies is inadequate if the teacher fails to make the students understand the importance of the skills being developed. This involves explaining the skills being taught and their significance. The teacher should connect these skills and the values they teach by applying them in real-life situations. Bean et al. (2018) highlighted the importance of discussing life skills in a sports context to improve learners' understanding of the life skills and values they learn in PE lessons. This ensures that students comprehend the practical significance of these skills in real-life scenarios and how to use them to respond to their surroundings and environment beyond PA or sports practice.

SUMMARY AND FUTURE DIRECTIONS

Instilling life skills and values through education is crucial in preparing the next generation for the volatile, uncertain, complex, and ambiguous world. PE is a vital tool for enhancing life skills and values as it provides knowledge, opportunities, and emotional expression, enhancing individuals' quality of life. Therefore, PE teachers should integrate life skills and values into their teaching strategies, ensuring lessons align with the syllabus, implementing effective teaching pedagogies, fostering student-centred approaches, stimulating reflective thinking, and creating engaging physical activities.

Teachers should be equipped with effective PE teaching pedagogies, and school leaders should recognise its significance and ensure a qualified PE teacher is designated for teaching. School leaders must also comply with the regulations set by the authority in education, which state that any other subject cannot replace PE. Establishing PE equal to other core subjects can contribute to the development of healthy and well-rounded individuals equipped with life skills and values to thrive in various domains of life (Valentini et al. 2018). Therefore, educational institutions may prioritise PE as an essential component in the curriculum to ensure the optimal development of their students.

Higher education institutions must develop a comprehensive curriculum and provide real-life experience for prospective PE teachers. Thus, the practicum programme should be enhanced, employing experienced lecturers to enhance pre-service teachers' educational experience. This ensures a supply of high-quality teachers with advanced teaching skills and outstanding traits.

REFERENCES

Aboshkair, K. A., Amri, S., Lian Yee, K., & Abu Samah, B. (2012). Assessment of implementation level of the physical education program in Selangor secondary schools, Malaysia, *Wulfenia Journal*, 19(10), 108–124.

Alharbi, M. (2020). Why Some join in and Others don't: Embodied Experiences of Male Students in Physical Education at a Saudi High School. *International Journal of Research in Educational Sciences*, 4(1), 529–557.

Ahmad, M., Rahman, M. F., Ali, M., Rahman, F. N., & Al Azad, M. A. S. (2019). Effect of extra curricular activity on student's academic performance. *Journal of Armed Forces Medical College, Bangladesh*, 11(2), 41–46. https://doi.org/10.3329/jafmc.v11i2.39822

Ai Ling, C., & Salamuddin, N. (2010). The implementation of physical education in secondary school: A preliminary study. *Proceedings of the International Seminar Comparative Studies in Educational System between Indonesia and Malaysia*, 955–971.

Amulya, K. (2020). Life skill education in classroom. *International Journal of Humanities and Social Science Invention*, 9(8). https://doi.org/10.35629/7722-0908020410

Arockiaraj, J. G. (2017). Contemporary issues and upcoming challenges in physical education and sports technology in South India. *International Journal of Applied Research*, 3(3), 498–500.

Bailey, R. (2006). Physical education and sport in schools: A review of benefits and outcomes. *Journal of School Health*, 76(8), 397–401.

Bean, C., Kramers, S., Forneris, T., & Camiré, M. (2018). The implicit/explicit continuum of life skills development and transfer. *Quest*, 70(4), 456–470. https://doi.org/10.1080/00336297.2018.1451348

Burns, R. D., Brusseau, T. A., Pfledderer, C. D., & Fu, Y. (2020). Sports participation correlates with academic achievement: Results from a large adolescent sample within the 2017 U.S. National Youth Risk Behavior Survey. *Perceptual and Motor Skills*, 127(2), 448–467. https://doi.org/10.1177/0031512519900055

Chen, A. (1998). Perception of boredom: Students' resistance to a secondary physical education curriculum. *Research in Middle Level Education Quarterly*, 21(2), 1–20. https://doi.org/10.1080/10848959.1998.11670117

Cronin, L., Marchant, D., Johnson, L., Huntley, E., Kosteli, M. C., Varga, J., & Ellison, P. (2020). Life skills development in physical education: A self-determination theory-based investigation across the school term. *Psychology of Sport and Exercise*, 49, 101711. https://doi.org/10.1016/j.psychsport.2020.101711

Cuevas-Campos, R., Fernández-Bustos, J. G., González-Cutre, D., & Hernández-Martínez, A. (2020). Need satisfaction and need thwarting in physical education and intention to be physically active. *Sustainability*, 12(18), 7312. https://doi.org/10.3390/su12187312

Danish, S., Forneris, T., Hodge, K., & Heke, I. (2004). Enhancing youth development through sport. *World Leisure Journal*, 46(3), 38–49. https://doi.org/10.1080/04419057.2004.9674365

Edivaldo Góis Junior. (2014). Gymnastics, hygiene and eugenics in Brazil at the turn of the twentieth century. *International Journal of the History of Sport*, 31(10), 1219–1231. https://doi.org/10.1080/09523367.2013.854776

Eng Hoe, W. (2009). Management and leadership issues in the implementation of an academic program: A case study of Physical Education Program. *The Journal of Administrative Science*, 6(2), 27–45.

Eng Hoe, W. (2013a). Contemporary issues in the teaching of PE in Malaysia. *Contemporary trends and research in sports, exercise and physical education*, 36–40.

Eng Hoe, W. (2013b). Contemporary issues in the teaching of PE in Malaysia. *Journal of Physical Activity, Sport and Exercise*, 1(1), 17–20.

Ferkel, R. C., Hutchinson, Z. T., Razon, S., True, L., Zupin, D., Jones, L. M., & Judge, L. W. (2019). The benefits of health-related fitness education in secondary PE. *The Physical Educator*, 76(4), 883–906. https://doi.org/10.18666/tpe-2019-v76-i4-8724

Fonyi, L., & Soon, C. C. (2021). Administrators' attitude towards the implementation of physical education in Selangor Primary Schools. *Education, Training and Counseling: Implication on the Post-COVID-19 World Pandemic*, 29(S1). https://doi.org/10.47836/pjssh.29.s1.16

Garn, A. C., Ware, D. R., & Solmon, M. A. (2011). Student engagement in high school physical education: Do social motivation orientations matter? *Journal of Teaching in Physical Education*, 30(1), 84–98. https://doi.org/10.1123/jtpe.30.1.84

Goudas, M. (2010). Prologue: A review of life skills teaching in sport and physical education. *Hellenic Journal of Psychology*, 7, 241–258.

Hashim, N. H. (2000). Teachers' understanding of the application of values purely in Malay language subjects in primary school [Research Report].

Hendricks, P. A. (1998). *Developing youth curriculum using the targeting life skills model*. Iowa State University, University Extension

Holt, N. L., Sehn, Z. L., Spence, J. C., Newton, A. S., & Ball, G. D. C. (2012). Physical education and sport programs at an inner city school: exploring possibilities for positive youth development. *Physical Education & Sport Pedagogy*, 17(1), 97–113. https://doi.org/10.1080/17408989.2010.548062

Hubball, H., & Robertson, S. (2004). Using problem-based learning to enhance team and player development in youth soccer. *Journal of Physical Education, Recreation & Dance*, 75(4), 38–43. https://doi.org/10.1080/07303084.2004.10609266

Jenny, S. E., & Rhodes, S. (2017). Physical education professionals developing life skills in children affected by poverty. *The Physical Educator*, 74(4), 653–671. https://doi.org/10.18666/tpe-2017-v74-i4-7524

Jha, N., & Shah, M. (2018). Reflective thinking: An insight. *International Journal of Research and Analytical Reviews*, 5(2), 1104–1106.

Juliana, J., & Afrianti, N. (2020). The effect of extracurricular activity toward English learning achievement of nursing students. *Premise: Journal of English Education*, 9(2), 183. https://doi.org/10.24127/pj.v9i2.3075

Madrona, P. G., Samalot-Rivera, A., & Kozub, F. M. (2017). Acquisition and transfer of values and social skills through a physical education program focused in the affective domain. *Motricidade*, 12(3), 32. https://doi.org/10.6063/motricidade.6502

Mahoney, J. L., Durlak, J. A., & Weissberg, R. P. (2018). An update on social and emotional learning outcome research. *Phi Delta Kappan*, 100(4), 18–23. https://doi.org/10.1177/0031721718815668

McKenzie, T. L., & Lounsbery, M. A. F. (2009). School physical education: The pill not taken. *American Journal of Lifestyle Medicine*, 3(3), 219–225. https://doi.org/10.1177/1559827609331562

McMurrer, J. (2008). Instructional time in elementary schools: A closer look at changes for specific subjects. *Arts Education Policy Review*, 109(6), 23–28. https://doi.org/10.3200/aepr.109.6.23-28

Ministry of Education. (2016). Physical and Health Education. Standard Curriculum for Secondary Schools, Form 1.

Mitchell, S. A., & Walton-Fisette, J. L. (2016). *The essentials of teaching physical education: Curriculum, instruction, and assessment.* Human Kinetics.

Mohd Nasiruddin, N. (2020). Self-efficacy and achievement goals among Malaysian physical education pre-service teachers (p. 3) [Dissertation].

Muska, M., & Ashworth, S. (2002). *Teaching physical education* (5th ed.). Benjamin Cummins.

Osborne, R., Belmont, R. S., Peixoto, R. P., de Azevedo, I. O. S., de Carvalho Junior, A. F. P., Osborne, R., Belmont, R. S., Peixoto, R. P. (2016). Obstacles for physical education teachers in public schools: An unsustainable situation. *Motriz: Revista de Educação Física*, 22(4), 310–318. https://doi.org/10.1590/s1980-6574201600040015

Simonton, K. L., & Garn, A. C. (2019). Negative emotions as predictors of behavioral outcomes in middle school physical education. *European Physical Education Review*, 26, 1356336X1987995. https://doi.org/10.1177/1356336x19879950

Swamy C. M. (2022). Current trends, issues and challenges in higher education with reference to physical education. *International Journal of Creative Research Thoughts*, 10(7), 453–455.

Syed Ali, S. K., Zahidi, M. A., & Samad, R. S. A. (2014). Influence of school environment in the teaching and learning of physical education. *Turkish Journal of Sport and Exercise*, 16(2), 70–70. https://doi.org/10.15314/tjse.201428108

Taylor, R. D., Oberle, E., Durlak, J. A., & Weissberg, R. P. (2017). Promoting positive youth development through school-based social and emotional learning interventions: A meta-analysis of follow-up effects. *Child Development*, 88(4), 1156–1171.

Valentini, M., Riccardi, F., Raiola, G., & Federici, A. (2018). Educational research: Motor area and relational area during children's personality development. *Journal of Physical Education and Sport*, 18, 2157.

Valkenborghs, S. R., Noetel, M., Hillman, C. H., Nilsson, M., Smith, J. J., Ortega, F. B., & Lubans, D. R. (2019). The impact of physical activity on brain structure and function in youth: A systematic review. *Pediatrics, 144*(4), e20184032. https://doi.org/10.1542/peds.2018-4032

Walsh, E. I., Smith, L., Northey, J., Rattray, B., & Cherbuin, N. (2020). Towards an understanding of the physical activity-BDNF-cognition triumvirate: A review of associations and dosage. *Ageing Research Reviews, 60,* 101044. https://doi.org/10.1016/j.arr.2020.101044

Wee, E. H. (2017). Quality control in physical education in Malaysia: Relooking at the national strategy for quality physical education. In *Empowering 21st century learners through holistic and enterprising learning* (pp. 197–209). https://doi.org/10.1007/978-981-10-4241-6_20

Wee, E. H., Cheng, W. F., & Chin, N. S. (2021). Teachers' perceived barriers to implementation of physical education. *Collegium Antropologicum, 45*(3), 191–200. https://doi.org/10.5671/ca.45.3.2

WHO. (1994). *Life skills education for children and adolescents in schools* (p. 1). Retrieved from https://iris.who.int/bitstream/handle/10665/63552/WHO?sequence=1

Wintle, J. (2022). Physical education and physical activity promotion: Lifestyle sports as meaningful experiences. *Education Sciences, 12*(3), 181. https://doi.org/10.3390/educsci12030181

Diverse Values and Life Skills Learnt
from Sports Context

Chapter Nine

Eiichiro Fukami

INTRODUCTION

Athletic Club Activities Providing Rich Sports Opportunities for Japanese Youth

In Japan, school athletic club activities have traditionally supported youth's sporting experiences. Physical education (PE) teachers and other school teachers, as well as managers and coaches of club activities, help ensure that students have the opportunity to engage in cooperative and enriching after-school sports opportunities, regardless of level or gender. According to the Courses of Study (MEXT, 2017a, p. 246),

> Athletic club activities should be independent, spontaneous, and enjoyable for students. Club activities, in which students participate voluntarily and on their own initiative, help to familiarize students with sports, culture, science, etc., improve their motivation to learn, and cultivate a sense of responsibility and cooperation, thereby contributing to the development of the qualities and abilities that education aims to promote.

The Japan Sports Agency (2018) points out that in order for students to develop the "zest for life" that balances intellectual, moral, and PE through school programmes, it is important for them to actively participate in athletic club activities to maintain and improve their physical and mental health throughout their lives, and to have an enriching sports life. When engaging in athletic club activities, independence in goal setting and practice is crucial for athletes. Coaches also play an important role in providing guidance and feedback by ensuring improvement and progress among their athletes. In particular, training and goal setting should be realistic and based on abilities. Moreover,

DOI: 10.4324/9781032688657-12

goals should be set for competitions and rankings in order to ensure steady and effective training during daily practice (Nose, 2007). This is important, as an authoritarian teaching approach that does not allow learners to contribute and make decisions would prove challenging for students to develop independence and creativity – qualities that are important in sports activities (Nagai, 2013). Therefore, coaches should respect their athletes' opinions and needs when constructing their training plans.

On the other hand, according to the recent "National Survey on Physical Fitness, Exercise Ability, and Exercise Habits" by the Japan Sports Agency (2018), both male and female students are divided into two main groups: those who actively participate in physical activity and those who do not exercise at all. In particular, 19.4% of female junior high school students spend less than 60 minutes per week in total physical activity, excluding PE classes. Under these circumstances, in order to create more opportunities for students to exercise, sports club activities are required to encourage the habit of physical activity that students enjoy, such as activities that are not competition-oriented but recreation-oriented, and activities that aim to build physical fitness. Therefore, sports education programmes should emphasise inclusiveness and education instead of competition.

The current concept of athletic club activities was first introduced to Japan by the United States following Japan's defeat in World War II. Specifically, under the guidance of the US GHQ,[1] traditional Japanese militarism was rejected and eliminated, and a new democratic education was introduced. Athletic club activities were considered to be even more effective than PE classes as a means of democratic education and human character building. This is because athletic club activities give students the opportunity to choose a sports they enjoy and a chance to work independently. Even today, students are expected to set individual and group goals and learn the importance of human relationships and the importance of effective team management through friendly competition with teammates and opponents under the guidance of coaches (Japan Sports Agency, 2018). However, many middle and high school students perceive athletic club activities differently. Most of the students engage in these extracurricular sports competitively, with expectations to represent their teams in competitions and games, and to win them. The national high school athletic championships are held two to three times a year for most sports at the high school level. Participation in these competitions is the goal of high school students in athletic clubs. The highly competitive games require student-athletes to compete against one another to qualify for the position to represent their prefectures and further compete for the top spot in the nation. But first, student-athletes must win regular competitions within their teams to compete. Therefore, while athletic club activities aim to build students' personalities, competition within these activities has encouraged students to instead focus on victory and breaking records(Japan Sports Agency, 2018, p. 12). For this reason, it is difficult for students to learn responsibility, cooperation, and even friendship through athletic club activities.

APPLIED INSIGHTS

The Role of Athletic Club Activities from a Historical Perspective

Athletic club activities have a long history and give rise to the popularity of many sports and the improvement of athletic performance in Japan (Nakazawa, 2011). When Japan first participated in the Olympic Games in Stockholm in 1912, two of the athletes in the track and field events were university students. In 1964, during the first Olympic Games in Asia that was held in Tokyo, 128 out of 355 Japanese athletes were student-athletes. This included 14 high school students (Fukami, 2023). Many top Japanese athletes were trained in school athletic club activities, and therefore, these activities were perceived to be favourable for the development of elite athletes. Through these activities, a number of Japanese high school student Olympic medalists in sports such as swimming, gymnastics, judo, and table tennis have been born.

Later on, athletic club activities contributed to another part of the history of school education in Japan. In the 1970s, more than 90% of junior high school students entered high school, leading to an increase in the number of students per teacher. As a result, teachers were unable to provide sufficient individualised instruction to all students in their classes, resulting in some students starting to lag behind in their school work (= OCHIKOBORE), and delinquency was observed. Subsequently, incidents of violence were rampant among students in and out of school. This became a national social problem, and in the 1980s, schools were made to deal with this problem of student delinquency. The main behavioural problems of delinquent students at that time were as follows. Students left the school during class without permission from teachers. Students smoked on campus. Students broke windows in the school buildings. Students fought with students from other schools. Students committed violence against teachers and students. The increase in these delinquent students was due to teachers' inability to get students to follow instructions (Noshige, 1980). To deal with this challenge, many schools sought to actively involve these students in athletic club activities to build trusting relationships with students to control incidences of delinquent behaviour and help them recover. Through these athletic club activities, teachers reported that student delinquency was actually prevented and reduced (Tosaka, 1981). Thus, these results suggest that athletic club activities play a role in improving student behaviour by tackling students' inability to adapt to and belong in school by promoting inclusivity in the activities (Ito, 1993).

Participation in athletic club activities provides students with an opportunity to represent the school in national tournaments, which could improve chances of entry and advancement to high school and college, which may impact students' future career paths. A survey by the Japanese Association of University Physical Education and Sports (2014) reported that 30.5% of universities across the country had a sports recommendation entrance examination. In particular, high school students can be recommended for admission to nationally recognised, academically prestigious universities by participating and excelling in national championship competitions. Therefore, students, as well as athletic coaches and schools, try to strengthen their athletic activities. In addition, there is a great advantage for universities in admitting top athletes through sports recommendation entrance examinations. By selecting athletes who can perform at world-class competitions such as the Olympics and World Championships, as well as at university championships, which attract a great deal of attention in Japan, universities can enhance their reputations by attracting media attention.

For instance, one of the most renowned college sports events in Japan, the "Hakone Ekiden," a round-trip college relay race between Tokyo and Hakone is broadcast live on television, recording an average viewership rating of approximately 30%. Over one million spectators support the event and athletes over the two days, making it a high-profile collegiate sports event that has gained the support of many citizens. Runners wearing uniforms with the university's name on them are featured in the media. By gaining attention through media outlets, the popularity and reputation of the university is improved. An example is Tokai University, which showed a significant increase in the number of applicants for the entrance examinations in 2019 after winning the competition for the first time (Onda et al., 2020). The sports recommendation entrance examination could thus potentially benefit both the school and high school students. While the sports recommendation entrance examination provides an avenue for many athletes to enter high schools and universities, it often exempts student-athletes from academic achievement tests. This results in the admission of student-athletes without sufficient academic ability (Miyata, 2016). As such, some students who are admitted with sports recommendations face difficulties in balancing their academic work and athletic activities, resulting in them neglecting their studies to focus on pursuing their athletic activities (Kubo, 2006). Furthermore, it is not uncommon for these students to drop out without graduating (Tomozoe, 2016). As many as 70% of the universities in Japan have indicated a need to provide student-athletes with academic support (Ito et al., 2014). To mitigate the problem, the Study Council on the Promotion of University Sports has focused on trying to help student-athletes balance their studies and athletic activities, and each university is encouraged to provide suitable forms of support (MEXT, 2017c). For example, Waseda University (2024) started the Waseda Athlete Program (WAP) in 2014. The WAP is a student-athlete development programme for all athletic divisions, which comprises 44 teams and approximately 2,700 athletes, and is the first in Japan. This programme aims to help student-athletes balance their academics and club activities, as well as develop their character, by combining social skills and a rich sense of humanity. Student-athletes not only achieve excellent athletic results but also learn the fundamentals of becoming leaders in various fields of society. This programme also provides student-athletes with opportunities to think about their own career development after graduation (or after they retire from competition). In addition, there is a system to reward the athletic teams and individual student-athletes with the most outstanding grade point average (GPA) each year.

Athletic Club Activities as a Potential Harm to Lifelong Sports

The promotion of athletic club activities has led to the emergence of additional problems. These activities have been cited as one of the main causes of the long working hours of teachers, which have become a social problem in recent years (Sankei Shimbun, 2019). According to the Organisation for Economic Co-operation and Development (OECD) Teaching and Learning International Survey (TALIS) (Sankei Shimbun, 2019), of junior high school teachers in 48 countries and regions around the world, it was found that Japanese junior high school teachers work approximately 54 hours per week. This exceeds the International Labour Organisation's (ILO) international standard of 48 hours per week, making it 1.4 times more than the average of participating countries. The ratio of extracurricular activities, such as club activities, was 3.7 times the average of the participating countries, the highest among the participating countries. This is a problem as teachers are needed to enhance the educational value of the activities and guide students along. Furthermore, students' involvement in practice games and tournaments on weekends and holidays adds to the workload of teachers.

Another challenge faced is the shortage of coaches for athletic club activities. Specifically, relative to the number of sports, there are insufficient coaches that specialise in each sports. Hence, sports are facilitated by teachers who have no experience in the field. According to the Japan Sports Association (JSPO, 2021), 26.9% of coaches in junior high schools and 25.3% in high schools had no experience in the sports they taught and did not specialise in PE. For them, the burden of coaching athletic club activities is heavy, and the risk of injury or accidents to student-athletes is high because they do not have the knowledge and skills necessary to effectively teach sports to students. A reason contributing to the shortage of coaches is that of family commitment. For example, coaches might not be able to commit to teaching in athletic clubs, as they may have to commit to looking after their family members, such as young children, children with disabilities, or elderly parents.

Finally, harassment and violence by coaches pose an additional challenge. As highlighted, there is a lot of emphasis placed on winning due to the amount of media coverage, recognition, prestige, and the advantages that such achievements promise. As such, students, parents, and coaches approach sports with a 'win-at-all-cost' mentality, which leads to an acceptance of harsh coaching by coaches toward their players. Harsh coaching in turn often escalates to harassment and violence. An example is the basketball coach who repeatedly used corporal punishment and violence against a team captain for his failure to play and lack of leadership in 2013, which led to the suicide of the player. In addition, a high school student-athlete who was selected for Japan's U18 volleyball national team committed suicide after being subjected to repeated verbal abuse by his advisor, which affected his dignity. As such, it has become extremely challenging to maintain the use of traditional methods of coaching in athletic clubs, and thus, a new approach to guiding student-athletes in athletic club activities should be sought and considered.

SUMMARY AND FUTURE DIRECTIONS

Discussion about the Transition of Athletic Club Activities to the Local Community

In recent years, Japan's declining birthrate has led to a decrease in the number of students enrolled in junior high schools, causing some athletic club activities to be suspended or discontinued, and it is no longer feasible for schools to continue athletic club activities on their own.

Furthermore, the shortage of experienced teachers who are able to coach sports activities effectively and the heavy workload for the teachers involved in extracurricular athletic club activity calls for an increasing demand to hire local sports coaches instead of involving school teachers. For instance, MEXT (2017b) has institutionalised rules that allow schools to hire local sports coaches to lead students in competitions and other events to reduce the burden of coaching club activities on school teachers. However, challenges associated with this plan include employment conditions and benefits, which are not always good, and the difficulty in hiring coaches, especially those who are willing to contribute to the holistic development of student-athletes, focusing on character building rather than primarily on skills and winning. To mitigate these, another plan has been developed. It aims to make teachers' participation in coaching club activities on off days non-mandatory and appropriately compensate teachers who continue engaging in coaching club activities on their off days. The main goal of this is to develop a sustainable and diverse local sports environment while reducing the working hours of teachers and ensuring that students have sufficient opportunities to continue being involved in sports. In addition, all coaches (teachers) ~~leaders~~ of athletic club activities are required to obtain a sports coach certification before leading athletes in tournaments. This new coach certification system is a framework for training excellent coaches who can not only acquire the coaching theory and medical sciences knowledge necessary for sports coaching but also enhance the ability and humanity of athletes and the value of sports (JSPO, 2019). Therefore, new coaches (teachers) who are certified are expected to provide a range of opportunities that meet the diverse interests of students.

On the other hand, with regard to plans for transitioning athletic activities from the school to community-based activities, the costs associated with implementing these activities outside of the school environment can be a challenge, as students have been using the facilities and equipment provided by their schools free of charge to implement sports.

According to a survey commissioned by the Japan Sports Agency (2022), the average annual cost per student would be 17,000 yen (about 115 USD) more if the club is operated outside the school. Hence, consideration should be made to seek government funding for the additional fees associated with externally based athletic club participation. This is to ensure that students can continue participating without having to worry about their financial situation. Plans to move athletic club activities outside the school have been discussed several times. Each time, however, the plans have not been successful, arising from several concerns relating to the cost of such programmes, the shortage of qualified coaches, and matters relating to the liable party should accidents and injuries occur with students. For future discussion, the "student perspective" and opportunities aligning with their interests should be considered. To date, there has been a rich sporting culture created for students through athletic club activities in Japan. It is important to consider the limitations and challenges of the current sports environment and work toward improving the conditions for both coaches and students to create a more conducive sports environment for students to develop holistically and grow. It would mark a major shift in Japan's sports education system should there be a shift towards incorporating athletic club activities outside school to improve the learning conditions for both students and coaches.

NOTE

1 Abbreviation for "General Headquarters." Established in Tokyo in 1945 as the high command for occupying and managing Japan after the Pacific War.

REFERENCES

Fukami, E. (2023). Social transition of athletic club activities. In H. Tomozoe (Ed.), *Regional sports club activities and athletic club activities in the new era: Its vision and mission* (pp. 117–129). Taishukan Shoten.

Ito, K., Kita, T., Takahashi, M., Nishigaki, K., Shigeto, S., & Kobayashi, K. (2014). Report of a survey about sports and club governing bodies and academic and career support. *College Physical Education*, 105, 132–135.

Ito, Y (1993). Characteristics of contemporary adolescents. In Y. Ochiai, Y. Ito, & M. Saito (Eds.), *Psychology of adolescence* (pp. 209–226). Yuhikaku.

Japan Sport Association (JSPO) (2019). The certified sports instructor. Retrieved from https://www.japan-sports.or.jp/coach/tabid58.html

Japan Sport Association (JSPO) (2021). Survey about the actual conditions of school athletic club activity coaches. Retrieved from https://www.japan-sports.or.jp/coach/tabid1280.html

Japan Sports Agency (2018). Comprehensive guidelines about the state of athletic club activities. Retrieved from https://www.mext.go.jp/sports/b_menu/shingi/013_index/toushin/1402678.htm

Japan Sports Agency (2022). *Study meeting about transition of athletic activities to the community* (4th meeting) proceedings. Retrieved from https://www.mext.go.jp/sports/b_menu/shingi/035_index/gijiroku/jsa_00005.html

Japanese Association of University Physical Education and Sports (2014). Report on the results of a survey about support for extracurricular sports activities at universities and junior colleges. Retrieved from https://2020.daitairen.or.jp/dtr2020/wp-content/uploads/2023/08/2014.pdf

Kubo, M. (2006). Second career issues of athletes and universities. In H. Tomozoe (Ed.), *Contemporary sports critique* (pp. 47–57). Soubun Kikaku.

Ministry of Education, Culture, Sports, Science and Technology (MEXT). (2017a). *Commentary on the curriculum guidelines for elementary schools: Section 7 health and physical education*. Toyokan Publishing.

Ministry of Education, Culture, Sports, Science and Technology (MEXT) (2017b). About club activity instructors. Retrieved from https://www.mext.go.jp/sports/b_menu/sports/mcatetop04/list/1405720_00010.htm

Ministry of Education, Culture, Sports, Science and Technology (MEXT). (2017c). *Study council about the promotion of university sports: Final summary. Toward Enhancing the Value of University Sports*. Retrieved from https://www.mext.go.jp/sports/b_menu/shingi/005_index/toushin/1383246.htm

Miyata, Y. (2016). *The runaway American college sports economics*. Toshindo.

Nagai, Y. (2013). *Youth sports: Bad adults will crush kids!* Asahi Shimbun Publications.

Nakazawa, A (2011). Why are teachers positively motivated to manage extracurricular sports activities in Japan: A sociological study of teacher's interpretations of the difficulties in combining sports with education. *Japan Journal of Physical Education, Health, and Sport Sciences*, 56(2), 373–390.

Nose, S (2007). Practical coaching methods about improving judo competitiveness. *Bulletin of Saitama University*, 56(1), 185–195.

Noshige, M (1980). Violence of children. *Physical Education*, 28(2), 26–27.

Onda, T., Room, A., Nishide, N., & Morozumi, H. (2020). *A study on media exposure of Hakone Ekiden and the number of applicants for university admission* (pp. 25–32). Bulletin of Tokai University.

Sankei Shimbun. (2019). Dated June 19th. Retrieved from https://www.sankei.com/nyushi/news/190619/nys1906190005-n1.html

Tomozoe, H. (2016). What is required of athletic club activities from now on. In Tomozoe, H. (Ed.), *Theory and practice of athletic club activities* (pp. 2–15). Taishukan Shoten.

Tosaka, H (1981). Aiming for schools with zero delinquency. *Physical Education*, 34(9), 43–47.

Waseda University. (2024). School of Sport Sciences, Admissions office entrance examination I: Top Athlete Entrance Examination. Retrieved from https://www.waseda.jp/fsps/sps/applicants/admissions/

Caught or Taught? Situating Approaches for Coaching
Life Skills through Sports

Chapter Ten

Martin Camiré

INTRODUCTION

Life skills research, as currently situated in the youth sports literature, can be traced back to the pioneering work of Steven Danish in the early 1980s (e.g., Danish, 1983). In the decades that have followed, life skills (e.g., time management, teamwork) have come to be defined as skills "that enable individuals to succeed in the different environments in which they live, such as school, home and in their neighbourhoods" (Danish et al., 2004, p. 40). In sports, Gould and Carson (2008) defined life skills as "internal personal assets, characteristics and skills such as goal setting, emotional control, self-esteem and hard work ethic that can be facilitated or developed in sports and are transferred for use in non-sports settings" (p. 60). As an extension of the Gould and Carson (2008) definition, Pierce et al. (2017) defined life skills transfer as the

> [o]ngoing process by which an individual further develops or learns/internalises a personal asset (psychosocial skill, knowledge, disposition, identity construction or transformation) in sports and then experiences personal change through the application of the asset in one or more life domains beyond the context where it was originally learned.
>
> (p. 194)

Taken together, these life skills definitions have guided the conduct of research and have enhanced our understanding of the variables shaping life skills development in sports. Inspired by these definitions, the purpose of the present chapter is to situate the most prevalent approaches for coaching life skills through sports by providing readers with applied insights as well as a summary and future directions.

DOI: 10.4324/9781032688657-13

APPLIED INSIGHTS

When studying, researching, and applying life skills, one key variable to consider is *intentionality*, referred to as the extent to which deliberate decisions are made (or not) to create opportunities for athletes to develop life skills. In initial conceptualisations, intentionality was explored dichotomously and composed of two approaches (Turnnidge et al., 2014). The *implicit* approach encompasses a focus on the coaching of sports skills with little/no attention paid to the coaching of life skills and life skills transfer. In the implicit approach, it is postulated that the inherent features of sports (e.g., competition, relationships, motivational climate), if experienced adaptively, implicitly help athletes develop life skills that are transferrable. In other words, the basic premise of the implicit approach is that even if coaches do not intentionally teach life skills, by structuring the sports context in adaptive ways, youth can still acquire life skills as they develop positive relationships and compete in healthy manners in sports (Holt et al., 2017). Some empirical evidence has shown that athletes can implicitly develop life skills through sports and then transfer these skills to non-sports settings, with minimal/no intervention from coaches (Chinkov & Holt, 2016; Jones & Lavallee, 2009).

Conversely, the *explicit* approach encompasses a focus on the concurrent coaching of sports skills, life skills, and life skills transfer. In the explicit approach, coaches intentionally plan life skills messages, initiatives, and activities that provide youth opportunities to discuss and practice life skills in and out of sports. The basic premise of the explicit approach is that such messages, initiatives, and activities increase youth's awareness and confidence as coaches deliberately explain to athletes the life skills they possess and the contexts in which such life skills can be transferred (Pierce et al., 2017). Empirical research has highlighted the importance of coaching life skills explicitly while also emphasising the notion of transfer. For example, Camiré et al. (2012) demonstrated how coaches who deliberately taught life skills (e.g., getting older athletes to mentor younger athletes to develop their leadership skills) enhanced their athletes' ability to transfer life skills outside of sports. Moreover, Allen et al. (2015) showed how peer group transfer debriefs were useful in getting athletes to share their successes and challenges with transferring life skills. When athletes engaged in such debriefs, they learned from one another and got exposed to varying ways through which they can apply their life skills at school, at home, and in the community.

The implicit and explicit approaches offer a useful framework for positioning life skills development and transfer. However, by situating them as distinct processes, the framework fails to consider the inherent complexity and entanglement of how life skills are developed and transferred. It should also be noted that recent models articulate that development is maximised when coaches teach life skills in an integrated (implicit/explicit) manner. For instance, Holt et al. (2017) clearly indicated in their model of positive youth development (PYD) through sports that "[t]he combined effects of a PYD climate and a life skills focus will produce more PYD outcomes than a PYD climate alone" (p. 38). Similarly, Bean et al. (2018) stated in their implicit/explicit continuum of life skills development and transfer that youth can expect to experience greater positive developmental outcomes when coaches start with implicit approaches and then gradually build up their coaching repertoire to include explicit approaches.

It should be noted that in the context of sports, coaches have been situated as important actors responsible for overseeing life skills development and transfer processes due to several reasons. First, sports is positioned as a practice with inherent skill-building features that must be prioritised if athletes are to attain desired levels of mastery and performance. In such environments, coaches are ideally positioned to act as frontline providers of sporting experiences and teach not only physical, technical, and tactical skills but also life skills. Second, sports is fundamentally a social activity through which coaches can help youth develop a wide range of social life skills (e.g., interacting effectively with teammates, coaches, and referees) that can be transferred outside of sports (e.g., interacting effectively with colleagues, managers, and community leaders). Third, due to the time they spend with youth during (e.g., practices, games) and surrounding (e.g., locker room, team bus), sports coaches can serve as important complementary (i.e., youth with good family/social situations) or compensatory (i.e., youth with challenging family/social situations) resources. Taken together, these reasons position coaches as powerful social agents in sports who can complement and extend the efforts of parents, teachers, and community leaders in developing the life skills of young people. In the following section, strategies are provided to help coaches teach life skills in sports through combined implicit and explicit approaches.

ESTABLISHED STRATEGIES FOR COACHING LIFE SKILLS

Camiré et al. (2011) offered five key principles coaches can use to coach life skills through sports. These five principles consist of (a) carefully developing one's coaching philosophy (e.g., taking time to reflect on one's coaching priorities), (b) developing meaningful relationships with athletes (e.g., getting to know athletes and their interests outside of sports), (c) intentionally integrating developmental strategies in one's coaching practice (e.g., actively discussing the importance of perseverance to achieve one's goals), (d) not just talking about life skills but getting athletes to practice life skills (e.g., planning practice drills for athletes to experience working as a cohesive unit), and (e) coaching athletes on how life skills transfer to non-sports settings (e.g., explaining how leadership skills developed in sports can also be applied in the classroom). In a similar fashion, to help coaches facilitate life skills transfer, Pierce et al. (2018) offered seven key strategies, which consist of (a) prioritising the coaching of life skills and recognising the need to intentionally foster transfer (e.g., situating life skills not as add-ons but as integral elements of coaching), (b) fostering life skills mastery and reinforcing life skills transfer beyond sports (e.g., sharing life skills stories with athletes that facilitate retention), (c) maintaining positive coach-athlete relationships (e.g., asking athletes about events in their daily lives), (d) creating opportunities for athletes to apply life skills outside of sports (e.g., volunteering as a team at a local animal shelter), (e) developing partnerships with key social agents (e.g., sharing with teachers and parents one's life skills coaching plan for the season), (f) providing life skills boosters (e.g., getting former athletes to share the importance of life skills with current athletes), and (g) facilitating athlete reflection (e.g., promoting peer discussions on life skills transfer). When applied deliberately and consistently, these principles and strategies provide coaches with a solid foundation for coaching life skills through sports.

In efforts to help coaches move beyond dichotomous (i.e., implicit or explicit) approaches to life skills development and transfer, Bean et al. (2018) theorised how the coaching of life skills occurs on a six-level continuum of intentionality, with the levels complementing one another and acting as building blocks. Level 1 consists of coaches working to structure the sports context by designing the programme and setting rules while level 2 consists of facilitating a positive climate by modelling positive behaviour and fostering positive relationships. Levels 3 and 4 are reached when coaches make deliberate efforts to discuss (level 3) and practice (level 4) life skills in sports. Levels 5 and 6 are reached when coaches make deliberate efforts to discuss (level 5) and practice (level 6) life skills transfer beyond sports. The Bean et al. (2018) continuum was used to theoretically anchor the Coaching Life Skills in Sports Questionnaire (Camiré et al., 2021), which was subsequently converted into a life skills self-assessment tool for coaches (Kramers et al., 2022). The self-assessment tool can serve as an important indicator for coaches, enabling them to assess their level of intentionality in coaching life skills through sports. English, French, Portuguese, and Spanish versions of the self-assessment tool were created and complemented by an instructional video.

ADVANCEMENTS AND EVOLUTIONS FOR COACHING LIFE SKILLS

The principles, strategies, and models created to help coaches coach life skills have made key contributions to coaching science/practice. Yet, some researchers have argued for the need to evolve the coaching of life skills. For example, Ronkainen et al. (2021) critiqued how the concept of life skills reduces what youth learn from sports to skills aimed at economic productivity. Moreover, Wilson Outley and Blyth (2020) critiqued the underlying logics of coaching life skills such as resilience to equity-owed youth, explaining how such approaches fail to tackle the oppressive inequalities that make the world unjust and thus require resilience in the first place.

Camiré et al. (2022) provided concrete examples of how coaching can be advanced by evolving life skills to take on expanded meanings and applications. For example, in its conventional delineation, teamwork entails working together to achieve a common goal. However, when positioned outside of a goal-achievement perspective, teamwork can take on alternative meanings focused on relationships and personal growth that can be derived from significant opportunities for socialisation. In this sense, teamwork can evolve to be situated as a life skill enabling youth to live a variety of social experiences by interacting with culturally diverse individuals and groups who may hold different belief systems. Teamwork, as an evolved life skill, becomes focused on solidarity, cultural awareness, and openness to different ways of being and doing. Similarly, in the life skills literature, leadership has traditionally been defined as an ability to influence and/or guide individuals, teams, or organisations. By evolving this definition and positioning leadership as influence/guidance for advancing social advocacy, youth can learn valuable leadership skills that can galvanise community efforts for change and compel a more socially just society. In this sense, by coaching leadership from a social advocacy perspective, coaches can help athletes feel more aware/confident and better prepared to stand up for teammates and victims of harassment because of their racial/ethnic background, gender identity, or sexual orientation. Evolving life skills such as teamwork and leadership in these manners helps advance the narrative from individual development to societal development, enabling life skills to shed their normative connotations and become transformative in their capacity for social change.

FROM NORMATIVE TO TRANSFORMATIVE APPROACHES TO COACHING LIFE SKILLS

As several researchers have noted, the conventional approach to coaching life skills in sports focuses on the individual, with life skills positioned as important forms of capital youth must acquire to strive for upward social mobility in competitive capitalistic societies (Kwauk, 2022). When societal logics privilege individuality and meritocracy, life skills act as key attributes that youth must internalise to successfully overcome difficult social realities. This conventional approach to coaching life skills is referred to as *normative*, whereby the skills taught to youth are those that help promote social order through ideals of personal responsibility, functionality, and obedience to dominant social norms. The premise is simple: if we coach youth in the life skills they need to deal with their problems and overcome their life challenges, then the economic apparatus benefits through reduced chances of youth engaging in illicit activities, being unemployed, and being unnecessary burdens to society (Coakley, 2021). The normative approach to coaching thus has its limits, as it generally does not account for systemic issues, such as racism, sexism, and ableism, thereby failing to address the inequalities affecting many youth. By prioritising the moulding of individuals as opposed to the changing of society (i.e., fix the youth, not the system), discrimination remains mostly unaddressed.

Conversely, the *transformative* approach connects the coaching of life skills to social justice, with relationality taking centre stage. At its core, the transformative approach is focused on change, deployed with the deliberate intent to destabilise normative ways to situate sports. By prioritising relationships over individual success, the transformative coaching of life skills facilitates a collective well-being that helps shape a more just world. To coach life skills transformatively, coaches must adopt a critical praxis by positioning their work within historically shaped, culturally diverse, and power laden discourses. As an extension of the Bean et al. (2018) continuum, Camiré (2023a) created the two continua model for life skills teaching, providing coaches with a tangible blueprint for how they can be implicit or explicit in their approaches to coaching life skills doing so normatively or transformatively. In the following sections, brief descriptions are offered of the four main approaches to coaching life skills found in the two continua model.

Normative Implicit

Life skills coaching approaches deemed normative implicit are those focused on sports skills, with little/no attention paid to life skills or social justice. Coaches who deploy normative implicit approaches help maintain the status quo, do not address systemic barriers, and abide by the Great Sports Myth that sports has inherent powers to promote development and fix social ills. In normative implicit coaching climates, the dominant meritocratic culture of sports is sustained, whereby the onus of change is on youth to take responsibility for creating better lives for themselves through gruelling regimes of resilience in the face of constant oppression and inequality.

Normative Explicit

Life skills coaching approaches deemed normative explicit are those where sports skills and life skills are intentionally addressed but where social justice remains unaddressed. In this approach, coaches take deliberate steps to discuss and practice life skills with their athletes but fail to question ongoing social injustices and inequalities. The prevailing normative social order is maintained and athletes are taught that the more life skills they develop, the better equipped they will be to thrive as productive citizens. No "disclaimer" is provided that equity-owed youth will need to navigate and overcome a world that is filled with unequally distributed life hurdles.

Transformative Implicit

Life skills coaching approaches deemed transformative implicit are those that afford youth possibilities for solidarity. Working with the concept of transformative relationality, coaches enact conditions for peer interactions that are devoid of the toxicity, misogyny, and heteronormativity commonly experienced in sports. Solidarity that is transformative goes beyond conventional notions of support. Specifically, coaches create pedagogical climates in which youth experience their well-being as always already entangled in their peers' well-being. When coaches create settings that position solidarity and well-being as relational and entangled, it sets the stage for reflexivity. Youth develop increased abilities to introspect and situate the state of their existence within broader historical, social, and cultural contexts where agency is shared through complex sets of relations. In practical terms, coaches who foster solidarity and reflexivity equip youth to actively challenge a multitude of stereotypes and microaggressions with the goal of enhancing collective well-being.

Transformative Explicit

Life skills coaching approaches deemed transformative explicit are those enacted by coaches who intentionally coach social justice life skills. For example, coaches can help their athletes develop collective dignity, situated as a relational feeling of care brought forth through the recognition that one's personal worth is always already entangled in the worth of others. Another example of a social justice life skill is *reciprocity*, a relational responsibility that goes beyond normative notions of personal responsibility. Youth who act reciprocally seek benefits for themselves *and* others simultaneously, thereby promoting collective well-being. Coaches can also help youth enhance their *critical consciousness* by enabling them to develop their critical reflection, political efficacy, and critical action. Practically speaking, this requires coaches to help youth (a) grasp how systems of power maintain social inequalities, (b) increase beliefs in their capacity to fight for social justice, and (c) act in proactive manners in the name of social change. Although the inherent benevolence of sports has been evangelised to far too great a degree (i.e., Great Sports Myth), coaches who adopt transformative approaches to coaching life skills can indeed work towards maximising the power of sports as one of many relevant sites for instigating social change.

SUMMARY AND FUTURE DIRECTIONS

In the present chapter, several approaches for coaching life skills through sports were advanced. Pertaining to the "caught versus taught" debate, although life skills may be developed implicitly through the simple practice of sports, it is suggested that coaches make deliberate efforts to coach life skills explicitly. The explicit approach does not guarantee larger returns on investment than the implicit approach, but a combination of implicit/explicit strategies does increase the likelihood that youth will be more aware (e.g., appreciate the life skills they have developed) and feel more confident (e.g., be self-assured in using their life skills) in the life skills application process. To foster climates conducive to coaching life skills, coaches should continuously look to evolve their coaching philosophy and enact pedagogies of care that promote strong coach-youth and youth-youth relationships.

The chapter also examined how normative approaches to coaching life skills contrast with transformative approaches. The position taken is that transformative approaches have the potential to better prepare youth to not only confront a mostly unjust world but actively strive to change it for the better. Yet, despite their potential, it must be noted that transformative approaches rarely ensue without challenges, risks, and drawbacks. A dosage of reality is needed by realising that those benefiting from the status quo will not relinquish their stranglehold on power without a fight. That being said, coaches who wish to explicitly coach life skills transformatively must be acutely aware of the challenges that lay ahead of them. Such challenges also extend to athletes who apply social justice life skills in schools and communities where the social, cultural, and political reality may make social activism quite burdensome and fraught with perils and hardships. Bearing those notions in mind, transformative life skills coaching must be positioned as difficult yet necessary work intended to dismantle the oppressive societal forces weighing down many youth's opportunities to live life well.

In terms of future directions, it is essential to consider what next steps may lie ahead for coaching life skills through sports. Recently, Camiré et al. (2023) raised key interrogations as to whether we should transition from PYD and life skills approaches in youth sports research, providing several arguments intended to stir dialogue in the field. One argument in particular invites researchers to reimagine life skills coaching through a posthumanist lens, which may offer great potential to enact transformative change. As it pertains to life skills, Camiré (2022) introduced the concept of *relationally adaptive know hows* in an attempt to challenge our narrow and stratified way of thinking about the development that occurs in sports. When life skills are situated as relationally adaptive know hows, they move from stable entities encased in bounded human beings to relational enactments actualising in fleeting moments at the intrasection of person and environment. Situating life skills through a posthumanist lens spurs theorising in unconventional directions and invites researchers to think beyond humanist, essentialist, and homogenising views of life skills. As it relates to coaching, Camiré (2023b) instigated a reimagining through the lens of agential realism. Historically, coaching science has been concerned with linear one-way knowledge flows, studying coaches who enact coaching practices for athletes who perform athletic feats. From an agential realist lens, attention shifts from the coach to coaching intra-action, effectively ending the coach's reign as the focus of inquiry. Instead, coaching becomes a performance of shared agency entangling human (e.g., coaches, athletes, referees, parents) and nonhuman (e.g., fields of play, weather, equipment) entities, thereby multiplying who and what gets accounted for in the study of coaching. From this lens, coaching becomes a relational phenomenon through which coach and athlete co-articulate one another in entangled influences involving humans, animals, playing surfaces, technologies, and other agentic entities. In sum, the merits of posthumanism lie in compelling researchers to brave beyond their intellectual comfort zones and seek alternative ways to theorise life skills and coaching beyond their conventional renditions.

REFERENCES

Allen, G., Rhind, D., & Koshy, V. (2015). Enablers and barriers for male students transferring life skills from the sports hall into the classroom. *Qualitative Research in Sport, Exercise and Health*, 7(1), 53–67. https://doi.org/10.1080/2159676X.2014.893898

Bean, C., Kramers, S., Forneris, T., & Camiré, M. (2018). The implicit/explicit continuum of life skills development and transfer. *Quest*, 70(4), 456–470. https://doi.org/10.1080/00336297.2018.1451348

Camiré, M. (2022). A move to rethink life skills as assemblages: A call to postqualitative inquiry. *Qualitative Research in Sport, Exercise and Health*, 14(6), 900–915. https://doi.org/10.1080/2159676X.2021.2002395

Camiré, M. (2023a). The two continua model for life skills teaching. *Sport, Education and Society*, 28(8), 915–928. https://doi.org/10.1080/13573322.2022.2073438.

Camiré, M. (2023b). Sport coaching as intra-action: An agential realist diffraction. *Sports Coaching Review*. https://doi.org/10.1080/21640629.2023.2242180

Camiré, M., Forneris, T., Trudel, P., & Bernard, D. (2011). Strategies for helping coaches facilitate positive youth development through sport. *Journal of Sport Psychology in Action*, 2(2), 92–99. http://doi.org/10.1080/21520704.2011.584246

Camiré, M., Newman, T., Bean, C., & Strachan, L. (2022). Reimagining positive youth development and life skills in sport through a social justice lens. *Journal of Applied Sport Psychology*, 34(6), 1058–1076. https://doi.org/10.1080/10413200.2021.1958954

Camiré, M., Santos, F., Newman, T., Vella, S., MacDonald, D. J., Milistetd, M., Pierce, S., & Strachan, L. (2023). Positive youth development as a guiding framework in sport research: Is it time to plan for a transition? *Psychology of Sport & Exercise*, 69, 102505. https://doi.org/10.1016/j.psychsport.2023.102505

Camiré, M., Trudel, P., & Forneris, T. (2012). Coaching and transferring life skills: Philosophies and strategies used by model high school coaches. *The Sport Psychologist*, 26(2), 243–260. https://doi.org/10.1123/tsp.26.2.243

Camiré, M., Turgeon, S., Kramers, S., Rathwell, S., Bean, C., Sabourin, C., & Pierce, S. (2021). Development and initial validation of the coaching life skills in sport questionnaire. *Psychology of Sport & Exercise*, 53, 101845. https://doi.org/10.1016/j.psychsport.2020.101845

Chinkov, A. E., & Holt, N. L. (2016). Implicit transfer of life skills through participation in Brazilian jiu-jitsu. *Journal of Applied Sport Psychology*, 28(2), 139–153. https://doi.org/10.1080/10413200.2015.1086447

Coakley, J. (2021). Neoliberalism and community sport coaching in the United States: Meeting challenges with an informed strategy. In B. Ives, P. Potrac & L. Nelson (Eds.), *Community sport coaching: Policies and practice* (pp. 25–44). Routledge. https://doi.org/10.4324/9781003159063-4

Danish, S., Forneris, T., Hodge, K., & Heke, I. (2004). Enhancing youth development through sport. *World Leisure*, 46(3), 38–49. https://doi.org/10.1080/04419057.2004.9674365

Danish, S. J. (1983). Musings about personal competence: The contributions of sport, health, and fitness. *American Journal of Community Psychology*, 11(3), 221–240. https://doi.org/10.1007/BF00893365

Gould, D., & Carson, S. (2008). Life skills development through sport: Current status and future directions. *International Review of Sport and Exercise Psychology, 1*(1), 58–78. https://doi.org/10.1080/17509840701834573

Holt, N., Neely, K., Slater, L., Camiré, M., Côté, J., Fraser-Thomas, J., MacDonald, D., Strachan, L., & Tamminen, K. A. (2017). A grounded theory of positive youth development through sport based on results from a qualitative meta-study. *International Review of Sport and Exercise Psychology, 10*(1), 1–49. https://doi.org/10.1080/1750984X.2016.1180704

Jones, M. I., & Lavallee, D. (2009). Exploring the life skills needs of British adolescent athletes. *Psychology of Sport and Exercise, 10*(1), 159–167. https://doi.org/10.1016/j.psychsport.2008.06.005

Kramers, S., Camiré, M., Ciampolini, V., & Milistetd, M. (2022). Development of a life skills self-assessment tool for coaches. *Journal of Sport Psychology in Action, 13*(1), 54–64. https://doi.org/10.1080/21520704.2021.1888832

Kwauk, C. T. (2022). Empowering girls through sport: A gender transformative approach to life skills? In J. DeJaeghere & E. Murphy-Graham (Eds.), *Life skills education for youth: Critical perspectives* (pp. 91–111). Springer. https://doi.org/10.1007/978-3-030-85214-6_5

Pierce, S., Gould, D., & Camiré, M. (2017). Definition and model of life skills transfer. *International Review of Sport and Exercise Psychology, 10*(1), 186–211. https://doi.org/10.1080/1750984X.2016.1199727

Pierce, S., Kendellen, K., Camiré, M., & Gould, D. (2018). Strategies for coaching for life skills transfer. *Journal of Sport Psychology in Action, 9*(1), 11–20. https://doi.org/10.1080/21520704.2016.1263982

Ronkainen, N., Aggerholm, K., Ryba, T., & Allen-Collinson, J. (2021). Learning in sport: From life skills to existential learning. *Sport, Education and Society, 26*(2), 214–227. https://doi.org/10.1080/13573322.2020.1712655

Turnnidge, J., Côté, J., & Hancock, D. J. (2014). Positive youth development from sport to life: Explicit or implicit transfer? *Quest, 66*(2), 203–217. https://doi.org/10.1080/00336297.2013.867275

Wilson Outley, C., & Blyth, D. (2020). Race, antiracism, and youth development: From awareness to sustained action. *Journal of Youth Development, 15*(5), 1–15. https://doi.org/10.5195/jyd.2020.1005

The Art of Teaching Values and Life Skills
Part 4

Chapter Eleven

The Intentional Approach to Teaching Values and Life Skills

Yvonne Seng

INTRODUCTION

An expanding corpus of research highlights the role of physical education and sports (PES) in positive youth development (PYD) (Jacobs & Wright, 2018). PYD empowers youth through a strength-based and asset-focused approach (Holt et al., 2020; Lerner, 2005), and PES offers an accessible and engaging platform for PYD that appeals to the sports-inclined youth (Martinek & Hemphill, 2020). PES is increasingly recognised as a valuable platform for fostering PYD, promoting values and life skills (VLS) and 21st-century competencies vital for holistic youth development (Federico, 2019; Newman, 2020; Santos et al., 2019).

Historically, PES has been instrumental in youth development. Extensive research attests to its efficacy in promoting a broad spectrum of positive youth developmental outcomes (Bean & Forneris, 2017; Koh & Camiré, 2015; Newman, 2020). However, researchers have cautioned against undiscerning evangelism on the inherent benefits of PES participation (Camiré & Santos, 2019). They argue that the initial belief that PES automatically leads to positive youth outcomes may have been overstated. Mere participation in PES does not inherently guarantee positive developmental outcomes; instead, it requires intentionality to promote PYD through PES (Camiré & Santos, 2019). Walker (2019) and Kerrick (2015) define intentionality as the purposeful and strategic decisions and actions to create opportunities to optimise developmental outcomes. Many studies also support this notion of intentionality (e.g., Bean & Forneris, 2017; Camiré et al., 2012; Gould et al., 2013; Newman et al., 2023). The academic consensus affirms PES as a powerful catalyst for PYD, contingent upon thoughtful design, intentional implementation, and adept facilitation by trained adults (Newman et al., 2023).

DOI: 10.4324/9781032688657-15

While interest in this field of research has increased significantly in recent years, a notable gap exists in understanding how practitioners intentionally apply strategies to teach VLS and ensure their application extends beyond PES, especially in the Asian context. Walker (2019) noted the substantial influence of cultural backgrounds on youth's learning, values, behaviours, thoughts, emotions, and identity. Additionally, Morgan et al. (2006) highlighted the cultural disparities in the pedagogical approaches used by physical education teachers and sports coaches (PETSC) in Singapore and the United Kingdom. Nonetheless, limited studies in non-Western settings have been conducted to address this gap (Koh et al., 2016; Ma & Shek, 2019; Xie et al., 2021), highlighting the urgent need for culturally relevant PES-PYD interventions that are effective and resonant with Asian youth (Ma & Shek, 2019).

Considering the growing interest and persistent gaps in this area, this chapter introduces the T^2VLS_{PES} Framework and intervention as a comprehensive tool to guide the intentional and effective design and implementation of PES-PYD. Validated by Seng (2022), the T^2VLS_{PES} Framework and dual cyclical intervention will significantly contribute to the ongoing discourse on PYD in PES, providing actionable insights for educators, sports practitioners, and policymakers worldwide.

APPLIED INSIGHTS

PES-Based PYD Intervention

Early interventions in youth development are crucial in mitigating adolescent risks and enhancing PYD (Ma & Shek, 2019). The scope of PES-PYD interventions has evolved beyond physical health to include cognitive, affective, social, and lifestyle development (Bailey, 2006). Empirical evidence suggests that an intentional approach is imperative for effective PES-PYD interventions (Bean & Forneris, 2017; Koh et al., 2016; Newman et al., 2023). PETSC play a pivotal role in offering an optimal learning experience in PES that significantly impacts the development of VLS and fosters PYD. However, recent studies highlight that PETSC lack intentional approaches and concrete strategies to develop VLS through PES (Santos et al., 2019). Although evidence-based guidelines have been made more accessible, a research-practice gap remains (Gaion et al., 2020). Consequently, the T^2VLS_{PES} Framework and intervention aim to bridge this gap by introducing a comprehensive training plan for the PETSC.

Studies also indicate that involving classroom teachers and parents (CTP) as supportive social agents in PES-PYD programmes enhances youth development (Santos et al., 2019). Koh et al. (2016) highlighted that the involvement of CTP was instrumental in facilitating the transfer of values to contexts beyond PES, accentuating the significance of their support in promoting PYD. Conclusively, integrating these elements into the PES-PYD intervention is vital for its success (Jacobs & Wright, 2018).

T²VLS$_{PES}$ Framework and Intervention

A robust and well-structured framework is crucial for shaping the development of effective PES-PYD interventions (Whitley et al., 2019). It provides a systematic structure and coherent alignment to existing PYD literature and best practices, ensuring the intervention is evidence-based and theoretically grounded. Moreover, Newman et al. (2017) suggest that inadequate theoretical insight into PES-PYD and the role of stakeholders might compromise the success of these interventions. Some sports-based PYD interventions have documented the application of frameworks, models, and theoretical approaches; however, their use remains notably inconsistent (Whitley et al., 2019). For instance, some studies lack clear alignment between the chosen framework and the research objectives. This inconsistency can compromise the validity and reliability of the research findings, making it challenging to draw meaningful conclusions (Wright et al., 2010). While the PYD framework has been a predominant theoretical lens for enhancing our knowledge of the psychosocial growth in youth for more than two decades (Bruner et al., 2023), there is a need for a critical examination of its limitations and to consider alternative conceptual approaches to studying PES-PYD (Camiré et al., 2023).

Considering the complexity of teaching and facilitating the transference of VLS through PES, the development of the T²VLS$_{PES}$ Framework was conscientiously guided by thorough research. The framework integrates best practices that align with existing literature to offer practical guidance for practitioners. This rigorous approach ensures the integration of critical elements into the comprehensive framework to bridge existing research gaps. The T²VLS$_{PES}$ Framework advances existing conceptual PYD models and frameworks to provide practitioners and policymakers with an extensive compendium for designing comprehensive interventions to develop VLS more intentionally. It serves as a strategic resource for PETSC, educational leaders, and organisations to frame their intentional approach to teaching and facilitating the transference of VLS through PES. After an extensive review of the existing literature on PYD frameworks, Petitpas et al.'s (2005) framework was selected to guide the development of the T^2VLS_{PES} Framework and intervention. The framework provides a practical, evidence-based, and theory-grounded approach to planning youth sports programmes that promote psychosocial development. Petitpas et al.'s (2005) framework offers a practical, theory-based method for designing youth sports programmes that foster psychosocial development. It identifies four critical areas for effective PYD: a psychologically safe and motivating context well-supported by positive external assets, opportunities for developing internal assets, and continuous evaluation and research. These components are crucial for creating a structured intervention to develop VLS through PES.

The T^2VLS_{PES} Framework adapted Petitpas et al.'s (2005) framework to synthesise the insights from the PYD literature and the best practices of exemplary PETSC into the four critical areas: (1) context, (2) external assets, (3) internal assets, and (4) research and evaluation. The T^2VLS_{PES} Framework guides practitioners from the preparation to the delivery phase. The preparation stage begins with establishing a psychologically safe environment that supports autonomy, motivation, and engagement, as well as training supportive and caring adults. The delivery stage involves implicit and explicit teaching and facilitating the transference of VLS, which are essential for navigating life challenges and addressing the assessment and challenges to evaluate the intervention. The synthesised research findings and best practices from Seng's (2022) study are well-fitted in the T^2VLS_{PES} Framework depicted in Figure 11.1.

The T^2VLS_{PES} Framework encapsulates the four critical areas essential for a robust PES-PYD intervention:

Context

A safe and supportive environment is fundamental for physical, psychological, cognitive, and social growth during the youth's critical development period (Newman, 2020). Effective PES-PYD interventions foster a psychologically safe climate where youth feel secure,

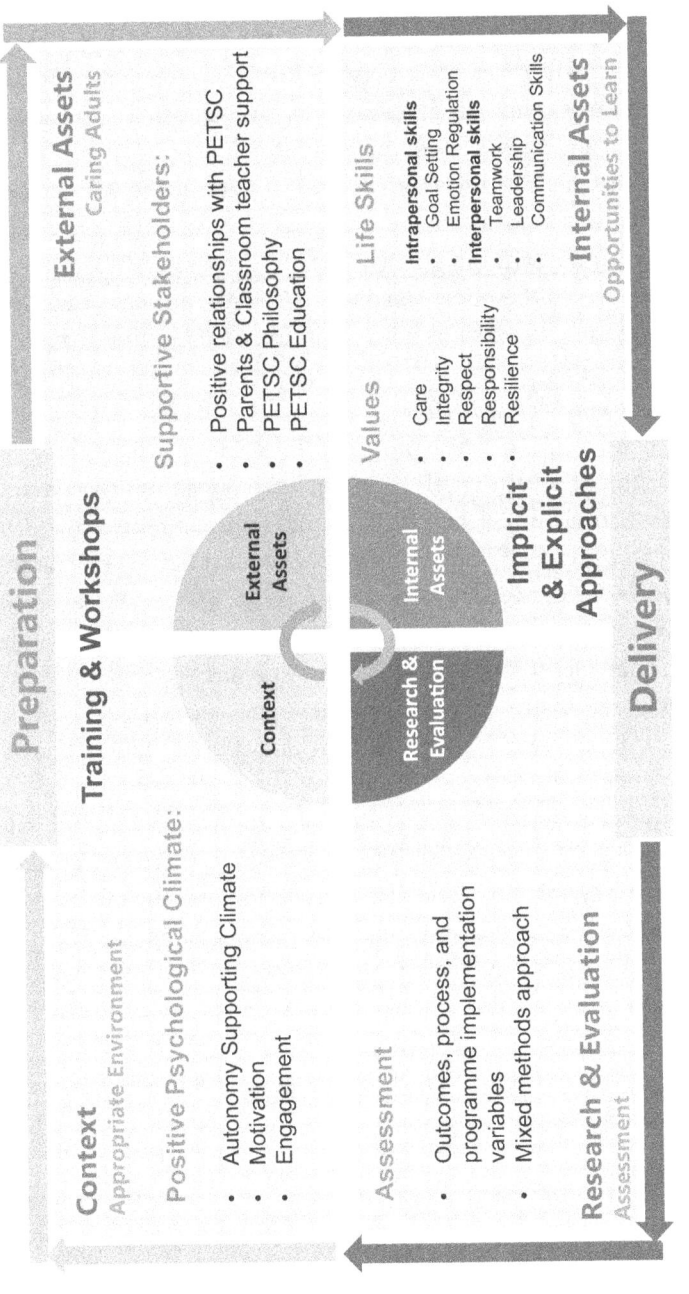

Figure 11.1 T²VLS_PES Framework – A framework for PES-based PYD intervention Seng (2022)

motivated, and respected (Federico, 2019; Holt et al., 2020). The strong correlations observed among motivation, engagement, and PYD outcomes accentuate the importance of a supportive and motivating environment (Hansen & Larson, 2007). A motivating climate can provide a psychologically safe environment that encourages positive youth outcomes. Autonomy support has been identified as a crucial component of the motivational climate in the PES setting; it fosters intrinsic motivation and engagement (Deci & Ryan, 2008). Furthermore, autonomy-supportive climates promote PYD and significantly influence the effectiveness of PYD programmes (Federico, 2019). Supportive relationships with adults like PETSC in an autonomy-supportive climate enhance youth's psychosocial, social, and physical growth (Barkoukis et al., 2020).

Consequently, PETSC must purposefully create a psychologically safe environment where youth feel safe, encouraged, motivated and respected when planning the PES-PYD intervention (Federico, 2019). This intentional structure of an appropriate context has to begin at the intervention's preparation stage. According to the T^2VLS_{PES} Framework, the intervention includes training the PETSC to support youth autonomy with strategies to establish autonomy-supportive climates.

The intervention incorporates strategies from the exemplary PETSC and existing PYD research.14 outstanding Singapore PETSC, acknowledged for their substantial contributions to youth's positive development, were interviewed to examine how they teach and facilitate the transference of VLS through PES and assist in transferring these acquired VLS beyond the PES context. The findings were synthesised with the PYD literature to formulate the strategies in the T^2VLS_{PES} intervention (Seng, 2022). These strategies include providing choices, offering rationales, acknowledging feelings, creating opportunities for initiative, giving informational feedback, avoiding over-control, structuring reward systems thoughtfully, building on strengths, facilitating decision-making, and limiting ego involvement (Table 11.1). The success of the PYD intervention is significantly influenced by the expertise and skillfulness of those implementing it. Hence, comprehensive training for the PETSC is crucial to optimising PES's potential as a context for developing and transferring VLS through PES (Koh & Camiré, 2015). However, research highlighted that PETSC lack concrete strategies and skills to promote the development of VLS (Santos et al., 2019). Most PETSC education focuses on athletic performance

Table 11.1 T²VLS$_{PES}$ Strategies to Build Autonomy-Supportive Climate (Seng, 2022)

ASC Strategies	Explicit Actions
a) Provide choices within limits	• Provide a range of activities for students to choose from • Clarify responsibilities, expectations and consequences • Involve students in decision-making and solution finding
b) Offer rationales for activity	• Explain the relevance of activities/tasks/rules/tactics • Allow students to make informed choices
c) Acknowledge feelings and perspectives	• Be warm and caring • Inquire about students' feelings and perspectives • Provide emotional support
d) Create opportunities to demonstrate initiative	• Assign students with responsibilities of leading warm-ups, setting targets, resolving problems
e) Provide informational feedback	• Provide factual, non-judgemental feedback • Provide positive and constructive feedback to facilitate competence satisfaction
f) Avoid overt control and criticism	• Focus on improvement and mastery • Convey trust with warmth and affection • Avoid judgemental criticism
g) Structure reward system thoughtfully	• Avoid rewards for tasks that students are enjoying • Provide rewards only when necessary
h) Build on strengths and affirm competency	• Acknowledge students' strengths • Affirm improvement and mastery to promote a sense of competency • Provide genuine encouragement
i) Provide opportunities for decision-making	• Plan for decision-making activities/tasks • Allow sufficient time for decision-making
j) Limit ego involvement in activities	• Avoid activities/tasks that involve ego • Facilitate self-improvement • Avoid comparison

enhancement, with very little attention given to PYD (Bean et al., 2018). Furthermore, most PETSC perceive that PYD occurs incidentally through mere participation in PES (Santos et al., 2019). This gap underscores the need for targeted comprehensive PYD training within PETSC education to fully harness the potential of PES in the development of VLS.

In the T_2VLS^{PES} intervention, a series of workshops are specially designed for the PETSC to enhance their knowledge and skills. The PETSC participate in a pre-intervention workshop focusing on strategies to foster autonomy-supportive climates. At the start of the workshop, the trainer will highlight the importance of creating an autonomy-supportive environment to enhance youth's motivation and engagement in the PES-PYD intervention. Through the workshop, the PETSC develop a good understanding of the strategies and the explicit actions backed by scholarly research for implementing these strategies (Table 11.1) (Seng, 2022). For example, PETSC can involve the youth in decision-making to promote autonomy. With the guidance of the trainer, these strategies are integrated into every lesson plan (Appendix A), ensuring each PES session intentionally fosters an autonomy-supportive environment conducive to holistic growth in youth. The motivational climate established by PETSC critically influenced the quality of motivation and engagement and, ultimately, the intervention's overall effectiveness.

External Assets

In the T^2VLS_{PES} Framework, the external assets refer to the involvement of caring adults to teach, support, and facilitate the transference of VLS beyond PES. Research confirms that PYD flourishes in nurturing and supportive environments, with PETSC and CTP playing a pivotal role in PES settings (Petitpas et al., 2005; Santos et al., 2019). Integrating the efforts of schools and families is pivotal to the success of the T^2VLS_{PES} intervention.

During the pre-intervention workshop, PETSC receive a comprehensive overview of the ten-week T^2VLS_{PES} intervention, understanding the intervention background, objectives, design, and timeline. The PETSC will then engage in a discussion on values, life skills, and the ten targeted VLS in this intervention to establish a clear understanding of the operational definitions (see Appendix B). Emphasis will be placed on aligning PETSC's personal beliefs, values, and teaching philosophy with the intervention's goals. Such alignment ensures a coherent and purposeful approach to fostering PYD through PES, thereby enhancing the effectiveness of the intervention (Martens & Vealey, 2023; Xie et al., 2021).

Contrary to expectations, research indicates a significant gap in the formal training for PETSC regarding teaching VLS and their application beyond the PES context. PETSC lack the concrete strategies and skills to teach and facilitate the transfer of PYD (Santos et al., 2019). Moreover, some PETSC continue to assume that the VLS acquired in PES automatically transfer to other life domains (Camiré, 2015). To bridge these gaps, it is paramount for PETSC to undergo training in implicit and explicit strategies for effective teaching of VLS, along with strategies to facilitate the transference of VLS beyond the PES context. During the pre-intervention workshop, each strategy is thoroughly explained, preparing the PETSC to proficiently apply these strategies as detailed in Tables 11.2 and 11.3 (Seng, 2022). For example, the PETSC can role model the VLS taught and provide opportunities for the youth to demonstrate the VLS during PES. At the end of each session, the PETSC can facilitate transfer by explaining how the VLS can be useful in other contexts.

Table 11.2 T^2VLS_{PES} Strategies to Teach VLS (Seng, 2022)

Strategies to Teach Values and Life Skills
Implicit approach
• Develop a philosophy and align with organisation
• Develop a positive relationship with students
• Create awareness in VLS development
• Take advantage of teachable moments
• Act as a role model
Explicit approach
• Provide explicit instructions
• Teach systematically
• Focus on one skill at a time
• Teach general concepts – provide examples of how this skill applies in non-sports settings
• Provide opportunities to display skills – set situations
• Set goals/targets
• Provide encouragement/feedback
• Foster team spirit
• Discussion/debrief
• Make students accountable
• Reflection
• Teacher-parent Involvement
• Use of social media

Table 11.3 T²VLS$_{PES}$ Strategies to Facilitate the Transference of VLS (Seng, 2022)

Strategies Facilitate the Transference of VLS beyond the PES Context
Implicit approach
• Automatic transfer
Explicit approach
• Provide practice opportunities for transfer of VLS
• Purposeful discussion
• Provide similar elements and settings in sports context to other contexts
• Explain how VLS can be useful in other contexts
• Ask students to put VLS into practice in another area of life
• Build confidence in the ability to transfer
• Structure debriefs at the end of the session
• Encourage reflection on the youth's transfer experience

Subsequently, four more reflective workshops are conducted at the end of each week of intervention to enable PETSC to assess the effectiveness of the strategies with the trainer. In the second half of the intervention, the PETSC gained more autonomy in selecting the strategies, reinforcing their grasp on them. This iterative process deepens understanding of the strategies and gives the youth a second engagement with the VLS. Through repeated exposure and reflection, both the PETSC and youth develop a more nuanced understanding, allowing for more meaningful internalisation and application.

In the T²VLS$_{PES}$ intervention, the CTP play a critical role alongside the PETSC by reinforcing the VLS taught in the intervention. Before the intervention, CTP will participate in a dedicated workshop to clarify their role in reinforcing VLS learned and facilitating the transference to the classroom and home contexts. The workshop outlines the intervention objectives, schedule, and key terms. It focuses on effective transfer strategies and observational skills for identifying and reinforcing VLS in the classroom or at home. Additionally, each CTP receives a handbook with behavioural checklists to systematically track progress throughout the ten-week duration. The comprehensive approach ensures that CTP can provide valuable insights and feedback at the end of the intervention. The primary goal of the CTP workshop is to empower the CTP with the essential tools and knowledge to support and extend the learning of VLS beyond PES contexts.

The T²VLS$_{PES}$ intervention exemplifies an intentional approach to PES-PYD with the collaborative roles of PETSC and CTP in the development and transference of VLS. Through the strategic planning of the targeted pre-intervention workshop, PETSC and CTP are equipped with essential tools to teach VLS and facilitate their transference beyond PES. The purposeful integration of implicit and explicit strategies for promoting VLS ensures a comprehensive framework that contributes to a robust PES-PYD intervention.

Internal Assets

In a psychologically safe environment, coupled with supportive and well-trained PETSC and CTP, the T²VLS$_{PES}$ intervention is ready to enter the delivery phase. At this phase, the PETSC systematically present opportunities for the youth to acquire internal assets vital for navigating life challenges and opportunities. The internal assets in this intervention are the ten VLS as defined in Appendix B. This intervention seamlessly integrates the PES and PYD instructions, aligning with the perspective of Hellison and Walsh (2002), who advocate that simultaneous teaching of both results in deeper learning than addressing them separately.

During the pre-intervention workshop, the PETSC are guided to use the T²VLS$_{PES}$ lesson plan template (Appendix A) to integrate both PES and VLS instructions and activities. They will first design the learning activities to achieve the PES lesson objectives. Thereafter, they will select the most appropriate strategies to promote an autonomy-supportive climate, teach VLS, and facilitate transference beyond PES. The strategies are designed to be infused into the PES activities without compromising the acquisition of the sports skills. As depicted in the sample lesson plan (Appendix A), for example, PETSC can integrate the teaching of responsibility by providing explicit instructions for the youth to take responsibility to get free to receive a pass. At the same time, they should be accountable for defending without infringing on the three-feet rule. PETSC can provide rationales for the three-feet rule, allowing youth to make decisions in an autonomy-supportive environment to foster autonomy. Additionally, PETSC can facilitate purposeful discussions and encourage the youth to reflect on how the VLS acquired can be applied in classroom and home contexts.

Kolb's (1984) experiential learning theory (ELT) provides a framework for understanding how individuals learn through experience, reflection, and applying knowledge to real-world contexts, making it particularly relevant to the learning of the internal assets in this intervention. This theory's key experiential and reflective processes have been proven to be highly beneficial in the PES context (Bethell & Morgan, 2011). It includes a four-stage cyclical model that involves concrete experience, reflective observation, abstract conceptualisation, and active experimentation.

At the start of the intervention, PETSC utilise the newly acquired strategies to teach VLS explicitly, providing concrete learning experiences through intentionally designed activities. In the second stage, the youth reflect on their experiences guided by reflective questions in their T^2VLS_{PES} journal (e.g., "How did I demonstrate integrity during PE?" "How can I apply integrity at home?"). These reflections, a vital component of Kolb's model, turned experiences into educational moments. In the third stage, the youth plan the application of VLS in classroom and home environments and, finally, apply VLS in various contexts, demonstrating the transference. The experiential learning process is depicted in Figure 11.2.

This experiential learning allows youth to construct knowledge, develop skills, and continuously derive value from their experiences. Their success in learning and transference of targeted VLS to the classroom and home contexts is facilitated by opportunities presented by PETSC and supported by CTP.

Research and Evaluation

Many programmes lack adequate planning for evaluation, and only a few conduct longitudinal evaluations post-intervention. Vella et al. (2012) highlighted the importance of longitudinal evaluations to determine the maintenance effect of interventions and assess the transference to real-world contexts beyond the intervention period. The T^2VLS_{PES} intervention addresses this by incorporating longitudinal evaluations in its protocols, assessing the effects six months after the end of the intervention. This approach monitors and ensures the continual impact of the VLS learning beyond the intervention's time frame and context. The evaluation protocol includes three data

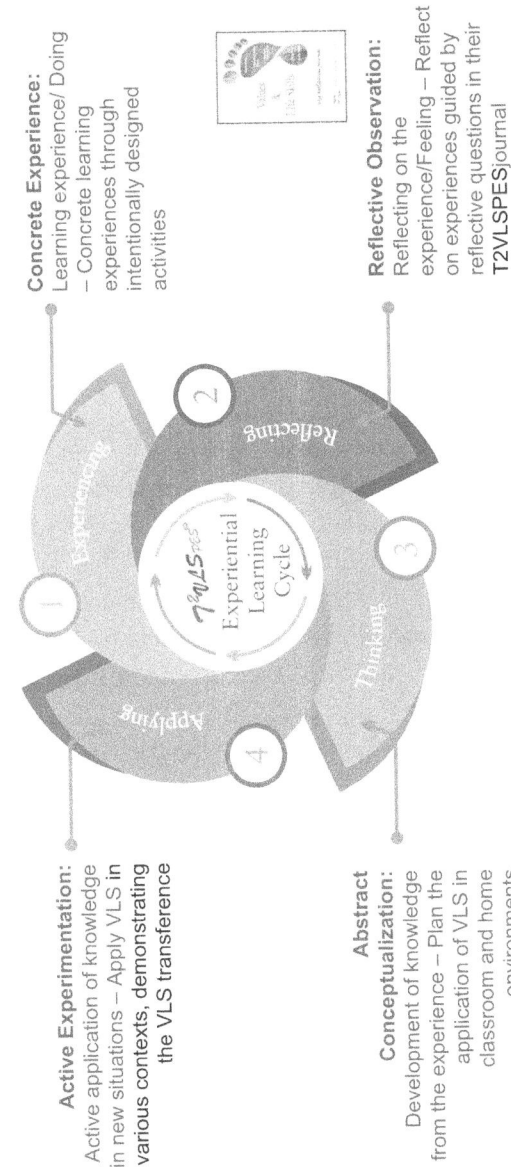

Figure 11.2 The experiential learning cycle for the youth's learning experience in T²VLS_PES

11 The Intentional Approach to Teaching Values and Life Skills

Concrete Experience:
Learning experience/Doing – Concrete learning experiences through intentionally designed activities

Reflective Observation:
Reflecting on the experience/Feeling – Reflect on experiences guided by reflective questions in their T2VLSPESjournal

Abstract Conceptualization:
Development of knowledge from the experience – Plan the application of VLS in classroom and home environments

Active Experimentation:
Active application of knowledge in new situations – Apply VLS in various contexts, demonstrating the VLS transference

collection points using validated instruments: before the intervention, immediately afterwards, and six months later (Seng, 2022). Mixed methods are recommended for assessing and evaluating the intervention due to their innovative approach to complex research (Salehi & Golafshani, 2010). The complementary nature of quantitative and qualitative methods provides a comprehensive way to tackle intricate research questions and yields more nuanced insights (Tashakkori & Teddie, 1998).

T²VLS$_{PES}$ Dual Cyclical Intervention

Based on the T²VLS$_{PES}$ Framework, the dual cyclical intervention design in Figure 11.3 depicts the cyclical flow of the intervention. The outer cycle illustrates the four critical components of the framework that guided the planning and training stages to prepare the PETSC to intentionally teach and facilitate the transference of the VLS and promote an autonomy-supportive climate. The implicit and explicit strategies are integrated into the delivery stage to optimise the effectiveness of the intervention. The inner cycle focuses on the youth's experiential learning within an autonomy-supportive climate. This includes engaging the youth in concrete experience, reflecting on these experiences, and applying the knowledge gained to real-world contexts. These two cycles complement each other to bring deeper and more meaningful learning (Seng, 2022).

This ten-week T²VLS$_{PES}$ intervention has been implemented in Seng's (2022) study. The PETSC's intentionality in promoting VLS through PES and the facilitation of the transference to the classroom and home contexts has been reported to have positive and significant effects on VLS outcomes. The positive maintenance and transference effects also highlighted the internalisation of the VLS learned and the long-term effects of the intervention. The internalisation of the acquired VLS would enable the students to gain greater benefits in the long term, providing the value compass and life skills to face the demands and challenges in life and become productive and contributing citizens in the community.

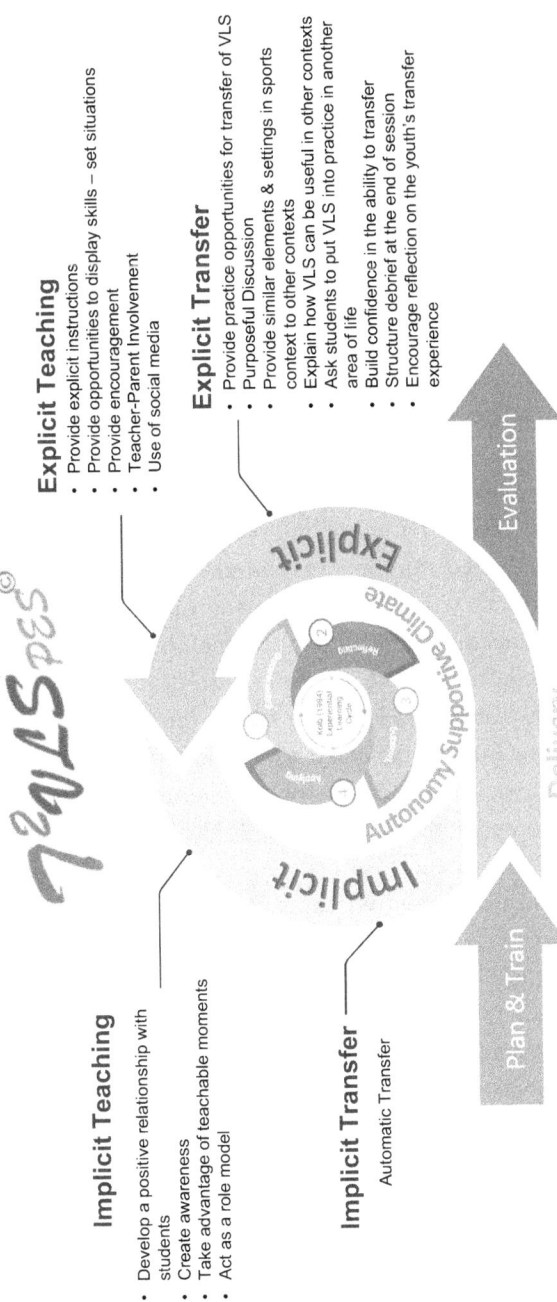

Figure 11.3 T²VLS$_{PES}$ dual cyclical intervention (Seng, 2022)

Explicit Teaching
- Provide explicit instructions
- Provide opportunities to display skills – set situations
- Provide encouragement
- Teacher-Parent Involvement
- Use of social media

Explicit Transfer
- Provide practice opportunities for transfer of VLS
- Purposeful Discussion
- Provide similar elements & settings in sports context to other contexts
- Explain how VLS can be useful in other contexts
- Ask students to put VLS into practice in another area of life
- Build confidence in the ability to transfer
- Structure debrief at the end of session
- Encourage reflection on the youth's transfer experience

Implicit Teaching
- Develop a positive relationship with students
- Create awareness
- Take advantage of teachable moments
- Act as a role model

Implicit Transfer
- Automatic Transfer

SUMMARY AND FUTURE DIRECTIONS

This chapter examines the intricacies of the intentional teaching approach and facilitating VLS transference through PES with the comprehensive and robust T²VLS$_{PES}$ Framework and intervention. The framework amalgamates insights from existing PYD research and the exemplary practices of Singapore's PETSC to design a well-structured and intentional intervention. The T²VLS$_{PES}$ intervention incorporates both implicit and explicit strategies to foster an autonomy-supportive climate conducive to learning VLS (Seng, 2022). The PETSC and CTP are equipped with essential strategies and tools to develop VLS through PES intentionally, optimising the effectiveness of the intervention. The intervention participants undergo the cyclical learning process through experiential learning, allowing them to construct knowledge through reflection, conceptualisation, and application.

However, the ambitious nature of the T²VLS$_{PES}$ to cover extensive content within a compact ten-week intervention presents a notable challenge. The limited duration may hinder thorough coverage and reinforcement of all ten VLS, and ensuring each aspect receives adequate attention and practice within the timeframe is crucial but demanding. It is recommended that the duration of the intervention be extended to allow for deeper learning. With a longer duration, the T²VLS$_{PES}$ intervention can be expanded to a whole-school approach, aligning the VLS schedule with the school curriculum and integrating the stakeholders more effectively (Xie et al., 2021). Literature has also suggested that a direct partnership between the PETSC and parents to increase parental involvement warrants future research (Xie et al., 2021).

In conclusion, the T²VLS$_{PES}$ Framework and intervention significantly contribute to the discourse in PES-PYD. With its potential applicability and generalisability within and beyond Asia, T²VLS$_{PES}$ offers valuable insights for educators and policymakers to enhance the intentional approach to teach and facilitate the transference of VLS through PES (Seng, 2022).

APPENDIX A

Sample of T²VLSPES Lesson Plan

Sports Skills: Attacking and Defending Moves in Netball
Targeted Life Skills: Responsibility

Group Activities	Strategies to Teach VLS	Strategies to Facilitate Transfer VLS	Strategies to promote Autonomy-Supportive Climate
Activity (Basics 1):	**Provide explicit instructions**	**Purposeful Discussion**	**Provide opportunities for decision making**
Attacking Moves: Straight Leads to receive a pass	Provide clear instructions on the straight lead drills and highlight that they are **responsible for making moves to free themselves to receive the ball.**	Ask how they can demonstrate **responsibility in class and at home.** Provide some examples.	Decision-making task: Players will get to **decide which direction they want to do the straight leads after practice.** Emphasize that they have a choice. Discuss **how their decision will impact** on the team play. Ask **what decisions they make in school and at home** and **how their decisions can affect others.**
In groups of 4: 1 thrower and 3 workers			
■ Make straight lead to the ball			
■ Make lead to the right			
■ Make lead to the left			
■ Decide on the direction and make the lead to receive a pass			
Activity (Basics 2):	**Make athletes accountable**	**Encourage reflection on the youth's transfer experience**	**Offer rationales for activity structures**
Defending Moves: 3 feet-Hands-Over when defending an opponent with the ball	The onus is on the players to ensure they defend without infringing the rules of the game. Highlight that they are responsible to **adhere to the rules to avoid losing possession for the team.**	Ask how they can demonstrate **responsibility in other situations on the court.** Get the students to **reflect on how they can transfer the values learned in PES to other contexts like home and the classroom.**	**Offer rationales:** Explain why there is a need to ensure 3-feet before hands-over. Make links to the importance of maintaining personal space in other context: Personal space is crucial for ensuring physical and psychological well-being, limiting disease transmission, and fostering respectful, non-threatening interactions.
Partner work:			
■ A will toss the ball up and jump to receive the ball.			
■ B will hop back to establish 3-feet before putting the arms up			

The Intentional Approach to Teaching Values and Life Skills

APPENDIX B

Operational Definition of Key Terms

Variables	Operational definitions
Values	"[T]he principles and fundamental convictions which act as general guides to behaviour, the standards by which particular actions are judged to be good or desirable" (Halstead & Taylor, 2000, p. 169).
Life Skills	"[T]hose skills that enable individuals to succeed in the different environments in which they live, such as school, home and in their neighbourhoods. Life skills can be behavioural (communicating effectively with peers and adults) or cognitive (making effective decisions); interpersonal (being assertive) or intrapersonal (setting goals)" (Danish et al., 2004, p. 40).
Care	Act with kindness and compassion and contribute to the betterment of the community and the world. (Doing favours and good deeds for others who are in difficulty.)
Integrity	Uphold ethical principles and have the moral courage to stand up for what is right. (Willingness to take action, despite unfavourable circumstances, to preserve what is perceived as morally right.)
Resilience	Demonstrate emotional strength and persevere in the face of challenges. Show courage, optimism, adaptability, and resourcefulness. (Ability to recover from or adjust to difficulties or discouragement.)
Respect	Demonstrate respect when they believe in their own self-worth and the intrinsic worth of people. (Willingness to treat others with courtesy and due attention despite the existence of differences.)
Responsibility	Taking private and public ownership of their feelings, behaviours, and commitments. (Recognise they have a duty to themselves, their families, community, nation, and the world, and fulfil their responsibilities with love and commitment.)
Communication skills	Ability to communicate with others.
Goal Setting	Development of an action plan designed to motivate and guide a person or group towards a goal.
Leadership	Influencing, directing, and motivating other group members towards collective success.

(Continued)

Variables	Operational definitions
Teamwork	Ability to work with others in a group for a common purpose.
Intrinsic Motivation	Energises and sustains activities and is characterised by personal enjoyment, interest, or pleasure.
Engagement	A state of optimal functioning, resulting from both personal and contextual factors that support behavioural integration and encourage satisfaction of psychological needs. (Jowett et al., 2016)
Autonomy-Supportive	Encouraged to make choices and take initiatives while criticisms, pressures, and controls are minimised. These behaviours convey a message of trust in athletes' abilities, thus influencing athletes' perceptions of competence. (Mageau & Vallerand, 2003)

REFERENCE

Bailey, R. (2006). Physical education and sport in schools: A review of benefits and outcomes. *Journal of School Health*, 76(8), 397–401. https://doi.org/10.1111/j.1746-1561.2006.00132.x

Barkoukis, V., Chatzisarantis, N., & Hagger, M. S. (2020). Effects of a school-based intervention on motivation for out-of-school physical activity participation. *Research Quarterly for Exercise and Sport*, 1–15. https://doi.org/10.1080/02701367.2020.1751029

Bean, C., & Forneris, T. (2017). Is life skill development a by-product of sports participation? Perceptions of youth sport coaches. *Journal of Applied Sport Psychology*, 29(2), 234–250. https://doi.org/10.1080/10413200.2016.1231723

Bean, C., Kramers, S., Forneris, T., & Camiré, M. (2018). The implicit/explicit continuum of life skills development and transfer. *Quest*, 70(4), 456–470. https://doi.org/10.1080/00336297.2018.1451348

Bethell, S., & Morgan, K. (2011). Problem-based and experiential learning: Engaging students in an undergraduate physical education module. *Journal of Hospitality, Leisure, Sport and Tourism Education*, 10(1), 128–134.

Bruner, M. W., McLaren, C. D., Sutcliffe, J. T., Gardner, L. A., Lubans, D. R., Smith, J. J., & Vella, S. A. (2023). The effect of sport-based interventions on positive youth development: A systematic review and meta-analysis. *International Review of Sport and Exercise Psychology*, 16(1), 368–395.

Camiré, M., & Santos, F. (2019). Promoting positive youth development and life skills in youth sport: Challenges and opportunities amidst increased professionalization. *Rui Resende Hugo Sarmento*, 5(1), 27–34.

Camiré, M., Santos, F., Newman, T., Vella, S., MacDonald, D. J., Milistetd, M., Pierce, S. & Strachan, L. (2023). Positive youth development as a guiding framework in sports research: Is it time to plan for a transition? *Psychology of Sport and Exercise*, 2023, 102505. https://doi.org/10.1016/j.psychsport.2023.102505

Camiré, M., Trudel, P., & Forneris, T. (2012). Coaching and transferring life skills: Philosophies and strategies used by model high school coaches. *The Sport Psychologist*, 26(2), 243–260. https://doi.org/10.1123/tsp.26.2.243

Danish, S. J., Forneris, T., Hodge, K., & Heke, I. (2004). Enhancing youth development through sport. *World Leisure Journal*, 46(3), 38–49. https://doi.org/10.1080/04419057.2004.9674365

Deci, E. L., & Ryan, R. M. (2008). Self-determination theory: A macrotheory of human motivation, development, and health. *Canadian Psychology*, 49(3), 182–185. https://doi.org/10.1037/a0012801

Federico, M. (2019). *Does sports build positive youth development? A synthesis of the research literature* (Master dissertation, State University of New York).

Gaion, P., Milistetd, M., Santos, F., Contreira, A., Arantes, L., & Caruzzo, N. (2020). Coaching positive youth development in Brazil: Recommendations for coach education programs. *International Sport Coaching Journal*, 7(1), 82–88. https://doi.org/10.1123/iscj.2018-0106

Gould, D., Carson, S., & Blanton, J. (2013). Coaching life skills. In P. Potrac, W. Gilbert, & J. Dension (Eds.), *Routledge handbook of sports coaching* (pp. 259–270). Routledge.

Halstead, J. M., & Taylor, M. J. (2000). Learning and teaching about values: A review of recent research. *Cambridge Journal of Education*, 30(2), 169–202.

Hansen, D. M., & Larson, R. W. (2007). Amplifiers of developmental and negative experiences in organized activities: Dosage, motivation, lead roles, and adult-youth ratios. *Journal of Applied Developmental Psychology*, 28(4), 360–374. https://doi.org/10.1016/j.appdev.2007.04.006

Hellison, D., & Walsh, D. (2002). Responsibility-based youth programs evaluation: Investigating the investigations. *Quest*, 54(4), 292–307. https://doi.org/10.1080/00336297.2002.10491780

Holt, N. L., Deal, C. J., & Pankow, K. (2020). Positive youth development through sport. In G. Tenenbaum, & R. C. Eklund, (Eds.). *Handbook of sport psychology* (pp. 429–446). John Wiley & Sons. https://doi.org/10.1002/9781119568124.ch20

Jacobs, J. M., & Wright, P. M. (2018). Transfer of life skills in sport-based youth development programs: A conceptual framework bridging learning to application. *Quest*, 70(1), 81–99. https://doi.org/10.1080/00336297.2017.1348304

Jowett, G. E., Hill, A. P., Hall, H. K., & Curran, T. (2016). Perfectionism, burnout and engagement in youth sport: The mediating role of basic psychological needs. *Psychology of Sport and Exercise*, 24, 18–26.

Kerrick, J. (2015). *The transformative effect of youth sports: Forging an intentional path towards enriching children's lives through sports*. Jones Media Publishing.

Koh, K. T., & Camiré, M. (2015). Strategies for the development of life skills and values through sport programmes. In H. K. Leng & N. H. Yang (Eds), *Emerging trends and innovation in sports marketing and management in Asia* (pp. 241–256). IGI Global. https://doi.org/10.4018/978-1-4666-7527-8.ch014

Koh, K. T., Ong, S. W., & Camiré, M. (2016). Implementation of a values training program in physical education and sport: Perspectives from teachers, coaches, students, and athletes. *Physical Education and Sport Pedagogy*, 21(3), 295–312. https://doi.org/10.1080/17408989.2014.990369

Kolb, D. A. (1984). *Experiential Learning: Experience as the source of learning and development.* Prentice Hall.

Lerner, R. M. (2005). Promoting positive youth development: Theoretical and empirical bases. White paper prepared for the workshop on the science of adolescent health and development, National Research Council/Institute Of Medicine. National Academies of Science.

Ma, C. M., & Shek, D. T. (2019). Objective outcome evaluation of a positive youth development program: The Project PATHS in Hong Kong. *Research on Social Work Practice,* 29(1), 49–60. https://doi.org/10.1177/10497315177112

Mageau, G. A., & Vallerand, R. J. (2003). The coach-athlete relationship: A motivational model. *Journal of Sports Science,* 21(11), 883–904. https://doi.org/10.1080/0264041031000140374

Martens, R., & Vealey, R. S. (2023). *Successful coaching.* Human Kinetics.

Martinek, T., & Hemphill, M. A. (2020). The evolution of Hellison's teaching personal and social responsibility model in out-of-school contexts. *Journal of Teaching in Physical Education,* 39(3), 331–336. https://doi.org/10.1123/jtpe.2019-0222

Morgan, K., Sproule, J., McNeill, M. C., Kingston, K., & Wang, J. C. K. (2006). A cross-cultural study of motivational climate in physical education lessons in the UK and Singapore. *International Journal of Sport Psychology,* 37(4), 299–316.

Newman, T. J. (2020). Life skill development and transfer: They're not just meant for playing sports. *Research on Social Work Practice,* 30(6), 643–657. https://doi.org/10.1177/1049731520903427

Newman, T. J., Alvarez, M. A. G., & Kim, M. (2017). An experiential approach to sport for youth development. *Journal of Experiential Education,* 40(3), 308–322. https://doi.org/10.1177/1053825917696833

Newman, T.J., Black, S., Santos, F., Jefka, B., & Brennan, N. (2023). Coaching the development and transfer of life skills: A scoping review of facilitative coaching practices in youth sports. *International Review of Sport and Exercise Psychology,* 16(1), 619–656. https://doi.org/10.1080/1750984X.2021.1910977

Petitpas, A. J., Cornelius, A. E., Van Raalte, J. L., & Jones, T. (2005). A framework for planning youth sport programs that foster psychosocial development. *The Sport Psychologist,* 19(1), 63–80. https://doi.org/10.1123/tsp.19.1.63

Salehi, K., & Golafshani, N. (2010). Commentary: Using mixed methods in research studies-an opportunity with its challenges. *International Journal of Multiple Research Approaches,* 4(3), 186–191. https://doi.org/10.5172/mra.2010.4.3.186

Santos, F., Gould, D., & Strachan, L. (2019). Research on positive youth development-focused coach education programs: Future pathways and applications. *International Sport Coaching Journal,* 6(1), 132–138. https://doi.org/10.1123/iscj.2018-0063

Seng, Y.B.G. (2022). Teaching and facilitating the transference of values and life skills through physical education and sports in Singapore schools (Doctoral dissertation, National Institute of Education, Nanyang Technological University). NIE Digital Repository. https://hdl.handle.net/10497/24366

Tashakkori, A., & Teddie, C. (1998). *Mixed methodology: Combining qualitative and quantitative approaches.* SAGE Publications.

Vella, S. A., Oades, L. G., & Crowe, T. P. (2012). Validation of the differentiated transformational leadership inventory as a measure of coach leadership in youth soccer. *The Sport Psychologist*, 26(2), 207–223. https://doi.org/10.1123/tsp.26.2.207

Walker, A. (2019) Culturally relevant pedagogy, identity, presence, and intentionality: A brief review of literature. *Journal of Research Initiatives*, 4(3), 11. https://digitalcommons.uncfsu.edu/jri/vol4/iss3/11

Whitley, M.A., Massey, W.V., Camiré, M., Boutet, M., & Borbee, A. (2019). Sport-based youth development interventions in the United States: A systematic review. *BMC Public Health*, 19, 89. https://doi.org/10.1186/s12889-019-6387-z

Wright, P. M., Li, W., Ding, S., & Pickering, M. (2010). Integrating a personal and social responsibility program into a wellness course for urban high school students: Assessing implementation and educational outcomes. *Sport, Education and Society*, 15(3), 277–298. https://doi.org/10.1080/13573322.2010.493309

Xie, F. M. F., Koh, K. T., & Falcão, R. W. (2021). Strategies and methods for teaching values transference from physical education to the classroom and home: A case study. *Asia Pacific Journal of Education*, 1–18. https://doi.org/10.1080/02188791.2021.1926919

Preparing Coaches to Teach Life Skills: The Need for a Behaviour Change Perspective in Coach Education Programmes

Chapter Twelve

Carlos Ewerton Palheta and Michel Milistetd

INTRODUCTION

Coach Education Programmes (CEPs) represent an intervention model formulated to promote coach development (Cushion et al., 2010). Participation in CEPs presents itself as a learning opportunity capable of enhancing coaches' knowledge of specific content. However, despite their potential, CEPs have shown to be ineffective when evaluated for their ability to transform coaches' practices (Stodter & Cushion, 2019; MacDonald et al., 2020). Having the expectation of efficacy regarding practice is consistent with the nature of coaching. After all, it's in practice that coaches express their knowledge into actions. For instance, they must effectively communicate to teach concepts, establish positive relationships, and manage conflicts in the sports environment (Becker, 2013). Therefore, the formulation of CEPs needs to be grounded to not only enhance knowledge but also transform practice. From this perspective, adopting principles from implementation science is an alternative for formulating effective CEPs.

In implementation science, a successful or failed intervention can be explained by the models and techniques adopted in its formulation (Nilsen, 2020). In CEPs, these aspects are not consistently clarified, contributing to their inefficacy. Considering behaviour change models and techniques is an alternative to address this situation and formulate effective CEPs (Allan et al., 2018). The Behaviour Change Wheel (BCW) (Michie et al., 2014) is a behaviour change model developed to assist in the characterisation, formulation, and evaluation of interventions. The BCW has the COM-B system at its centre, presenting Capability, Opportunity, and Motivation (COM-B) as the essential elements for acquiring and maintaining a target Behaviour. In addition to COM-B, the BCW describes intervention functions and

DOI: 10.4324/9781032688657-16

policy categories that can support this behaviour (Michie et al., 2014). Recently, the model has been useful in developing coaches' leadership (Lawrason et al., 2019) and examining behaviours conducive to teaching life skills (Preston et al., 2021).

Life skills refer to competencies, values, and attitudes capable of assisting in everyday problem-solving, fostering character development, and promoting citizenship (Gould & Carson, 2008). Respect, teamwork, perseverance, and communication are examples of life skills that can be cultivated through sports. Children and adolescents increase their chances of developing life skills when coaches show supportive behaviours for this purpose (Williams et al., 2022). Consequently, CEPs focused on teaching life skills have been developed in many countries (Koh et al., 2017; Camiré et al., 2018; Santos et al., 2019). The BCW can assist in the development of these CEPs, given their challenge in transforming coaches' practices (Santos et al., 2019; MacDonald et al., 2020). The aim of this chapter is to present the utilisation of the BCW as a possibility to assess and formulate CEPs. To achieve this goal, we will elucidate the components of the BCW. Subsequently, we will adopt the BCW to evaluate the aspects that render CEPs ineffective. Lastly, we will contextualise the assumptions of life skills teaching within the BCW to justify its application in CEP formulation.

THE BEHAVIOUR CHANGE WHEEL

The BCW is a synthesis of 19 behaviour change frameworks (Michie et al. 2014). Michie et al. (2011) sought to consider the strengths and overcome the limitations of each to design the BCW. A three-layered wheel represents the model with components interacting nonlinearly with each other (Michie et al., 2011) (Figure 12.1).

From the BCW perspective, every intervention has a target behaviour. The centre of the BCW is occupied by the COM-B system, which identifies the target behaviour as a result of the interaction among the components of Capability, Opportunity, and Motivation. Each component encompasses subcomponents that specify them (Table 12.1).

To achieve the goal of an intervention, certain elements of the COM-B model are modified to either increase or decrease their impact on the target behaviour, depending on the intervention's objective

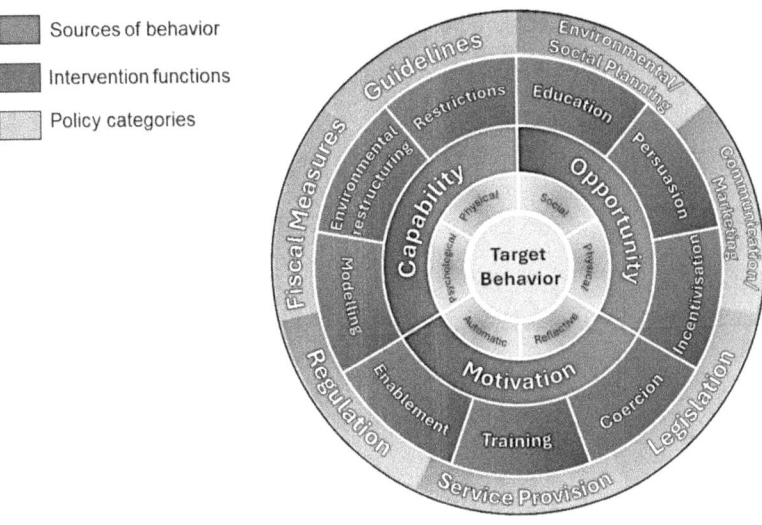

Figure 12.1 BCW (Michie et al., 2011)

Table 12.1 COM-B System (Michie et al., 2011)

Capability	Physical	Physical ability, strength, and endurance
	Psychological	Knowledge and mental processes
Opportunity	Physical	Environment, time, resources, and locations
	Social	Interpersonal influences, cultural norms, and language
Motivation	Automatic	Emotional reaction, desires, and impulses
	Reflective	Reflection about plans, intentions, and beliefs

(Michie et al., 2011). The BCW does not prescribe specific methods of intervention, such as lectures, workshops, or rule-setting. Instead, it characterises these interventions based on the functions they can have on the components of the COM-B model (Table 12.2).

Finally, encompassing the COM-B system and the intervention functions are seven policy categories. These categories represent the decisions and initiatives of authorities that can support the delivery of intervention functions (Table 12.3).

Table 12.2 Intervention Functions (Michie et al., 2011)

	Intervention Functions	Able to Change
Education	Increasing knowledge or understanding	Psychological capability Reflective motivation
Persuasion	Using communication to induce positive or negative feelings or stimulate action	Reflective motivation Automatic motivation
Incentivisation	Creating expectation of reward	Reflective motivation Automatic motivation
Coercion	Creating expectation of punishment or cost	Reflective motivation Automatic motivation
Training	Imparting skills	Physical capability Psychological capability
Restrictions	Using rules to reduce the opportunity to engage in the target behaviour (or to increase the target behaviour by reducing the opportunity to engage in competing behaviours)	Physical opportunity Social opportunity
Environmental restructuring	Changing the physical or social context	Physical opportunity Social opportunity automatic motivation
Modelling	Providing an example for people to aspire to or imitate	Automatic motivation
Enablement	Increasing means/reducing barriers to increase capability or opportunity	Physical capability Psychological capability Automatic motivation Physical opportunity Social opportunity

HOW CAN THE BCW EXPLAIN THE INEFFICACY OF CEPs?

The initial premise of the BCW is that every intervention should be formulated around a target behaviour. This premise allows the anticipation of factors that may influence outcomes and enables the selection of the best intervention methods (Michie et al., 2014). CEPs demonstrate difficulties in specifying the target behaviour. These difficulties can be explained by considering the characteristics of CEPs in university-based, large-scale, and small-scale interventions (Trudel et al., 2010).

Table 12.3 Policy Categories (Michie et al., 2011)

Policy Categories		Can Support the Functions
Communication/ marketing	Using print, electronic, telephonic, or broadcast media	Education, persuasion incentive, coercion, modelling
Guidelines	Creating documents that recommend or mandate practice; this includes all changes to service provision	Education, persuasion, incentive, coercion, training, restriction, environmental restructuring, enablement
Fiscal measures	Using the tax system to reduce or increase the financial cost	Incentive, coercion, training, environmental restructuring, enablement
Regulation	Establishing rules or principles of behaviour or practice	Education, persuasion, incentive, coercion, training, restriction, environmental restructuring, qualification
Legislation	Making or changing laws	Education, persuasion, incentive, coercion, training, restriction, environmental restructuring, enablement
Environmental/ social planning	Designing and/or controlling the physical or social environment	Environmental restructuring, enablement
Service provision	Delivering a service	Education, persuasion, incentive, coercion, training, modelling, enablement

University-based CEPs take place within the realm of higher education (Trudel et al., 2010). In this context, the training is focused on the development of broad competencies through human, biological, and social bases (Milistetd et al., 2014). This generic and broad characteristic of such CEPs makes defining a target behaviour challenging and undermines their effectiveness. For instance, in Brazil, the professionalisation of coaches occurs within university-based CEPs, which proves ineffective in preparing coaches for specific areas of practice, such as high-performance sports (Milistetd et al., 2017).

Large-scale CEPs are usually organised by national organisations offering professional certification (Trudel et al., 2010). This context aims to certify many coaches simultaneously (Milistetd et al., 2017). Consequently, it's common to bring together coaches with heterogeneous learning needs from diverse organisational cultures at different stages of professional development. In attempting to cater to all, large-scale CEPs tend to establish broad objectives based on issues disconnected from the reality coaches face in their various work contexts (Lara-Bercial & Bales, 2022). Thus, they become ineffective when coaches lack the contextual demand to exhibit the behaviours intended by the CEPs.

Small-scale CEPs represent localised and specific intervention initiatives (Trudel et al., 2010). Clubs are examples of institutions that develop this type of CEP. In this context, learning needs might be more evident (Cushion et al., 2019) and could favour the definition of a target behaviour. However, they may still be guided by broad parameters, even if contextualised. For instance, the vision, mission, and values of institutions might guide the initial steps in formulating CEPs. However, these are broad pieces of information that don't specify behaviours and hinder changes in coaching practice (Anderson & Jefferson, 2019).

The second premise of the BCW is the use of the COM-B system in intervention planning (Table 12.1) (Michie et al., 2014). Through COM-B, it's evident that CEPs do not address all necessary components for transforming coaches' practices (Hummell et al., 2023). They tend to be highly prescriptive and limited to the transmission of technical content (Milistetd et al., 2017). As a result, they often enhance coaches' knowledge of specific content areas but remain ineffective in changing coaching practice (Stodter & Cushion, 2019; MacDonald et al., 2020). From the BCW perspective, it's possible to suggest that this inefficacy happens because CEPs focus on only one of the COM-B components: Capability. Notably, the absence of practical experience (i.e., Opportunity) and means that encourage deliberate reflection (i.e., Motivation) are often identified as limitations of CEPs (Culver et al., 2019; Stodter & Cushion, 2019; Trudel et al., 2020; Goorevich et al., 2023).

The third premise of the BCW is the definition of intervention functions (Table 12.2) (Michie et al., 2014). It's important to clarify that the BCW guides planning based on functions rather than methods of intervention. Practical workshops, conferences, and mentoring are examples of methods of intervention offered in CEPs (Milistetd et al., 2021). Defining the methods does not clarify their functions. Thus, CEPs are ineffective when they select methods without planning the necessary intervention functions. Goorevich et al. (2023) assessed the impact of web-based coach education and found that the chosen method didn't engage participants. Coaches also reported that the method did not provide opportunities for practice and reflective motivation (Goorevich et al., 2023). From the BCW perspective, the programme should adopt the functions of incentive, training, and persuasion. These functions might require other intervention methods. However, not necessarily, as more than one function can be served by a single method. For instance, coach developers' mentoring is an intervention method capable of enhancing coaches' knowledge (Education function), encouraging action (Persuasion function), and inspiring them (Modelling function) (Culver et al., 2019; Jones et al., 2023).

The fourth premise of the BCW is that the policy categories can determine the sustainability of the intervention (Table 12.3) (Michie et al., 2014). For instance, in Brazil, national laws (a policy category) are crucial to sustain coaches' professionalisation within university-based CEPs (Milistetd et al., 2014). This example considers governmental actions, yet policy categories can also be restricted to the intervention context. Milistetd et al. (2021) considered policy categories restricted to a multisports club to plan and conduct a small-scale CEP. Categories like communication/marketing, environmental/social planning, and service provision sustained the CEP for two years. However, the mechanisms designed to support coaches' development weren't sustained when the service provision (consultants' involvement) ended (Milistetd et al., 2021).

CEPs FOR TEACHING LIFE SKILLS

Proposing a plan based on the BCW demands that its premises be considered, starting with the definition of the target behaviour. To define it, we can consider that intentional teaching is a determining factor for life skills development (Bean & Forneris, 2016; Holt et al., 2017; Pierce et al., 2018). This suggests that determining intentional teaching as the target behaviour is a promising path. However, this step is pivotal in CEP development and requires deeper analysis to specify

Table 12.4 Implicit/Explicit Continuum of Life Skills (Bean et al. 2018)

Explicit	6	Practicing transfer	Forge links with parents, teachers, and community members/provide opportunities to apply life skills beyond sports/enable reflection of life skills application beyond sports
	5	Discussing transfer	Discuss transferring and its importance/increase awareness of transfer opportunities/enhance confidence for transfer/enable reflection on transfer talks
	4	Practicing life skills	Intentionally create opportunities to practice life skills in sports/enable reflection on life skills application in sports
	3	Discussing life skills	Define life skills/talk about life skills and their importance/enhance confidence for life skills development/enable reflection on life skills talks
Implicit	2	Facilitating a positive climate	Model positive behaviours/foster positive relationships/support efficacy and mattering/take advantage of naturally-occurring teaching moments
	1	Structuring the sports context	Recognise the inherent demands of sports/design the practice/set rules

the target behaviour (Michie et al., 2014). Thus, a good alternative is to consider the implicit/explicit continuum, which presents six levels of intentionality in teaching life skills (Bean et al., 2018) (Table 12.4). In levels 3 to 6, it's possible to specify the behaviours that should be adopted to express teaching intentionality for life skills (highlighted in Table 12.4).

After specifying the target behaviour, it's necessary to decide which components of the COM-B to alter (Michie et al., 2011).

An analysis regarding Capability reveals that coaches lacking specific knowledge about teaching life skills remain at the implicit level and don't reach the levels of explicit teaching (Palheta et al., 2021).

Consequently, coaches' ways of teaching life skills are often inconsistent (Camiré & Santos, 2019). This limitation highlights the need to alter the Capability component, specifically the psychological aspect, to enhance coaches' knowledge. Knowing how to provide leadership opportunities, role modelling, and being able to communicate effectively with young athletes, parents, and other community members are skills that can be developed to foster higher levels of intentionality (Gould & Carson, 2008; Preston et al., 2021).

An examination regarding Opportunity reveals that coaches need practical experience. This is crucial for applying knowledge and recognising new learning needs (Camiré et al., 2014; Stodter & Cushion, 2019). Thus, some contextual aspects negatively influence Opportunity for teaching life skills. Coaches face challenges in teaching life skills when stakeholders have heightened expectations for competitive performance (Preston & Fraser-Thomas, 2018; Preston et al., 2021; Palheta et al., 2022). Coaches also note that factors such as the short duration and low frequency of training sessions limit life skills teaching (Koh et al., 2016; Palheta et al., 2022). These examples indicate that the CEP should alter both subcomponents of Opportunity, physical and social.

Lastly, a look for Motivation reveals that coaches often exhibit one of its subcomponents, automatic Motivation. At times, automatic motivation for teaching life skills stems from coaches' personal dispositions, such as their own personalities (Sackett & Gano-Overway, 2017) and how they recognise their professional role (Palheta et al., 2021). Personal life events, such as becoming a parent, can also trigger automatic Motivation to teach life skills (Camiré et al., 2014; Palheta et al., 2021). If these characteristics are observed in a preliminary analysis, the CEP can focus on altering only the reflective Motivation. This subcomponent remains necessary because even coaches who value teaching life skills need to recognise it as a complex process supported by specific pedagogical approaches and dependent on their plans, intentions, and beliefs (Holt, 2016).

To alter the components, intervention functions and policy categories enabling their delivery are properly selected. Therefore, choosing means with the Education function should enable psychological Capability and reflective Motivation. Courses, workshops, whether in-person or online, are means capable of imparting knowledge and motivating coaches' practice transformation (Koh & Camiré, 2015;

Camiré et al., 2018). The Training function should also be important to enable knowledge application in practice. One option is to provide a pilot implementation phase for programmes (Strachan et al., 2016; Camiré et al., 2018). To support these functions, the Service Provision category may be necessary. Formulating means for Education and Training should require the involvement of expert groups capable of imparting knowledge, arousing motivation, and overseeing the implementation phase (Milistetd et al., 2021).

To alter physical Opportunity, the Environmental Restructuring function might be useful in transforming coaches' working contexts. This transformation should allow adjustments in the structure of training sessions when difficulties in teaching life skills are recognised, as observed by Koh et al. (2016) and Palheta et al. (2022). To alter social Opportunity, the Enablement function can produce methods to clarify life skills teaching objectives to stakeholders. This initiative should reduce barriers created by expectations focused on competitive performance and align new expectations related to life skills teaching (Petitpas et al., 2005). Environmental/Social planning and Guidelines are categories that should aid in the delivery of selected functions. These categories may be achievable in small-scale CEPs where the settings of a specific context can be better controlled (Trudel et al., 2010).

APPLIED INSIGHTS

Michie et al. (2014) present a pragmatic perspective on using BCW. Following the authors' guidance, if used to prepare CEPs, the sequence of actions should be as follows:

1. Define life skills teaching in behavioural terms for coaches. How does teaching life skills manifest in the behaviour of coaches?
2. Select the target behaviour. What behaviour should be developed?
3. Specify the target behaviour.
4. Identify what needs to change. Do coaches need Capability, Opportunity, and Motivation to teach life skills?
5. Identify the intervention's functions. Which functions (Table 12.2) should favour a change in coaches' capability, opportunity, and motivation?
6. Identify policy categories. Which policy categories (Table 12.3) should support the delivery of the CEP?

SUMMARY AND FUTURE DIRECTIONS

In this chapter, we aimed to present the possibility of formulating CEPs for life skills teaching. To achieve this aim, we adopted a behaviour change perspective and selected the BCW as a lens to assess characteristics and anticipate possibilities within CEPs. The utilisation of BCW needs to be grounded in the view that interventions with coaches should not only enhance knowledge but also transform practice. Other models that highlight practice transformation as an expected outcome of coaches' learning also endorse this perspective.

We know that the process of coaches' development is complex, and the use of theoretical models often fails to support this complexity and can be flawed in certain aspects. Nevertheless, BCW can be beneficial in the coach education field by considering psychological, social, and environmental factors. While the BCW doesn't grant full control over the complexity of learning, it should at least facilitate predicting various factors that influence intervention outcomes. Therefore, despite its pragmatic purpose, its use isn't meant to prompt coaches into automatic behaviours without permission for critical perceptions. Instead, it's aimed at creating initiatives that foster learning considering its complexity.

To expand on the ideas presented in this chapter, it will be necessary to use the BCW to assess and formulate CEPs in different contexts. The use of BCW has recently been happening because investigations suggest a behavioural change perspective in the coach education field. In Brazil, we have used the model to evaluate a CEP specifically focused on life skills teaching. This case should clarify certain conditions regarding BCW utilisation in this context.

REFERENCES

Allan, V., Vierimaa, M., Gainforth, H. L., & Côté, J. (2018). The use of behaviour change theories and techniques in research-informed coach development programmes: A systematic review. *International Review of Sport and Exercise Psychology*, 11(1), 47–69.

Anderson, M., & Jefferson, M. (2019). *Transforming organizations: Engaging the 4Cs for powerful organizational learning and change*. Bloomsbury Business

Bean, C., & Forneris, T. (2016). Examining the importance of intentionally structuring the youth sport context to facilitate psychosocial development. *Journal of Applied Sport Psychology*, 28, 410–425. doi: https://doi.org/10.1080/10413200.2016.1164764

Bean, C., Kramers, S., Forneris, T., & Camiré, M. (2018). The implicit/explicit continuum of life skills development and transfer. *Quest*, 70, 456–470.

Becker, A. J. (2013). Quality coaching behaviours. In P. Potrac, W. Gilbert, & J. Denison (Eds.) *Routledge handbook of sports coaching* (pp. 184–195). Routledge.

Camiré, M., Kendellen, K., Rathwell, S., & Felber Charbonneau, E. (2018). Evaluation of the pilot implementation of the coaching for life skills program. *International Sport Coaching Journal*, 5, 227–236. doi: https://doi.org/10.1123/iscj.2018-0006

Camiré, M., & Santos, F. (2019). Promoting positive youth development and life skills in youth sport: Challenges and opportunities amidst increased professionalization. *Journal of Sport Pedagogy and Research*, 5(1), 27–34.

Camiré, M., Trudel, P., & Forneris, T. (2014). Examining how model youth sport coaches learn to facilitate positive youth development. *Physical Education and Sport Pedagogy*, 19(1), 1–17.

Culver, D. M., Werthner, P., & Trudel, P. (2019). Coach developers as 'facilitators of learning' in a large-scale coach education programme: One actor in a complex system. *International Sport Coaching Journal*, 6(3), 296–306.

Cushion, C., Nelson, L., Armour, K., Lyle, J., Jones, R., Sandford, R., & O'Callaghan, C. (2010). *Coach learning and development: A review of literature*. Project Report. Sports Coach UK, Leeds.

Cushion, C. J., Griffiths, M., & Armour, K. (2019). Professional coach educators in-situ: A social analysis of practice. *Sport, Education and Society*, 24(5), 533–546. https://doi.org/10.1080/13573322.2017.1411795

Goorevich, A., Boucher, C., Schneider, J., Silva-Breen, H., Matheson, E. L., Tinoco, A., & LaVoi, N. M. (2023). Acceptability and preliminary efficacy testing of a web-based coach development program addressing gender essentialism among coaches of adolescent girls. *International Sport Coaching Journal*, 1(aop), 1–13.

Gould, D., & Carson, S. (2008). Life skills development through sport: Current status and future directions. *International Review of Sport & Exercise Psychology*, 1, 58–78. doi:https://doi.org/10.1080/1750984070183 4573

Holt, N. L. (Ed.). (2016). *Positive youth development through sport*. Routledge.

Holt, N. L., Neely, K. C., Slater, L. G., Camiré, M., Côté, J., Fraser-Thomas, J., Tamminen, K. A. (2017). A grounded theory of positive youth development through sport based on results from a qualitative meta-study. *International Review of Sport and Exercise Psychology*, 10, 1–49. doi:10.1080/1750984X.2016.1180704

Hummell, C., Herbison, J. D., Turnnidge, J., & Côté, J. (2023). Assessing the effectiveness of the transformational coaching workshop using behavior change theory. *International Journal of Sports Science & Coaching*, 18(1), 3–12.

Jones, T., Allen, J., & Macdonald, S. (2023). The "Face" of coach development: A systematic review of the role of the coach developer. *International Sport Coaching Journal*, 1(aop), 1–19.

Koh, K. T., & Camiré, M. (2015). Strategies for the development of life skills and values through sport programmes: Review and recommendations. *Emerging trends and innovation in sports marketing and management in Asia*, 241–256.

Koh, K. T., Camiré, M., Bloom, G., & Wang, J. (2017). Creation, implementation, and evaluation of a values-based training program for sport coaches and physical education teachers in Singapore. *International Journal of Sports Science & Coaching, 12*, 795–806. doi: https://doi.org/10.1177/1747954117730987

Koh, K. T., Ong, S. W., & Camiré, M. (2016). Implementation of a values training program in physical education and sport: perspectives from teachers, coaches, students, and athletes. *Physical Education and Sport Pedagogy, 21*(3), 295–312.

Lara-Bercial, S., & Bales, J. (2022). *The challenge of doing coach education and development in the 21st century: Education in sport and physical activity: Future directions and global perspectives.*

Lawrason, S., Turnnidge, J., Martin, L. J., & Côté, J. (2019). A transformational coaching workshop for changing youth sport coaches' behaviors: A pilot intervention study. *The Sport Psychologist, 33*(4), 304–312.

MacDonald, D. J., Camiré, M., Erickson, K., & Santos, F. (2020). Positive youth development related athlete experiences and coach behaviors following a targeted coach education course. *International Journal of Sports Science & Coaching, 15*(5–6), 621–630.

Michie, S., Atkins, L., & West, R. (2014). *The behaviour change wheel: A guide to designing interventions* (1st ed., pp. 1003–1010). Silverback Publishing.

Michie, S., Van Stralen, M. M., & West, R. (2011). The behaviour change wheel: a new method for characterising and designing behaviour change interventions. *Implementation Science, 6*(1), 1–12.

Milistetd, M., Ramos, V., Saad, M. A., Sales, W., & Nascimento, J. V. (2017). Formação de Treinadores para o Esporte de Elite. In L. R. Galatti, A. J. Scaglia, P. C. Montagner, & R. R. Paes (Eds.), *Desenvolvimento de treinadores e atletas - Pedagogia do esporte* (Vol. 1, pp. 39–62). Unicamp.

Milistetd, M., Trudel, P., Culver, D., Cortela, C. C., Tozetto, A., Lima, C. O., & Souza, V. (2021). A second look at a 24-month collaborative initiative to develop coaches in a multisport club. *Journal of Sport Pedagogy and Research, 7*(6), 51–62.

Milistetd, M., Trudel, P., Mesquita, I., & Nascimento, J.V. (2014). Coaching and coach education in Brazil. *International Sport Coaching Journal, 1*(3), 165–172. doi:10.1123/iscj.2014-0103

Nilsen, P. (2020). Making sense of implementation theories, models, and frameworks. *Implementation Science, 3*, 53–79.

Palheta, C. E., Ciampolini, V., Nunes, E. L. G., Santos, F., & Milistetd, M. (2021). Between intentionality and reality to promote positive youth development in sport-based programs: A case study in Brazil. *Physical Education and Sport Pedagogy, 26*(2), 197–209.

Palheta, C. E., Ciampolini, V., Santos, F., Ibáñez, S. J., Nascimento, J. V., & Milistetd, M. (2022). Challenges in promoting positive youth development through sport. *Sustainability, 14*(19), 12316.

Petitpas, A. J., Cornelius, A. E., Van Raalte, J. L., & Jones, T. (2005). A framework for planning youth sport programs that foster psychosocial development. *The Sport Psychologist, 19*(1), 63–80.

Pierce, S., Kendellen, K., Camiré, M., & Gould, D. (2018). Strategies for coaching for life skills transfer. *Journal of Sport Psychology in Action, 9*, 11–20. doi:10.1080/21520704.2016.1263982

Preston, C., Allan, V., & Fraser-Thomas, J. (2021). Facilitating positive youth development in elite youth hockey: Exploring coaches' capabilities, opportunities, and motivations. *Journal of Applied Sport Psychology*, 33(3), 302–320.

Preston, C., & Fraser-Thomas, J. (2018). Problematizing the pursuit of personal development and performance success: An autoethnography of a Canadian elite youth ice hockey coach. *The Sport Psychologist*, 32(2), 102–113.

Sackett, S. C., & Gano-Overway, L. A. (2017). Coaching life skills development: Best practices and high school tennis coach exemplar. *International Sport Coaching Journal*, 4(2), 206–219.

Santos, F., Camiré, M., MacDonald, D. J., Campos H., Conceição, M., & Silva, A. (2019). Process and outcome evaluation of a positive youth development focused online coach education course. *International Sport Coaching Journal*, 6, 1–12. doi: 10.1123/iscj.2017-0101

Stodter, A., & Cushion, C. J. (2019). Evidencing the impact of coaches' learning: Changes in coaching knowledge and practice over time. *Journal of Sports Sciences*, 37(18), 2086–2093.

Strachan, L., MacDonald, D. J., & Côté, J. (2016). Project SCORE! Coaches' perceptions of an online tool to promote positive youth development in sport. *International Journal of Sports Science & Coaching*, 11(1), 108–115.

Trudel, P., Gilbert, W., & Werthner, P. (2010). Coach education effectivenes. In J. Lyle & C. J. Cushion (Eds.), *Sports coaching: Proffessionalisation and practice* (1st ed., pp. 135–152). Churchill Livingstone Elsevier

Trudel, P., Milestetd, M., & Culver, D. M. (2020). What the empirical studies on sport coach education programs in higher education have to reveal: A review. *International Sport Coaching Journal*, 7(1), 61–73.

Williams, C., Neil, R., Cropley, B., Woodman, T., & Roberts, R. (2022). A systematic review of sport-based life skills programs for young people: The quality of design and evaluation methods. *Journal of Applied Sport Psychology*, 34(2), 409–435.

Integration

Chapter Thirteen

Swee Meng Wong, Alice Koh and Thomas Yong

INTRODUCTION

In Singapore, sports is the most popular genre of co-curricular activity in schools. Indeed, the goal of school sports competitions is to provide quality competition experiences for student-athletes to support character development through the pursuit of sporting excellence. There is a strong emphasis on sports participation as an important student development experience for character and citizenship education (Ministry of Education [MOE], Singapore, 2022). In fact, the completion of the module Values and Principles in Sports is a prerequisite for all school coaches. This has contributed to the general understanding amongst teachers and coaches of school sports teams that character development is an important goal of sports participation and competition, which are believed to be natural contexts with the potential for fostering and developing character.

However, in our 30+ years of experiences as athletes, teachers and coaches, and policymakers and curriculum developers in Singapore's school sports scene, our observation is that this often seems to break down in practice. Anecdotal evidence suggests that this is because teachers and coaches often find it difficult to achieve both athletic development and character education, with one tending to be achieved at the expense of the other. We explain this paradox and provide suggestions for programme design in school sports that allows for the integration and synergy of both athletic and character development pursuits so that athletic development is enhanced while building character, and good character is also built while developing sporting skills.

DOI: 10.4324/9781032688657-17

DOES SPORTS BUILD CHARACTER?

Singapore's view that sports participation and competition are natural contexts with the potential for fostering and developing character is neither new nor unique. Indeed, such an idea has been in existence since the Ancient Greeks and been popular among educators for more than a century (Bredemeier & Shields, 2006). Proponents of the stance that sports can build character have highlighted the positive benefits related to children's physical, social, intellectual, emotional, individual, and even financial domains of learning (e.g., Bailey et al., 2012, 2013; Camiré & Trudel, 2010; Newman & Kim, 2017; Walters et al., 2012). For example, the majority of athletes interviewed in the study by Camiré and Trudel indicated that teamwork was one of the most important values that they developed through participating in sports.

With the understanding that the sporting environment and experience are both physically and emotionally demanding, sports participation can reveal an individual's positive and negative character traits when tensions and pressure from the desire to win increases. As such, many researchers have argued that participation in sports can have a positive impact on children's character development. This is possible as they continuously refine and practise their values and principles in their various sporting experiences to attain positive character development (Arnold, 1984), which can include both performance and moral character (Lickona and Davidson, 2005). Performance character has a mastery orientation and consists of qualities such as diligence and resilience. Such qualities are essential for realising one's potential in any area of endeavour, such as the sporting arena and the workplace but are morally neutral in that they can also be employed for unethical ends. On the other hand, moral character has a relational orientation that enables one to treat others with respect and care and use ethical means to achieve our goals.

However, others have produced findings that suggest a negative relationship between participation in sports and character development, pointing out that participation in sports may not lead to positive benefits and positive character building for all children (e.g., Doty, 2006; Dunn & Dunn, 1999; Gerdy, 2000; Kochanek et al., 2019; Krauuse & Priest, 1993). For example, Doty (2006) observed that some players showed a lack of respect for referees by shouting at and arguing with referees during the game. This is despite having been taught to show respect to the referees.

The debate between the two camps has settled on the consensus that sports and physical activities do not automatically promote, develop, or facilitate character and its unique virtues. Instead, character development can be facilitated, taught, and learned through a sporting experience if the activities are appropriately and intentionally planned within a structured and supportive environment to develop character and achieve its intended positive benefits (Bredemeier & Shields, 2006; Doty, 2006; Omar-Fauzee et al., 2012; Parker & Stiehl, 2004). More specifically, sports settings that encourage sportsmanship and fair play rather than winning and losing will tend to support greater positive character development (Coakley, 2001; Hellison, 2003; Parker & Stiehl, 2004).

There is also consensus that given the complex demands of designing and facilitating the learning experience required, key partners, including teachers, coaches, parents, and sports administrators, must be involved in character development efforts (Doty, 2006; Omar-Fauzee et al., 2012). Amongst these adults, the leadership and behaviour of the coach are key (Bredemeier & Shields, 2006). As such, the role of the coach and their contribution to both positive and negative sports participation in children in the complex sporting environment have gained significant research attention (Ferris et al., 2016; Keegan et al., 2009). For example, Bredemeier and Shields (1995) and Beller (2002) have highlighted that intentional and well-organised character education efforts in sports programmes with appropriate teaching and coaching strategies provide powerful contexts for the teaching and learning of good moral habits.

ATHLETIC DEVELOPMENT AND CHARACTER DEVELOPMENT AS CONTRADICTORY GOALS

However, the consensus in the academic community does not seem to have contributed to coaching practice in Singapore. There are few school sports programmes that seem to have effectively met the dual goals of athletic and character development. This can be seen in a study by Koh et al. (2016), which observed that although teachers and coaches of Singapore's school sports teams were strong believers of character education being built into sporting activities, they had limited knowledge and tools for doing so. This is in line with scholarship that posits that youth sports leaders (e.g., coaches, recreation leaders) range from being unable to explain the rationale for their coaching practices to having implicit knowledge of coaching strategies for facilitating sports towards youth development. Yet, even the group with implicit knowledge of facilitating sports towards youth development struggles to articulate specific practices for doing so (Newman & Kim, 2017). Following a training programme on character education through sports, teachers and coaches in the Singapore study mentioned earlier (i.e., Koh et al., 2016) reported a better understanding of how to do so but still found the time required to write the value-focussed lesson plans a challenge.

Similar to what Crossan and Bednar (2018) have found in other countries, we have observed that many coaches of school sports teams in Singapore believe that athletic and game development is more important than personal development. One reason for this is the misplaced faith that character building is a natural by-product of participation in sports. They therefore do not plan for character building in their programmes. On the other hand, there are also coaches who view athletic development and character education as two separate entities. Thus, when it comes to programme planning, these teachers and coaches feel the pressure from the shortage of time to do both. They therefore focus only on athletic and game development which they feel should be the foremost priority for sports coaches. As a result, these coaches who focus only on athletic and game development miss out on key moments in their programming to develop sustainable characteristics in athletes.

AN INTEGRATIVE AND SYNERGISTIC APPROACH

Given the situation described in the previous section, *is there then the possibility of synergy so that athletic development is enhanced while building character, and good character is also built while developing sporting skills?* We agree with the experts in the field cited earlier that this is not only possible, but also desirable and inevitable by understanding and leveraging the nature of athletic development and the natural opportunities for character education that come with it. This is even more so in the context of school sports, which is a key concern of the authors.

Learning, training, and competing in sports involves the building of character, as athletes will need to learn to work and communicate with others, manage their emotions, and manage failures and disappointment (Bredemeier & Shields, 2006). Martinkova (2012) also suggests there are values that are "inherent" to competitive sports where coaches do not need to do anything special beyond training athletes in the given sports discipline. These values tend to be associated with what Lickona and Davidson (2005) have called "performance character." In the realm of sports, this involves values, such as the effort to improve, the effort to win, perseverance, stamina (Martinkova, 2012).

Vealey and Chase (2016) also pointed out that sports is a particularly fertile context to teach moral and life lessons because competition involves striving to achieve one's goals against the opponent who is trying to prevent it. Although some writers (Shields & Bredemeier, 2009; Kochanek et al., 2019) have pointed out that the Latin roots of the word "competition" suggest that the essence of competition is about striving with rather than against the opponent for mutual excellence, this difference does not negate the understanding that sports provide an excellent context for character development as the continual striving to improve oneself to attain greater heights remains core to the process. This can be seen in the works of many writers (Hedstrom & Gould, 2004; Proios et al., 2004; Popescu & Masari, 2011; Santos et al., 2021) who have noted that participation in sports and competition provides a rich and authentic context in which character is both tested and honed.

Moreover, schools and sports are both social institutions and inevitably convey values through their structure and culture (Shields & Bredemeier, 2008). This could happen explicitly through the institutions' mission statements and core values or rules and regulations. Even when not explicitly articulated, moral considerations exist in the "hidden curriculum" (Narvaez, 2006) in the way teachers and coaches treat their athletes, the coaching styles that they adopt, and every day decisions made that have an impact on the team. For example, when a "star" athlete continues to be fielded despite repeated unsportsmanlike behaviour, the message to other athletes is that winning is more important than sportsmanship.

Beyond the understanding that sports is a natural and inevitable context where character development takes place is the conception that the building of character improves sporting development. Such a conception is perhaps the most important in convincing teachers and coaches that athletic development and character development are not contradictory but synergistic. Borrowing from research organisational management and leadership research, it is suggested that values-driven leadership may lead to positive results for staff and the organisation (Crossan & Bednar, 2018). As suggested by the authors (p. 113),

> [W]e could speculate that teams with value driven coaches would be less likely to have player injury and sickness; their players would be more likely to recover from defeat and be less affected by inconsistent referees; and be more likely to remember team plays.

Therefore, when extended to the sporting arena, the belief that the building of character improves sporting development is highly plausible.

This belief is borne out in a study that examined how coaches of university sports teams achieved excellence and success for their teams over an extended period. In the study, Vallee and Bloom (2005) found that successful coaches expressed genuine concern for the personal development of their athletes and sought to help their athletes become champions both in and out of sports. To do so, these coaches deliberately spent time to build self-confidence, nurture maturity, and create a sense of ownership in their athletes during training. Applying the learning from the study, Vallee then led a college and a varsity team to successes that were sustained for an extended period of time after taking the helm of each team for only two to three years (Vallee & Bloom, 2016). The varsity team even obtained a combined regular season and playoff winning percentage of greater than 80% and won five consecutive Canadian national championships. What was even more significant about the teams' successes was that both teams had previously been unsuccessful and insignificant teams.

APPLIED INSIGHTS

There is therefore strong reason to believe that the goals of athletic development and character building can be synergistic. Part of this can be explained by the positive effect on athlete motivation, which in turn leads to better trust in their coaches, sportsmanship, and other positive attitudes to sports (Stupuris et al., 2013) that support better sporting performance. As such, while the training in sports-specific physical, psychomotor, tactical, and psychological domains are essential aspects of any school sports programmes, the character development aspect should not be neglected. While this might present a dilemma to teachers and coaches, resulting in the paradox discussed earlier, we believe that it is not a question of more training hours but a matter of working smarter (Narvaez, 2006) and leveraging the natural opportunities within any school sports programmes for doing so. As stated by Beller (2002), well-organised, sports character education can provide powerful contexts for the teaching and learning of good moral habits. In other words, the building of character through sports can be done through systematic or non-systematic approaches and involve formal and/or informal processes. Here, we offer two suggestions for how this can be done through (1) nurturing a safe culture and climate that pursues excellence and (2) intentional programme design.

Nurturing a Safe Culture and Climate That Pursues Excellence

In an extensive study spanning two years, Lickona and Davidson (2005) concluded that schools that have effective character education programmes utilised everything in the life of a school, such as the routines, curriculum planned or unplanned, co-curricular activities, or discipline practices, in other words, the culture and climate, to foster excellence and ethics. The same can be said of school sports programmes which are a subset of a school. To help teachers and coaches have a simple handle on how they can shape the culture and climate of their programmes, we suggest that they should focus on shaping a team culture and training climate that is safe and pursues excellence.

Physical and psychological safety should be the basis for all learning, including athletic and character development, as it is unlikely that the learning of athletic skills or moral lessons will be effective when athletes are in a state of fear (Beard & Wilson, 2018; Newman et al., 2018; Smetana, 2006; Vallee & Bloom, 2005). Beyond just a baseline level of safety, teachers and coaches should also aim to nurture a sense of belonging to the team. This is because the nurturing of values such as justice, compassion, fairness, respect, and responsibility requires the context of a community to which one feels attached (Smetana, 2006; Vallee and Bloom, 2005).

According to Shields and Bredemeier (2009), excellence is a journey that is never fully completed, and it is the pursuit (journey) of excellence, which is about the continual improvement of oneself that matters. In their research, Donoso-Morales et al. (2017) found that successful coaches created and sustained a culture of excellence demanding high levels of commitment, nurturing daily habits, and core values such as hard work and discipline.

How, then, can teachers and coaches nurture a team culture and training climate that is safe and pursues excellence? We believe that we do not need to look far, as extant knowledge in sports psychology on motivation can provide us with most of the answers. For example, researchers have long found that low task orientation and high ego orientation are associated with higher endorsement of "unsportspersonlike" play and the rating of aggressive acts as more acceptable. (Bredemeier & Shields, 2006). Studies (e.g., Leo et al., 2015; Stupuris et al., 2013) have also observed that motivational climates in sports trainings affect athletes' moral behaviours. Of direct relevance is Nicholls' developmental theory of achievement motivation which sports researchers have applied to settings in youth sports (Duda, 1987; Shields & Bredemeier, 2008).

Based on theories of achievement motivation, a task (mastery) orientation is one where individuals focus on mastery of the task, skill development, exerting effort, and self-improvement. The alternative is an ego (performance) orientation where social comparison becomes the indicator of success, and the emphasis is on outperforming others (preferably with minimal effort) to attain recognition and status (Smith & Smoll, 2009). It is generally accepted that a mastery orientation is preferred to an ego orientation as studies have shown that the latter is associated with negative behaviours such as inconsistent efforts, higher levels of performance anxiety, reduced persistence or withdrawal in the face of failure, decreased intrinsic motivation for sports involvement, and a willingness to use deception and illegal methods in order to win (Duda, 1987; Roberts et al. 2007 as cited in Smith & Smoll, 2009, p. 174). As such, an ego orientation can be seen to be contradictory to the pursuit of excellence and should be discouraged in school sports. This is because when an athlete's goal is to appear superior over others rather than to improve themselves, the pursuit of personal, task-specific goals necessary for improvement is undermined (Kochanek et al., 2019).

While individuals would have characteristics of both orientations, they tend towards different ones in different situations, with the motivational climate influencing their orientations (Bredemeier & Shields, 2006; Shields & Bredemeier, 2008). To nurture athletes who favour a task orientation, teachers and coaches should promote a mastery climate where teachers, coaches, or parents define success in terms of self-improvement, task mastery, and exhibiting maximum effort and dedication (Ames, 1992, as cited in Smith & Smoll, 2009). To promote a mastery climate where athletes feel safe and pursue excellence, teachers and coaches can achieve the following:

- Emphasise participation, effort, continual improvement, and task mastery rather than innate ability and competitive outcomes (Smetana, 2006; Bredemeier & Shields, 2006).
- Help athletes appreciate the important role of mistakes in the learning process (Bredemeier & Shields, 2006).
- Value every athlete in the team equally regardless of their athletic abilities (Vallee & Bloom, 2005)
- Be aware of each athlete's sports and competition readiness (Kochanek et al., 2019; Purcell, 2005)
- Focus on the common good and promote cooperation and collective responsibility rather than team rivalry (Bredemeier & Shields, 2006; Power et al., as cited in Smetana, 2006)
- Encourage student agency and independence by involving athletes in decision-making and dialogues on team matters (Bredemeier & Shields, 2006; Morris, 2019; Newman et al., 2018; Vallee & Bloom, 2016)
- Make the principle of respect (Smetana, 2006) for all by all (including adults and spectators) an integral part of the team culture and climate.
- Ensure that the training environment and any equipment used are properly maintained and safe for use.

Intentional Programme Design

Past studies (Crossan & Bednar, 2018; Koh & Camiré, 2015; Koh et al., 2016; Newman & Kim, 2017; Newman et al., 2018) have pointed to the importance of the intentionality of teachers and coaches involved in sports and that their attitudes and behaviours are key to successful character education through sports. To convince teachers and coaches who might be more concerned with preparing athletes for competition than building their character, it is important that we leverage the rich and naturally occurring opportunities that are part and parcel of most, if not all sports programmes and competitions (Shields & Bredemeier, 2009; Newman et al. 2018; Proios et al., 2004; Santos et al., 2021). Such an idea is not new, as researchers (Crossan & Bednar, 2018; Fullinwider, 2006; Martinkova, 2012) have examined values that are inherent to sports participation and competition such as discipline and sportsmanship.

These naturally occurring opportunities could range from simple events where direct teaching and messaging methods would usually suffice to rich experiences that call for more systematic constructivist experiential-based approaches. *How then, can we intentionally design the sports programme to leverage these valuable events and experiences in sports so that there is synergy between athletic and character development?* We suggest that this could be done with the understanding of the phases in a typical sports programme and the key events and experiences that an athlete would go through in such a programme. In the following sections, we give an example of each, as well as suggestions for other events and experiences that teachers and coaches could utilise for character development.

In Singapore, a typical school sports programme would include preparatory, competitive, and transition phases (MOE, 2023), with each phase including various key experiences that an athlete would go through. The main athletic development focus in the preparatory phase is to develop students' physical fitness, psychomotor, fundamental and basic technical skills to build the foundation for more intense and sports-specific technical skills in the competitive phase that follows. Tactically, the focus is on learning individual tactics with some introduction to team tactics.

An example of an event that takes place in this phase would be the first training session of the season when new members join the team. Besides icebreaking and induction activities conducted to help team members get to know one another, the occasion also provides a good opportunity for emphasising the messages relating to teamwork and respect for diversity. While this might appear simple and intuitive, sports coaches who are naturally more concerned about athletic development can easily overlook such events and the naturally occurring opportunities for character building.

As training moves from the preparatory to the competitive phase, the athletic development focus shifts towards more technical and sports-specific skills required in a competitive setting. There will also be more focus on team tactics and mental skills that are required for competition. A significant event that athletes would have to go through in this phase would be the selection (and deselection) of players for the competition. In comparison to the icebreaking and induction activities mentioned in the previous paragraph, the event of selection is a much richer "experience" characterised by being a real-world problem (Morris, 2019) with real and immediate consequences (Newman et al., 2018).

Table 13.1 outlines some other possible opportunities that teachers and coaches could utilise in their sports programmes. However, it should be noted that simply allowing athletes to go through the events would not be sufficient, and guidance from teachers and coaches is essential.

Table 13.1 Suggested Key Events and Learning Opportunities

Preparatory Phase: Key Events and Learning Opportunities
Icebreaking and Induction of New Team Members
For all athletes (through icebreaking and team-building activities)
• Teamwork
• Respect teammates, teachers, and coaches, and appreciate diversity
For senior team members (through organising and planning the activities)
• Self-confidence
• Organisational skills
• Perspective taking
Setting of Team Rules and Expectations during First or Second Training Session
For all athletes (through dialogue and coming to a consensus on team rules and expectations)
• Commitment to striving for and giving one's best
• Responsibility to self and team
Election of Team Captains and Other Appointment Holders
For all athletes (through dialogue and voting)
• Respect for the democratic process
• Understanding of civic processes and responsibilities
• Concern for common good beyond individual friendships
For elected appointment holders
• Managing power and responsibility

(Continued)

Table 13.1 *(Cont.)*

Goal Setting

For all athletes (through setting individual and team goals guided by teachers and coaches)

- Self-awareness
- Growth mindset
- Commitment to striving for and giving one's best

Mental Skills Training in Sports

For all athletes

- Arousal and emotional regulation
- Metacognition

Competitive Phase: Key Events and Learning Opportunities

Taking Part in Competition

For all athletes

- Respect for competitors and officials
- Arousal and emotional management
- Sportsmanship
- Adaptability

Transition Phase: Key Events and Learning Opportunities

Postseason Reflection

For all athletes (through reflection on and evaluation of goals set)

- Metacognition
- Self-evaluation
- Understanding one's strengths and weaknesses

End of Season Gathering and Farewell

For all athletes (through thanking others who have helped them and the team)

- Appreciation and gratitude

Experienced teachers and coaches would not find the events suggested in Table 13.1 new or unfamiliar. As such, all they would need to do is to identify and make explicit the key messages and lessons that they hope to transmit or reinforce through these events. The advantage of such an approach would be, firstly, that there is no need for the planning of additional and unnecessary events in the already crowded training programme. Secondly, such events provide an authentic and engaging context in which athletes learn and practise the identified character education "lessons" in a pursuit that they are passionate in and can relate to. As noted by Beard and Wilson (2018), experiences that have significance for the learner provide engagement and therefore potential for change to the person.

To help athletes learn from the rich experiences inherent to sports, we believe that we can learn from experiential education and learning approaches which have been more commonly associated with outdoor and adventure education. This belief aligns with Donoso-Morales et al. (2017), Koh et al. (2016), and Newman and his colleagues (Newman & Kim, 2017; Newman et al., 2018), who have seen the potential of adopting experiential-based approaches to values education and positive youth development. This arises from the understanding that sports-based positive youth development and experiential-based programming share many key design features, as well as best practices (Newman & Kim, 2017).

We suggest that firstly, athletes should be allowed to experience the real and immediate consequences (Newman et al., 2018) that follow the experience. The consequences in turn lead to different emotions, positive or negative, that can underpin learning (Beard & Wilson, 2018). The experience of selection (and deselection) mentioned earlier is understandably one of joy for some and one of disappointment for others. Either way, the cognitive and emotional dissonance creates a state of disequilibrium (Manners et al., 2004; Nalani et al., 2021) that requires the athlete to sense-make (Beard & Wilson, 2018) and learn from the experience. For example, the state of joy provides a suitable context for discussing the lesson of complacency, while the state of disappointment would be suitable for conversations about resilience and understanding one's strengths and weaknesses. Similarly, Shields and Bredemeier (2008) have also cited the works of Larson and colleagues (2000, 2005), who found that youths reported experiences that combined challenge, deep concentration, and heightened intrinsic motivation during sports and suggested that such experiences are essential for developing the ability to direct attention and effort that can be associated with the development of moral will.

To facilitate this, teachers and coaches can use the four-stage learning cycle by Kolb (1984), as cited in Koh et al. (2016), which guides educators and learners in transforming experience into learning to guide the design of the learning experience. As they do so, considerations that teachers and coaches would do well to keep in mind include:

- Be aware of the different experiences in sports participation and possible consequences that offer powerful opportunities for learning. Besides the team selection mentioned earlier, the most significant experience for most athletes would be participation in competition. Table 13.2 provides some suggested consequences of competition that offer such powerful learning opportunities.

Table 13.2 Suggested Possible Experiences for Learning Arising from Participating in Competition

Possible Experiences	Possible Consequences	Possible Learning Goals
Before competition	• Readiness for competition	• Self-discipline and responsibility
During competition	• Reaction to situations e.g. poor umpiring, rough play from opponents • Consequences of game decisions made • Conflicts with teammates	• Arousal and emotional management • Metacognition • Teamwork
Outcome of competition	• Winning or losing • Achieving or falling short of targets set	• Humility in victory and grace in defeat • Reflection on strengths and weaknesses

- Allow students to sense-make through critical reflection instead of giving explicit "answers" or telling them what they should be thinking. While this will be more time-consuming, the process of transforming experience into meaning by an individual is what leads to the learning and not the answers themselves.
- Facilitate and guide athletes in their sense-making (when necessary) by asking clarifying, sensing, and influencing questions (Ministry of Education [MOE], 2022).

SUMMARY AND FUTURE DIRECTIONS

In this chapter, we have suggested two approaches that would allow teachers and coaches to take a more deliberate and systematic approach to the integration of athletic and character development. While effective application of the two should have permeated somewhat most aspects of the sports programme, they should also not neglect the impact of less structured approaches like role modelling and teachable moments. Role modelling is an informal process of character education where children imitate and learn from the actions of significant adults (Beller, 2002; Vealey & Chase, 2016), whether the adult intended for it to happen or not. Similarly, teachable moments arise frequently in sports due to the dynamic nature of sports (Arnold, 1984; Newman et al., 2018; Santos et al., 2021) and how adults respond to (or not) the moment would convey the priorities of the adult. As such, teachers and coaches would need to ensure that they recognise and cultivate teachable moral moments as they arise in training and competition and "walk the talk" (Vealey & Chase, 2016, p. 625), and ensure that their words and actions support what they are doing to promote a mastery climate where athletes feel safe and pursue excellence.

However, more crucial than the approaches is the intention and attitudes of the adults involved (Berkowitz & Bier, 2005; Crossan & Bednar, 2018; Newman & Kim, 2017; Newman et al., 2018). Past studies have noted that successful character education through sports is very much affected by the attitudes and behaviours of adults delivering the programmes (Koh and Camiré, 2015; Newman & Kim, 2017). Unfortunately, while policymakers and curriculum developers have articulated the intention to use sports to promote athletic and character development (Bailey et al., 2009 as cited in Koh & Camiré, 2015; Ministry of Education Singapore [MOE], n.d.; Ministry of Education [MOE], Singapore 2022), this might not be the case with teachers and coaches managing sports teams for various reasons discussed. As such, it would be important for those who wish to see the successful character development of athletes through sports to start by influencing the hearts and minds of the teachers and coaches directly working with youth athletes. It is hoped that what we have explained about the paradox and the approaches suggested would help teachers and coaches to see that athletic development and character education are synergistic rather than contradictory and thus put greater effort into integrating the two in their sports programmes. In addition, it would be crucial for adults involved to be trained and familiar with how they could apply the suggested approaches in their work in school sports.

REFERENCES

Arnold, P. J. (1984). Sport, moral education and the development of character. *Journal of Philosophy of Education*, 18(2), 275–281.

Bailey, R. P., Hillman, C., Arent, S., & Petitpas, A. (2012). Physical activity as an investment in personal and social change: The human capital model. *Journal of Physical Activity and Health*, 9, 1053–1055.

Bailey, R. P., Hillman, C., Arent, S., & Petitpas, A. (2013). Physical activity: An underestimated investment in human capital? *Journal of Physical Activity and Health*, 10, 289–308.

Beard, C., & Wilson, J. P. (2018). *Experiential learning: A practical guide for training, coaching and education*. Kogan Page.

Beller, J. (2002). Positive character development in school sport programs. *ERIC Digest*, 12, 1–8. https://files.eric.ed.gov/fulltext/ED477729.pdf

Berkowitz, M. B., & Bier, M. C. (2005). *What works in character education: A research-driven guide for educators*. Researchgate. https://www.researchgate.net/profile/Marvin-Berkowitz-2/publication/251977043_What_Works_In_Character_Education/links/53fb5ea60cf22f21c2f31c28/What-Works-In-Character-Education.pdf

Bredemeier, B., & Shields, D. (1995). *Character development and physical activity*. Human Kinetics.

Bredemeier, B. L., & Shields, D. L. (2006). Sports and character development. *Research Digest*, 7(1), 1–8. https://www.govinfo.gov/app/details/GOVPUB-HE20-PURL-gpo42236

Camiré, M. & Trudel, P. (2010). High school athletes' perspectives on character development through sport participation. *Physical Education & Sport Pedagogy*, 15, 193–207. https://doi.org/10.1080/17408980902877617.

Coakley, J. (2001). Sport and children: Are organised programs worth the effort. In J. Coakley (Ed.), *Sport in society: Issues and controversies* (7th ed., pp. 109–136). McGraw-Hill Inc.

Crossan, W., & Bednar, M. (2018). A critical evaluation of the development and use of values in coaching. *AUC Kinanthropologica*, 54(2), 96–117.

Donoso-Morales, D., Bloom, G. A., & Caron, J. G. (2017). Creating and sustaining a culture of excellence: Insights from accomplished university team-sport coaches. *Research Quarterly for Exercise and Sport*, 88(4), 503–512. http://doi.org/10.1080/02701367.2017.1370531

Doty, J. (2006). Sports build character?! *Journal of College and Character*, 7(3), 1–9.

Duda, J. L. (1987). Toward a developmental theory of children's motivation in sport. *Journal of Sport Psychology*, 9, 130–145.

Dunn, J. G., & Dunn, J. C. (1999). Goal orientations, perceptions of aggression, and sportspersonship in elite male youth ice hockey players. *The Sport Psychologist*, 13, 183–200.

Ferris, K., Ettekal, A., Agans, J., & Burkhard, B. (2016). Character development through youth sport: High school coaches' perspectives about a character-based education program. *Journal of Youth Development*, 10, 127–140. https://doi.org/10.5195/JYD.2015.13.

Fullinwider, R. K. (2006). *Sports, youth and character: A critical survey*. ERIC. Retrieved December 4, 2023, from https://files.eric.ed.gov/fulltext/ED491127.pdf

Gerdy, J. (2000). *Sport in school: The future if an institution*. Teachers College Columbia.

Hedstrom, R., & Gould, D. (2004, January 11). *Research in youth sports: Critical issues status*. (Issue 1) [White Paper Summaries of the Existing Literature]. Researchgate. Retrieved from https://www.researchgate.net/publication/247397067_Research_in_Youth_Sports_Critical_Issues_Status

Hellison, D. (2003). *Teaching responsibility through physical activity*. Human Kinetics.

Keegan, R. J., Harwood, C. G., Spray, C. M., & Lavallee, D. E. (2009). A qualitative investigation exploring the motivational climate in early career sports participants: coach, parent and peer influences on sport motivation. *Psychology of Sport and Exercise*, 10, 361–372.

Kochanek, J., Matthews, A., Wright, E., Disanti, J., Neff, M., & Erickson, K. (2019). Competitive readiness: Developmental considerations to promote positive youth development in competitive activities. *Journal of Youth Development, 14*(1), 48–69. https://doi.org/10.5195/jyd.2019.671

Koh, K. T., & Camiré, M. (2015). Strategies for the development of life skills and values though sport programmes. In H. Leng, & N. Hsu (Eds.), *Emerging trends and innovation in sports marketing and management in Asia* (pp. 241–257). IGI Global. Retrieved from https://www.researchgate.net/publication/273058531_Strategies_for_the_Development_of_Life_Skills_and_Values_through_Sport_Programmes_Review_and_Recommendations

Koh, K. T., Koh, S. W., & Camire, M. (2016). Implementation of a values training program in physical education and sport: Perspectives from teachers, coaches, students, and athletes. *Physical Education and Sport Pedagogy, 21*(3), 295–312. http://doi.org/10.1080/17408989.2014.990369

Krauuse, J., & Priest, R. (1993). Sport value choices of US Military cadets – A longitudinal study of the class of 1993 (Unpublished manuscript, Office of Institutional Research, U.S. Military Academy. West Point, NY).

Leo, F. M., Sanchez-Miguel, P. A., Sanchez-Oliva, D., Amado, D., & Garcia-Calvo, T. (2015). Motivational climate created by other significant actors and antisocial behaviors in youth sport. *Kinesiology, 47*(1), 3–10.

Lickona, T., & Davidson, M. (2005). *Smart and good high schools: Integrating excellence and ethics for success in school, work, and beyond.* (A Report to the Nation). Cortland, NY: Center for the 4th and rth Rs (Respect and Responsibility).

Manners, J., Durkin, K., & Nesdale, A. (2004). Promoting advanced ego development among adults. *Journal of Adult Development, 11*(1), 19–27. https://www.researchgate.net/publication/227062563

Martinkova, I. (2012). Teaching values in movement activities: Inherent and added values. *Acta Universitatis Carolinae, Kinanthropologica, 48*(2), 111–119. https://karolinum.cz/data/clanek/724/Kinan_2_2012_10_martinkova.pdf

Ministry of Education. (2022). *Character and Citizenship Teaching and Learning Guide* [Internal Working Document].

Ministry of Education, Singapore. (2022). *Establishing Clarity, Planning and Delivery of Student Development Experiences (Secondary)* [Internal Working Document].

Ministry of Education, Singapore. (2023). *Annex D5 - Physical Sports Co-curricular Activities* [Manuscript submitted for internal working document].

Ministry of Education, Singapore. (n.d.). *Co-Curricular Handbook* [Internal Working Document].

Morris, T. H. (2019). Experiential learning – a systematic review and revision of Kolb's model [Accepted Manuscript (pre-published)]. Google Scholar. https://researchspace.bathspa.ac.uk/13077/1/13077.pdf

Nalani, A., Gomez, C., & Garrod, A. C. (2021). Constructive disequilibrium and transformative pedagogy: Developing global citizens in faraway spaces. *Journal of the Scholarship of Teaching and Learning, 21*(4), 151–163. http://files.eric.ed.gov/fulltextEJ1340423.pdf

Narvaez, D. (2006). Integrative ethical education. In M. Killen & J. G. Smetana (Eds.), *Handbook of moral development* (pp. 703–732). Lawrence Erlbaum Associates, Publishers.

Newman, T. J., & Kim, M. (2017). *An Experiential Approach to Sport for Youth Development* [Manuscript submitted to Journal of Experiential Education, March 2017. Original version prior to peer-review]. Researchgate. https://www.researchgate.net/publication/314462876

Newman, T. J., Kim, M., Tucker, A. R., & Alvarez, A. G. (2018). Learning through the adventure of youth sport. *Physical Education and Sport Pedagogy.*, 23(3), 280–293. https://doi.org/10.1080/17408989.2017.1413708

Omar-Fauzee, M. S., Nazarudin, M. N., Saputra, Y. M., Taweesuk, D., Latif, R. A., & Soh, K. G. (2012). The strategies for character building through sports participation. *International Journal of Academic Research in Business and Social Sciences*, 2(3), 48–58.

Parker, M., & Stiehl, J. (2004). Personal and social responsibility. In D. Tannehill & J. Lund (Eds.), *Standards-based physical education curriculum development*. Boston, MA: Jones and Bartlett, 131–153.

Popescu, V., & Masari, G.-A. (2011). Comparative Analysis of athletes' fair play attitude according to specific variables conditioned by sports training and competition. *Procedia Social and Behavioral Sciences*, 12, 24–29. Retrieved from https://www.researchgate.net/publication/248392430_Comparative_Analysis_of_athletes%27_fair_play_attitude_according_to_specific_variables_conditioned_by_sports_training_and_competition?enrichId=rgreq-e23a881e46a5e190015a88c08786a842-XXX&enrichSource=Y292ZX

Proios, M., Doganis, G., & Athanalidis, I. (2004). Moral development and form of participation, type of sport, and sport experience. *Perceptual and Motor Skills*, 99, 633–642. Retrieved from https://www.researchgate.net/publication/8167737_Moral_Development_and_Form_of_Participation_Type_of_Sport_and_Sport_Experience

Purcell, L. (2005). Sport readiness in children and youth. *Paediatrics & Child Health*, 10(6), 343–344. Retrieved from https://www.ncbi.nlm.nih.gov/pmc/articles/PMC2722975/

Santos, L. L. M., Vissoci, J. R. N., & Olivera, L. P. (2021). Systematic review of the literature about moral in the sport context. *Saud Pesq*, 14(1). Retrieved from https://www.researchgate.net/publication/350068224

Shields, D. L., & Bredemeier, B. J. (2009). *True competition: A guide to pursuing excellence in sport and society*. Human Kinetics.

Shields, D. L., & Bredemeier, B. L. (2008). Sport and the development of character. In L. P. Nucci & D. Narvaez (Eds.), *Handbook of moral and character education*. Taylor & Francis. Retrieved from https://www.academia.edu/download/31312948/_Larry_Nucci__Handbook_of_Moral_and_Character_Educ(BookFi.org).pdf#page=517

Smetana, J. G. (2006). Social-cognitive domain theory: Consistencies and variations in children's moral and social judgements. In M. Killen & J. G. Smetana (Eds.), *Handbook of moral development* (pp. 119–153). Lawrence Erlbaum Associates, Publishers.

Smith, R. E., & Smoll, F. L. (2009). Motivational climate and changes in young athletes' achievement goal orientations. *Motivation and Emotion*, 2009(33), 173–183.

Stupuris, T., Sukys, S., & Tilindiene, I. (2013). Relationship between adolescent athletes' values and behavior in sport and perceived coach's character development competency. *Baltic Journal of Sport and Health Sciences*, 4(91), 37–45. Retrieved from https://www.researchgate.net/publication/333139262

Vallee, C. N., & Bloom, G. A. (2005). Building a successful university program: Key and common elements of expert coaches. *Journal of Applied Sport Psychology*, (17), 179–196. http://doi.org/10.1080/10413200591010021

Vallee, C. N., & Bloom, G. A. (2016). Four keys to building a championship culture. *International Sport Coaching Journal*, 3, 170–177.

Vealey, R. S., & Chase, M. A. (2016). *Best practice for youth sport*. Human Kinetics.

Walters, S. R., Schluter, P. J., Oldham, A. R. H., Thomson, R. W., & Payne, D. (2012). The sideline behaviour of coaches at children's team sports game. *Psychology of Sport and Exercise*, 13(2), 208–215.

Practical Strategies for Using a Trauma-Informed Approach to Support Life Skills Transferability through Physical Education and Sports

Chapter Fourteen

Kalyn McDonough and Jenn M Jacobs

INTRODUCTION

It has been widely acknowledged that physical education and sports (PES) have the potential to teach life skills along with sports skills to student-athletes (Koh et al., 2016), promote positive youth development (Holt et al., 2017), and have implications for social justice (Camiré et al., 2022). Prior research has established support for explicitly integrating life skills and values within PES activities, which can help facilitate the transfer of these lessons beyond the learning context (Bean et al., 2018). Despite these critical opportunities, very real challenges exist across communities and sporting organizations that affect practitioners' abilities to engage and thoughtfully support young people in learning life skills within programs and facilitating transfer into their lives off the field. These challenges include factors such as a global pandemic, poverty, racism, and community violence, among others, which can equate to stress and trauma in childhood. These community and individual-level traumas can impact young people's abilities to access PES activities, constructively engage, and successfully transfer life skills learned through their involvement. Recognizing the pervasiveness of childhood trauma, there is a need to adopt trauma-informed approaches in PES activities, which can support *all* young people. Our chapter will provide an overview of what we currently know about childhood trauma and the role that PES can play in facilitating spaces of healing. Integrated throughout the chapter are the voices and expertise of practitioners from sports-based organizations who are working to apply these concepts with young people in PES settings. The chapter will conclude with practical strategies that coaches and practitioners can utilize to intentionally integrate life skills into their PES activities, utilizing a trauma-informed approach to support transferability.

DOI: 10.4324/9781032688657-18

Life Skills through PES

The mechanisms through which PES is able to impart valuable physical, cognitive, behavioral, and social skills among participants have been thoroughly explored in recent research (Jacobs & Wright, 2018; Pierce et al., 2017). It has been summarized that due to the authentic experiences that arise during PES experiences, coaches and instructors are in opportune positions to help participants recognize and practice psychosocial skills. Similar to the physical skill development that is inherent to physical activity, life skills should be taught through demonstration, modeling, and application (Danish & Hale, 1981; Jacobs & Wright, 2018). Youth can then be empowered to utilize life skills outside the PES context to help them prosper in their prospective life contexts, such as school, home, and social domains (Danish et al., 2005).

Life skill content in PES can take many different routes, where coaches can focus on interpersonal skills (e.g., teamwork, conflict resolution, leadership) or intrapersonal skills (e.g., perseverance, self-regulation, authenticity). Importantly, one integral aspect of teaching life skills through PES is finding ways to creatively integrate values and life skills within activities. This intentional integration of life skills in program design and instruction aligns with the idea that these skills need to be "taught" rather than "caught" (Hodge, 1989).

Transferability

Transferability of life skills in PES is the intentional action of making connections between the skills learned in the PES context (e.g., leadership, responsibility) and the application of those skills in different life contexts (Jacobs & Wright, 2018). The transfer process therefore involves three distinct yet interacting elements: (a) the individual, (b) the sports/learning context (e.g., where the sports and life skills are being taught), and (c) the transfer contexts (e.g., home, school, community, social settings) (Pierce et al., 2017).

There is a multitude of research that captures the various facilitators and barriers to the transfer of life skills through PES, with a strong consensus that transfer occurs when youth are supported in thinking about the relevance of lessons outside of sports and are motivated to adopt those behaviors in their prospective life contexts (Jacobs & Wright, 2018). Notably, this process is heavily influenced by a socioecological framework, which suggests that individuals cannot learn behaviors isolated from their environments. Research points to several factors that impact the complex transfer process, including youth factors (i.e., age, gender, race, maturity, psychological processes, internal assets), coaching characteristics (values, philosophy, training), and environmental norms (social climate, socioeconomics, dominant values, external assets) (Jacobs & Wright, 2018; Pierce et al., 2019), but currently, we have a more limited understanding of the impact of childhood trauma in this complex process.

Childhood Trauma

Childhood trauma is considered a global public health issue and refers to stressful, dangerous, or life-threatening events that leave a child feeling overwhelmed or helpless (CCTASI, 2023). In understanding what makes an event traumatic, it has been described as the "Three E's of Trauma," which include the event, the experience, and the effect (SAMHSA, 2014). The event refers to the threat or experience of harm, whether once or multiple times. The experience refers to the young person's perception of the event, which is unique to each child, where perception and experience of an event as "traumatic" will vary. Lastly, the effect is the immediate or long-term impact of the experience. What we are coming to learn and understand through years of study is the pervasiveness of childhood trauma, the varying forms of traumatic experiences, and their very real impact on children's lifelong development (Felitti et al., 1998).

"Adverse childhood experiences," or ACEs, are a group of potentially traumatic events that have been used to study childhood trauma. They include experiences such as violence, abuse, or neglect; witnessing violence in the home; or growing up in a household with substance abuse issues, mental health challenges, or instability through parental divorce, absence, and/or incarceration (CDC, 2023). In the United States, more than 46% of young people (or 34 million children) under the age of 18 have had at least one ACE, and more than 20% have had at least two (RWJF, 2018). In a global study on ACEs involving 21 countries and 51,945 adults, 38.8% of respondents reported experiencing at least one ACE before the age of 18 (Kessler et al., 2010). Not surprisingly, the study also found that ACEs were highly interrelated, meaning that a child experiencing one type of adversity increased their likelihood of experiencing other adversities. Although ACEs are reported among all young people, because of structural inequities, higher rates are seen among low-income and minoritized populations (RWJF, 2018).

Although the reported rates of ACEs are already high, the original classification of ACEs does not account for community context and, thus, may not accurately account for traumatic experiences that result from living in high-crime and high-poverty communities (Giovanelli & Reynolds, 2021). Situating childhood trauma within community contexts helps us consider what other events could result in traumatic experiences for young people, but to date, they have been less explored. Although it is too recent to understand its long-term effects, the COVID-19 global pandemic, for some children, resulted in the loss of family members, fear of the unknown, increased social isolation, and fractures in key developmental milestones, which have the potential to equate to traumatic experiences. For other children, adverse experiences did not come by way of a recent global pandemic but rather through long-standing societal injustices resulting in poverty, racism, and discrimination (Wade et al., 2014). Unfortunately, if young people are not supported with adequate resources, traumatic experiences can lead to long-term negative outcomes.

Outcomes associated with childhood traumatic experiences reveal negative impacts that are pervasive and long-standing. Without adequate support, an adverse experience can bubble over into an intolerable level of stress for a young person, impacting their brain and body, and affecting social, emotional, and cognitive development (Center on the Developing Child, n.d.). Due to the impact on the brain and body, traumatic experiences have been associated with detriments in physical and mental health, challenges in learning, increased substance use, and decreased life expectancy (Mersky et al., 2013; Felitti et al., 1998).

This is not an attempt to stigmatize all young people as "traumatized" but rather to move to an understanding of a universal experience of trauma and highlight the necessity of building our own collective capacity to create spaces of healing for our young people while also working to change community conditions that place some young people at greater risk for traumatic experiences. Broadening this understanding of childhood adversity further underpins the need to infuse PES spaces with a trauma-informed approach, which can support young people in productively engaging and transferring valuable lessons learned in PES.

Sports as Spaces of Healing

What is encouraging and galvanizing is that when constructed to do so, PES is uniquely positioned to support healing and provide a buffer against the negative effects of trauma. Specifically, it is the supportive relationships, physical activity, predictable and manageable stress, and opportunities for competency and skill-building that make PES such a valuable opportunity to support young people (Folco, 2023; CHJS, n.d.). So much so that child trauma expert Dr. Bruce Perry said,

> Sports is naturally structured to provide relational dosing that is much more therapeutically sensitive than traditional therapy. If we make coaches 5% more trauma-informed, or developmentally sensitive, we will have more therapeutic impact on children than if we trained an entire new cohort of trauma therapists.
>
> (CHJS, n.d., p. 13)

The Center for Healing and Justice through Sports (CHJS) is a national organization based in the United States and is focused on increasing awareness and access to healing-centered sports. They expand on the facets of sports that make it such a powerful intervention and provide quick tips for practitioners interested in infusing these concepts into their programs:

> At CHJS, we recognize trauma as the wrenching away of control when it's needed the most. Acknowledging that traditional sports systems strip athletes of their power and control, we advocate for a paradigm shift. By intentionally redesigning sports experiences, we can transform these spaces into healing-centered environments. By focusing on the power of positive relationships, we acknowledge the innate human need for connection and belonging. Through patterned, repetitive movement, we offer a pathway for regulation, enabling young people to access their higher cognitive functions. By introducing manageable patterns of stress, we empower young people with choices and success, fostering resilience and competence.
>
> So how do we do it? We make a series of small, biologically respectful pivots, which are mindful of what the brain needs for regulation.

Focus on supportive relationships.

Our brains are wired for connection. We need trusted relationships to feel safe.

- DON'T: Expect all kids to "fit this system or find somewhere else to play."
- DO: Create unity through a team handshake. Young people will feel like a part of something special.

Use movement to do more than train.

Sports is full of opportunities to introduce somatosensory movement through patterned, repetitive rhythmic activities. This type of movement is naturally regulating and allows our brains to move from survival mode to accessing its higher functions.

- DON'T: Isolate and contain dysregulated young people. Connect and move with them.
- DO: Incorporate opportunities for movement, like a ritual or routine, prior to challenges (think pre-foul shot routine in basketball) and in moments of dysregulation.

Create manageable patterns of stress.

The answer to overwhelming stress or trauma isn't no stress. It's the introduction of "good" stress- that is moderate, predictable, and controlled and if dosed appropriately, will lead to increased levels of resilience and competence.

- DON'T: Assume that all young people enjoy high stakes competition.
- DO: Give choice. Create three versions of a drill (beginner, middle, advanced). Let the athlete choose. In five minutes, call a reset where the athlete can stay, or switch to a different level.

> These biologically respectful pivots serve as the foundation for a transformative approach to sports that supports young people in their physical pursuits and nurtures their mental and emotional well-being. By implementing these changes, we pave the way for sports to serve as a healing tool, empowering ALL young people to navigate the challenges of life, heal from trauma, and thrive.
> –Jillian Green Loughran, CHJS

Trauma-Informed Life Skill Transfer

Recognizing what we are learning about healing-centered sports, it is crucial to examine how trauma may be an additional contextual factor that can greatly impact young people's ability to access, learn, and transfer valuable life skills from PES to other areas of their lives. The Practice Spotlight, see Figure 14.1, describes a youth sports program intentionally designed to support a youth population with elevated rates of reported trauma, highlighting many of the concepts we will discuss moving forward.

Thus, there are key considerations within the sports/learning context and the transfer process that can be strengthened in order to adopt trauma-informed principles. Specifically, it is important that young people recognize the value of lessons learned and where they might be able to apply them. Unfortunately, youth from disenfranchised backgrounds may experience challenges recognizing the applicability of life skills given that their sports contexts may differ significantly from their life contexts (Jacobs et al., 2017). Consequently, if we are structuring programs that empower young people to understand the ways that they can deal with difficult emotions, to regain a sense of control, to calm themselves through physical activity, and to reengage their executive functioning in stressful situations, this can have universal and transcending utility and value. If young people are supported adequately in learning and practicing these skills and experience benefits, this can increase their motivation for application in other settings. Therefore, the purpose of this next section is to explore a specific case study of a program focused on life skill transfer with youth who are incarcerated. Because there is a dearth of literature exploring the transfer process with youth populations who have

> **Practice Spotlight**
>
> I started Rising Phoenix Sports Program because I recognized the gap in resources for girls+ in juvenile detention centers. The potential for sports to support survivors of family violence and/or sexual abuse stood out to me in particular, as an estimated 80%-90% of justice-involved girls have experienced this type of trauma (Epstein et al., 2015). Compared to other therapies and outlets, the physicality of sports allows survivors of violence to connect with their bodies while exploring competition, leadership, collaboration, and countless other life lessons learned through sports. These qualities, when paired with a thoughtful, girl-centered curriculum and trauma-sensitive coaching techniques, are quite effective in helping youth develop protective life skills.
>
> Rising Phoenix Sports Program coaches abide by three non-negotiables: Adaptability, Positivity, and Consistency. Adaptability comes into play at nearly every practice, as we make on-the-fly adjustments to our drill plan depending on the energy of our athletes. Positivity is crucial in each session, as our athletes experience negativity from their fellow residents, facility staff, and themselves on a daily basis. Learning and growing are immensely difficult when stifled by negativity and put-downs. We aim to uplift our athletes and foster a culture where they lift up each other, as well as themselves. This is a goal that comes over time, which is why Consistency is such an important non-negotiable. Consistency in the way we show up for practices, run our drills, and prompt reflective conversations is particularly meaningful to athletes who have not experienced much consistency in life. Prior to incarceration, many justice-involved youth have tumultuous lives, and may not have many consistently caring adult relationships. We greatly value the privilege we have as coaches to support our athletes in their healing through the simple act of showing up.
>
> These three non-negotiables are designed to meet athletes where they are, rather than forcing them to participate in a way that makes them uncomfortable and could disengage them from the program completely. We will often never know the full stories of what our athletes have endured, but by remaining Adaptable, Positive, and Consistent, we aim to use sports to decrease our athletes' risk of recidivism, revictimization, and retraumatization.
>
> -Alannah Scardino, Rising Phoenix Sports Program

Figure 14.1 Practice spotlight

reported elevated rates of trauma, such as incarcerated youth (Abram et al., 2004), greater clarity is needed to understand how individual and environmental factors impact a student's ability to transfer. This work can help to enhance prior models of life skills transfer in sports-based youth development, including reconceptualizing trauma as a contextual factor influencing both the learning and transfer process (Jacobs & Wright, 2018).

APPLIED INSIGHTS

Case Example: Project FLEX

Project Fitness Leadership EXperience (FLEX) represents a partnership between a state juvenile justice department and a university. FLEX follows a sports-based youth development curriculum to impart life skills through the power of sports and provide a psychologically and physically safe place for youth who are incarcerated to participate in sports and fitness activities. The ultimate aim of the program is to teach life skills to the program participants so that they may transfer the life skills to their different environments both while incarcerated and post-incarceration.

Youth in the program are serving sentences at one of three state facilities near a major US city that has struggled with gang violence for decades. Most youth have been convicted of crimes related to gun use and will serve multiyear sentences that begin in juvenile facilities and may continue in adult facilities. Mirroring national demographics, most youth (90%) housed in these state facilities are youth of color and fall between the ages of 15 and 20 years old, with an average age of 17 years. Two of the facilities where FLEX is run are all-male facilities, with those sites housing between 40 and 200 individuals, while one facility houses female youth. Within facilities, youth are restricted to the grounds for the entirety of their sentence, except in special cases. They inhabit single occupancy rooms with a small window, built-in bed and desk, plastic chair, toilet, and small sink. Personal belongings are limited to soft-cover books, special journals without any spiral/metal objects, and toiletries provided by the state or purchased with personal funds through the facility commissary.

Many of the youth are placed in substance abuse programs, offering mental health services, including therapy and journaling. Youth who have not earned their high school diploma attend school on-site daily, where classrooms of two to four youths participate in online schooling. High school graduates may participate in employment, including food services or janitorial services. Extracurricular activities are offered weekly by external volunteers, including religious services, creative writing groups, art programs, and FLEX.

FLEX programs are run by graduate students at the partnering university who are studying a variety of sports-related (e.g., sports psychology, sports management) or social services (e.g., public administration, sociology) degrees. The majority of graduate students leading FLEX programs are students of color (75%) and males (75%). Instructors receive a variety of training familiarizing them with basic pedagogical strategies, and contextual training on juvenile justice and carceral settings.

FLEX has several programmatic offerings, but their flagship element delivers bi-weekly sports sessions to groups of youth on-site at the prison facilities. These sessions take place in a gym setting for blocks of an hour and follow a format aligned with the teaching personal and social responsibility model (Hellison, 2011), where priorities such as relationship-building, social interaction, and life skill development are at the centerfold of the program. Sessions include between 5 and 15 youths and are led by 2 graduate instructors. A typical session starts with a discussion around the life skill of the day, followed by a teambuilding activity to reinforce the skill. Next, gameplay commences and the life skill is identified by the instructor throughout the authentic experiences that arise through the sports (e.g., conflict resolution during a disagreement, leadership during timeouts, perseverance when losing). Finally, a discussion and reflection on the life skill concludes the session. There is a de-emphasis on skill-building, and instead collaborative games are set up for youth to demonstrate, practice, and reflect on the life skill of the session.

Trauma-Informed Practical Strategies

The following section describes trauma-informed practical strategies that coaches and practitioners can utilize while intentionally integrating life skills into PES. While the lessons will be presented through the lens of working in a carceral setting, these strategies may be modified to fit educational and community-based settings as well.

Addressing Youth Hierarchy of Needs: Start at the Most Basic

Maslow's hierarchy of needs represents one of the most foundational concepts in psychology, finding that any individual's motivation for engaging in future behaviors is directly impacted by a tiered set of conditions to be met from their socioecological environment (1954). Maslow posits that in order for "actualization" to be achievable, these baseline needs must be met: (a) physiological needs (e.g., food, water, shelter), (b) safety needs (e.g., security, access to health care) (c) social needs (e.g., caring adult figures, social interaction, play), and (d) esteem needs (e.g., encouragement, respect, discipline, learning life skills).

Expectedly, restrictive settings, such as prisons and detention centers, introduce a multitude of components that may violate the basic human needs outlined in Maslow's model. Consequently, how can instructors expect to successfully teach life skills that are designed to support self-actualization when basic supportive conditions are not being met in the environment? In FLEX's program design phase, we observed that sportss inherently necessitate physical body contact in intimate ways, and this appeared to be problematic and even threatening for many participants. Over time, we learned that youth might feel threatened when their backs are to the door, when they are huddled up in close proximity to others, and in confined spaces with just one other individual present. Understanding the effects of trauma now, we believe that this did not just result in disengagement from the program; it often meant introducing more critical threats to psychological and physical safety. Thus, it was essential to establish trust as a means to secure safety and alleviate threats.

In an attempt to build trust, we established some foundational strategies related to *transparency* and *consistency*. In carceral settings, youth are not often afforded the opportunity of knowledge (e.g., information around schedules), and therefore, we are deliberate about sharing our program schedule (e.g., when and how long to expect us to be on-site) and being transparent about schedule disruptions (e.g., facility logistical conflicts, conflicts with instructors' schedules). In training our instructors, we were forthcoming that, for some youth, we may be the only outside programming they receive all week, so being consistently present with a positive demeanor is crucial. One rationale when focusing on this principle centered around the fact that much of youths' daily lives possess inconsistency around scheduling, relationships (e.g., staff and peer turnover), and feelings of safety (e.g., daily fights, isolation from caring individuals), so FLEX strives to represent one entity that can challenge this. Providing programming that can successfully be executed on a regular basis, being a consistent and positive face, and being transparent when conflicts arise are important practical strategies to consider.

Addressing the Elephant in the Room: "Yes, we're in Jail, but..."

It is challenging to build a growth-oriented climate in a context where most factors do not support psychosocial growth. For example, in carceral settings, peer support and family contact are scarce. Opportunities for pride from accomplishments and incentives for positive behavior are rarely incorporated into detention structures. In truth, there are limited opportunities for self-actualization. Therefore, outside programs have the onus and privilege to create an atmosphere that is empowering and facilitative of growth opportunities.

Within the reality of the prison context, one must consider how to reframe the successful transfer of life skills. In restrictive settings such as prison, it is oftentimes unreasonable and even unsafe to encourage youth to adopt and implement life skills taught in PES due to the incongruency between the sports setting and the prison setting (Jacobs et al., 2017). In these cases, best practices point to parents, teachers, and other key social agents in their environments to help coordinate efforts, but in these contexts, these structures may not exist. As an example, we have observed the very complex dynamic that fighting holds in the prison setting and have learned that it's neither realistic nor beneficial to encourage youth not to fight at all costs, as is a principle in many out-of-school programs. Instead, in line with some research, our program frames the successful transfer of life skills as individuals *thinking about* and *considering* the impact of their choices versus simply adopting the behavior (Jacobs & Wright, 2018). Instead, our ultimate goal is to increase intrinsic motivation and foster mastery of transfer versus measurable behavioral change. We have found that journal writing in the form of musical lyrics or stories is one way to foster this type of reflection for thinking about transfer of life skills.

Addressing the Power of Culture: Step into Their Worlds

Lastly, a foundational aspect of supporting youth in the FLEX setting is finding commonality through addressing their culture and ecosystem. We strive to speak their language and understand the structures of their daily lives so they do not feel burdened or pressured to explain them. For example, we spend time getting to know the language components that are inherent to prison culture (e.g., "TRD" stands for "target release date"). We work with facility partners to understand security codes so that we are aware of the challenges youth face on a daily basis. Beyond the prison terminology, we show interest in their personal cultural practices related to handshakes, common phrases, fashion trends, etc. Much of this is achieved through curiosity, for example, "Hey, I see that date written on your shoes – that must mean something to you?" This also looks like adopting nonacademic words when talking about life skills, as some phrases may be triggering or elicit a lack of engagement. Instead of teamwork, leadership, and authenticity, we could identify "brotherhood," "leading the pack," and "keeping it real" as life skills. Finally, as is the case in many sports settings, we adopt "trash talk" as a program value with the understanding that in many contexts, it's a form of mutual respect and inclusivity. While many of these components violate what stand as best practices in the sports-based youth development (SBYD) field, at FLEX, we adopt an attitude of meeting the youth where they are and operating with their context at the epicenter of our practice.

SUMMARY AND FUTURE DIRECTIONS

Project FLEX represents one case of how an SBYD program utilizes a trauma-informed lens to support life skill transfer among its youth participants. Theoretically, the idea is that sports offers a structured, supportive environment for youth participants to identify opportunities to practice life skills, which makes them more likely to see connections to apply the skills to life contexts such as school, community, and home settings (Holt et al., 2017). Although the context of a juvenile facility may seem far from applicable to other youth settings, it in many ways epitomizes several of the critical challenges (and opportunities) to access, engagement, and transfer of valuable life skills through PES. The value of sharing FLEX's intentional program structure is not necessarily to promote strict adoption of their structure, but to advocate for an intentional, trauma-informed structure within PES programming in order to support transferability. FLEX's example highlights that an intentional structure integrating and practicing life skills should be informed by the context/environment of the program, grounded in culture, and remain authentic to youth participants and educators. Thus, it highlights the necessary inclusion of trauma as a contextual factor to be considered in prior life skills models in sports, which can influence both the in-program learning and the transfer process (Jacobs & Wright, 2018). If we truly want to see a commitment to life skill transferability in PES, we must be willing to throw out our traditional ideals of what PES should look like and radically commit to building structures that are reflective of and responsive to youth participants, to context of programs, and to the universal experience of trauma.

REFERENCES

Abram, K. M., Teplin, L. A., Charles, D. R., Longworth, S. L., McClelland, G. M., & Dulcan, M. K. (2004) Posttraumatic stress disorder and trauma in youth in juvenile detention. *Archives of General Psychiatry*, 61, 403–410.

Bean, C., Kramers, S., Forneris, T., & Camiré, M. (2018). The implicit/explicit continuum of life skills development and transfer. *Quest*, 70(4), 456–470.

Camiré, M., Newman, T. J., Bean, C., & Strachan, L. (2022). Reimagining positive youth development and life skills in sport through a social justice lens. *Journal of Applied Sport Psychology*, 34(6), 1058–1076.

Center for Child Trauma Assessment, Services, and Interventions (CCTASI). (2023). What is child trauma? Retrieved from https://cctasi.northwestern.edu/child-trauma/

Center on the Developing Child. (n.d.). *Toxic stress*. Harvard University. Retrieved from https://developingchild.harvard.edu/science/key-concepts/toxic-stress/

Centers for Disease Control and Prevention (CDC). (2023). Adverse childhood experiences. Retrieved from https://www.cdc.gov/violenceprevention/aces/index.html

Danish, S. J., Forneris, T., & Wallace, I. (2005). Sport-based life skills programming in the schools. *Journal of Applied School Psychology*, 21, 41–62. doi:https://doi.org/10.1300/J370v21n02_04

Danish, S. J., & Hale, B. D. (1981). Toward an understanding of the practice of sport psychology. *Journal of Sport Psychology*, 3, 90–99. doi:https://doi.org/10.1123/jsp.3.2.90

Felitti, V. J., Anda, R. F., Nordenberg, D., Williamson, D. F., Spitz, A. M., Edwards, V., Koss, M. & Marks, J. S. (1998). Relationship of childhood abuse and household dysfunction to many of the leading causes of death in adults. *American Journal of Preventive Medicine*, 14(4), 245–258.

Folco, M. (2023). The neurobiological impact of trauma on youth development: Restoring relationships and regulation through sport. *Child and Adolescent Social Work Journal*, 40, 1–11.

Giovanelli, A., & Reynolds, A. J. (2021). Adverse childhood experiences in a low-income black cohort: The importance of context. *Preventive Medicine*, 148, 106557.

Hellison, D. (2011). *Teaching responsibility through physical activity* (3rd ed.). Human Kinetics.

Hodge, K. P. (1989). Character-building in sport: Fact or fiction. *New Zealand Journal of Sports Medicine*, 17, 23–25.

Holt, N. L., Neely, K. C., Slater, L. G., Camiré, M., Côté, J., Fraser-Thomas, J., MacDonald, D., Strachan, L. & Tamminen, K. A. (2017). A grounded theory of positive youth development through sport based on results from a qualitative meta-study. *International Review of Sport and Exercise Psychology*, 10(1), 1–49.

Jacobs, J. M., Lawson, M., Ivy, V. N., & Richards, K. A. R. (2017). Enhancing the transfer of life skills from sport-based youth development programs to school, family, and community settings. *Journal of Amateur Sport*, 3(3), 20–43.

Jacobs, J. M., & Wright, P. M. (2018). Transfer of life skills in sport-based youth development programs: A conceptual framework bridging learning to application. *Quest*, 70(1), 81–99.

Kessler, R. C., McLaughlin, K. A., Green, J. G., Gruber, M. J., Sampson, N. A., Zaslavsky, A. M., & Williams, D. R. (2010). Childhood adversities and adult psychopathology in the WHO World Mental Health Surveys. *The British Journal of Psychiatry*, 197(5), 378–385.

Koh, K. T., Ong, S. W., & Camiré, M. (2016). Implementation of a values training program in physical education and sport: Perspectives from teachers, coaches, students, and athletes. *Physical Education and Sport Pedagogy*, 21(3), 295–312.

Maslow, A. H. (1954). *Motivation and personality*. New York: Harper and Row.

Mersky, J. P., Topitzes, J., & Reynolds, A. J. (2013). Impacts of adverse childhood experiences on health, mental health, and substance use in early adulthood: A cohort study of an urban, minority sample in the US. *Child Abuse & Neglect*, 37(11), 917–925.

Pierce, S., Erickson, K., & Dinu, R. (2019). Teacher-coaches' perceptions of life skills transfer from high school sport to the classroom. *Journal of Applied Sport Psychology*, 31(4), 451–473.

Pierce, S., Gould, D., & Camiré, M. (2017). Definition and model of life skills transfer. *International Review of Sport and Exercise Psychology*, 10(1), 186–211.

Robert Wood Johnson Foundation. (2018). Traumatic experiences widespread among U.S. Youth, New Data Show. Retrieved from https://www.rwjf.org/en/library/articles-and-news/2017/10/traumaticexperiences-Widespread-among-us--youth--new-data-show.html

Substance Abuse and Mental Health Services Administration (SAMHSA). (2014). SAMHSA's concept of trauma and guidance for a trauma-informed approach. Retrieved from https://ncsacw.acf.hhs.gov/userfiles/files/SAMHSA_Trauma.pdf

The Center for Healing and Justice through Sport (CHJS). (n.d.) Why trauma-informed sport is vital: A white paper. Retrieved from https://chjs.org/wp-content/uploads/2022/02/CHJS-WhitePaper.pdf

Wade Jr, R., Shea, J. A., Rubin, D., & Wood, J. (2014). Adverse childhood experiences of low-income urban youth. *Pediatrics*, 134(1), e13–e20.

Theory to Practice
Part 5

Whole-School Approach
Fifteen
Ferdinand Xie Fai Mar and Koon Teck Koh

INTRODUCTION

Physical education and sports (PES) provide students and athletes with opportunities for social and moral development (Aksoy & Gürsel, 2017). PES is defined as "structured, supervised physical activities that take place at school and during the school day" (Bailey, 2006, p. 398). Empirical evidence suggests the positive impact of PES stems from approaches employed by physical education (PE) teachers and sports coaches that explicitly address opportunities for development among their students and athletes (Koh et al., 2016; Pierce et al., 2017). The emergence of studies highlighting the advantages of PES for teaching life skills and values has led to the creation of several programmes designed to develop students and athletes holistically (Koh et al., 2016; Balderson & Martin, 2011; Madrona et al., 2017). Researchers on life skill promotion have shown that youth must internalise and transfer life skills to other domains to gain maximum benefits from their learning process (Pierce et al., 2017). In turn, studies examining values promotion have indicated that the regularity in which teachers, coaches, and parents reinforce values is among the factors that impact a learner's ability to internalise and apply such values (Bailey, 2006; Pierce et al., 2018).

As students spend the majority of their time in school and at home, the effectiveness of PES programmes is largely determined by the interaction and support received in these contexts, which may include teachers, coaches, and parents who play a crucial role in the process of learning and transferring life skills (Koh et al., 2016; Bailey, 2006; Camiré et al., 2012). Several studies have highlighted the importance of values transference beyond PES and the role of parents and classroom teachers in reinforcing these values (Koh et al., 2016, 2017a, 2017b; Gordon, 2020; Madrona et al., 2017). As such, applied research is warranted in this context to help teachers and coaches acquire the

DOI: 10.4324/9781032688657-20

knowledge and tools necessary to effectively teach values (Koh et al., 2017a). Unfortunately, most programmes that aim to teach values through sports were designed in Western countries and are not always successfully implemented in Asian contexts due to cultural differences in the way students learn, practice values and what values are deemed important to them (Hoon, 2004; Joy & Kolb, 2009).

To meet this demand in Asian contexts, Koh et al. (2016) designed and implemented a Values-Based Training Programme (VTP) in Singapore that aimed to equip PES practitioners with the knowledge to plan and teach values systematically and explicitly. Results from their study revealed that students and athletes who participated in the VTP showed a deeper understanding of the values taught in the programme than those who did not. In a subsequent study, the same participants highlighted that the collaboration between teachers, coaches, and parents facilitated the effective transfer of values (Koh et al., 2017b). In addition, the study found that an open and effective communication system between these key stakeholders supported the values transference process and increased the likelihood that transfer occurred beyond PES contexts. Despite the positive results, few studies have examined the strategies and methods of values transference. For example, the work by Aksoy and Gürsel (2017) has shown that strategic planning plays an important role in helping organisations coordinate activities involving multiple people and groups for the effective transfer of learning. Jacobs and Wright (2021) also highlighted that transfer is a multi-dimensional experience that includes cognitive processes. Specifically, getting learners thinking about the meaning, thinking beyond the self, and thinking through situations are key success factors that would facilitate transformative learning. Hence, the current study adopted strategic planning by engaging teachers, coaches, and parents in the design and implementation of an intervention programme to guide them in teaching and transferring values to students. To achieve this purpose, the current study conducted a preliminary needs assessment study followed by an intervention programme. The aim of the preliminary needs assessment study was to guide the development of the intervention programme. Hence, the preliminary study involved three PES practitioners who were previously participants of Koh et al.'s VTP (2017a).

PRELIMINARY STUDY

Two female PE teachers and one female sports coach between 31 and 53 years old participated in the preliminary study. The PE teachers had more than 13 years of experience, and the coach had more than 8 years of experience. In addition, one of the PE teachers was the head of her school's PE Department. Individual interviews were conducted with the participants to understand their experiences transferring values to their student-athletes during their participation in Koh et al.'s VTP (2017a). The needs assessment study revealed that participants believed that (a) values were not transferred beyond PES because of the lack of engagement of key stakeholders (e.g., Character and Citizenship Education (CCE) teachers and parents) in the transference process; (b) challenges like additional workload and different beliefs of the CCE teachers and parents must be overcome to facilitate better engagement; (c) a cross-departmental approach supported by school leaders to teach and transfer values intentionally and regularly may facilitate value transference beyond PES more effectively. The findings were used to guide the development of the following intervention programme.

INTERVENTION PROGRAMME

Based on the participants' experiences from the preliminary study, an appropriate intervention programme was developed (cf. Balderson & Martin, 2011). Eight participants from a high school in Singapore volunteered to participate in the study. They included two PE teachers (aged 34 and 47 years old) who had a minimum teaching experience of eight years, two CCE teachers (aged 31 and 41 years old) who had a minimum teaching experience of three years, two students (aged 14 and 16 years old), and their parents (aged 43 and 45 years old), respectively. Participants were divided into two groups based on the school's classes (i.e., one lower secondary level and one upper secondary level each) and their relationship. More specifically, each group consisted of one student, their parents, PE teacher, and CCE teacher (see Figure 15.1).

The five-week intervention programme is composed of two phases: training and implementation phase. In the training phase, six participants attended a series of workshops that were designed to teach

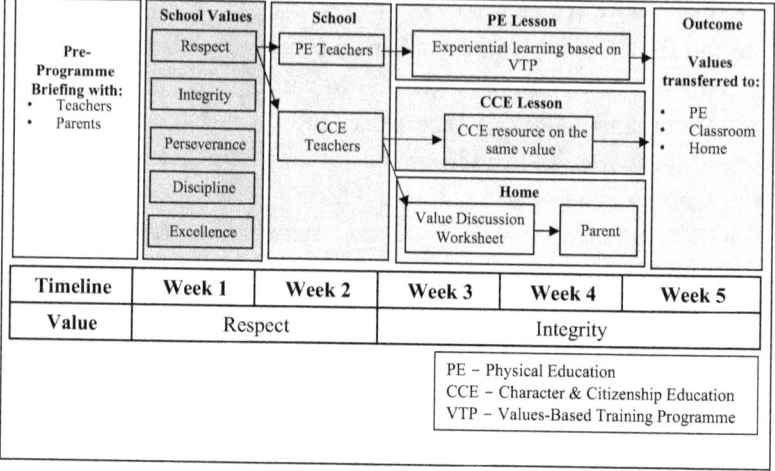

Figure 15.1 Relationships between participants in groups one and two
Note: Numbers in Parenthesis = Age of participants; M = Male; F = Female.

PE teachers, CCE teachers, and parents how to build sustainable and collaborative partnerships among themselves while facilitating values transference from PES classes to classroom and home. The intervention programme was supplemented with the use of explicit approaches that promote a better understanding of values (Koh et al., 2016). Thus, it consisted of four topics deemed important steps in the values teaching and transfer processes using a whole-school approach: (a) involvement of stakeholders and communication, (b) use of CCE lessons, (c) use of discussion worksheet, and (d) development of values action plan.

Involvement of Stakeholders and Communication

Two briefing sessions, each lasting an hour, were conducted for PE teachers, CCE teachers, and parents to equip them with the information required to facilitate values transference. More specifically, it guided CCE teachers on how to explicitly plan and transfer values in the classroom and guided parents on how to use the worksheets to facilitate in-depth discussions of values at home with their children. Furthermore, being aware of the values being taught helped minimise the additional work required to communicate with CCE teachers and parents after a value is taught and transferred beyond PES.

Use of Character and Citizenship Education Lessons

The intervention programme utilised CCE lessons to transfer values from PES to the classroom. According to Singapore's Ministry of Education (2014), every secondary school in Singapore is required to set aside two hours weekly for CCE lessons. With dedicated hours for values education, CCE teachers may be more motivated to reinforce values in their classrooms. In addition, as CCE resources are readily available in most schools, CCE teachers can use existing lesson plans of similar values and modify them to suit the values taught and transferred by PES practitioners. As the programme was supplemented with the use of explicit approaches, CCE teachers were trained on how to explicitly plan and transfer these values in their classroom during a briefing session held in the school.

Use of Discussion Worksheet

In this study, the findings from the needs assessment revealed that engaging the help of parents increased the workload of teachers. To address this issue, a values discussion worksheet (Table 15.1) was created to encourage students to seek their parents' assistance in facilitating values transference at home. They also served as a mode of communication between teachers and parents, reducing the workload required to contact parents. The questions in the worksheet were designed using Socratic Questioning Techniques (Paul & Elder, 2016) and Bloom's Digital Taxonomy (Churches, 2009) to promote reflection and foster a deeper understanding of the values taught in school and transferred to the home setting.

Development of Values Action Plan

According to Nagy and Fawcett (2017), detailed action plans can ensure intervention programmes meet their objectives. For the present work, the preliminary needs assessment study served this purpose by facilitating the development of a values action plan (Table 15.2).

Figure 15.2 illustrates how a school value was transferred regularly by teachers and parents. For example, if the value of an intervention was "Respect" followed by "Integrity," teachers and parents were briefed on the values-based programme and the action plan prior to the programme's implementation. This allowed PE teachers and CCE teachers to focus on the same values in their respective lessons for

Table 15.1 A Sample of the Values Discussion Worksheet for Respect

Name: _____ Date: _____
Class: _____

RESPECT

The following questions require you to discuss with your parents/guardian and write down their responses:

1. What is the meaning of **respect**?

You	Parent/Guardian

1a. Do you agree with your parent/guardian's definition of respect? Explain.

2. Who should we show **respect** to?

You	Parent/Guardian

3. Name one person you **respect** a lot in your life. Explain why you respect this person.

You	Parent/Guardian

4. Ask your parent/guardian about a time when you failed to show respect to them. Knowing this, how would you behave differently if you were given another chance? Write down your answers below.

_____
_____
_____

5. Discuss with your parent/guardian the role that respect play in a country like Singapore and write down your answers below.

_____
_____
_____
_____

Table 15.2 Values Action Plan

Action Step	Person(s) Responsible	By Values	Desired Outcome
Pre-programme briefing with teachers on the intervention programme conducted by the first author	• First author • Teachers	Before implementation of intervention programme	Teachers understand their role in the intervention programme and are aligned with the programme's objectives
Pre-programme briefing with parents on the intervention programme conducted by the first author	• First author • Parents	Before implementation of intervention programme	Parents understand their role in the intervention programme and are aligned with the programme's objectives
Values transferred intentionally during PE lessons through experiential learning based on Koh et al.'s (in press) VTP	• PE teachers	Respect – two weeksIntegrity – three weeks	Students gain a greater understanding of the values learned during PE lessons
Same values transferred during CCE lessonsAssign the values discussion worksheet after class	• CCE teachers	Respect – two weeksIntegrity – three weeks	Same values are reinforced by the CCE teacher to facilitate values transference to classroom
Values discussion between students and parents through values discussion worksheet	• Parents • Students	Respect – two weeksIntegrity – three weeks	Same values are reinforced by parents through discussion of values to facilitate values transference to home

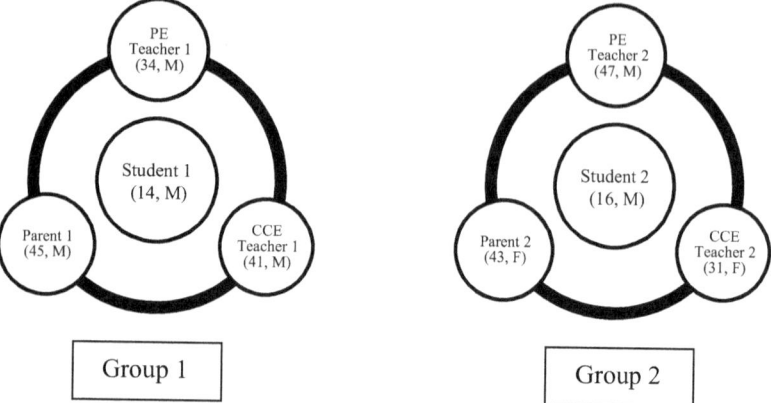

Figure 15.2 Example of how the value of *respect* is transferred by PE teachers, CCE teachers, parents, and children from school to home

consistency. The values were intentionally planned so that PE teachers could explicitly teach and transfer them beyond the PE context through experiential learning, as described in the VTP (Koh et al., 2017a). Subsequently, CCE teachers would reinforce the same values taught during PE lessons in their classes. At the end of their lesson, CCE teachers assigned students with the values discussion worksheet as homework. Students are required to complete the worksheet with their parents at home.

APPLIED INSIGHTS

The findings revealed that having a whole-school approach, such as the intervention programme guided by careful strategic planning (e.g., using a values action plan, involving parents and their students), can show positive results in the teaching and transfer of values beyond the PE context. Firstly, it successfully engaged CCE teachers and parents in the values transference process that was otherwise difficult due to time constraints or negative attitudes of CCE teachers and parents in the values inculcation and transfer process (Koh et al., 2017a; Pierce et al., 2018).

> Whatever the PE teachers taught [in] their lessons, we didn't communicate to the other subject teachers initially because everybody was busy... The [intervention programme] gave us a structure, everybody

knew what everybody else was doing. I think it was good that in a way when you told the kids to go back and talk to their parents, that relieved the work of having to be the ones telling parents what was going on [in school].

(CCE1)

Understanding their role in the transference process, parents in the present study discussed how the values discussion worksheets were effective as a form of communication and guidance.

Usually, we didn't know what the school was doing, but this worksheet allowed us to know about the school's initiative. We thought 'if we know what the school is doing, we can work with the school to help teach the same value'. The question in the worksheet helped because sometimes we didn't know how to help our children.

– (P1)

CCE2 also described how she initially had doubts about the worksheet's feasibility but was surprised at the outcome as she was reading the completed worksheets, saying, "I was impressed that my kids went home to do the worksheet with their parents. I thought they would not take it seriously…but they really put in the effort."

Lastly, CCE teachers appreciated their engagement and involvement in the values transference process because they believed they were playing a greater role in teaching values and acknowledged that "this is the role and responsibility of the CCE teacher (CCE1)." PE2 agreed that tapping onto CCE lessons was "more feasible as it would avoid taking away teaching time that classroom teachers require to complete their syllabuses."

The programme's ability to overcome these difficulties can be attributed to the adopted strategic planning processes (Aksoy & Gürsel, 2017). More specifically, findings from the preliminary needs assessment study revealed the challenges faced by PES practitioners in Singapore which were used to guide the design of the intervention programme (Koh et al., 2017a).

Another strength of this approach was the alignment of values being transferred by these key stakeholders. It allowed students to be exposed to the same values in different contexts during the same timeframe. Such an approach is consistent with the alternative Teaching Personal and Social Responsibility Model proposed by Gordon (2020) that places transfer at the core of the programme. Findings from the present study may be used to guide schools in teaching and transferring values, especially since values education is a high priority for the Ministry of Education in Singapore. This can be achieved through professional development workshops organised by the Ministry aiming to teach PE and CCE teachers strategic planning and strategies to engage parents and students effectively. Outside of Singapore, our findings may be used to inform policymakers and educators who are keen to implement values or life skills transfer beyond PES.

The effectiveness of employing explicit and implicit approaches to facilitate the transfer of values has been widely documented (Koh et al., 2017a; Camiré et al., 2012; Lee & Martinek, 2013). Specifically, the present study contributes to the existing literature by involving all key stakeholders who teach values and their transfer (i.e., students, PE teachers, CCE teachers, and parents). It demonstrated what explicit methods (i.e., use of scenarios, videos, and values discussion worksheets) and implicit methods (e.g., use of teachable moments) can be used to teach and transfer values beyond the context they were learned.

Although participants reported evidence of values transferred from PE to home and classroom settings, one of the CCE teachers from the present study did not observe the same outcome in the classroom, attributing it to the short time frame between the implementation and evaluation process. Other studies support this finding, revealing the transfer of learning between different contexts is not immediate, as students require time to make mindful abstraction from the learning context for the transfer of learning to occur (Koh et al., 2017a; Lee & Martinek, 2013; Perkins & Salomon, 1992). Therefore, more time should be provided for students after the programme to reflect on the values taught and transfer opportunities.

In addition, participants also felt that addressing the schools' values action plan could improve the programme. These suggestions further reinforced the importance of strategic planning when developing an effective and sustainable values-based intervention programme, as there is no one-size-fits-all model that will be effective for all contexts (Nagy & Fawcett, 2017; Pierce et al., 2018). More importantly, the results of the present study highlighted the importance of engaging different key stakeholders in co-designing and implementing the values programme in a context-specific setting (Aksoy & Gürsel, 2017; Görgüt and Tutkun (2018); Koh et al., 2017b). Continued efforts to explore strategies and methods of values transference with different populations, cultures, and contexts are needed to advance this line of research.

Findings from the present study suggest that practitioners must be properly trained to employ explicit and implicit approaches for values to be learned and transferred beyond PES contexts. Hence, to maximise the effectiveness of both approaches, it is recommended that key stakeholders such as school leaders, teachers, and parents should be involved in the development of an intervention programme. Briefing sessions should also be conducted to ensure clarity about the process and provide the necessary support to the process of learning and transferring values. It will also be helpful for schools to plan a yearly curriculum that includes values and share them with teachers, students, and parents so that they can be emphasised by different stakeholders, at the same time, in different contexts, to reinforce learning and facilitate transfer.

SUMMARY AND FUTURE DIRECTIONS

The purpose of the present study was to identify the strategies and methods that facilitated the transfer of values learned in PE lessons to the classroom and home settings using a whole-school approach. Our results provide insights into the importance of involving all key stakeholders in teaching values and facilitating students' transferring from PE lessons to classroom and home. In addition, the use of strategic planning processes, including conducting a preliminary needs assessment study, development of a values action plan, and use of transfer strategies and methods, proved to be beneficial.

As our understanding of effective strategies and methods of values transference is still in its infancy, more empirical evidence involving key stakeholders (e.g., school leaders such as vice-principal/principal, head of department, and youth) is required to improve the understanding of this burgeoning field. Future studies should explore other school contexts (e.g., junior schools, colleges, independent schools) and countries with a larger sample size to investigate the transfer strategies and methods used by students of different educational levels and cultural backgrounds. Lastly, the duration of the intervention programme may have been insufficient for values transference. Future studies should consider a longer intervention period to determine the programme's effectiveness.

REFERENCES

Aksoy, G., & Gürsel, F. (2017). The implementation of personal and social responsibility model in physical education classes: An action research. *Education and Science*, 42, 415–431.

Bailey, R. (2006). Physical education and sport in schools: A review of benefits and outcomes. *Journal of School Health*, 76, 397–401. https://doi.org/10.1111/j.1746-1561.2006.00132.x

Balderson, D., & Martin, M. (2011). The efficacy of the personal and social responsibility model in a physical education setting. *PHEnex Journal*, 3, 1–15.

Camiré, M., Trudel, P., & Forneris, T. (2012). Coaching and transferring life skills: Philosophies and strategies used by model high school coaches. *The Sport Psychologist*, 26, 243–260. https://doi.org/10.1123/tsp.26.2.243

Churches, A. (2009). Bloom's digital taxonomy. Retrieved from http://burtonslifelearning.pbworks.com/f/BloomDigitalTaxonomy2001.pdf (accessed 18 June 2018).

Gordon, B. (2020). An alternative conceptualisation of the teaching personal and social responsibility model. *Journal of Physical Education, Recreation & Dance*, 91(7), 8–14. https://doi.org/10.1080/07303084.2020.1781719

Görgüt, İ. & Tutkun, E. (2018). Views of physical education teachers on values education. *Universal Journal of Educational Research*, 6, 317–332. https://doi.org/10.13189/ujer.2018.060215

Hoon, C. Y. (2004). Revisiting the Asian values argument used by Asian political leaders and its validity. *Indonesian Quarterly*, 32(2), 154–174.

Jacobs, J. M., & Wright, P.M. (2021). Thinking about the transfer of life skills: Reflections from youth in a community-based sport programme in an underserved urban setting. *International Journal of Sport and Exercise Psychology*, 19(3), 380–394.

Joy, S., & Kolb, D. (2009) Are there cultural differences in learning style? *International Journal of Intercultural Relations*, 33, 69–85. https://doi.org/10.1016/j.ijintrel.2008.11.002

Koh, T., Camire, M., Regina, S., & Soon, W. (2017b). Implementation of a values training program in physical education and sport: A follow-up study. *Physical Education and Sport Pedagogy*, 22, 197–211. https://doi.org/10.1080/17408989.2016.1165194

Koh, T., Camire, M., & Wang, C. (2017a). Creation, implementation, and evaluation of a values-based training program for sport coaches and physical education teachers in Singapore. *International Journal of Sport Sciences & Coaching* 12, 795–806. https://doi.org/10.1177/1747954117730987

Koh, T., Ong, S., & Camirie, M. (2016). Implementation of a values training program in physical education and sport: Perspectives from teachers, coaches, students, and athletes. *Physical Education and Sport Pedagogy*, 21, 295–312. https://doi.org/10.1080/17408989.2014.990369

Lee, O., & Martinek, T. (2013). Understanding the transfer of values-based youth sport program goals from a bioecological perspective. *Quest*, 65, 300–312. https://doi.org/10.1080/00336297.2013.791871

Madrona, Pedro & Samalot-Rivera, Amaury & Kozub, Francis. (2017). Acquisition and transfer of values and social skills through a physical education program focused in the affective domain. *Motricidade*, 12, 32. https://doi.org/10.6063/motricidade.6502.

Ministry of Education. (2014). 2014 Syllabus: Character and citizenship education (secondary school). Retrieved from https://www.moe.gov.sg/education/syllabuses/character-citizenship-education (accessed 18 June 2018).

Nagy, J., & Fawcett, S. (2017). Developing a strategic plan. Retrieved from https://ctb.ku.edu/en/table-of-contents/structure/strategic-planning/vmosa/main (accessed 18 June 2018).

Paul, R., & Elder, L. (2016). *The art of Socratic questioning*. The Foundation for Critical Thinking.

Perkins, D., & Salomon, G. (1992). *Transfer of learning - Contribution to the international encyclopedia of education*. Pergamon Press.

Pierce, S., Gould, D., & Camiré, M. (2017). Definition and model of life skills transfer. *International Review of Sport and Exercise Psychology*, 10, 86–211. https://doi.org/10.1080/1750984X.2016.1199727

Pierce, S., Kendellen, K., Camiré, M., & Gould, D. (2018). Strategies for coaching for life skills transfer. *Journal of Sport Psychology in Action*, 9, 11–20. https://doi.org/10.1080/21520704.2016.1263982

Teaching Values and Life Skills to Different Age Groups

Chapter Sixteen

Koon Teck Koh and Muhammad Shufi Bin Salleh

INTRODUCTION

A significant portion of children's time is spent in school. Hence, schools play an important role in exposing growing children to a range of values and beliefs, presenting a critical opportunity for teaching essential values and life skills. Within the context of the school system, physical education and sports (PES) have been found to provide a favourable context for inculcating values and life skills (VLS; Cronin et al., 2018). PES refers to the "structured, supervised physical activities that take place at school during the school day" (Bailey, 2006, p. 398). The PES environment promotes engagement, teamwork, and social interactions between children, and in the process, it facilitates in imparting important life skills such as decision-making and, social and self- awareness (Claudia, 2022).

In Singapore, physical education (PE) lessons are compulsory for all students to attend in public schools. They occur once to twice a week in both primary (7–12 years old) and secondary (13–16 years old) schools. These PE lessons aim to enable students to demonstrate, individually and with others, the physical skills, practices, and values to enjoy a lifetime of active and healthy living (Ministry of Education [MOE], 2016). More specifically, during PE lessons, students are exposed to a variety of physical activities, games, and sports. Through intentional planning and facilitation by trained teachers, these activities provide a conducive environment that has the potential to facilitate cognitive, affective, character, and social development (MOE, 2016). For instance, by the end of secondary school, students would have had a chance to engage in school recreational competitions organised at the school's level. Important VLS like teamwork and communication among team members can be learned and practiced beyond PES settings (Koh et al., 2016). Such opportunities help students develop

DOI: 10.4324/9781032688657-21

important life skills, learn to overcome challenges and setbacks and to be more confident from a young age (MOE, 2016).

The importance of PES in helping students develop the values needed to succeed in adulthood was highlighted in the opening address by the former minister of education, Singapore, Mr. Ong Ye Kung, at the 2020 National School Games (MOE, 2018, 2020). During the opening ceremony, he stated,

> Each competition and Co-Curricular Activities (CCA) experience is a lesson in character building, providing valuable learning opportunities for students beyond the classroom. These experiences will continue to be essential for holistic learning and character education for our students.
> (MOE, 2020)

Acknowledging the role PES plays in students' learning of VLS, frameworks, and syllabi of PE lessons and sports CCA has been updated to include VLS integration and to improve the environment and maximise teaching of VLS through PES (MOE, 2015). Furthermore, few courses are available for PE teachers and sports coaches (PETSCs). In particular, the values and principles in sports (VPS) certification is mandatory for PETSCs who are looking to teach in MOE schools and is also needed for PETSCs' application for the National Registry of Coaches (NROC).

PES provides a good opportunity for children to learn VLS; however, for lessons to be impactful, it is important for teachers to be able to plan and facilitate learning of VLS intentionally during lessons (Koh et al., 2016), while at the same time considering their students from a developmental standpoint and planning lessons that will be appropriately catered to their age.

APPLIED INSIGHTS

Theories

To guide the development of VLS teaching in PES, the teaching pedagogy is guided by several unique theories and frameworks, such as Implicit/Explicit Approaches and Continuum of Life Skills Development (Bean et al., 2018), Experiential Learning Theory (Kolb, 1984), Teaching Games for Understanding (TGfU; O'Connor, 2019), and Mosston's Spectrum of Teaching Styles (Mosston & Ashworth, 1990).

The teaching of VLS can happen through both the implicit and the explicit approaches (Turnnidge et al., 2014). In the implicit approach, teachers and coaches do not intentionally plan how they intend to incorporate the teaching of sports skills with VLS development in their lessons. The learning of VLS is typically left to chance. This approach is often favoured by practitioners as they believed that learners may learn on their own as they engage in the activities in the PES setting (Camiré & Kendellen, 2016). Furthermore, these learners may unconsciously or consciously transfer these learnings beyond the sports contexts as they reach a certain level of maturity (Holt et al., 2017).

In the explicit approach, PE teachers and coaches intentionally integrate within their teaching and coaching practice specific VLS teaching pedagogies. This entails providing opportunities for youth to discuss and practice life skills both in and out of sports. Teaching in a more explicit manner can potentially increase learners' awareness as they are guided more explicitly on a regular basis. In addition, the transfer of learning becomes more conscious due to the promotion of metacognitive processing through discussion and reflection episodes (Pierce et al., 2017).

Over the last decade, several studies were done to evaluate the impact of these two approaches to identify which approach was more appropriate. For instance, Chinkov and Holt (2016) found support for the implicit approach, while Weiss, Bolter, and Kipp (2016) found support for the explicit approach. However, this implicit/explicit dichotomy may be too simplistic as pitting one approach against another may undermine the complexities surrounding the teaching and learning of values (Bean & Forneris, 2016).

Bean et al. (2018) introduced an implicit/explicit continuum of life skills development and transfer to address the research gap. The authors suggest that VLS teaching could fall along a continuum comprising six levels of intentionality, whereby the intentionality levels increase with each level. Levels 1 and 2 are more implicit in nature, while levels 3–6 are more explicit in nature. Each level exists as a building block, with level 6 being the highest level of intentionality. In addition, life skills should be discussed and practiced before transference. At the highest level of the implicit/explicit continuum, PETSCs could create and design opportunities for students/athletes to transfer their knowledge to non-PES contexts. These are thought to be more effective than discussion.

Additionally, Kolb's (1984) Experiential Learning Theory (ELT) suggests learning occurs through a process of experience transformation. New knowledge and skills are created through concrete experience, reflective observation, abstract conceptualisation, and active experimentation (Kolb, 1984). In the context of PES, *concrete experience* refers to the direct experience of engaging in physical activity and sports. For example, in the three-on-two defensive concept in basketball, learners may be able to learn VLS, such as *perseverance* and *communication with the team*, besides the technical skills. After the players have gone through the activity, the coach can engage them in *reflective observation* – i.e., reflecting on their experience, especially the defenders, who are in an extremely disadvantaged situation. Some may experience success in stopping the offence, forcing the opponents to make a mistake (a turnover) and regain possession of the ball. The coach can then guide players in *abstract conceptualisation*, which involves using reflective observation to develop new ideas or concepts. In this case, the effective ways of defending the attackers, including the importance of values of *perseverance* – i.e., never giving up despite being in a disadvantaged situation – and life skills – i.e., *communication* with teammates to experience success. Finally, *active experimentation* refers to the process of putting new or modified knowledge into practice in other situations. In this case, the coach needs to guide the players on how to apply the VLS that they have learned in basketball in their daily lives, such as in their academic studies, personal relationships, or future careers.

The ELT is unique and effective in VLS development in the PES context. It is very different from the traditional and ineffective approach where practitioners just talk about the importance of any value and life skill and learners have no concrete experiences to reflect. As Beard and Wilson (2002) highlighted, reflection is important for the extraction and transfer of information to other domains in life. Without the concrete experience to guide reflection and internalise the learning, participation in PES remains an experience for learners and may not benefit from the development of VLS.

A teaching pedagogy that could be applied to facilitate reflection is the TGfU approach (O'Connor, 2019). This approach encourages greater participation and involvement of the learners. For example, learners will be exposed to a game situation first, understanding problems encountered and the skills required for the game. The role of the instructor is to set rules for the game, ask specific questions, and guide learners to understand the need to learn the skill/concept for each lesson. Using this approach, the motivation of the learners wanting to learn the skill/concept is likely to be high. In this process, various skills, such as critical thinking, communication, and decision-making, are learned and can be applied in different ways and levels according to students' abilities. In addition, students/athletes are given the opportunity and autonomy in decision-making and problem-solving, which will enhance their knowledge and skills (Beni et al., 2019; Mandigo et al., 2019; Stolz & Pill, 2014). Generally, a non-linear teaching pedagogy is more useful for reflection to raise awareness of the lesson objectives compared to direct instructions/teaching (Aarskog, 2021).

Teaching Styles

Several teaching styles arise from Mosston's Spectrum of Teaching Styles (Mosston & Ashworth, 1990). The styles incorporating decision-making among students/athletes promote an autonomy-supportive climate, which will benefit the well-being of the learners and significantly predicts VLS. The following are some examples to consider.

The Practice Style

VLS are defined and modelled by PETSCs before putting them into practice through carefully designed lessons based in an authentic environment. Students decide the order of tasks, location for practice, pace, and rhythm. Good examples of demonstrating VLS during practice are acknowledged and reinforced appropriately to encourage students to model positive behaviour.

The Reciprocal Style

Students take on greater responsibility in their learning. A cooperative learning environment is established – for example, through working in pairs, whereby one student is an observer and the other a doer. Observers are fully responsible for providing feedback to doers using resources such as a performance checklist, rubric, or a video recording tool, with support from PETSCs. This allows students to become more aware of the behaviours, which facilitates internalisation. Teachers can observe how the students provide feedback to each other and facilitate the reflection on the importance of *respecting* each other's learning ability and highlight the need to develop life skills, such as *social awareness* when working with others.

The Self-Check Style

This style focuses on self-evaluation of performance against a set of checklists provided by the teacher. For example, how to execute an underarm serve in badminton. When using this style, the teacher needs to ensure that the activities are suited to students' abilities and interests. Students should be readily supported by PETSCs when they have queries, as they may interpret the checklists differently and hence be unable to perform the desired movements. Again, PETSCs could harness the planned activities and highlight the learning objectives in sports skill (underarm serve), as well as the values (e.g., *integrity*: be honourable and follow the rules even when no one is watching). Words of encouragement should be provided when challenges and setbacks are encountered by the students, and use these teachable moments to reflect and highlight the relevant VLS and how they can be transferred beyond PES.

The Inclusion Style

PETSCs should plan activities with varying difficulty to include students of different abilities in attempting the same task. Students can decide on factors like difficulty, equipment, and space according to their abilities when performing the tasks. Difficulty levels can be adjusted till one is sufficiently challenged. Upon task completion, students can decide to maintain the same level, reduce, or increase the difficulty, depending on their progress. Using this style can develop values such as *excellence* (personal improvement – e.g., shooting from 3 metres away from the goal post successfully in a soccer lesson and progressing to 6 metres eventually) or *resilience* (keep on trying to get the ball into the target, and never give up).

The various teaching styles illustrated can impact learners from different age groups significantly. Hence, the following section highlights how the teaching styles can be adapted to suit different age groups for effective teaching and learning.

Adapting Teaching Styles to Different Ages

Children's abilities vary according to the developmental stage they are in, which should affect the teaching styles used. For instance, primary school students would understand the instructions better through demonstrations than just verbal cues. Cognitive changes occur with brain development, social interactions, and learning from others (Diamond, 2013; Sternberg & Grigorenko, 2001). This happens earlier in females. In addition, primary school children develop basic skills like memory, attention, and processing speed through reading, mathematics, and writing. Task complexity increases at the secondary level as critical thinking, complex problem-solving skills, and abstract reasoning are developed. Hence, to develop effective and engaging lessons and optimise learning and development, cognitive challenges should match students' age.

Primary school children depend more on adults and will require more support through tasks. Thus, they benefit more from structured social interactions with adult supervision and clear instructions. As such, explicit instructions to exchange "high fives" after scoring a goal, and to pat each other on the shoulder and say, "It's ok, let's keep going," if a goal is conceded or to check two to three teaching cues in their classmate's performance instructed to provide feedback and being gracious by exchanging "high fives" before swapping roles, would help them. Autonomous motivation is enhanced when children are allowed to provide feedback to their classmates (Teraoka et al., 2021). Additionally, explicit instructions adapted for young children would provide concrete behaviour for them to visualise instructions. For instance, young children can be encouraged to set targets, count the number of successful attempts, and then take time to practice and improve.

To promote inclusivity, young children can be initially given two choices of learning. For instance, two types of throwing distances, two sizes of ball, or two targets to work on. The number of choices can be gradually increased according to difficulty. By providing choices, children's basic psychological needs are fulfilled, which increases their autonomous motivation (Leptokaridou et al., 2016; Perlman & Goc Karp, 2010). However, the class context and students' abilities should also be considered when planning lessons to maximise the benefits of providing choices (Perlman, 2010; Teraoka et al., 2021) and to cater to students of varying levels of competence (Mandigo et al., 2008).

Secondary school students are more independent and will have formed many social relationships with similarly aged peers (Rubin et al., 2011; Wentzel & Caldwell, 1997). Hence, less explicit instructions can be used. Examples include motivational quotes, such as, "Talent may win games but teamwork win championships," instructions to affirm or encourage fellow teammates after a goal is scored or conceded, or structured feedback like, "Say one good thing that was observed and an area for improvement." Graciousness can also be emphasised by getting students to thank their peers for the feedback before exchanging roles. Additionally, task cards can be utilised for self-assessment against a set of criteria in a checklist or rubric.

As older students gain self-awareness and social skills, social identity, self-expression, and peer acceptance become more important to them (Thompson, 1994). Thus, social pressures pose a great challenge to them. Hence, teaching styles employed should promote greater autonomy, flexibility, freedom, and opportunity for collaboration with peers. To instil a greater sense of autonomy and encourage students to make informed decisions, choices with a wider range of difficulty levels can be offered. Questions and feedback should be objective to create a safe and supportive learning environment.

The following section highlights some pedagogies in teaching core values in primary and secondary school settings.

Teaching Core Values

Primary Level

In a PES setting, values such as *respect*, *responsibility*, and *sportsmanship* can be easily incorporated into learning activities. For example, when in the one-on-one modified mini-tennis lesson, students can be asked to keep the rally going as long as possible within the playing area, with one bounce of the ball permitted. The goal is to 'score' the highest rally in a game. Here, students must *respect* the rules and be *responsible* for keeping the "score" and adhering to the rules, even though no one is watching them. If they follow the requirements, it is a demonstration of *sportsmanship*. The teacher can highlight and reinforce the positive VLS demonstrated. Such a student-centric approach can be used where students are responsible for decision-making and problem-solving (Siedentop, 1998). The process increases awareness of sports rules and how decisions made can have consequences (Siedentop et al., 2019). Students learn to organise, self-reflect, and regulate in the process (Chow & Atencio, 2014; Crotti et al., 2021). Also, an autonomous environment which enhances students' development is provided in the process (Schmidt et al., 2018).

PETSCs can also encourage their students to take care of school equipment and facilities by being responsible for it, keeping it clean, and admitting to causing any damage. When peers are talking, PETSCs should get their students to pay attention. These instil respect for others.

Sportsmanship should be modelled or highlighted by PETSCs. Students should be corrected when they lack sportsmanship and asked to consider their actions from an alternative perspective to guide their reflection. If failure occurs, areas for improvement and strengths should be discussed to cultivate a growth mindset. Encouragement can be given from time to time to build perseverance and resilience.

As much as students should be motivated to improve, challenges should be integrated without overwhelming them. PETSCs should focus on students' mental well-being and assist them in developing a healthy stress-coping mechanism when faced with stress and obstacles. An example is relaxation strategies like positive self-talk (Lang et al., 2016; Lang et al., 2017). Additionally, activities should match children's imaginative and playful nature, and more positive and encouraging tones should be used when teaching young (Griggs & Stevens, 2010; Mercier, 1993).

Secondary Level

Higher levels of cognitive and social ability at this stage allow for more advanced PES lessons in addition to the methods for the primary level. For example, besides taking charge of equipment by ensuring they are well maintained and cleaned, students can be instructed to set up, return, and store or maintain equipment. Leadership roles can be assigned to ensure this.

Based on students' strengths, other leadership positions can also be established and assigned to build confidence and enhance students' strengths while teaching them to lead, set examples for others, make decisions, reflect on their actions and their consequences, and practice responsibility. Examples of other leadership roles include leaders for warm-ups and game captains. These roles can be rotated to provide other students the opportunity to lead too.

PETSCs should also encourage students to communicate and collaborate. These can be instilled through team sports. An example would be in netball, where verbal communication and teamwork are needed to successfully achieve aims. The learning environment should be inclusive by involving individuals from different backgrounds and levels of ability. For instance, less proficient teammates can be given encouragement and advice instead of being excluded. This cultivates respect and creates a sense of belonging in all individuals. Competition can be incorporated. However, to minimise aggression that may arise, students should be taught to respect authority, their opponent, and the referee's decision.

Resources can also be provided to encourage students to be responsible for their personal fitness, which instils a sense of self-responsibility. Opportunities can also be provided for learners to develop knowledge and skills associated with physical fitness and well-being. As well as how to self-assess levels of fitness or physical activity, goal-setting, and safe and developmentally appropriate training principles.

Students can also be encouraged to reflect and relate their learning to non-PES contexts. When teaching older children, a more challenging and critical tone can be used, especially when providing feedback relating to fair play and sportsmanship or if safety is compromised.

SUMMARY AND FUTURE DIRECTIONS

Overall, PES provides a good environment for teaching VLS. Theories guide PETSCs in teaching VLS to maximise students' learning. However, lesson plans should focus on student-centricity, autonomy, and physicality to enhance motivation. In addition, PES lessons should be planned to match students according to their age and stages of development to ensure that they reap the benefits of PES and are able to understand and apply the lessons taught in PES, as well as in non-sports contexts.

Future Directions

While there have been efforts to train PETSCs in teaching VLS through PES, being able to create an effective programme catering to different groups of students is challenging (Seng et al., 2022). Training programmes have been developed and evaluated. However, sample size and study designs (e.g., perception from the participants using surveys or interviews) were often cited as limitations to the evaluation of the programmes (Koh et al., 2017; Seng et al., 2022). Future directions should aim to address these gaps, such as using objective and quantifiable data to understand what is going on during lessons and triangulating with the perception data to determine the effectiveness of the programme.

Another challenge within PES is the volume of outcomes and priorities within a PES programme needing to be attended to. Therefore, discourse around how VLS outcomes in PES will be monitored and evaluated, alongside the physical, cognitive, and fitness-related outcomes measures expected within/across a PES should be examined. Specifically, how can PE teachers accomplish all these goals within the time allocated for teaching and learning? Consequently, it is useful to consider students' differing levels of ability and maturity to establish a balance programme outcome in physical, cognitive, fitness, values, and life skills development. Hence, more research is needed to develop a greater understanding of integrating sports skills with VLS teaching across students of different age groups.

REFERENCES

Aarskog, E. (2021). 'No assessment, no learning': exploring student participation in assessment in Norwegian physical education (PE). *Sport, Education and Society*, 26(8), 875–888. https://doi.org/10.1080/13573322.2020.1791064

Bailey, R. (2006). Physical education and sport in schools: a review of benefits and outcomes. *Journal of School Health*, 76(8), 397–401. https://doi.org/10.1111/j.1746-1561.2006.00132.x

Bean, C., & Forneris, T. (2016). Examining the importance of intentionally structuring the youth sport context to facilitate positive youth development. *Journal of Applied Sport Psychology*, 28(4), 410–425. https://doi.org/10.1080/10413200.2016.1164764

Bean, C., Kramers, S., Forneris, T., & Camiré, M. (2018). The implicit/explicit continuum of life skills development and transfer. *Quest*, 70(4), 456–470. https://doi.org/10.1080/00336297.2018.1451348

Beard, C., & Wilson, J. P. (2002). *The power of experiential learning: A handbook for trainers and educators*. ERIC.

Beni, S., Ní Chróinín, D., & Fletcher, T. (2019). A focus on the how of meaningful physical education in primary schools. *Sport, Education and Society*, 24(6), 624–637. https://doi.org/10.1080/13573322.2019.1612349

Camiré, M., & Kendellen, K. (2016). Coaching for positive youth development in high school sport Coaching for Positive Youth Development in High School Sport | 11 | v2 (taylorfrancis.com) (pp. 126–136). Routledge. https://doi.org/10.4324/9781315709499-11

Chinkov, A. E., & Holt, N. L. (2016). Implicit Transfer of Life Skills Through Participation in Brazilian Jiu-Jitsu. *Journal of Applied Sport Psychology*, 28(2), 139–153. https://doi.org/10.1080/10413200.2015.1086447

Chow, J. Y., & Atencio, M. (2014). Complex and nonlinear pedagogy and the implications for physical education. *Sport, Education and Society*, 19(8), 1034–1054. https://doi.org/10.1080/13573322.2012.728528

Claudia, W. M. Y. (2022). The physical education pedagogical approaches in nurturing physical literacy among primary and secondary school students: A scoping review. *International Journal of Educational Research*, 116, 102080. https://doi.org/10.1016/j.ijer.2022.102080

Cronin, L. D., Allen, J., Mulvenna, C., & Russell, P. (2018). An investigation of the relationships between the teaching climate, students' perceived life skills development and well-being within physical education. *Physical Education and Sport Pedagogy*, 23(2), 181–196. https://doi.org/10.1080/17408989.2017.1371684

Crotti, M., Rudd, J. R., Roberts, S., Boddy, L. M., Fitton Davies, K., O'Callaghan, L., Utesch, T., & Foweather, L. (2021). Effect of linear and nonlinear pedagogy physical education interventions on children's physical activity: A cluster randomized controlled trial (SAMPLE-PE). *Children*, 8(1), 49. https://www.mdpi.com/2227-9067/8/1/49

Diamond, A. (2013). Executive functions. *Annual Review of Psychology*, 64, 135–168. https://doi.org/10.1146/annurev-psych-113011-143750

Griggs, G., & Stevens, T. (2010). Teaching social skills in physical education to elementary school students with autism spectrum disorders. *Journal of Physical Education, Recreation & Dance*, 81, 8–12.

Holt, N. L., Neely, K. C., Slater, L. G., Camiré, M., Côté, J., Fraser-Thomas, J., MacDonald, D., Strachan, L., & Tamminen, K. A. (2017). A grounded theory of positive youth development through sport based on results from a qualitative meta-study. *International Review of Sport and Exercise Psychology*, 10(1), 1–49. https://doi.org/10.1080/1750984X.2016.1180704

Koh, K. T., Camiré, M., Lim Regina, S. H., & Soon, W. S. (2017). Implementation of a values training program in physical education and sport: A follow-up study. *Physical Education and Sport Pedagogy*, 22(2), 197–211. https://doi.org/10.1080/17408989.2016.1165194

Koh, K. T., Ong, S. W., & Camiré, M. (2016). Implementation of a values training program in physical education and sport: perspectives from teachers, coaches, students, and athletes. *Physical Education and Sport Pedagogy*, 21(3), 295–312. https://doi.org/10.1080/17408989.2014.990369

Kolb, D. (1984). *Experiential Learning: Experience as the Source of Learning and Development: Kolb, David A.: 9780132952613: Amazon.com: Books* (Vol. 1). Prentice Hall.

Lang, C., Feldmeth, A. K., Brand, S., Holsboer-Trachsler, E., Pühse, U., & Gerber, M. (2016). Stress management in physical education class: An experiential approach to improve coping skills and reduce stress perceptions in adolescents. *Journal of Teaching in Physical Education*, 35(2), 149–158. https://doi.org/10.1123/jtpe.2015-0079

Lang, C., Feldmeth, A. K., Brand, S., Holsboer-Trachsler, E., Pühse, U., & Gerber, M. (2017). Effects of a physical education-based coping training on adolescents' coping skills, stress perceptions and quality of sleep. *Physical Education and Sport Pedagogy*, 22(3), 213–230. https://doi.org/10.1080/17408989.2016.1176130

Leptokaridou, E. T., Vlachopoulos, S. P., & Papaioannou, A. G. (2016). Experimental longitudinal test of the influence of autonomy-supportive teaching on motivation for participation in elementary school physical education. *Educational Psychology*, 36(7), 1135–1156. https://doi.org/10.1080/01443410.2014.950195

Mandigo, J., Holt, N., Anderson, A., & Sheppard, J. (2008). Children's motivational experiences following autonomy-supportive games lessons. *European Physical Education Review*, 14(3), 407–425. https://doi.org/10.1177/1356336X08095673

Mandigo, J., Lodewyk, K., & Tredway, J. (2019). Examining the impact of a teaching games for understanding approach on the development of physical literacy using the passport for life assessment tool. *Journal of Teaching in Physical Education*, 38(2), 136–145. https://doi.org/10.1123/jtpe.2018-0028

Mercier, R. (1993). Student-Centered Physical Education—Strategies for Teaching Social Skills. *Journal of Physical Education, Recreation & Dance*, 64(5), 60–65. https://doi.org/10.1080/07303084.1993.10609979

MOE. (2015). Co-Curricular Activities (CCAs). Retrieved from http://www.moe.gov.sg/education/secondary/cca/

MOE. (2016). *Physical education teaching & learning syllabus primary, secondary & pre-university*. Ministry of Education, Student Development Curriculum Division. Retrieved from https://www.moe.gov.sg/-/media/files/primary/physical_education_syllabus_2014.pdf

MOE. (2018). Speech by Mr. Ng Chee Meng, Minister for Education (Schools) at the Opening Ceremony of the National School Games 2018. Retrieved from https://www.moe.gov.sg/news/speeches/20180124-speech-by-mr-ng-chee-meng-minister-for-education-schools-at-the-opening-ceremony-of-the-national-school-games-2018

MOE. (2020). National School Games 2020- Enhancing Co-Curricular Experiences. Retrieved from https://www.moe.gov.sg/news/press-releases/20200121-national-school-games-2020-enhancing-co-curricular-experiences

Mosston, M., & Ashworth, S. (1990). *The spectrum of teaching styles. From command to discovery*. ERIC.

O'Connor, J. (2019). Exploring a pedagogy for meaning-making in physical education. *European Physical Education Review*, 25(4), 1093–1109. [Record #139 is using a reference type undefined in this output style.]

Perlman, D. (2010). Change in affect and needs satisfaction for amotivated students within the sport education model. *Journal of Teaching in Physical Education*, 29(4), 433–445. https://doi.org/10.1123/jtpe.29.4.433

Perlman, D., & Goc Karp, G. (2010). A self-determined perspective of the Sport Education Model. *Physical Education and Sport Pedagogy*, 15(4), 401–418. https://doi.org/10.1080/17408980903535800

Pierce, S., Gould, D., & Camiré, M. (2017). Definition and model of life skills transfer. *International Review of Sport and Exercise Psychology*, 10(1), 186–211. https://doi.org/10.1080/1750984X.2016.1199727

Rubin, K. H., Bukowski, W. M., & Laursen, B. (2011). *Handbook of peer interactions, relationships, and groups*. Guilford Press.

Schmidt, R. A., Lee, T. D., Winstein, C., Wulf, G., & Zelaznik, H. N. (2018). *Motor control and learning: A behavioral emphasis*. Human kinetics.

Seng, Y. B. G., Koh, K. T., & Liem, G. A. D. (2022). *Teaching and facilitating the transference of values and life skills through physical education and sports in Singapore schools [electronic resource]*. National Institute of Education, Nanyang Technological University.

Siedentop, D. (1998). What is sport education and how does it work? *Journal of Physical Education, Recreation & Dance*, 69(4), 18–20. https://doi.org/10.1080/07303084.1998.10605528

Siedentop, D., Hastie, P., & Van der Mars, H. (2019). *Complete guide to sport education*. Human Kinetics.

Sternberg, R. J., & Grigorenko, E. L. (2001). *Environmental effects on cognitive abilities*. Lawrence Erlbaum Associates Publishers.

Stolz, S., & Pill, S. (2014). Teaching games and sport for understanding: Exploring and reconsidering its relevance in physical education. *European Physical Education Review*, 20(1), 36–71.

Teraoka, E., Jancer Ferreira, H., Kirk, D., & Bardid, F. (2021). Affective learning in physical education: A systematic review. *Journal of Teaching in Physical Education*, 40(3), 460–473. https://doi.org/10.1123/jtpe.2019-0164

Thompson, R. A. (1994). Emotion regulation: A theme in search of definition. *Monograph Society Research and Child Development*, 59(2–3), 25–52.

Turnnidge, J., Côté, J., & Hancock, D. J. (2014). Positive youth development from sport to life: Explicit or implicit transfer? *Quest*, 66(2), 203–217. https://doi.org/10.1080/00336297.2013.867275

Weiss, M. R., Bolter, N. D., & Kipp, L. E. (2016). Evaluation of The First Tee in promoting positive youth development: Group comparisons and longitudinal trends. *Research Quarterly for Exercise and Sport*, 87(3), 271–283. https://doi.org/10.1080/02701367.2016.1172698

Wentzel, K. R., & Caldwell, K. (1997). Friendships, peer acceptance, and group membership: Relations to academic achievement in middle school. *Child Development*, 68(6), 1198–1209. https://doi.org/10.1111/j.1467-8624.1997.tb01994.x

How We Know It Has Worked
Part 6

Strategies to Evaluate the Intentional Teaching
of Values and Life Skills in Sports

Chapter Seventeen

Koon Teck Koh and Shun Xin Koong

INTRODUCTION

Participation in sports programmes provides a conducive environment for students and athletes to develop sports skills, values, and life skills, which will enable them to navigate through challenges in the environment and be successful in life (Camiré et al., 2012; Schwartz, 1992). However, such positive developmental outcomes are not automatic unless the programmes are well-planned and facilitated by trained instructors (Koh et al., 2016). Equally important is to guide the learners to apply these skills beyond the context of sports. To achieve these goals, Bean et al. (2018) suggested that explicit planning and teaching of values and life skills are crucial when delivering a sports programme, in which coaches intentionally integrate sports skills with values and life skills development during their lessons. Also, providing proper guidance to the athletes for application in real life scenarios.

Learning is continuous, and it is essential to monitor the progress of the learners to ensure that the delivery of lessons is effective. As such, it is essential to establish and utilise appropriate methods, such as pre- and post-programme evaluations, that are useful for measuring the progress of athletes accurately. Unfortunately, tracking and evaluating the effectiveness of values and life skills development can be challenging, as they are deeply personal and multifaceted. In addition, the existing literature mainly focuses on perception studies – i.e., using surveys or interviews with the participants, such as students, athletes, teachers, and coaches on the programme effectiveness (Camiré et al., 2020; Koh et al., 2016). The limitation of using such a methodology can be subjected to participants' recall bias, and what exactly happens during the coaching session remains unclear (Koh et al., In Press).

Past studies showed that intentional planning, delivering, and debriefing are critical success factors for the effective development of sports skills, values, and life skills in sports (Bean et al., 2018; Koh et al.,

DOI: 10.4324/9781032688657-23

2016). Careful planning, assessment, facilitation, and reflection by the coach are crucial in ensuring that sports programmes promote positive behaviours and attitudes which serve to benefit athletes not just within a sports-driven context but also beyond it (Almeida et al., 2023). Hence, there is an urgent need to explore using objective tools such as systematic observation to capture coaches' behaviours during a coaching session so that they are better informed and their athletes will benefit from their coaching. It is also our aim to address the existing gap in the literature.

To achieve these goals, we propose having a systematic observation instrument through a free Coaching Observation Tool (COT) mobile application developed by the first author that has the potential to produce quantifiable data (e.g., behaviours exhibited during a coaching session reported by percentages). The objective data would facilitate coaches in identifying aspects of their practice that can be improved and making the necessary changes accordingly. It would also allow them to provide support and guidance that are suitable for their athletes' needs and work toward achieving their goals in acquiring values and life skills that would allow them to excel in life personally, socially, and academically.

The following section aims to provide insight into the different tools and strategies used to track and evaluate values and life skills acquisition and coaching effectiveness in the context of sports.

APPLIED INSIGHTS

Tracking Athlete's Learning

Surveys

A quantitative way to track athlete's learning in values and life skills is through surveys. One of the common tools used is the Prosocial and Antisocial Behaviour in Sports Scale (PABSS; Kavussanu & Boardley, 2009). The survey was developed by garnering an extensive sample of athletes. In the process, specific behaviours across the four categories were observed and included in the scale (Kavussanu & Boardley, 2009). This tool has been validated and investigated for reliability and proven to be a valid and reliable tool for assessing sports-related prosocial and antisocial behaviour demonstrated among athletes in sports (Kavusannu et al., 2013). There are four categories in the 20-item scale (Kavussanu & Boardley, 2009), 2 relating to prosocial behaviour (toward teammates and toward opponents) and another 2 relating to antisocial behaviour (similarly, towards teammates and opponents) (Kavussanu & Boardley, 2009; Li et al., 2015). The scale has been used extensively in past research examining moral behaviour in the sports context (Kavussanu & Al-Yaaribi, 2021). This is attributed to the fact that it was developed to effectively measure athletes' social behaviour (Trigueros et al., 2020).

The Life Skills Transfer Survey (LSTS) developed by Weiss et al. (2014) is another tool that can be used to measure the transfer of life skills beyond sports. It consists of 50 items with 8 subscales such as (1) Meeting and Greeting, (2) Managing Emotions, (3) Goal Setting, (4) Resolving Conflicts, (5) Making Healthy Choices, (6) Appreciating Diversity, (7) Getting Help, and (8) Helping Others (Weiss et al., 2014), and is a self-report measure (McCarthy et al., 2022). It has been used to examine youth development golf programme, and positive results were reported (Weiss et al., 2016). This tool has been validated and tested for reliability and generalisability across various sports settings apart from golf. The LSTS reflects how youth perceive themselves to be able to transfer the life skills they have learnt outside the sports setting, making it a valuable tool in research on life skills transfer to improve life skills teaching (Weiss et al., 2014). The LSTS can be administered before life skills have been taught to athletes in the planning stage. This provides insight into athletes' behaviours before the life skills programme through PES. After the programme, a post-programme survey can be administered. The results from the pre- and post-programme can be compared to determine the progress made by the athletes to determine the programme effectiveness.

Activity Cards

Activity cards can be used to monitor athletes' behaviours (Moss et al., 2013). The card could inform stakeholders such as parents or classroom teachers of the values or life skills that were taught to the athletes. The definition of the value or life skill could be integrated into the activity card to establish a common understanding among various parties, such as the coach, parents, and classroom teachers of the value. Athletes will be asked to provide a transfer plan that allows them to practice and display the observable behaviours relating to the values or life skills in which they have been taught outside the sports context. The stakeholder concerned can then observe the athletes' behaviours and verify the plan if a behaviour is observed. Two sample activity cards can be found in Figures 17.1 and 17.2.

These activity cards can be used by physical education teachers and sports coaches (PETSCs) to track the learning and transfer of values and life skills in all settings. Such activity cards can be easily created by PETSCs. It can also be made available to athletes in an electronic format using personal devices (e.g., WhatsApp, Line) for quick and effective communication among the stakeholders. This communication and monitoring process is important, as it involves all the key stakeholders in facilitating the reinforcement and transference of values and life skills learnt beyond PES.

Values Transfer Plan

Dear parents,

Your child has learned one of the school values i.e. RESPECT this week. It means

- Being polite, kind and caring to others.
- Honouring rules in family and school.

He/she has outlined the following plan: *(This part is to be written by the student/athlete before giving it to the parents for verification)*:

- Greet family members before any meals
- Adhere to house rules

Please help to verify his/her plan by putting a tick against your child's plan based on your observation at home:

Your Child's Plan	Your Observation At Home	
	(Yes)	(No)
Greet family members before any meals		
Adhere to house rules		

We hope that through this engagement, we can help your child transfer the values learned beyond school. Together, we can help to develop him/her to be a better and productive citizen who can make positive contribution to the society.

Thank you for your kind assistance.

From: _____ (Name of Teacher/Coach)

Verified by father/mother/guardian (name): _____

Signature: _____

Date: _____

Figure 17.1 A simple of the values transfer card

Name: _____   Date: _____

Class: _____

<u>RESPECT</u>

The following questions require you to <u>discuss</u> with your parents/guardian and write down their responses:

1. What is the meaning of *respect*?	
You	Parent/Guardian

1a. Do you agree with your parent/guardian's definition of respect? Explain.	

2. Who should we show *respect* to?	
You	Parent/Guardian
3. Name one person you *respect* a lot in your life. Explain why you respect this person.	
You	Parent/Guardian

4. Ask your parent/guardian about a time when you failed to show respect to them. Knowing this, how would you behave differently if you were given another chance? Write down your answers below.

_____

_____

5. Discuss with your parent/guardian the role that respect play in a country like Singapore and write down your answers below.

_____

_____

_____

Figure 17.2 A sample of a discussion card focusing on the values of respect

Limitations

While most of these observation tools and activity cards sought to track the progress of athletes through observing, surveying, or discussing a plan for changing their behaviours, these methods have limitations, as they are based on recall and reporting through oneself or their parents or teachers. Consequently, they may lead to the inability to recall accurately and social desirability bias (Krumpal, 2013). This limits the validity and reliability of the results obtained (Camiré et al., 2020; Vella et al., 2013).

The following section highlights the development of the systematic observation tools that are used in enhancing coaching practice and making a case for having a mobile application that has the potential to quantify coaching behaviours that are related to the teaching of sports skills, values, and life skills, and transference beyond sports setting.

Tracking Coaching Behaviours
Systematic Observation Tools

Systematic observation instruments have been used to collect data on coaches' behaviours during practices (Lacy & Darst, 1984). They allowed researchers to identify and understand the influence of coaches' behaviours on selected athlete's developmental outcomes. The depth and volume of the data collected gave systematic observation tools a reputation of being a valuable device that enables coaches to enhance quality coaching practices. However, its potential as a coach development tool is eclipsed by an over-concentration on data collection and behaviour categorisation (Cope et al., 2022).

Recent research using systematic observation tools has gone beyond merely identifying and categorising behaviours. For example, Raya-Castellano et al. (2021) used a combination of systematic observations via filming coaches, coding behaviours, debriefing interviews, workshops, assigned tasks, and reflective interviews to explore and enhance coaches' skills in giving post-match, video-based feedback. In addition, Wagner et al. (2023) developed a systematic observation instrument named PlayerScore and applied it to handball athletes to examine individual player performance in team competitions. While there have been processes and methods used to study coaching behaviours, the focus was primarily on coaching and enhancing sports skills. To date, there is no application for quantifying coaching behaviours related to values and life skills development during sports coaching sessions. Hence, there is an urgent need to address this gap in the literature.

Coaching Observation Tool

As mentioned earlier, systematic observation tools have been used commonly in sports settings, as they could produce objective data on the behaviours exhibited by coaches during a coaching session. Coaches can use the data generated for targeted self-reflection to enhance future practice and promote coach development (Koh et al., 2015). The Arizona State University Observation Instrument (ASUOI) developed by Lacy and Darst (1984) is one of the tools that is widely used to systematically observe coaching behaviours to enhance coaching practices in sports settings (Lacy & Goldston, 1990). It is easy to use, and the data generated are useful for targeted reflection to enhance subsequent training planning and practice. However, like other systematic observation tools, it is mainly focusing on quantifying behaviours that are related to sports skills development, which is a limitation.

To overcome this limitation, adaptation of the ASUOI to include coaching behaviours related to the teaching of values and life skills is needed to make it relevant to the sports coaching context. Two new subcategories, "with Values" and "With Transfer," were added to the current seven categories of behaviour in the ASUOI. The current categories that have been modified to include the subcategories are (1) pre-instruction, (2) concurrent instruction, (3) post-instruction, (4) questioning, (5) positive modelling, (6) negative modelling, and (7) praise. "With Values" would be achieved when a PES lesson incorporates values, while "With Transfer" is achieved when PETSCs teach their athletes the application of values out of PES. This tool has been renamed the Coaching Observation Tool (COT).

COT is a fully automated free mobile application with a few unique features. For example, videos of the coaching session can be taken while coding is taking place with COT. When the coach is providing "positive modelling with values" to the athletes, the coder/observer can use the recording function to capture this moment. It will be tabbed with this behaviour category for ease of referencing after the lesson and serves as a positive reinforcement and affirmation of the values and life skills coaching practice. The time spent in each category is calculated and tallied to quantify (by percentage) and identify the amount of time spent on teaching sports skills, values, and life skills during the lesson.

COT follows ASUOI's ten-second interval coding method – i.e., five seconds observe and the next five seconds code. However, instead of referring to the stopwatch manually, it comes with an automatic prompt to observe and a code function that is extremely helpful to the coder. More importantly, the COT can help coaches develop in several ways, such as self-reflection, collaborative learning, and mentoring others.

Self-reflection: By referring to the amount of time planned on teaching sports skills, values, and life skills (by percentage) and the actual amount of time spent on each lesson, PETSCs can use the objective data generated from the COT to reflect on their coaching practice and engage in critical reflection to enhance the quality of the coaching sessions in future (Koh et al., 2015). For example, a coach may plan to spend about 70% of the time on teaching sports skills and 30% on teaching values and life skills. However, if the actual amount of time shown on sports skills is 60%, and only 5% of time was spent on teaching values and life skills, the coach needs to reflect on what happened and explore ways (e.g., talking to experienced coaches) to improve future practice in incorporating values and life skills more intentionally and effectively. Based on a few studies conducted in Singapore, coaches often allocate more time to teaching values and life skills, but the actual amount of time spent in this area is often exceptionally low, which is consistent with the literature if they are not trained. Nonetheless, by providing the objective observation data to these coaches with just over two data points with an interval of two weeks, positive improvements in coaching values and life skills intentionally were observed (Koh et al., In Press).

Collaborative Learning: Collaboration is seen as an important part of helping to improve PETSCs' teaching. In the post-pandemic era, the use of technology has gained traction and increasing attention, as it allows people to work together remotely. As highlighted, observation tools are advantageous in helping PETSCs evaluate their teaching more objectively and quantitatively. Incorporating technology such as COT to allow better access and collaboration. This app serves as a platform to help PETSCs track the progress of their teaching of values and life skills in PES. The app allows users to code lessons based on video-recorded lessons that can be uploaded to the app, after which users are able to code the lessons based on the different dimensions of the modified ASUOI. Findings from the coding data suggest that the mobile application is a useful tool to evaluate the effectiveness of a coaching lesson by comparing the planned and actual percentage of time allocated to sports skills, values, and life skills development.

For instance, in a study evaluating the effectiveness of a Values and Principles in Sports (VPS) coach training course, the COT app was used to quantify coaches' behaviours in teaching sports skills, values, and life skills during lessons and transfer beyond sports setting (Koh et al., In Press). Twenty-seven coaches and athletes from their teams (n = 85) participated in the study. Fourteen coaches attended the VPS course, which aimed to equip them with knowledge and skills for promoting values-driven coaching practices. Findings suggested that the VPS course contributed to understanding and awareness related to teaching values in sports and the transfer of values outside of sports. The authors believe that the enhanced ASUOI mobile application can be a valuable tool to help coaches reflect on their coaching practice using objective assessments of time use in delivered sessions. While there may be concerns about time-based assessment of coaching behaviours, the authors argue that providing this information is helpful for increasing coaches' awareness of their own actions. Equally, it helps to support them in critically reflecting on achieving effective coaching outcomes and how to enhance future practice (Koh et al., 2015). This applies to sports skills, values, and life skills development. In addition, the enhanced ASUOI pp was useful in helping coaches evaluate their values-driven coaching, and it facilitated their discussions with their colleagues and mentors.

Additionally, a study that examined the creation and implementation of the enhanced ASUOI mobile application for values-driven lessons by practitioners 16 sports practitioners provided further evidence that the app helped these sports practitioners reflect and refine their lessons through the comparison of planned lessons and actual lessons in the areas of sports skills, values and life skills and transfer. This was evident with 44% of the PETSCs showing increased engagement in values and skill development and 56% of them incorporating more values and transfer in their lessons as shown through their teaching behaviours (Koh, 2023).

Therefore, as evident, the app provides PETSCs with feedback on their coaching. With the feedback, PETSCs could have greater awareness of their plans to create and deliver lessons that are values-driven in nature. The use of the app allows PETSCs to share their videos and coding with other users such as their colleagues or mentors. This allows PETSCs to collaborate with them to ensure coding of their lessons is more accurate with fewer internal biases that might affect one's personal judgement. With the coded data, a review can be done by the coach individually or between the coach and a peer whom he feels comfortable talking to. The data could also be sent to a mentor whom the coach respects to guide the review process and identify key learning areas that the coach or peer might have overlooked. These can be done remotely through mobile devices, making it convenient for everyone. By having an objective review process, PETSCs can receive objective data for themselves, which would help them refine their lessons and be more intentional in planning and delivering value-driven and impactful coaching sessions to their athletes.

SUMMARY AND FUTURE DIRECTIONS

Despite the challenges faced when attempting to quantify and evaluate the progress of inculcating values and life skills in PES, various tools have been established. Some of these tools are based on self-reports and recall, limiting the potential they have in accurately quantifying progress. Observation tools have been developed to facilitate the evaluation process. While it is important to track the development of values and life skills in athletes, the progress of PETSCs and their teaching pedagogies are also critical areas to consider evaluating too. The ASUOI has been identified as an ease to use tool and was modified to a fully automated and user-friendly mobile application to serve as an objective observation tool to guide PETSCs in evaluating their values-driven lessons. We believe that COT offers greater convenience and attraction to facilitate collaboration between PETSCs, their colleagues, and their mentors to help PETSCs achieve a more objective, accurate, and effective evaluation of their effort in promoting values-driven coaching practice.

Future Directions

However, as the coding process is still tedious and time-consuming, the COT app could be enhanced by harnessing the benefits of artificial intelligence (AI) to facilitate the coding process. As such, future research could aim to train AI in the coding process of the values-driven lessons. This would save the time needed to obtain a coded lesson and quantifiable data relating to the lesson. The time saved could be spent on reflection and review processes instead. The reflection and review processes are important in coaching practices, as they are fundamental parts of PETSCs' professional development. Through reflection, coaching effectiveness can be enhanced to facilitate athlete development (Costello et al., 2023).

The AI mechanism can also be developed to provide feedback and resources to PETSCs to improve their lessons. This would allow them to have a clearer understanding of their current coaching practices and have a better plan of how they could strive to improve their lessons to integrate values and life skills and their transfer more effectively. The feedback provided could also serve as a starting point for discussion with fellow colleagues and mentors to help with critical reflection and better improvement of lesson plans.

REFERENCES

Almeida, L., Dias, T., Corte-Real, N., Menezes, I., & Fonseca, A. (2023). Positive youth development through sport and physical education: A systematic review of empirical research conducted with grade 5 to 12 children and youth. *Physical Education and Sport Pedagogy*, 1–27. https://doi.org/10.1080/17408989.2023.2230208

Bean, C., Kramers, S., Forneris, T., & Camiré, M. (2018). The implicit/explicit continuum of life skills development and transfer. *Quest*, 70(4), 456–470. https://doi.org/10.1080/00336297.2018.1451348

Camiré, M., Kendellen, K., Rathwell, S., & Turgeon, S. (2020). Evaluating the coaching for life skills online training program: A randomised controlled trial. *Psychology of Sport and Exercise*, 48, 101649. https://doi.org/10.1016/j.psychsport.2020.101649

Camiré, M., Trudel, P., & Forneris, T. (2012). Coaching and transferring life skills: Philosophies and strategies used by model high school coaches. *The Sport Psychologist*, 26(2), 243–260. https://doi.org/10.1123/tsp.26.2.243

Cope, E., Cushion, C. J., Harvey, S., & Partington, M. (2022). Re-visiting systematic observation: A pedagogical tool to support coach learning and development. *Frontiers in Sports and Active Living*, 4, 962690. https://doi.org/10.3389/fspor.2022.962690

Costello, K., Jewitt-Beck, R., & Leeder, T. M. (2023). Coach developers and reflective practice: Evaluating exercises, mechanisms and challenges in facilitating reflection within novice coach education. *Reflective Practice*, 24(3), 279–294. https://doi.org/10.1080/14623943.2023.2174963

Kavussanu, M., & Al-Yaaribi, A. (2021). Prosocial and antisocial behaviour in sport. *International Journal of Sport and Exercise Psychology*, 19(2), 179–202. https://doi.org/10.1080/1612197X.2019.1674681

Kavussanu, M., & Boardley, I. D. (2009). The prosocial and antisocial behavior in sport scale. *Journal of Sport Exercise Psychology*, 31(1), 97–117. https://doi.org/10.1123/jsep.31.1.97

Kavussanu, M., Stanger, N., & Boardley, I. D. (2013). The prosocial and antisocial behaviour in sport scale: Further evidence for construct validity and reliability, *Journal of Sports Sciences*, 31(11), 1208–1221. https://doi.org/10.1080/02640414.2013.775473

Koh, K.T. (2023). *Teaching values and life skills through physical education and sports programmes*. National Institute of Education.

Koh, K.T., Komar, J., Newman, T.J., & Tan, E. [In Press]. The effects of a Values and Principles in Sports coach education course designed to promote values-driven coaching styles. *International Journal of Sport Science & Coaching*.

Koh, K. T., Mallett, C. J., Camiré, M., & Wang, C. K. J. (2015). A guided reflection intervention for high performance basketball coaches. *International Sport Coaching Journal*, 2(3), 273–284. https://doi.org/10.1123/iscj.2014-0135

Koh, K. T., Ong, S. W., & Camiré, M. (2016). Implementation of a values training program in physical education and sport: Perspectives from teachers, coaches, students, and athletes. *Physical Education and Sport Pedagogy*, 21(3), 295–312. https://doi.org/10.1080/17408989.2014.990369

Krumpal, I. (2013). Determinants of social desirability bias in sensitive surveys: A literature review. *Quality & Quantity*, 47(4), 2025–2047.

Lacy, A. C., & Darst, P. W. (1984). Evolution of a systematic observation system: The ASU coaching observation instrument. *Journal of Teaching in Physical Education*, 3(3), 59–66. https://doi.org/10.1123/jtpe.3.3.59

Lacy, A. C., & Goldston, P. D. (1990). Behavior analysis of male and female coaches in high school girls basketball. *Journal of Sport Behavior*, 13, 29–39.

Li, C., Koh, K. T., Wang, C. K. J., & Chian, L. K. (2015). Sports participation and moral development outcomes: Examination of validity and reliability of the prosocial and antisocial behavior in sport scale. *International Journal of Sports Science & Coaching*, 10(2–3), 505–513.

McCarthy, M. K., Harris, B. S., & Gregg, K. (2022). The effectiveness of teaching life skills through sport-based interventions for youth at risk. *National Youth Advocacy and Resilience Journal*, 5(2), n2.

Moss, E., O'Connor, A., & Peterson, R. (2013). *Behavior monitoring*. https://doi.org/10.13140/RG.2.1.5057.3845

Raya-Castellano, P. E., Reeves, M. J., Fradua-Uriondo, L., & McRobert, A. P. (2021). Post-match video-based feedback: A longitudinal work-based coach development program stimulating changes in coaches' knowledge and understanding. *International Journal of Sports Science & Coaching*, 16(6), 1259–1270. https://doi.org/10.1177/17479541211017276

Schwartz, S. H. (1992). Universals in the content and structure of values: Theoretical advances and empirical tests in 20 countries. In M. P. Zanna (Ed.), *Advances in experimental social psychology* (Vol. 25, pp. 1–65). Academic Press. https://doi.org/10.1016/S0065-2601(08)60281-6

Trigueros, R., Alias, A., Gallardo, A. M., García-Tascón, M., & Aguilar-Parra, J. M. (2020). Validation and adaptation of the prosocial and antisocial behaviour in sport scale to the Spanish context of physical education. *International Journal of Environmental Research and Public Health*, 17(2), 477. https://doi.org/10.3390/ijerph17020477

Vella, S. A., Oades, L. G., & Crowe, T. P. (2013). A pilot test of transformational leadership training for sports coaches: Impact on the developmental experiences of adolescent athletes. *International Journal of Sports Science & Coaching*, 8(3), 513–530. https://doi.org/10.1260/1747-9541.8.3.513

Wagner, H., Hinz, M., Melcher, K., Radic, V., & Uhrmeister, J. (2023). The player-score: A systematic game observation tool to determine individual player performance in team handball competition. *Applied Sciences*, 13(4), 2327. https://www.mdpi.com/2076-3417/13/4/2327

Weiss, M. R., Bolter, N. D., & Kipp, L. E. (2014). Assessing impact of physical activity-based youth development programs: Validation of the Life Skills Transfer Survey (LSTS). *Research Quarterly for Exercise and Sport*, 85(3), 263–278.

Weiss, M. R., Bolter, N. D., & Kipp, L. E. (2016). Evaluation of The First Tee in promoting positive youth development: Group comparisons and longitudinal trends. *Research Quarterly for Exercise and Sport*, 87(3), 271–283. https://doi.org/10.1080/02701367.2016.1172698

Eighteen

Strategies to Evaluate the Intentional Teaching of Values and Life Skills in Sports: Sports Singapore's Perspective

Eliza Tan, David Chin, Noor Hisham, Caleb Khoo and Federico Carreres

INTRODUCTION

The Game-for-Life (GFL) Framework developed by Sports Singapore (SportSG) aims to guide sports educators (e.g., sports coaches and physical education teachers) to be more intentional in facilitating the learning of values and life skills in their coaching and teaching process. The GFL framework centres around the use of sports activities and role-learning for the learning and development of performance, social and moral values, and attributes (see Figure 18.1). This enables trainers, educators, and coaching professionals to plan and generate more teachable moments, where values/attributes can be infused into any sporting experience to develop character and leadership through sports.

Over the years, the framework has been applied in multiple contexts (e.g., coaching education, physical education curriculum, intervention programmes for youth-at-risk, sports academies, and club programmes). The chapter will discuss the evaluation strategies and tools that have been developed to evaluate the learning and application of values and life skills at various levels. Evaluation strategies and tools discussed will be around three main areas:

1 Assessing Values-based Coaching and Teaching Practices in Coach Education
2 Measuring the Effects of Intentional Values-Focused Sports Programmes on Student and Youth Development
3 Case Example: SportSG's Integrated Approach for Programme Evaluation

DOI: 10.4324/9781032688657-24

GAME FOR LIFE FRAMEWORK
for character & leadership development through sport

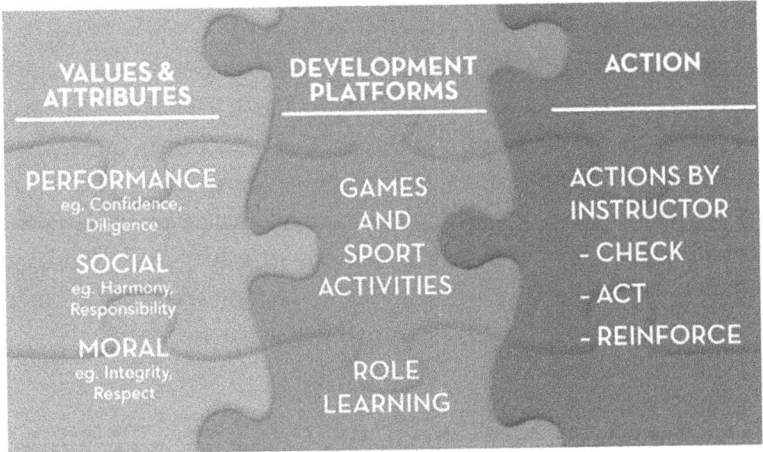

Figure 18.1 Elements that make up the GFL Framework (Sports Singapore, 2013)

The evaluation tools are designed for use by different stakeholder groups and depend on whether the key focus is coach development or youth development. These strategies and tools are contributed by SportSG's Character and Leadership Development Team and its key partners who have applied the GFL framework in their various contexts from the Ministry of Social and Family Development, Republic Polytechnic, Saint Hilda's Secondary School, Punggol Secondary School, and the University of Alicante (Spain).

APPLIED INSIGHTS
Assessing Values-based Coaching and Teaching Practices in Coach Education

It is important that evaluation strategies do not just focus on the outcome of whether the learners (e.g., youths) developed values and life skills without taking into consideration the coaching and teaching practices of the sports educator. Having customised evaluation strategies is critical for developing coaching and teaching practices for teaching life skills and values because it moves beyond evaluating solely on results on whether values and/or life skills have been developed in the learners but focuses on developing the sports educator involved.

Assessing the Professional Practice of Coaching through Portfolios

SportSG's training partner, Republic Polytechnic, adopts a portfolio-based workplace learning approach where aspiring sports coaches are required to document evidence of learning in their workplaces (Boud & Solomon, 2001). Therefore, a coach's learning environment is assessed based on normal work tasks and is not based on artificial or contrived scenarios (Norcini, 2003) delivered in a classroom or assessed by traditional exams and graded assignments. To ensure all participants in the sports coaching diploma programme have a common reference point when it comes to values-based coaching, Republic Polytechnic uses SportSG's GFL Framework as the basis for participants to build their professional practice portfolios.

The Portfolio Evaluation Rubric

An analytic rubric is used by lecturers to evaluate evidence captured in the coaching portfolio. The rubric's performance criteria are designed to help coaching students focus on developing higher-order transferable skills required for lifelong learning, including planning, research, execution, getting feedback, and reflection for action on how to be a better sports coach.

Each performance criterion of the rubric is defined in the following:

Performance Criteria	Description
Planning	The ability to design a session plan based on the GFL template that is specific to the coach's sports and athletes
Research	The ability to source and cite applications of values-based coaching from academic research to support their professional practice
Execution	The ability to demonstrate and capture evidence of professional skills in coaching based on the session plan in an authentic context
Feedback	The ability to seek and utilise feedback from athletes, peer coaches, and other stakeholders
Reflection	The ability to reflect on coaching experiences to improve future practice
Structure and format	The ability to present a work portfolio that is coherent and professionally appealing to stakeholders
Oral questioning	The ability to answer questions and elaborate on their portfolio without prompting and apply skills to unfamiliar contexts

The descriptors in the analytic rubric (see Table 18.1) are designed to evaluate the depth of coaching students' understanding of their portfolio work, their communication skills, and their ability to critically engage with the material in a broader context. The effectiveness of an analytic rubric lies in its clarity, relevance, and ability to provide guidance that can help a coach understand the skills they are to demonstrate in the portfolio. Each descriptor also provides guidance on what is expected at each level of competency so that coaches can use the rubric as a self-assessment tool to develop their portfolio as well as for their own professional and personal growth. To ensure interrater reliability so that there is a common interpretation of student performance (Reddy & Andrade, 2010), benchmarking of several portfolios is done by all lecturers involved in the portfolio assessment. Thereafter, each candidate is then interviewed by a panel of two of the lecturers to verify that the work during a 20-minute oral questioning session.

Supporting Coaches in Practice through Mentoring and Observations

As part of continuing coach education, SportSG also supports coaches in practice through a structured mentoring programme that is anchored by the GFL framework to enhance values-based coaching practices. As part of the mentoring programme, a clear list of coaching competencies and an observation tool (see Figure 18.2) has been developed to evaluate a coach's application of learnings of GFL framework principles within his/her coaching process.

This tool guides the mentor on areas to pay attention to when observing the coach in action and helps the mentee identify the coaching competencies he/she is strong in and competencies which are areas for growth. This method of evaluation will also serve as a reflective tool for the coaches involved, facilitating continuous improvement to their values-driven coaching/teaching practices. Beyond mentoring, this observation tool can also be used for seasonal or end-year evaluations from administrators, other coaches, or educators as a form of continuous professional development, co-learning, and/or competency assessment for quality assurance to enhance coaching practices that integrate the teaching of values and life skills.

Table 18.1 Republic Polytechnic Portfolio Evaluation Rubric

Performance Criteria	Level 3	Level 2	Level 1	Level 0
Planning	Shows mastery in strategic planning and innovatively integrating diverse elements that help all athletes learn the desired skills and values	Exhibits proficient planning skills that include strategies to help most athletes learn the desired skills and values	Creates plans that are tailored to specific goals that are somewhat focused on integrating skills and values	Demonstrates basic planning abilities; plans are often generic and may lack detail
Research	Integrates recent research approaches from credible academic sources that directly support the professional practice of values-based coaching	Conducts in-depth research from credible sources that is broad and applied to actionable practices for values-based coaching	Research gathers mostly relevant information from credible sources that are somewhat specific to a values-based portfolio	Research does not apply learning from academic research articles and is not specific to a values-based portfolio
Execution	Demonstrates exceptional execution of values-driven coaching that consistently imparts all desired skills and values	Consistently implements values-driven coaching session plan that imparts identified skills and values	Execution follows the session plan and shows values-driven coaching in a somewhat consistent manner	Execution does not follow the session plan and lacks demonstration of values-based coaching competencies

Feedback	Feedback is sought from diverse stakeholders, including athletes, that helps improve significant aspects of coaching both skills and values through sports	Feedback is sought from diverse stakeholders, including athletes, that helps improve aspects of both coaching skills and values through sports	Feedback comes from one other stakeholder that helps improve some aspects of coaching skills or values through sports	Feedback from stakeholders is weak and does not improve the practice of teaching skills and values through sports
Oral questioning	Independently articulates in-depth insights on coaching values and skills, including application to unfamiliar contexts	Explains and elaborates concepts independently and makes relevant connections to other contexts	Explains and elaborates with some prompting for familiar contexts but lacks depth and clarity	Answers basic questions with frequent prompting and unable to elaborate on details
Structure and format	Portfolio is easy to navigate, visually appealing, coherent throughout, and can be published with minor edits	Portfolio is easy to navigate, visually appealing, coherent for most parts, and can be published with moderate edits	Portfolio is somewhat difficult to navigate, lacks visual appeal and coherence, but can be published with major edits	Portfolio is difficult to navigate, is not coherent, has no visual appeal, and is not suitable for publishing

263 Strategies to Evaluate the Intentional Teaching

Coaching Values and Life Skills through Physical Education and Sports

Coach Name: _____ Venue: _____ Date: _____ Time: _____ Report: 1 / 2 / 3

COACHING COMPETENCIES (In the boxes provided, indicate:)

+	when competency is a Strength
∆	when the competency is an Area for Growth
√	when competency demonstrated is neither a strength nor weakness
NA	when there is no opportunity for coach to demonstrate the competency

PROCESSES	COACHING COMPETENCIES	COMMENTS (Strengths, Areas for Growth and Suggestions)
PLANNING	• Clear training outcomes for skills and values development for the session • Designs appropriate learning activities to facilitate training outcomes • Determines appropriate values/attributes and observable behaviours that can be brought out through the learning activities • Develops an appropriate time schedule for learning of skills and values • Plans key questions to ask to facilitate learning of skills and values • Demonstrates ability in using the Game-for-Life framework/template	
LESSON DELIVERY	• Engages learners in active participation through meaningful individual/group practices • Gives clear cues/instructions and effective demonstrations • Provides clear definitions/meanings for learners to demonstrate values-based behaviours through actions during learning activities • Asks appropriate questions and elicit responses pertaining to facilitate learning of skills/strategies and values associated with the sports • Appropriate time spent between imparting skills and values • Concludes lesson by drawing the skills and values learned from learners	
ASSESSMENT & FEEDBACK	• Gives specific, timely and relevant feedback to learners (verbal / non-verbal) • Acknowledges and affirms positive skills and behaviours • Addresses non-desired behaviours and performance timely and appropriately • Able to draw connections on how certain values and desired behaviours can be applied in daily life (when appropriate)	
MANAGEMENT	• Establishes a supportive learning environment • Establishes rules and routines that promote positive behaviours • Always ensures safety and well-being of learners	
OVERALL VALUES-DRIVEN APPROACH	• Able to integrate the learning and practice of character and values in coaching practice consistently • Able to guide learners towards expectations of positive character and values • Able to use a variety of push and pull strategies to reinforce development of values and skills. (e.g. highlighting, discussions, reflections, peer-teaching) • Is a good role model that exhibits character and values consistently through actions and words	

Figure 18.2 SportSG's GFL coaching competencies observation and feedback tool

MEASURING THE EFFECTS OF INTENTIONAL VALUES-FOCUSED SPORTS PROGRAMMES ON STUDENT/YOUTH DEVELOPMENT

At minimum, all programme evaluation systems should include tools for measuring athlete/student development (Gilbert, 2017). Beyond the technical skills of the sports, most stakeholders would also be interested in the eventual outcome of whether the end-user (e.g., students) has indeed developed some values and life skills through sports. To assess whether students have learnt any value(s), we need to first define the outcomes explicitly. When the students can identify the goal clearly (Deci & Ryan, 1994), they can better understand how and what behaviours to demonstrate.

Table 18.2 outlines examples of how observable values-based behaviours have been defined explicitly by the physical education department at Saint Hilda's Secondary School. Communicating these expectations at the start of the school term and reinforcing them at each lesson (where appropriate) helps students understand how they can demonstrate values and helps educators to assess if values have been demonstrated during lessons.

To deepen the intentional practice of teaching values, the students need to internalise the values and build a consistent value system. Dweck (2015) stipulates that helping students improve requires telling the truth about a student's current achievement and then, together, doing something about it. To achieve this, a set of rubrics for individual attributes for the student to self-evaluate after a series of lessons was also developed by Punggol Secondary School's physical education team (see Table 18.3). Self-reported evaluation aids students in being clearer on what behaviours to exhibit and to conceptualise the values which may lead to positive behaviours. It also allows students to have the autonomy to decide where they are developmentally.

In addition, students are informed at the start of the year of a summative inclusion in their holistic report for physical education (see Table 18.4) done by the physical education teacher at the end of the year. The educator will design sessions and lessons based on these rubrics to monitor student development throughout the year.

266 Coaching Values and Life Skills through Physical Education and Sports

Table 18.2 St. Hilda's Secondary's Observable Behaviours/Outcomes for Value of "Respect" to Be Demonstrated by Secondary Students

Game	Observable Behaviours		
	Respect for Self	Respect for Others	Respect for the Environment/Equipment
Basketball	Self-analysis in drill practice (chest pass, bounce pass, shooting)	Execute a successful chest pass by ensuring that the ball is thrown towards the partner's chest area	Set up and keep movable poles properly
Volleyball	Self-analysis in drill practice (serve, receive, set, hit)	Execute a toss high enough for your partner to return successfully	Refrain from dragging or pulling the nets/red-white tape to prevent metal poles from collapsing
Handball	Self-analysis in drill practice (passing, receiving, shooting, moving)	Run into space and call out for the ball when a teammate is in possession	Set up and keep movable goalposts properly
Outdoor education	Self-analysis in map reading competency	To communicate effectively with patience during pair work	Refrain from tampering with orienteering flags set up at respective checkpoints/recycle tin cans after cooking lesson

Table 18.3 Punggol Secondary School's Student Self-Evaluation Tool on the Value of "Strive for Excellence"

	"WOW" Level 4	"Got It" Level 3	"Getting There" Level 2	"Needs Work" Level 1
Personal accountability	☐ I am always able to complete assigned work on time, and through reflecting on the learning outcomes, I hold myself to high standards and initiate improvement in work and behaviour	☐ I am mostly able to complete assigned work on time, and I am aware of the learning outcomes to manage my efforts in work and behaviour	☐ I can sometimes complete assigned work on time and am able to make myself aware of the learning outcomes	☐ I need constant reminders to be on task, and I need a lot of motivation from others for me to put in the right efforts towards achieving the outcomes of the lesson/s
Focus (enthusiasm for learning)	☐ I am able to focus for almost 100% of the lesson. I set my learning goals early and have fully cleared all my doubts	☐ I am able to focus for much of the lesson, and I am able to identify several critical observation points for my learning	☐ I am able to focus for some of the lesson, but I need to be more "present" in order to maximise my learning time	☐ I did not manage to participate much in the learning as I allowed my distractions to get the better of me

Strategies to Evaluate the Intentional Teaching

Table 18.4 Punggol Secondary's Rubrics to Evaluate the Developmental Levels to Receive and Respond to the Values Taught (Krathworl et al., 1964) to Students Based on the School's Core Values and the Educational Values of Olympism

Strive for Excellence	Respect	Mental Resilience (Balance between Body, Will, and Mind)	Level of Development
Shows exceptional enthusiasm in learning, always actively participates in the lesson, and also consistently reflects to better oneself in terms of knowledge acquisition and skill performance	Is exemplary in upholding sportsmanship values and showing regard for others (peers and teachers) via use of tactful words, and showing kindness to others, and being fair always to teammates and opponents alike	Shows exceptional ability to find opportunities for learning when faced with adversity, is highly adaptable to situations, and has a strong value of self-esteem	Exceeding expectations
Is often enthusiastic in learning, actively participates in the lesson most of the time, hugely dedicated towards betterment of self in terms of knowledge acquisition and skill performance, and is also highly disciplined with reflections and practices	Often upholds sportsmanship values through showing regard for others (peers and teachers), respects social conventions via use of tactful words and showing kindness to others most of the times and is mostly fair to teammates and opponents alike	Is mostly able to find opportunities for learning when faced with adversity, shows ability to adapt to different situations and has a respectable sense of self-esteem	Achieving expectations

Shows moderate enthusiasm in learning, participates in the lesson adequately, shows tolerable dedication in terms of knowledge acquisition and skill performance, and also requires some prompting towards reflective practice	Is at times able to uphold sportsmanship values through showing regard for others (peers and teachers), respecting social conventions via use of tactful words, and showing kindness to others at times and is fair sometimes to teammates and opponents alike	Sometimes displays resilience to achieve outcomes for self and manage distractions and requires some affirmation from others in building self-esteem	Developing
Requires constant mediation from teacher/s or others to stay on track towards lesson objectives and requires ongoing intervention from others to apply thinking processes in finding solutions	Requires constant reminders to show regard for others (peers and teachers), often needs guidance to respect social conventions like using appropriate words and being kind to others, and rarely treats others fairly	Seldom displays resilience to achieve outcomes for self and manage distractions and requires much affirmation and encouragement from others in building self-esteem	Needs improvement

CASE EXAMPLE: SPORTSG'S INTEGRATED APPROACH FOR PROGRAMME EVALUATION

To evaluate programmes in a more systematic and structured manner, SportSG has adopted the Kirkpatrick training evaluation model (Kirkpatrick & Kirkpatrick, 2006) when considering the type of evaluation strategies and tools to develop to measure the effectiveness of developing values and life skills at various levels (see Figure 18.3). The model describes training effectiveness in terms of how individuals reacted, learnt, applied, and demonstrated results after receiving training.

Evaluating Effectiveness of GFL Sports Educators Workshops (Level 1 and 2) As SportSG is an institution that is actively involved in the development and upskilling of sports educators, it is important for us to have evaluation tools in place to assess whether training workshops conducted are effective for participant learning. Designing feedback forms to gather such data will allow us to continually review the content and delivery

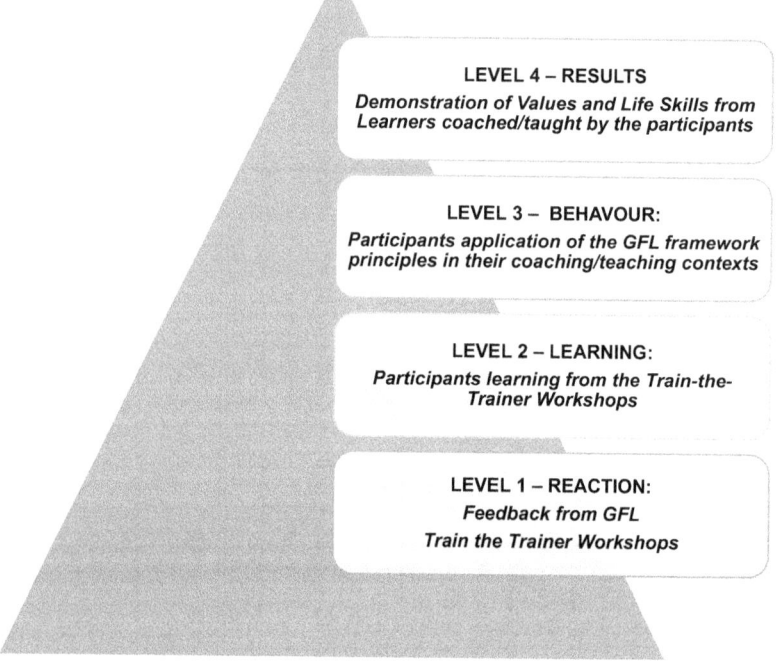

Figure 18.3 SportSG's application of the Kirkpatrick's training evaluation model

of sports educators' workshops to ensure they are relevant, engaging, and impactful for the participants so that they will be motivated to implement the learnings back in their environments.

Quick rating scales are used to assess the extent to which participants found the facilitator's delivery of the workshop to be engaging and the content taught to be relevant and adequate. To assess the knowledge and skills acquired, open-ended questions are also added in the feedback forms to provide greater insights into the learnings and takeaways of the participants. This helps provide data on the type of post-workshop support if required. Examples of such evaluation questions developed by SportSG and the University of Alicante (Spain) can be found in Appendix A.

Having these tools in place to evaluate participants' reactions to the sports educators' workshops allows facilitators to have a better understanding of participant learnings and takeaways, providing valuable feedback to aid in enhancing the content and design of future workshops to be more effective and engaging. Examples of training enhancements made because of participant feedback include the following:

1 **Diversifying training content**: Developing training modules that delve deeper into effective communication strategies and emphasise sports educators' role in positive reinforcement.
2 **Tailoring content to coaching philosophy**: Customising training materials to underscore the importance of creating a positive team culture, aligning with coaches' evolving philosophies.
3 **Scenario-based workshops**: Integrating scenario-based workshops into the training programme, allowing coaches/teachers to practice applying character development principles in challenging real-world situations.
4 **Individualised support strategies**: Include guidance on individualised approaches for coaches facing resistance, providing tools to address specific challenges encountered during implementation.
5 **Interactive case studies**: Develop interactive case studies that mirror common youth sports scenarios, allowing coaches/teachers to analyse, discuss, and apply character development principles in context.
6. **Peer learning community**: Establishing online platforms and/or forming communities of practice for sports educators to connect, share experiences, and learn from one another, creating a supportive community dedicated to character development through sports.

The next step would be to evaluate the applications of learnings by participants, and the results of their application. Hence, we developed an instrument consisting of two different scales to be used to assess the frequency of sports educators' application of GFL framework principles in their coaching and teaching practices, along with the frequency of demonstration of values-based behaviours by their learners. These are self-reported pre-post questionnaires on a 5-point, Likert-type scale that are meant to be filled out by the end-user (e.g., youths).

The first measure is a 15-item values inculcation practices scale that measures the frequency at which sports educators apply values-driven practices in their physical education (PE) lessons or coaching sessions. These items measure the extent to which sports educators identify, define, model, shape, and reinforce values-based behaviours during the PE lessons/coaching sessions (e.g., "During training, my coach explains how certain values can be demonstrated").

The second measure is a 15–20 item values scale that measures the frequency at which athletes/students demonstrated values-based behaviours during sports activities (e.g., "I accepted my role in the team and fulfilled it to the best of my ability"). The scales for each level were adapted from a variety of sources, such as the Goal Orientation Scale – Sports (1992), Reasons for Discipline Scale (1998), Athletic Coping Skills Inventory (2004), Attitudes to Moral Decision-Making in Youth Sports Questionnaire (2007), Prosocial and Antisocial Behaviour in Sports scale (2009), and Youth Experience Survey for Sports (2012), and contextualised to measure selected values emphasised by various stakeholder groups.

Additional questions and analyses were also performed to explore the possibility that integrating values during PE lessons/coaching sessions reduced levels of actual skill development and enjoyment of sports/game activities. To address this legitimate concern, students/athletes were asked, "How much did you enjoy learning during PE lessons/training sessions?" and "How confident are you now in playing the sports/activity?" using a 5-point Likert scale (1 = Not at all to 5 = Very much)

Results revealed positive relationships between skill development, enjoyment, and sports educators' application of GFL framework principles. In other words, the more frequently sports educators facilitated values inculcation through the framework during PE lessons/coaching sessions, the greater the students/athletes' perceived levels of enjoyment and actual game skill development.

This instrument has since been expanded to also include questions that go beyond the sporting context – under the Achieve-Connect-Thrive (ACT) SG Framework outlined in Figure 18.4, which posits that youths are best positioned to succeed in school and life when they have mastery over 13 core skills, including (i) **achieve** tasks and complete work, (ii) **connect** to others, and (iii) **thrive** as a person (Boston After School and Beyond, 2008). This is an important step to assess the transfer of the values and attributes learnt through sports to other contexts.

The ACT SG (Sports) Tool

Co-developed with the Ministry of Social and Family Development and National Council of Social Services, the ACT SG (Sports) tool

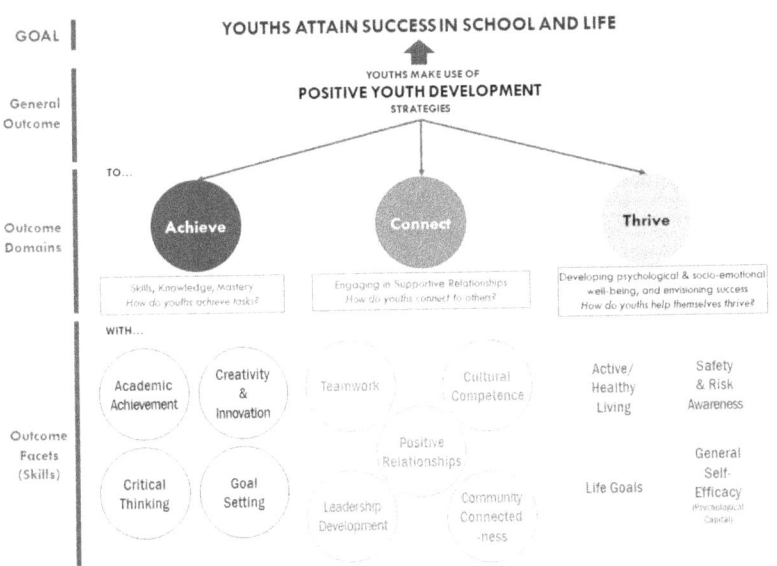

Figure 18.4 ACT SG Framework on 13 core skills for youth development (MSFD, 2019)

combines the scales explained earlier into three sections of questions that measure the following:

- Section A – 15 questions on the frequency of teaching values and/or life skills by the coach/youth worker
- Section B – 15 questions on the frequency with which youth has demonstrated selected values (Confidence, Respect, Excellence, Compassion, and Teamwork) during sports activities
- Section C – 39 questions on the 13 skills/outcomes under the ACT domains

Using this validated tool, agencies would be able to assess the effectiveness in three areas:

1 The coach/youth worker's frequency of teaching values
2 Changes in the youth's behaviours in the sports context
3 Outcome objectives beyond the sporting context in the three domains of ACT.

More information and a sample of the tool (MSFD, 2019) have been provided in Appendix B. While the tool has been contextualised for the youth-at-risk sector, it can also be used for the general youth population, as the same principles apply.

Gathering Qualitative Data through Interviews and Open-Ended Questions

To complement the quantitative data collected using the self-reported questionnaires, SportSG has also developed an interview guide consisting of open-ended questions for sports educators, athletes/students, and parents (see Appendix C). Gathering their responses for evaluation purposes can provide valuable insights, offering a first-hand account of their experiences with the programme or intervention and providing qualitative data that complements quantitative measures. These responses can also be used to assess the application of learning of participants (both sports educators and their learners) and an effective way to encourage critical thinking, self-assessment, and deeper understanding of the learning process.

Examples of some responses can be found in the following table:

Coach 1: During a heated match, I implemented the "sportsmanship timeout" concept. Pausing the game to address unsportsmanlike behaviour allowed me to emphasise the importance of respect. The positive change in players' conduct was evident in subsequent matches.
Coach 2: I integrated the "values-based challenges" into our training routine. These challenges, centred around teamwork and communication, not only made practices more engaging but also created a shared sense of accomplishment among the athletes.
Athlete 1: There was this friendly, where we beat the team ten to one at the final whistle. After I scored those goals, I was starting to get a little bit arrogant, and started doing these celebrations that were very flashy. Then at the end of the game, Coach told us, "You need to show some respect to the opponent. When you score a goal, you can do your crazy celebration after your first and second goal, but beyond that will be a bit too arrogant, a bit too overconfident," and it would throw us off our game. It's something that really impacted on me, so each time I try to score a goal I try to tone down now.
Athlete 2: There is greater emphasis on teamwork compared to last time. It's more asking to work with your teammates more than just taking the ball. It's like thinking about the team before yourself; there is slightly more emphasis on that. In the exercises, there's more possession games and emphasis on passing – more teamwork based and not just doing it yourself.
Parent 1: We found that the coaches were a lot more focused on the child and the skills. It's not about winning games; it's about the skills that you develop to become a better footballer. ... I think they emphasise a lot about teamwork, on understanding what your strengths are, where you can try to build up or where your weaknesses are, and they are very open about how the children can develop. ... With the kids, they talk to them at the end of the session, around what they are doing, what the need to do as a team, and what they need to do individually.

The previous sections have provided details on the tools used by SportSG to holistically evaluate its education programmes across multiple levels using varied evidence-based approaches (e.g., qualitative, quantitative, mixed methods) and the use of valid and reliable scales. However, when adopting these tools, it is important that data collected is disaggregated (e.g., by demographics) for more detailed analysis to explore what works, for whom, and why.

LIMITATIONS

Overall, while self-evaluation tools, criteria-based and observational assessments discussed in the previous sections, can offer valuable insights into the teaching and learning of values and life skills, it's crucial to acknowledge their limitations.

The nature of the questions, which are based on behaviours related to values and life skills, may lead to respondent bias and social desirability bias, as individuals may provide responses that align with their self-image and what they believe is socially desirable rather than being completely honest (Demetriou et al., 2015). Questionnaires also typically focus on specific values and life skills, potentially overlooking other important aspects of participants' beliefs and abilities.

Moreover, self-evaluation questionnaires are influenced by contextual factors, such as the lack of situational information, language barriers, and cultural bias, all of which can significantly impact the interpretation and accuracy of responses. The absence of external factors or circumstances in these questionnaires may pose challenges in accurately assessing certain traits or behaviours.

Additionally, limited recall ability and the variability of individuals' self-perceptions over time and across situations may affect the reliability of the results. Survey fatigue, depending on the questionnaire's length, may also contribute to decreased response quality, as respondents may hastily answer questions without fully considering their responses. Furthermore, constraints such as limited class/programme time, large class sizes, and competing curricular demands may constrain the extent to which assessments can be conducted effectively.

For observational assessments (e.g., teacher's evaluation or coaching observations) certain values and life skills, such as empathy or integrity, may be challenging to directly observe, leading to reliance on indirect indicators or self-reported measures. These assessments may not capture the full context or situational factors that could influence behaviour, potentially resulting in incomplete or inaccurate evaluations. The inherently subjective nature of observational assessments, reliant on the interpretation and judgement of the observer, who may have preconceived notions, introduces variability in the assessment process, potentially affecting the reliability and validity of evaluations.

These limitations highlight the complexity and challenges associated with evaluation and emphasise the need for careful consideration and supplementary measures to ensure comprehensive and accurate assessments.

OTHER CONSIDERATIONS AND SUPPLEMENTARY MEASURES

To enhance the effectiveness of self-evaluation tools, anonymity should be ensured in responses to minimise social desirability bias, as individuals tend to be more honest and open in their self-evaluations when they feel their responses are confidential. Secondly, providing adequate briefings prior to the self-assessment is crucial, as it educates individuals about common biases and encourages reflection on their own experiences and behaviours. Thirdly, regular monitoring through self-reflection exercises over time can help track changes and identify patterns in self-perceptions, mitigating the impact of temporary factors and promoting ongoing self-awareness.

Additionally, it is important to consider the developmental appropriateness of the tools, especially for young children, by translating them into the participant's language and adapting them to align with their developmental stage. Using simpler language and associating response options with visual cues, such as smiley faces, can aid in comprehension and engagement, facilitating a more accurate and meaningful self-evaluation process.

For observational assessments, providing training and calibration sessions for assessors is essential to ensure consistency and reliability in evaluations, reducing subjectivity and biases. Developing clear and

Figure 18.5 Examples of visual cues (MSFD, 2019)

specific assessment criteria for each value or life skill being evaluated is also crucial. This involves articulating the expected behaviours, attitudes, and outcomes, and providing examples or benchmarks to guide assessment. Additionally, tailoring assessment methods and criteria to the specific context and cultural background of the sporting environment of the participants should be considered.

SUMMARY AND FUTURE DIRECTIONS

Currently, the evaluation tools shared have a very strong focus on values-driven coaching/teaching practices and the development of values and life skills. Organisations should also consider developing holistic evaluation systems that are not only limited to this area but shed light on the overall coach's ability to (a) model and teach the programme's core values, (b) build trust and cohesion across the duration of the programme, (c) develop athlete competencies, and (d) help athletes perform at their peak in competitions (Gilbert, 2017).

Apart from the collection and analysis of quantitative outcomes data through the use of self-reported tools, programme evaluation is also amenable to and often times strengthened by a multi-method approach – i.e., examining and triangulating outcomes through qualitative interviews, performance metrics, objective indicators, observations, and feedback from multiple sources like peers, parents, opposing coaches, and teachers/staff.

More longitudinal studies/tools can also be developed to capture evidence and evaluate if having sports educators who embrace values-driven coaching practices translates into better sporting performance by their athletes on the field over a period and to assess the transfer of learning to other non-sporting contexts and domains (such as academics, day jobs). Future research could explore using other objective indicators for measuring players' demonstration of values-based behaviours.

In one sense, it could be more straightforward to design evaluations for athlete/student outcomes. Assessments can be purely formative, as we are not certifying them to be a sports educator. Designing an effective programme evaluation system for coaches and sports educators involves a creative tension between formative and summative assessment, especially if they are being accredited. Assessments of individuals are an invaluable opportunity to help sports educators improve while also providing evidence of programme growth and results when aggregated.

In conclusion, evaluations should be used for the purpose of informing future programming to make continuous improvements and adaptations that best fit/meet the needs of their youth athletes and/or student community. When selecting an evaluation strategy, it is important to consider the specific goals, context, and stakeholders involved, as well as the resources and time available for the evaluation. Each strategy offers unique benefits and considerations, and the choice of strategy should be most meaningful and practical for the persons (e.g., coaches/athletes) involved and the environments they are operating in.

If programme owners feel that there are specific or certain niche outcomes of their programmes which are not included in existing tools, they should consider administering other scales or collect the missing information in other ways for evaluation/research. Sports organisations and educators should not hesitate to experiment with revising the tools to create new ones that might work better in one's setting.

APPENDIX A: SAMPLE FEEDBACK QUESTIONNAIRES TO EVALUATE REACTION AND LEARNINGS OF SPORTS EDUCATORS WORKSHOPS

Instructions

For each of the following statements in regard to the **overall conduct of the trainer**, rate the extent to which you agree or disagree by ticking the corresponding circles below.

Coaching Values and Life Skills through Physical Education and Sports

	The Trainer	Strongly Disagree	Disagree	Slightly Disagree	Neutral	Slightly Agree	Agree	Strongly Agree
1	Demonstrates his understanding of the subject	○	○○	○○	○○	○○	○○	○○
2	Provides the contextual knowledge of the subject	○	○○	○○	○○	○○	○○	○○
3	Demonstrates his experience in the application of the subject	○	○	○	○	○	○	○
4	Is well aware of the rationale and "bigger picture" behind key concepts and practices of the subject	○	○	○	○	○	○	○
5	Was able to articulate his knowledge in a clear and concise manner	○	○	○	○	○	○	○
6	Was able to clarify my doubts	○○○	○○○	○○○	○○○○	○○○○	○○○	○○○○○
7	Is an active listener	○○○	○○○	○○○	○○○○	○○○○	○○○	○○○○○
8	Is a good facilitator	○○○	○○○	○○○	○○○○	○○○○	○○○	○○○○○
9	Provided constructive feedback	○○○	○○○	○○○	○○○○	○○○○	○○○	○○○○○
10	Demonstrates interest in my personal learning	○○	○○	○○	○○	○○	○○	○○
11	Motivates/inspires me to take ownership of my learning	○○	○○	○○	○○	○○	○○	○○
12	Helps me make sense of my learning	○	○○	○○	○○	○○	○○	○○
13	There was good interaction between the facilitator and the participants	○	○○	○○	○○	○○	○○	○○
14	Overall, the facilitator was prepared and well-organised	○	○	○	○	○	○	○
15	Do you have any other feedback/comments regarding the **delivery** of the workshop?							

Instructions

For each of the following statements in regard to the **overall conduct of the workshop**, rate the extent to which you agree or disagree by ticking the corresponding circles below.

		Strongly Disagree	Disagree	Slightly Disagree	Neutral	Slightly Agree	Agree	Strongly Agree
16	The duration of the practical session was adequate to try out the approaches.	O	O	O	O	O	O	O
17	The time allocated was sufficient.	O	O	O	O	O	O	O
18	The materials provided are adequate.	O	O	O	O	O	O	O
19	The materials provided are relevant and interesting.	O	O	O	O	O	O	O
20	Overall, I felt the workshop was useful for me.	O	O	O	O	O	O	O
21	Overall, I feel better equipped to teach values and leadership through sports.	O	O	O	O	O	O	O

22 Which topics did you find beneficial to your learning?
23 Were there any other topics that you felt should have been included in this workshop?
24 Would you require more assistance from SportSG to implement the Toolkit?
☐ Yes ☐ No
If yes, what other resources/assistance would you require?
25 Please share with us what attending this workshop meant for you.
26 Any other comments/suggestions on the workshop?

UNIVERSITY OF ALICANTE SPORTS EDUCATORS WORKSHOP FEEDBACK QUESTIONNAIRE

On a scale of 1 to 5, please rate the following statements below based on your experience of the workshop:

(1) Not at all (2) To a small extent (3) Moderately (4) To a large extent (5) Extremely

Cognitive Learning

I acquired a clear understanding of the key principles of character development in youth sports.	1	2	3	4	5
The training expanded my knowledge of effective strategies for instilling positive values in young athletes.	1	2	3	4	5
The materials provided during the training were helpful in enhancing my conceptual understanding of character development.	1	2	3	4	5

Behavioural Learning

I feel more confident in implementing practical character-building activities in my coaching sessions.	1	2	3	4	5
The training improved my ability to integrate positive values seamlessly into my coaching practices.	1	2	3	4	5
The training positively influenced my personal commitment to fostering a culture of sportsmanship.	1	2	3	4	5

Affective Learning

I now recognise the importance of character development in youth sports more than before the training.	1	2	3	4	5
My attitudes towards the role of coaches in shaping athletes' character have evolved as a result of the training.	1	2	3	4	5

(Continued)

Key Takeaways:
1. What specific concepts or strategies from the character development training did you find most valuable in your coaching role?
2. How has the training influenced your coaching philosophy, especially concerning character development and positive values?

Suggestions for Improvement:
3. In what ways could the character development training be enhanced to better meet your needs in youth sports?
4. Are there any additional resources or support that you believe would further contribute to your learning in this area?

APPENDIX B: ACT SG (SPORTS) TOOL TO EVALUATE APPLICATION OF LEARNINGS AND RESULTS ON DEVELOPING VALUES AND LIFE SKILLS

Section A

There are no right or wrong answers. Read each statement carefully and think about your experiences <u>during sports activities</u>. Circle the best number that shows how often you have demonstrated the behaviours <u>during the sports activities</u> in the **past six months**.

1	2	3	4	5
Never	Rarely	Sometimes	Often	Very Often

DURING SPORTS ACTIVITIES, MY COACH/INSTRUCTOR:

Not only focuses on learning a new skill but also on values as well	1	2	3	4	5
Identifies one or two values	1	2	3	4	5
Asks us whether we have learnt any values	1	2	3	4	5
Explains how certain values can be demonstrated	1	2	3	4	5
Discusses with us how our behaviours are related to certain values	1	2	3	4	5
Explains how values can be applied in our daily life	1	2	3	4	5
Shows us how we can demonstrate certain values	1	2	3	4	5
Gives us examples of values-based behaviours	1	2	3	4	5
Shares stories that exemplify certain values	1	2	3	4	5
Corrects our behaviours when we do not demonstrate the right values	1	2	3	4	5

(Continued)

Gives feedback on how we can better demonstrate certain values	1	2	3	4	5
Sets certain standards for demonstrating values-based behaviours	1	2	3	4	5
Praises us when we demonstrate the right values	1	2	3	4	5
Highlights to the group when we demonstrate positive values	1	2	3	4	5
Encourages us to demonstrate certain values	1	2	3	4	5

SECTION B

There are no right or wrong answers. Read each statement carefully and think about your experiences **during sports activities**. Circle the best number that shows how often you have demonstrated the behaviours **during the sports activities** in the **past six months**. For Q28–30, **select "Not Applicable" if you do not participate in sports activities with others**.

1	2	3	4	5
Never	Rarely	Sometimes	Often	Very Often

I cannot handle more difficult skills in the sports.	1	2	3	4	5
I am able to carry out skills as well as most of my teammates.	1	2	3	4	5
I can be counted on to understand and carry out my skills well.	1	2	3	4	5
I show respect to my teammates even if I do not agree with them.	1	2	3	4	5
I will play by the rules of the game.	1	2	3	4	5
I do not pay attention to my coach when he/she is coaching us.	1	2	3	4	5
It is important to me to do my best in what I set out to do.	1	2	3	4	5
I always do what I promise to do.	1	2	3	4	5
I do not have a skill or talent others can use.	1	2	3	4	5
I do not care about other people's feelings.	1	2	3	4	5
I try to help others whenever I can.	1	2	3	4	5
I can be counted on to help if someone needs me.	1	2	3	4	5

(Continued)

I value what my teammates can do for the team.	1	2	3	4	5	N/A
(To value means to think it is important.)						
I will do what it takes for the sake of the team.	1	2	3	4	5	N/A
I am committed to my team's objectives.	1	2	3	4	5	N/A
(Committed refers to willingness to spend time and effort. Objectives refer to what the team hopes to achieve together.)						

SECTION C

There are no right or wrong answers. Please answer all questions. Read each statement carefully and decide how well it describes you using the following scale. <u>Circle</u> the number that best describes you.

1	2	3	4	5
Strongly Disagree	Disagree	Neither Agree nor Disagree	Agree	Strongly Agree

I achieved better grades than I had expected.	1	2	3	4	5
My overall grades are good.	1	2	3	4	5
My school attendance is not good.	1	2	3	4	5
I am able to break down a problem into smaller parts to work through them.	1	2	3	4	5
I am unable to tell if the information I received is reliable.	1	2	3	4	5
I make decisions based on facts.	1	2	3	4	5
I am able to find creative ways to solve problems.	1	2	3	4	5
I try to learn things in a creative way.	1	2	3	4	5
(For example, I use acronyms to remember difficult concepts.)					
What I learn now will not be useful for me later on in life.	1	2	3	4	5
I do not know what my goals are.	1	2	3	4	5
(Goals are what I want to achieve in the future, e.g., swim the butterfly stroke.)					
The short-term goals I set for myself are realistic.	1	2	3	4	5
(Short-term goals refer to things I hope to achieve in the next year.)					
I have a plan to reach my long-term goals.	1	2	3	4	5
(Plan refers to knowing what to do to reach the goals.)					
(Long-term goals refer to things I hope to achieve in the next five to ten years.)					

(Continued)

I feel unsupported by adults in my life. *(adults include parents, relatives, teachers, religious leaders, etc.).*	1	2	3	4	5
I am able to talk things through with my friends or family to solve problems.	1	2	3	4	5
I care about how my actions affect other people.	1	2	3	4	5
I like to work with others to solve problems.	1	2	3	4	5
I am able to work on a project with others.	1	2	3	4	5
I do not like to work in a team.	1	2	3	4	5
I can be counted on to lead my peers when needed.	1	2	3	4	5
(Peers refer to others around my age, such as my classmates.)					
I try to set a good example for my peers.	1	2	3	4	5
(Peers refer to others around my age, such as my classmates.)					
I am unable to organise others to do something (e.g., organise an event).	1	2	3	4	5
I do not like spending time with others in my community. *(Community includes my neighbourhood, clubs, schools, associations, societies, and locations where I volunteer.)*	1	2	3	4	5
I do things that can make a difference in people's lives in the community.	1	2	3	4	5
It is important for me to be a good role model for others in the community.	1	2	3	4	5
I am aware of the traditions that other races practise.	1	2	3	4	5
I respect the different racial practices.	1	2	3	4	5
I do not enjoy being involved in my racial traditions.	1	2	3	4	5
I think my weight is unhealthy.	1	2	3	4	5
I take part in physical activities for at least seven hours a week every week.	1	2	3	4	5
(Physical activities refer to activities that involve a lot of body movement, e.g., riding a bicycle, running, doing household chores.)					
I am able to prepare food for myself with no help from others.	1	2	3	4	5
I do not have clear life goals.	1	2	3	4	5
(Life goals refer to things I hope to achieve throughout or at a later part of my life, e.g., being compassionate to others.)					
I believe I can achieve my life goals.	1	2	3	4	5
It is important for me to do my best in what I set out to do.	1	2	3	4	5
I am able to manage in difficult situations.	1	2	3	4	5
I can conduct myself well in front of others.	1	2	3	4	5

(Continued)

I cannot cope with the changes in my life.	1	2	3	4	5
I avoid taking part in activities that may get me into trouble.	1	2	3	4	5
I am against bullying.	1	2	3	4	5
I engage in harmful behaviours (For example, smoking, self-harm, using drugs, being violent).	1	2	3	4	5

APPENDIX C: SPORTSG'S INTERVIEW GUIDE TO EVALUATE APPLICATION OF LEARNINGS AND RESULTS ON DEVELOPING VALUES AND LIFE SKILLS

Sports Educators Interview Questions

- What was your experience designing PE lessons/training sessions to infuse values and leadership?
  - What were some of the key considerations or issues that you needed to take into account during this design process?
- What are some key success factors to ensure the design of PE lessons/training sessions achieves the desired outcomes of character and leadership development?
- Share one experience or story that highlighted the impact of using PE lessons/sports to inculcate values.
- What is one thing you would change to improve on subsequent PE lessons/trainings for values inculcation? Why?
- What advice would you give other coaches who want to design lessons for values inculcation?

Students/Athletes Interview Questions

- How have PE lessons/sports trainings been different as compared to before?
  - Did your coaches emphasise any other lessons other than learning a new skill in PE lessons/trainings?
  - Did you notice your teacher/coach discussing values during training?
- Are there any experiences that particularly stand out in your mind?
  - Was that experience positive or negative? Why?
  - What (values) did you learn from that experience?
- Could you share one specific experience or story in which positive values and behaviours took place during training?
  - What was meaningful about it?
  - What did your coach/teammates do?
- Overall, what impact has the sports training programme had on the way you feel about yourself?
- How will you continue to carry over what you have learnt and accomplished during training into your daily life?

(Continued)

Parents Interview Questions (for Sports Clubs/Academies)
- Why did you sign your child up for football training?
- What do you think is unique about the football trainings here at the club/academy?
- What positive values do you hope to see being developed in your child by taking part in sports/football?
- Could you share one specific experience or story in which you have witnessed positive values and behaviours from your child during the course of the programme?
  - What was meaningful about it?
- Overall, what impact do you think football training has had on your child?
  - Any specific positive changes?

REFERENCES

Boston After School and Beyond (2008). About the ACT Framework: ACT Skills. Retrieved from: https://insight.bostonbeyond.org/act-skills/about-act/

Boud, D., & Solomon, N. (2001). *Work-based learning: A new higher education?* McGraw-Hill Education (UK).

Deci, E. L., & Ryan, R. M. (1994). Promoting self-determined education. *Scandinavian Journal of Educational Research*, 38(1), 3–14.

Demetriou, C., Özer, B., & Essau, Cecilia. (2015). *Self-report questionnaires: The encyclopedia of clinical psychology* (1st ed).

Dweck C. S. (2015). Carol Dweck revisits the "growth mindset." Retrieved from https://www.edweek.org/ew/articles/2015/09/23/carol-dweck-revisits-the-growth-mindset.html

Gilbert, W. (2017). *Coaching better every season.* Human Kinetics

Kirkpatrick, D. L., & Kirkpatrick, J. D. (2006). *Evaluating training programs the four levels* (3rd ed.). Berrett-Koehler Publishers, Inc.

Krathwohl, D. R., Bloom, B. S., and Masia, B. B. (1964). *Taxonomy of educational objectives, Book II. Affective domain.* David McKay Company, Inc.).

Ministry of Social and Family Development (2019). ACT SG Framework and Tools for Programme Evaluation. Retrieved from https://www.msf.gov.sg/what-we-do/ncpr/initiatives/benchmarks-and-frameworks

Norcini, J. (2003). Work based assessment. Retrieved from https://www.ncbi.nlm.nih.gov/pmc/articles/PMC1125657/.

Reddy, Y. M., & Andrade, H. (2010). A review of rubric use in higher education. *Assessment & Evaluation in Higher Education*, 35(4), 435–448. https://doi.org/10.1080/02602930902862859

Sport Singapore. (2013). *Game for life: A guide to developing character and leadership.* Sports Singapore

Sports-Based Life Skills Interventions: Psychological Needs and Psychological Well-Being

Chapter Nineteen

Ken Hodge

INTRODUCTION

Sports-based life skills interventions are designed to help individuals develop psychosocial resources that promote success in multiple life domains (Bean et al., 2014, 2015; Danish et al., 2004; Hodge et al., 2013, 2016). Various populations ranging from adolescents to adults have engaged in life skills (LS) interventions in various life domains (e.g., in sports/physical activity, in adventure/outdoor education, at school, at work). LS interventions have been deemed beneficial for individuals to understand and apply skills to promote success in one life domain (e.g., sports) and to display competence and success in other life domains (e.g., at school, in work, at home). Sports psychology practitioners have typically employed interventions to enhance individuals' athletic performance based on a deficit-reduction approach (i.e., mental skills training; Brown & Fletcher, 2017). More recently, a number of practitioners have adopted strength-based, holistic lifespan approaches that focus on helping athletes develop psychosocial resources that benefit both *personal* excellence and *performance* excellence (Kendellen & Camiré, 2019; Miles & Hodge, 2020).

LS interventions are one strength-based, preventative approach to help athletes develop psychosocial resources to cope with the demands of both sports and non-sports experiences. LS interventions focus on developing transferable psychosocial resources, labelled LS, that can help individuals cope with demands associated with multiple life domains (Danish et al., 2004; Hodge et al., 2013, 2016; Miles & Hodge, 2020). LS have been defined as "those internal personal assets, characteristics and skills such as goal setting, emotional control, self-esteem, and hard work ethic that can be facilitated or developed in sports and are transferred for use in non-sports settings" (Gould & Carson, 2008,

p. 60). LS can be "behavioural (communicating effectively with peers and adults) or cognitive (making effective decisions); interpersonal (being assertive) or intrapersonal (setting goals)" (Danish et al., 2004, p. 40).

These skills enhance individuals' psychosocial resources and have been taught as skills that can be developed or refined in one life domain and transferred to other life domains through experience or from participating in deliberately structured programmes (Gould & Carson, 2008; Martin et al., 2022; Pierce et al., 2017). Nevertheless, the wide range of LS taught and the definitions used in interventions limit our ability to make comparisons about the relative effectiveness of these intervention programmes. If each LS intervention programme highlights a particular set of LS, then meaningful comparisons and any consensus about the relative worth of such programmes become problematic. It is argued in this chapter that one solution to this problem is to utilise an integrated conceptual model of LS development that seeks to articulate the key underlying psychological mechanisms that underpin optimal human functioning and specific outcomes such as psychological well-being (PWB).

Until recently, within the sports-based LS interventions literature, studies have been largely atheoretical (e.g., Kendellen et al., 2017; Weiss et al., 2013) and have mostly employed superficial or indirect measures of LS outcomes (e.g., Danish et al., 2004; Kramers et al., 2021; Martin et al., 2022; Yulong et al., 2024). These measures are, at best, only indirect assessments of any underlying psychological development that may have occurred as an outcome of an LS intervention. To truly assess underlying psychological development that may have occurred as an outcome of an LS intervention, we need direct measures of psychological mechanisms (e.g., basic psychological needs; Ng et al., 2011; Sheldon & Hilpert, 2012) that affect such development, as well as direct measures of specific, quantifiable LS outcomes (e.g., PWB; Ryff, 2013).

The purpose of this chapter is to move beyond descriptive evaluations to conceptually-driven investigations of LS programmes focused on PWB. In 2013, Hodge et al. developed a conceptual framework for LS interventions to address that limitation, and subsequent empirical findings confirmed the usefulness of that framework for positive LS outcomes. Hodge et al. (2013) advocated the inclusion of (i) the three basic psychological needs of autonomy, competence, and relatedness and (ii) the need-supportive motivational climate from basic needs theory (BNT; Standage & Ryan, 2020) into the Life Development Intervention (LDI) Framework (Danish et al., 2004). When these basic psychological needs are satisfied, people experience positive psychological development – the stated outcome goal of many LS programmes. By developing that framework, Hodge et al. (2013) sought to articulate the key underlying psychological mechanisms (i.e., basic psychological needs) that contribute to optimal human functioning and positive psychosocial development via life skill interventions. In this chapter, the Hodge et al. (2013) conceptual framework is adapted and updated to include additional BNT constructs and a specific focus on PWB as a key targeted outcome for LS interventions.

Empirical Investigations of the LDI/BNT Life Skills Model: Although further research is needed to fully test Hodge et al.'s (2013) LDI/BNT model, significant research findings support key aspects of the model. Two studies examined whether or not physical activity-based LS programmes (ranging from five to nine months) were perceived as supporting the three basic psychological needs of adolescent girls (Forneris et al., 2013) and whether or not a physical activity-based LS programme was perceived as providing a need-supportive motivational climate (Bean et al., 2019a). In addition, a third study examined whether or not a perceived need-supportive motivational climate predicted LS outcomes for adolescent girls (Bean et al., 2014). Other studies have also supported basic psychological needs satisfaction (Bae & Jin, 2023; Bean et al., 2018, 2019b, 2021; Forneris et al., 2013) and need-supportive motivational climates (Bean et al., 2016, 2019a) as significant contributors to positive outcomes for sports-related developmental experiences in youth sports, as well as PWB (Bean et al., 2019b).

In summary, these studies provided substantive empirical support for aspects of the LDI/BNT framework. More specifically, these LS programmes appeared to be effective at providing a need-supportive motivational climate and need satisfaction, and also appeared to support the development of LS. However, further quantitative research is needed to fully examine relationships between need-supportive motivational climates and need satisfaction within LS programmes and amongst need satisfaction, LS development, and specific measures of PWB.

Based on gaps in the life skills interventions literature with respect to specific LS outcomes, an integrated conceptual model (see Figure 19.1) is outlined that synthesises recent advances in PWB literature and links to life skills interventions processes proposed in Hodge et al.'s (2013) LDI/BNT framework. In particular, the integrated conceptual model includes the recently developed well-being enhancer of "beneficence" (Martela & Ryan, 2016, 2020; Martela et al., 2021) and an explicit focus on PWB as a key targeted outcome for LS interventions. Considerable research has shown strong positive relationships between PWB and self-determination theory (SDT) constructs (e.g., basic psychological need satisfaction, autonomous motivation, need-supportive motivational climates; see Ryan & Deci, 2001, 2017 for reviews). While SDT constructs relate to both hedonic PWB (i.e., feeling good; e.g., Reis et al., 2000) and eudaimonic PWB (i.e., functioning well; e.g., Gagné et al., 2003; Houge Mackenzie & Hodge, 2020), the major focus of this chapter and the integrated conceptual model (see Figure 19.1) is on eudaimonic PWB.

The integrated conceptual model outlines how LS interventions can foster eudaimonic PWB via satisfaction of the three basic

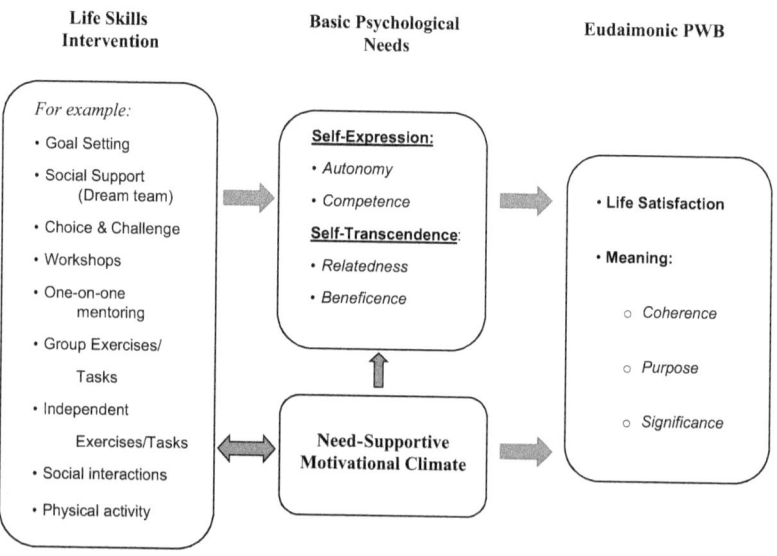

Figure 19.1 An integrated conceptual model of LS development to enhance eudaimonic PWB. Adapted from Houge Mackenzie and Hodge (2020)

psychological needs for autonomy, competence, and relatedness detailed in SDT (Martela et al., 2023), as well as the recently proposed well-being enhancer of 'beneficence' (Martela & Ryan, 2016; Martela et al., 2021). *Autonomy* is defined as having an authentic sense of self-direction and volition, and being the perceived origin of one's own behaviour (Beyers et al., 2024; Ryan & Deci, 2017). *Competence* refers to individuals feeling effective in their ongoing interactions with their environment and experiencing opportunities to exercise and express their capacities. *Relatedness* refers to feeling connected to others, caring about and being cared for by others, and having a sense of belonging both with other individuals and with one's community (Standage & Ryan, 2020). As a well-being enhancer, *beneficence* is characterised by feeling that one has a positive impact on the lives of other people and engaging in prosocial behaviour (Martela et al., 2018, 2021; Titova & Sheldon, 2022). The integrated conceptual model also identifies and differentiates amongst three proposed elements of eudaimonic PWB (i.e., coherence, purpose, significance; Martela & Steger, 2016) that may be supported when LS interventions satisfy basic psychological needs.

PSYCHOLOGICAL WELL-BEING RESEARCH

PWB models describe well-being in terms of a range of feelings arising from what people do and how they think and feel (Kahneman et al., 1999; Ryan & Huta, 2009). LS programmes can provide a sense of purpose and meaningfulness (e.g., eudaimonic PWB; Bean et al., 2019b; Ryan & Deci, 2001). Within PWB approaches, the complex and symbiotic nature of hedonic and eudaimonic elements has been vigorously debated (e.g., Huta & Waterman, 2014). The primary difference is that hedonic PWB is a more immediate, affective experience, whereas eudaimonic PWB is characterised as "a good and fulfilling way of life" focused on meaning and purpose (Ryan & Martela, 2016, p. 109). Ryan and Deci (2001) described well-being as "a multidimensional phenomenon that includes aspects of both the hedonic and eudaimonic conceptions of well-being" (p. 148). Eudaimonic PWB was the central focus of Ryff's (1989, 2013) foundational model of psychological well-being that integrated six psychological dimensions: *autonomy, environmental mastery, personal growth, positive relations with others, purpose in life,* and *self-acceptance*.

Psychological Well-Being via Psychological Need Satisfaction: As a sub-theory of self-determination theory, BNT (Ryan & Deci, 2017) posits that satisfying basic psychological needs is vital for psychological growth (e.g., autonomous motivation), subjective vitality (Ryan & Deci, 2017), and well-being (e.g., life satisfaction; psychological health). A large volume of evidence demonstrates how satisfying these psychological needs facilitates PWB (see Martela et al., 2023; Ryan & Deci, 2017 for reviews), while a smaller but substantive body of research demonstrates how ill-being results when these needs are thwarted or frustrated (Martela & Ryan, 2020; Martela et al., 2023; Titova & Sheldon, 2022; Vansteenkiste & Ryan, 2013).

Within the basic needs framework, Martela et al. (2018) distinguished between those basic psychological needs and well-being enhancers that support *self-expression* (autonomy and competence) and those that support *self-transcendence* (relatedness and beneficence [as a well-being enhancer]). Considerable research has demonstrated that satisfying these psychological needs for self-expression and self-transcendence predicts differences in well-being at (a) the level of daily well-being (Reis et al. 2000) and (b) the overall life satisfaction levels (Ryan & Huta, 2009). The influence of basic psychological need satisfaction on PWB has been documented across various life domains, such as work (Van den Broeck et al., 2010), education (Mouratidis et al., 2011), adventure education (Scarf et al., 2018), and sports (Stenling & Tafvelin, 2014), and across diverse cultural samples (e.g., Chen et al., 2015; Martela et al., 2023).

Recently, beneficence has been proposed as a well-being enhancer (as opposed to a potential basic psychological need) that relates to self-transcendence. Based on findings that prosocial behaviours and giving to others supports PWB, Martela and Ryan (2016) assessed whether 'acting benevolently' directly contributed to well-being, or whether this effect was mediated by satisfying needs for autonomy, competence, or relatedness. In a series of five studies, they found that while the three basic needs explained some of the variance, beneficence satisfaction predicted unique variance in eudaimonic PWB (Martela & Ryan, 2016). These findings supported eudaimonic notions that PWB is enhanced by acting in ways that benefit others, even in the absence of direct contact with beneficiaries.

Operationalising Eudaimonic PWB: Eudaimonic PWB is often referred to as leading a meaningful life, and research has robustly demonstrated that meaning in life plays an important role in PWB (see Martela et al., 2023 for review). However, scholars have increasingly debated the unidimensional nature of research on eudaimonic PWB as *meaning* and have proposed that meaning has specific, distinctive components. Drawing on theoretical developments in psychological research and philosophy, Martela and Steger (2016) distinguish between three core components of *meaning* in life: coherence, purpose, and significance. These three components are used in the integrated conceptual model (see Figure 19.1) to operationalise eudaimonic PWB outcomes. Briefly, *coherence* is a cognitive assessment of whether one's life makes sense in terms of following predictable patterns and structures. *Purpose* is motivational as it entails having clear goals, aims, and directions in one's life. *Significance* is evaluative, as it entails feeling that one's life has value, worth, and importance. These three facets are also proposed to be connected to overall meaning in life (Martela & Steger, 2016; Martela et al., 2023). Therefore, eudaimonic PWB is operationalised in these specific terms, as they provide a clear means for measuring important PWB outcomes.

AN INTEGRATED MODEL FOR LIFE SKILLS INTERVENTIONS AND EUDAIMONIC PWB

The integrated conceptual model includes LS interventions, SDT basic psychological needs, need-supportive motivational climates, and eudaimonic PWB (see Figure 19.1). The integrated conceptual model characterises eudaimonic PWB as occurring via satisfaction of the basic psychological needs of autonomy, competence, and relatedness, plus the well-being enhancer of beneficence, as well as need-supportive motivational climates. Such PWB development begins with participation in a LS intervention/programme (left side of Figure 19.1).

According to the integrated model, an LS intervention will only be successful in satisfying the three basic psychological needs and beneficence if the motivational climate created and nurtured by the LS leaders and/or peers is need-supportive (Bean et al., 2016, 2019a,b; Rocchi et al., 2017). A need-supportive motivational climate is created when a participant in an LS intervention is provided with choice and a rationale for tasks, their feelings are acknowledged, opportunities to show initiative and independent work are provided, participants are given non-controlling competence feedback, and the use of guilt-inducing criticism and overt control is avoided by LS leaders (Cheon et al., 2018; Mageau & Vallerand, 2003; Rocchi et al., 2017). If a need-supportive climate is created, then the greater the level of need satisfaction and internalisation, and the greater the likelihood that participants will report high levels of key eudaimonic PWB markers, such as meaning, purpose, significance (e.g., Houge Mackenzie & Hodge, 2020; Kouali et al., 2022; Martela & Steger, 2016; Martela et al., 2018; Ryan & Deci, 2017; Ryan & Martela, 2016) (right side of Figure 19.1).

The integrated model serves as a potential basis for theoretically informed best practice guidelines to support PWB across a range of LS interventions. With respect to creating a need-supportive motivational climate, there are numerous practical examples of leadership strategies from educational psychology (e.g., Cheon et al., 2018) and coaching literature (e.g., Mageau & Vallerand, 2003). Finally, a key applied issue in LS interventions is LS "transfer" from one domain (e.g., sports/physical activity) to another (e.g., home/school/work).

APPLIED INSIGHTS

Life skills development and transfer: The LS development and transfer process involves three interrelated stages: (a) LS learning, (b) LS transfer, and (c) LS application (to both the sports/physical activity domain and a non-sports domain). Life skills transfer has been described as an important process for LS development (Bean et al., 2022; Gould & Carson, 2008; Harmsel-Nieuwenhuis et al., 2022; Jacobs & Wright, 2018; Kendellen & Camiré, 2019; Martin et al., 2022; Pierce et al., 2017). Pierce et al. (2017, p. 194) defined the LS transfer process as

> [t]he ongoing process by which an individual further develops or learns and internalises a personal asset (i.e., psychosocial skill, knowledge, disposition, identity construction, or transformation) in sports and then experiences personal change through the application of the asset in one or more life domains beyond the context where it was originally learned.

Pierce et al.'s (2017) definition of LS transfer highlighted three concepts that LS intervention practitioners can employ to help athletes/

students remove the barriers to LS development and transfer. These concepts were (i) LS development encompasses skill acquisition and/or skill refinement; (ii) the athlete is central to the transfer process as he/she moves from one life context to another; (iii) the application context refers to any setting beyond sports where the LS is applied. Based on these concepts, LS intervention practitioners should purposefully design LS interventions to help athletes/students transform their understanding of LS to meet the demands of multiple application contexts (e.g., education, their career, at home, in their social life) (Bean et al., 2022).

The process of promoting need satisfaction and LS development begins with participation in the LS intervention. The specific content (i.e., workshops, exercises, activities, skills, homework) of LS interventions should provide opportunities for participants to learn LS that help satisfy one or more of the basic psychological needs for autonomy, competence, and relatedness (Hodge et al., 2013, 2016). As previously stated, LS interventions will only be successful in satisfying these three basic psychological needs (plus beneficence) if the motivational climate created and nurtured by the LS intervention practitioner/leader is need-supportive. The LS intervention setting is therefore considered a crucial factor in promoting the internalisation of values associated with LS development and LS transfer (Hodge et al., 2013, 2016; Martin et al., 2022). LS intervention practitioners/leaders who create a need-supportive motivational climate are more likely to promote need satisfaction in athletes/students; the more these three needs are satisfied, the more the value of LS will become internalised by the participant. The greater the level of need satisfaction and LS generalisation, the increased likelihood that athletes/students will be able to deploy their LS in multiple life domains (see Bean et al., 2022; Hodge et al., 2016; Martin et al., 2022; Pierce et al., 2017, for more details).

SUMMARY AND FUTURE DIRECTIONS

Reframing LS interventions in terms of satisfying psychological needs and PWB outcomes allows us to directly examine the role that LS interventions can play in enhancing eudaimonic PWB for individuals and communities. Despite shared values and objectives that include understanding eudaimonic PWB, psychologists and LS intervention researchers have remained largely isolated from one another.

Integrating these disparate yet complementary areas of research would yield great benefits. The integrated conceptual model (see Figure 19.1) has synthesised diverse areas of existing knowledge from psychology and LS interventions to illustrate promising new directions in research and practice. These integrations have the potential to transform our understanding of how LS interventions can promote PWB and optimal functioning for individuals and communities.

REFERENCES

Bae, J-S., & Jin, G. (2023). Life skills development in youth taekwondo trainees: The role of perceived caring climate and basic psychological needs. *The Journal of Korean Alliance of Martial Arts, 25*, 87–101.

Bean, C., Forneris, T., & Brunet, J. (2016). Investigating discrepancies in program quality related to youth volleyball athletes' needs support. *Psychology of Sport and Exercise, 26*, 154–163. https://doi.org/10.1016/j.psychsport.2016.07.001

Bean, C., Kramers, S. & Harlow, M. (2022) Exploring life skills transfer processes in youth hockey and volleyball. *International Journal of Sport and Exercise Psychology, 20*, 263–282. https://doi.org/10.1080/1612197X.2020.1819369

Bean, C., McFadden, T., Fortier, M., & Forneris, T. (2019b). Understanding the relationships between programme quality, psychological needs satisfaction, and mental well-being in competitive youth sport. *International Journal of Sport and Exercise Psychology, 19*, 246–264. DOI: https://doi.org/10.1080/1612197X.2019.1655774

Bean, C., Rocchi, M., & Forneris, T. (2019a). Using the Learning Climate Questionnaire to assess basic psychological needs support in youth sport. *Journal of Applied Sport Psychology, 32*, 585–606. https://doi.org/10.1080/10413200.2019.1571537

Bean, C., Shaikh, M., Kramers, S. & Forneris, T. (2021). Does context matter? Unpacking differences in program quality and developmental experiences across competitive and recreational youth sport. *International Journal of Sports Science & Coaching, 16*, 1204–1213. https://doi.org/10.1177/17479541211001879

Bean, C., Solstad, B., Ivarsson, A. & Forneris, T. (2018). Longitudinal associations between perceived programme quality, basic needs support and basic needs satisfaction within youth sport: A person-centred approach. *International Journal of Sport and Exercise Psychology, 18*, 76–92. DOI: https://doi.org/10.1080/1612197X.2018.1462234

Bean, C. N., Kendellen, K., & Forneris, T. (2014). Does participation in summer camp fulfill youth's basic needs and facilitate life skill development? *Journal of Sports & Exercise Psychology, 36*, S81.

Bean, C. N., Kendellen, K., Halsall, T., & Forneris, T. (2015). Putting program evaluation into practice: Enhancing the Girls Just Wanna Have Fun program. *Evaluation & Program Planning, 49*, 31–40.

Beyers, W., Soenens, B., Vansteenkiste, M. (2024). Autonomy in adolescence: A conceptual, developmental, and cross-cultural perspective. *European Journal of Developmental Psychology*. https://doi.org/10.1080/17405629.2024.2330734

Brown, D. J., & Fletcher, D. (2017). Effects of psychological and psychosocial interventions on sport performance: A meta-analysis. *Sports Medicine, 47*, 77–99. https://doi.org/10.1007/s40279-016-0552-7

Chen, B., Vansteenkiste, M., Beyers, W., Boone, L., Deci, E., Van der Kaap-Deeder, J., Duriez, B., Lens, W., Matos, L., Mouratidis, A., & Ryan, R. (2015). Basic psychological need satisfaction, need frustration, and need strength across four cultures. *Motivation & Emotion, 39*, 216–236. https://doi.org/10.1007/s11031-014-9450-1

Cheon, S. H., Reeve, J., & Ntoumanis, N. (2018). A needs-supportive intervention to help PE teachers enhance students' prosocial behavior and diminish antisocial behaviour. *Psychology of Sport & Exercise, 35*, 74–88.

Danish, S. J., Forneris, T., Hodge, K. & Heke, I. (2004). Enhancing youth development through sport. *World Leisure 3*, 38–49.

Forneris, T., Bean, C. N., Danish, S. J. & Fortier, M. (2013) Examining the relationship between Basic Needs Theory and life skills programming for female youth. *Journal of Sport & Exercise Psychology, 35*, S85.

Gagné, M., Ryan, R., & Bargmann, K. (2003). Autonomy support and need satisfaction in the motivation and well-being of gymnasts. *Journal of Applied Sport Psychology, 15*, 372–390.

Gould, D., & Carson, S. (2008). Life skills development through sport: Current status and future directions. *Sport & Exercise Psychology Reviews, 1*, 58–78.

Harmsel-Nieuwenhuis, L. et al. (2022). Life skills development and transfer amongst socially vulnerable adults through sports: A systematic review. *International Journal of Sport & Exercise Psychology*. https://doi.org/10.1080/1750984X.2022.2135125

Hodge, K., Danish, S., Forneris, T., & Miles, A. (2016). Life skills and basic psychological needs: A conceptual framework for Life Skills interventions. In N. Holt (Ed.), *Positive youth development through sport* (pp. 45–56). Routledge.

Hodge, K., Danish, S., & Martin, J. (2013). Developing a conceptual framework for life skills interventions. *The Counseling Psychologist, 41*, 1125–1152. https://doi.org/10.1177/0011000012462073

Houge Mackenzie, S., & Hodge, K. (2020). Adventure recreation and subjective well-being: A conceptual framework. *Leisure Studies, 39*, 26–40. https://doi.org/10.1080/02614367.2019.1577478

Huta, V., & Waterman, A.S. (2014). Eudaimonia and its distinction from hedonia: Developing a classification and terminology for understanding conceptual and operational definitions. *Journal of Happiness Studies, 15*, 1425–1456.

Jacobs, J., & Wright, P. (2018). Transfer of life skills in sport-based youth development programs: A conceptual framework bridging learning to application. *Quest, 70*, 81–99. https://doi.org/10.1080/00336297.2017.1348304

Kahneman, D., Diener, E., & Schwarz, N. (Eds.) (1999). *Well-being: Foundations of hedonic psychology*. Russell Sage Foundation.

Kendellen, K., & Camiré, M. (2019). Applying in life the skills learned in sport: A grounded theory. *Psychology of Sport & Exercise, 40*, 23–32. https://doi.org/10.1016/j.psychsport.2018.09.002

Kendellen, K., Camire, M., Bean, C., Forneris, T., & Thompson, J. (2017). Integrating life skills into Golf Canada's youth programs: Insights into a successful research to practice partnership. *Journal of Sport Psychology in Action, 8*, 34–46. https://doi.org/10.1080/21520704.2016.1205699

Kouali, D., Hall, C., Divine, A., & Pope, J. P. (2022). Motivation and eudaimonic well-being in athletes: A Self-Determination Theory perspective. *Research Quarterly for Exercise & Sport, 93*, 457–466.

Kramers, S., Camiré, M., Ciampolini, V. & Milistetd, M. (2021): Development of a life skills self-assessment tool for coaches. *Journal of Sport Psychology in Action*. https://doi.org/10.1080/21520704.2021.1888832

Mageau, G. A., & Vallerand, R. J. (2003). The coach-athlete relationship: A motivational model. *Journal of Sports Sciences, 21*, 883–904.

Martela, F., Gómez, M., Unanue, W., Araya, S., Bravo, D., & Espejo, A. (2021). What makes work meaningful? Longitudinal evidence for the importance of autonomy and beneficence for meaningful work. *Journal of Vocational Behavior, 131*, 103631.

Martela, F., Lehmus-Sun, A., Parker, P. D., Pessi, A. B., & Ryan, R. M. (2023). Needs and well-being across Europe: Basic psychological needs are closely connected with well-being, meaning, and symptoms of depression in 27 European countries. *Social Psychological and Personality Science, 14*, 501–514. https://doi.org/10.1177/19485506221113678

Martela, F., Ryan, R., & Steger, M. (2018). Meaningfulness as satisfaction of autonomy, competence, relatedness, and beneficence: Comparing the four satisfactions and positive affect as predictors of meaning in life. *Journal of Happiness Studies 19*, 1261–1282.

Martela, F., & Ryan, R. M. (2016). The benefits of benevolence: Basic psychological needs, beneficence, and the enhancement of well-being. *Journal of Personality, 84*, 750–764.

Martela, F., & Ryan, R. M. (2020). Distinguishing between basic psychological needs and basic wellness enhancers: The case of beneficence as a candidate psychological need. *Motivation and Emotion, 44*(1), 116–133.

Martela, F., & Steger, M.F. (2016). The three meanings of meaning in life: Distinguishing coherence, purpose and significance. *Journal of Positive Psychology, 11*, 531–545.

Martin, N., Camiré, M. & Kramers, S. (2022) Facilitating life skills transfer from sport to the classroom: An intervention assisting a high school teacher-coach, *Journal of Applied Sport Psychology, 34*, 1077–1101. DOI: https://doi.org/10.1080/10413200.2021.1917016

Miles, A. & Hodge, K. (2020). Life skills interventions in elite sport. In D. Tod & M. Eubank (Eds.), *Applied sport psychology: Current approaches to helping athletes* (pp. 148–164). Routledge.

Mouratidis, A., Vansteenkiste, M., Sideridis, G., & Lens, W. (2011). Vitality and interest-enjoyment as a function of class-to-class variation in need-supportive teaching and pupils' autonomous motivation. *Journal of Educational Psychology, 103*, 353–366.

Ng, J., Lonsdale, C., & Hodge, K. (2011). The Basic Needs Satisfaction in Sport Scale (BNSSS): Instrument development and initial validity evidence. *Psychology of Sport & Exercise*, 12, 257–264.

Pierce, S., Gould, D., & Camiré, M. (2017). Definition and model of life skills transfer. *International Review of Sport & Exercise Psychology*, 10, 186–211. https://doi.org/10.1080/1750984X.2016.1199727

Reis, H. T., Sheldon, K. M., Gable, S. L., Roscoe, R., & Ryan, R. (2000). Daily well-being: The role of autonomy, competence, and relatedness. *Personality & Social Psychology Bulletin*, 26, 419–435.

Rocchi, M., Pelletier, L., Cheung, S., Baxter, D. & Beaudry, S. (2017). Assessing need-supportive and need-thwarting interpersonal behaviours: The Interpersonal Behaviours Questionnaire (IBQ). *Personality & Individual Differences*, 104, 423–433.

Ryan, R. M. & Deci, E. L. (2001). On happiness and human potentials: A review of research on hedonic and eudaimonic well-being. *Annual Review of Psychology*, 52, 141–166.

Ryan, R. M., & Deci, E. L. (2017). *Self-Determination Theory: Basic psychological needs in motivation, development, and wellness.* Guilford Press.

Ryan, R. M., & Huta, V. (2009). Wellness as healthy functioning or wellness as happiness: The importance of eudaimonic thinking (response to the Kashdan et al. and Waterman discussion). *Journal of Positive Psychology*, 4, 202–204.

Ryan, R. M., & Martela, M. F. (2016). Eudaimonia as a way of living: Connecting Aristotle with self-determination theory. In J. Vitterso (Ed), *Handbook of eudaimonic well-being* (pp. 109–122). Springer.

Ryff, C.D. (1989). Happiness is everything, or is it? Explorations on the meaning of psychological well-being. *Journal of Personality and Social Psychology*, 57, 1069–1081.

Ryff, C. D. (2013). Psychological well-being revisited: Advances in the science and practice of eudaimonia. *Psychotherapy & Psychosomatics*, 83, 10–28.

Scarf, D., Kafka, S., Hayhurst, J., Jang, K., Boyes, M., Thomson, R., & Hunter, J. A. (2018). Satisfying psychological needs on the high seas: Explaining increases self-esteem following an adventure education programme. *Journal of Adventure Education & Outdoor Learning*, 18, 165–175.

Sheldon, K. M., & Hilpert, J. C. (2012). The balanced measure of psychological needs (BMPN) scale: An alternative domain general measure of need satisfaction. *Motivation & Emotion*, 36, 439–451.

Standage, M., & Ryan, R. M. (2020). Self-determination theory in sport and exercise. In G. Tenenbaum & R. Eklund (Eds.), *Handbook of Sport Psychology* (pp. 37–56). Wiley.

Stenling, A., & Tafvelin, S. (2014). Transformational leadership and well-being in sports: The mediating role of need satisfaction. *Journal of Applied Sport Psychology*, 26, 182–196.

Titova, L., & Sheldon, K. M. (2022). Thwarted beneficence: Not getting to help lowers mood. *The Journal of Positive Psychology*, 17, 21–33.

Van den Broeck, A., Vansteenkiste, M., De Witte, H., Soenens, B., & Lens, W. (2010). Capturing autonomy, competence and relatedness at work: Construction and initial validation of the work-related basic need satisfaction scale. *Journal of Occupational & Organizational Psychology*, 83, 981–1002.

Vansteenkiste, M., & Ryan, R.M. (2013). On psychological growth and vulnerability: Basic psychological need satisfaction and need frustration as a unifying principle. *Journal of Psychotherapy Integration, 23*, 263–280.

Weiss, M., Stuntz, C., Bhalla, J., Bolter, N., & Price, M. (2013) 'More than a game': impact of The First Tee life skills programme on positive youth development: project introduction and Year 1 findings. *Qualitative Research in Sport, Exercise and Health, 5*, 214–244. https://doi.org/10.1080/2159676X.2012.712997

Yulong, C., Kohei, S., Takao, B., & Hironobu, T. (2024). Typology of acquiring life skills and mental health in international students in Japan during COVID-19. *Asian Journal of Sport & Exercise Psychology.* https://doi.org/10.1016/j.ajsep.2024.03.001

Index

[Page numbers in *italics* denote figures, page numbers in **bold** denote tables, and n refers to a note]

abstract conceptualization 46–47, 231
ACEs *see* adverse childhood experiences
Achieve-Connect-Thrive (ACT) SG Framework 273
achievement motivation theories 186–187
ACT SG (Sports) tool 273–274, 283–287
action 47
action-reflection process 46
active experimentation 46–47, 231
activism 22–23
activity cards 247–249
adaptability 74
adultification 17–18, 25n2
adventure education 31–32, 191
adventure therapy 48
adverse childhood experiences (ACEs) 200–201
after-school programmes 100
agential realism 137
Aksoy, G. 216
Alharbi, M. 107
Allen, G. 129
animalization 17–18, 25n3
anticipatory set 79–80
approaches: explicit 80–83, 86, 129–130, **172**, 224, 230; forward-looking 99; four-stage 5; implicit 77–80, 129–130, **172**, 224, 230; normative 133–134; normative explicit 134–135; normative implicit 134; strengths-based 52–53; systems-based 29; to teaching VLS 75–83; TGfU 231–232; transformative 134, 136–137; transformative explicit 135–136; transformative implicit 135; whole-school 10, 222
Arizona State University Observation Instrument (ASUOI) 251
assessing Point A 49–50
athletic club activities 119–120; potential harm to lifelong sports 123–124; role in Japan from historical perspective 120–122
athletic development 189; and character building 184–185, **189–190**, 192
Atkinson, O. 39
autonomy 293
autonomy support 148, 161, 235; strategies to build **149**

basic needs theory (BNT) 291, 294
BCW *see* Behaviour Change Wheel
Beamish, Nick 97–98
Bean, C. 35, 76, 130–132, 230, 245
Beard, C. 190, 231
Bednar, M. 182
Behaviour Change Wheel (BCW) 165–167, *167*, 175; and inefficacy of CEPs 168–171
behavioural reinforcements 82–83
behaviours, controlling 17
Beller, J. 181, 185

beneficence 293–294
Beni, S. 18
bioecological theory 59–60, 63
Biological Model of Life Skills Development (BMLSD) 61–62, 61, 67–69
Black, S. 48
Bloom, G. A. 184
Blyth, D. 132
BMLSD *see* Biological Model of Life Skills Development
BNT *see* basic needs theory
Bodey, K. J. 80
Bolter, N. D. 230
boredom 112
Bredemeier, B. 181, 186, 191
Bronfenbrenner, Urie 58–61, 63, 65–66, 69
Brown, B. E. 5

Camiré, M. 45, 64, 66, 129, 131–132, 134, 137, 180
Capability, Opportunity, and Motivation (COM-B) 165–167, **167**, 172–174; in intervention planning 170
care 7, 160
Career Club programme 97, 100
Carson, S. 64, 128
Carson-Sackett, S. 35
CCE teachers *see* Character and Citizenship Education (CCE) teachers
Center for Healing and Justice through Sport (CHJS) 202–204
CEPs *see* Coach Education Programmes
certification 39
Chalk Talk 83
Character and Citizenship Education (CCE) teachers 217–219, 222–223
character building 91, 180–182, 188; and athletic development 184–185, **189–190**
Chase, M. A. 183
check-in activities 78–79
Chen, A. 112

childhood trauma 198, 200–201
China 92–93, 95–97
Chinkov, A. E. 230
classroom culture 10–11
classroom teachers and parents (CTP) 145, 152–153
Coach Beyond 77, 85
Coach Education Programmes (CEPs) 165–166; and BCW 168–171; large-scale 170; small-scale 170; for teaching life skills 171–175; university-based 169
coaches 35–36, 48, 51; harassment and violence by 123–124; shortage of 123; supporting 261; tracking behaviours 250–254
Coaching Life Skills in Sport Questionnaire 132
Coaching Observation Tool (COT) 246, 251–254
coaching practices: assessing 259–261; facilitative 49
coherence 295
collaboration 11–12
collaborative learning 112–113, 252–254
COM-B *see* Capability, Opportunity, and Motivation
commitment 74, 100
communication 75, 94, 218–219, 231, 237; skills 160; with stakeholders 12
communities 20–22, 99
competence 293
competition 4, 13, 183; possible learning from **192**
concrete experience 46, 231
conflict resolution 75
consistency 208
controlling behaviours 17
COT *see* Coaching Observation Tool
COVID-19 pandemic 201
Critical Coaching on the Wave (Critical CotW) model 46, 48–49, 55; six steps 49–54

critical consciousness 49, 135–136
Crossan, W. 182
CTP *see* classroom teachers and parents
cultural context 13, 144, 209–210
culturally responsive pedagogy 37

"Daily" programme 97–98
Danish, Steven 128
Darst, P. W. 251
Davidson, M. 183, 185
debriefing 47, 53–54, 84
decision-making 94
developmental stages 234–235
Dewey, J. 46
dignity 135
discipline 74
discussion card 249
diversity 33
Donoso-Morales, D. 186, 191
Doty, J. 180
Dweck, C. S. 265
dyad 63

education function 173
effort 74, 81
ego orientation 186–187
ELT *see* experiential learning, theory
empowerment 99
enablement function 174
engagement 161
environmental restructuring function 174
evaluations 245; core values development **268–269**; of GFL sport educators workshops 270–271; longitudinal 154, 156; self-reported 265, **267**; strategies and tools 258–279; *see also* tracking
excellence, pursuit of 186–187
exosystem 66
expectations 99
experiential learning 84; facilitated 45–46, 48; five-stage model of 46–47; in T²VLS$_{PES}$ Framework 155; theory (ELT) 46–47, 154, 231

explicit approaches 80–83, 86, 129–130, **172**, 224, 230; normative 134–135; transformative 135–136

facilitated experiential learning 45–46, 48
Facilitated Wave model 48
facilitative coaching practices 49
family 96
Fawcett, S. 219
feedback 47, 81; sample questionnaires 279–283
First Tee programme 98
FLEX *see* Project Fitness Leadership EXperience
focus 47
Fonyi, L. 107
forward-looking approach 99
four-stage approach 5
four-stage learning cycle 46–47, 191
Freire, G. L. M. 68

Game-for-Life (GFL) Framework 258, 259
Gandolfi, H. E. 16
Gano-Overway, L. A. 35
Generation Z 67–68
goal setting 160
Gordon, B. 224
Gould, D. 64, 67–68, 128
Great Sport Myth 134, 136, 182
guidance 94
Gürsel, F. 216

Hakone Ekiden 121–122
harmony 7
Hassanin, R. 66–67
healing, spaces of 202–204
Hellison, Don 31, 153
Hendricks, P. A. 109
hidden curriculum 183
hierarchy of needs 207–208
Hodge, K. 291
Holt, N. L. 59, 130, 230

homework 100–101
honesty 74
Hong Kong 94–97

ideological outcomes 94–95
ILO *see* International Labour Organization
implicit approaches 129–130, **172**, 224, 230; normative 134; to teaching VLS 77–80; transformative 135
inclusion style 233
inclusivity 234–235
individuality 99
integrity 7, 74, 160
intentionality 51–52, 129, 158, 172; in programme design 187–192; six-level continuum 132; in teaching VLS 157, **159**
International Labour Organization (ILO) 123
interpersonal skills 94, 110
interventions: and COM-B 170–171; and eudaimonic PWB 295–296; functions **168**, 170–171, 173–174; programmes 217–222; sustainability 171
intrinsic motivation 161

Jacobs, J. 64, 216
jail 208–209
Japan 118–123, 125
Japan Sports Agency 118–119, 125
Japanese Association of University Physical Education and Sports 121
Jones, M. 64
Joplin, L. 46–48

Kendellen, K. 45, 64
King, Billie Jean 29
Kipp, L. E. 230
Kirkpatrick training evaluation model 270
knowledge transfer 53
Koh, K. T. 181, 191, 216

Kolb, D. 46–47, 154, 191, 231
Kramers, S. 66

Lacy, A. C. 251
Larson, R. W. 191
Lavallee, D. 64
LDI framework *see* Life Development Intervention (LDI) framework
LDI/BNT Life Skills model 291–293
leadership 99, 133, 160; values-driven 184
learning 47–48; collaborative 112–113, 252–254; designing experience 51–52; facilitating 52–53; key opportunities for **189–190**; from participation in competition **192**; tracking 246–250; *see also* experiential learning; problem-based learning (PBL); social and emotional learning (SEL)
Lee, O. 96
licensure 39
Lickona, T. 183, 185
Life Development Intervention (LDI) framework 291
life skills xi, 3, 74, 160, 166; research 128; social justice 45–46; through PES 199; WHO definition 109
Life Skills Scale for PE (LSSPE) 92
life skills transfer 68, 76, 128, 296–297; T^2VLS_{PES} Framework strategies **152**; trauma-informed 204–205
Life Skills Transfer Survey (LSTS) 247
LiFEsports 77–83
Loughran, Jillian Green 202–204
Lower-Hoppe, L. 10

macrotime 67
Malaysia 106–110
Martela, F. 294–295
Martin, N. 66
Martinkova, I. 183
Maslow's hierarchy of needs 207
mastery orientation 186–187

meaning 295
measuring: effects of programmes on PYD 272–274; *see also* tracking
mental health and well-being 13, 34, 236; *see also* psychological well-being (PWB)
mentorship 99; to support coaches 261
mesosystems 66
mesotime 68
Michie, S. 166, 174
microsystems 65, 69n1
microtime 68
Mills, M. 16
mini-games 110–112
Mitchell, S. A. 111
modelling 8–9
Mohd Nasiruddin, N. 107
moral character 180
Morgan, K. 144
Mosston's Spectrum of Teaching Styles 232–233
motivation 94
motor skills 111
mystery motivators 83

Nagy, J. 219
national education framework 5
National Federation of High School State Associations (NFHS) 34, 36, 39
neoliberalism 17, 25n1
Newman, T. J. 48, 80, 145, 191
normative approach 133–134; explicit 134–135; implicit 134
normative experiences 17

observation: reflective 46, 231; to support coaches 261; systematic 250–254
observational assessments 277–279; limitations 276–277
Olympic Games 120
operational definitions 160–161
Organisation for Economic Co-operation and Development (OECD) 123

outdoor activities 102, 191
Outward Bound 31–32

pair and share activities 78–79
participation, process of 32
pedagogy, culturally responsive 37
performance: character 180, 183; orientation 186–187
Perry, Bruce 202
perseverance 74, 231
Personal and Social Responsibility model 96
personal characteristics 64–65
personal fitness 237
Petitpas, A. J. 98, 146
physical education (PE) 30, 38; classrooms 100; K–12 30–31; teachers 32–33
physical fitness 101
Pierce, S. 36, 59–60, 64–65, 76, 128, 131, 296
planning 75
Play It Smart programme 95–96, 100
PlayerScore 250
plus sport 75–76, 79, 86
policy categories **169**, 173–174
pop sports 101
portfolio(s) 260–261; evaluation rubric **262–263**
positionality 54
positive classroom culture 10–11
positive youth development (PYD) 58, 75, 130, 143; critical (CPYD) 49; evaluations 272–274; outcomes 45; PES-based intervention 144–145
posthumanism 137
post-neoliberalism 18–20
practice 83; assessing 259–261; coaching 49; style 232
preparation 75, 78
primary school children 234–235; teaching core values to 235–236
prison 208–209
problem-based learning (PBL) 111

problem-solving 75, 94–95
processes, proximal 62–64, 68
Process-Person-Context-Time (PPCT) model 59–61
programmes: about VLS in PES contexts 95–100; design 187–192; of interventions 217–222; measuring effects on PYD 272–274
Project Effort programme 96, 100
Project Fitness Leadership EXperience (FLEX) 205–210
Prosocial and Antisocial Behaviour in Sport Scale (PABSS) 246–247
proximal processes 62–64, 68
psychological well-being (PWB) 290, 292–293; eudaimonic 292–296; hedonic 292–293; models 293; via psychological need satisfaction 294
psychosocial competencies 110
purpose 295
PWB *see* psychological well-being
PYD *see* positive youth development

qualitative data, gathering 274–275

Raya-Castellano, P. E. 250
reciprocal style 232–233
reciprocity 135
reflective observation 46, 231
reflective thinking 112
reflective writing 85
reinforcement 10
relatedness 293
relationally adaptive know hows 137
relaxation strategies 236
Republic Polytechnic 260
resilience 6–7, 99, 160
respect 6, 160, 235; example of transfer 222; observable behaviours/outcomes **266**; sample values discussion worksheet **220**
responsibility 6, 74, 98, 160, 235
Rising Phoenix Sports Program 205
Roberts, G. 48

role modelling 192
Ronkainen, N. 132
routines 78
Ryan, R. M. 294
Ryff, C. D. 293

safety 79–80, 93, 99, 185, 187
Safety, Ownership, Achievement, Respect (SOAR) 80
school-based sport 33–34, 38; coaches 35–36; negative outcomes 35; structure 34–35
schools 16, 18, 38; post-neoliberal 18–20, 24–25
SDT *see* self-determination theory
secondary school students 235; teaching core values to 236–237
SEL *see* social and emotional learning
self-check style 233
Self-Control, Effort, Teamwork, and Social Responsibility (SETS) 77, 83
self-determination theory (SDT) 292–293
self-evaluation tools 277; limitations 275–277
self-expression 294
self-reflection 54, 84–85, 252
self-transcendence 294
Seng, Y. B. G. 144
sense of belonging 185
sense-making 192
service provision category 174
SHAPE America *see* Society of Health and Physical Educators of America (SHAPE America)
shaping 9
Shields, D. 181, 186, 191
significance 295
Singapore 5, 144, 148, 179, 181–182, 188, 216–217, 219, 223–224, 228–229, 252; *see also* Sport Singapore (SportSG)
SOAR *see* Safety, Ownership, Achievement, Respect

social and emotional learning (SEL) 109
social justice 17, 20, 24; definition 20–21; life skills 45–46; promotion of 22–23
social pressures 235
Society of Health and Physical Educators of America (SHAPE America) 30, 39
solidarity 135
Soon, C. C. 107
spaces of healing 202–204
sport plus 75–76, 86
Sport Singapore (SportSG) 258–261, 270, 274–275; coaching competencies tool 264; Interview Guide 287–288
sportsmanship 235
stakeholders: collaboration with 11–12; involvement 218–219
Steger, M. F. 295
strategies: to build autonomy support **149**; established 131–132; evaluation 258–279; to facilitate VLS transfer **152**; relaxation 236; to teach VLS **151**; trauma-informed 207–210
strengths-based approach 52–53
structure 79–80
student-centred instruction 111–112
Subijana, C. L. 68
support 47; of coaches 261; *see also* autonomy support
supportive team culture, fostering 50–51
surveys 246–247; limitations 276
synergy 182
systematic observation tools 250–254
systems 65–67
systems-based approach 29

T²VLS$_{PES}$ Framework 144, 147; context 146, 148–150; dual cyclical intervention 156; experiential learning cycle 155; external assets 150–153; internal assets 153–154; and intervention 145–146, 158; research and evaluation 154, 156; strategies to facilitate VLS transfer **152**; strategies to teach VLS **151**
taken-for-granted truths and processes 18
task: intensity 83; orientation 186–187
teachable moments 81–82, 192–193
Teaching and Learning International Survey (TALIS) 123
teaching core values: at primary level 235–236; at secondary level 236–237
Teaching Games for Understanding (TGfU) approach 231–232
Teaching Personal and Social Responsibility (TPSR) model 31, 97
teaching styles 232–233; for different ages 234–235
team culture 50–51
team games 4
teamwork 75, 133, 161, 237
theories 229–232; achievement motivation 186–187; basic needs 291, 294; bioecological 59–60, 63; experiential learning 46–47, 154, 231; self-determination 292–293
thinking ahead 99
Three E's of Trauma 200
time 67–68
TPSR model *see* Teaching Personal and Social Responsibility (TPSR) model
tracking: athletes' learning 246–250, 265–**269**; coaching behaviours 250–254, 259–261; limitations 249–250
traditional sports activities 101
training function 174
transfer 83, 224; of knowledge 53; of life skills 68, 76, 128, 204–205, 296–297
transferability 199–200
transformative approach 134, 136–137; explicit 135–136; implicit 135
transparency 208
trash talk 210
Trudel, P. 180

Turgeon, S. 34
Turnnidge, J. 76
two continua model 134

UNESCO 106
United Kingdom 144
United States of America 30–31, 33–34, 36, 39, 75, 119, 200, 202

Vallee, C. N. 184
values xi, 3, 74, 109, 160; identifying 5
values action plan **221**; development of 219–222
values and life skills (VLS) 3, 143; approaches to teaching 5, 75–83; *see also* approaches; in PES contexts 95–100; and T²VLS$_{PES}$ Framework 144–158
values transfer card 248
Values-Based Training Programme (VTP) 216

Vealey, R. S. 183
Vella, S. A. 154
visual cues 277

Wagner, H. 250
Walker, A. 144
Walsh, D. 97, 153
Walton-Fisette, J. L. 111
Waseda Athlete Program (WAP) 122
wave, as metaphor 48–49
Weiss, M. R. 98, 230, 247
What? So What? Now What? 53, 84
What's Important Now? (WIN) 82
whole-school approach 10, 222
Wilson, J. P. 190, 231
Wilson Outley, C. 132
Wong, A. 4
World Health Organization (WHO) 109
Wright, P. 64, 216

For Product Safety Concerns and Information please contact our EU representative GPSR@taylorandfrancis.com
Taylor & Francis Verlag GmbH, Kaufingerstraße 24, 80331 München, Germany

www.ingramcontent.com/pod-product-compliance
Lightning Source LLC
Chambersburg PA
CBHW071400300426
44114CB00016B/2135